Living Oil

Living Oil

PETROLEUM CULTURE IN THE AMERICAN CENTURY

Stephanie LeMenager

OXFORD
UNIVERSITY PRESS

OXFORD
UNIVERSITY PRESS

Oxford University Press is a department of the University of Oxford.
It furthers the University's objective of excellence in research, scholarship,
and education by publishing worldwide.

Oxford   New York

Auckland   Cape Town   Dar es Salaam   Hong Kong   Karachi
Kuala Lumpur   Madrid   Melbourne   Mexico City   Nairobi
New Delhi   Shanghai   Taipei   Toronto

With offices in

Argentina   Austria   Brazil   Chile   Czech Republic   France   Greece
Guatemala   Hungary   Italy   Japan   Poland   Portugal   Singapore
South Korea   Switzerland   Thailand   Turkey   Ukraine   Vietnam

Oxford is a registered trademark of Oxford University Press
in the UK and certain other countries.

Published in the United States of America by
Oxford University Press
198 Madison Avenue, New York, NY 10016

© Oxford University Press 2014

First issued as an Oxford University Press paperback, 2016

Library of Congress Cataloging-in-Publication Data
LeMenager, Stephanie, 1968–
Living oil : petroleum culture in the American century / Stephanie LeMenager.
pages cm. — (Oxford Studies in American Literary History ; 5)
Includes bibliographical references and index.
ISBN 978-0-19-989942-5 (hardcover : alk. paper); 978-0-19-046197-3 (paperback : alk. paper)
1. American literature—History and criticism.   2. Ecocriticism.
3. Petroleum industry and trade—United States.   4. Environmental
protection in literature.   5. Environmental policy in literature.
6. Petroleum in literature.   I. Title.
PS169.E25L36 2014
810.9'36—dc23
2013016997

for my parents

{CONTENTS}

{ACKNOWLEDGMENTS}

There is no solitary writing, although writing, particularly for academics, can feel like the loneliest practice on earth. When I began writing this book I felt powerfully moved to do so by the places I lived and worked, Ventura and Santa Barbara, California. Those places, and Los Angeles, the metropolis nearest to them that in many respects shapes their culture, gave me a reason to keep going outside, as I dutifully tried to confine myself to the office to consider what a book about oil might look like, or what it might do. My first thanks go to these sites of oil production, oil culture, and environmentalism. Closely related to these places are the people in them, my neighbors, local activists, and colleagues who spoke to me about oil and environmentalism and about how both developed in Southern California. Bud Bottoms, Paul Relis, Dick Flacks, Harvey Molotch, Brian Segee of the Environmental Defense Center in Santa Barbara, Paul Jenkin of Ventura Surfrider, Melinda Gandara, and my neighbors, Connie Howard and Jack and Karen "next-door," all gave me plenty to think about in regard to oil and Southern California's imbrication in it. They also allowed me to conceive, if tentatively, that an academic book might forge some relationship to the larger world. In brief, thank you for extending the dialogue.

I hope my dedication of the book to my parents makes clear that they, too, extended the dialogue, by reminding me of the beauties and casualties of the American twentieth century every day. My father Spencer LeMenager's commitment to oil and to Texas served me better than any text in making clear that environmental attachment doesn't only come in one ideological color.

Beyond personal connections to the topic there have been a multitude of professional influences. Some of these are clearly marked in the body of the book, others not—but they are no less important for that. Lawrence Buell, Rob Nixon, Joni Adamson, Stacy Alaimo, Ursula Heise, Jennifer James, and Paul Outka have opened ways of thinking within the field of ecocriticism that spurred my intellectual development to a degree that even I can't fully estimate. Buell's work on environmental memory, Nixon's and Heise's acute analyses of scale, Adamson's and Nixon's reimagining of environmental justice, Alaimo's extensions of material feminism into questions of ecology, James's and Outka's theoretical and archival contributions to the imbrications of the U.S. environment and race—for such exciting, committed work, I offer thanks. As is evident from my introduction, I also am indebted to Jenny Price, Richard White, and William Cronon for making environmental history a genuinely interdisciplinary mode and model for stylistically strong academic prose. Those historians know how to tell stories. Jenny, in particular, has held my feet to the fire about the dangers of academic jargon, and I thank her for her mentorship and friendship. A generation of wonderful younger ecocritical scholars, including Allison Carruth, Janet Fiskio, Karen Salt, and Theresa Shewry, also contribute to my way of thinking and writing about the environment, if not about oil per se. The arts community at the University of California, Santa Barbara, including Dick Hebdige, Marko Peljhan, Lisa Jevbratt, and Bruce Caron, pushed me toward visual culture and beyond it, into new media and activist performance. Their dynamic methods of thinking through making, and Matt Coolidge's experiments in theorizing and performing place at Los Angeles's Center for Land Use Interpretation, have been in some respects more foundational to this book than scholarship ostensibly closer to its interests. On the explicit question of oil within environmental cultural studies, Rob Nixon, Imre Szeman, Jennifer Wenzel, Patricia Yaeger, and Mike Ziser directly and productively challenged some of the assumptions of this book, and I hope to report that they made it better. Rob earns my deeper thanks for his mentorship since our meeting at the University of Wisconsin back in 2000.

Byron Caminero-Santangelo generously worked with me to compile a reading list about oil in the Niger Delta, and he read an early draft of the section of this book that treats it. Cheryll Glotfelty, Laurie Monahan, Harvey Molotch, and Tess Shewry were also constructive, challenging draft readers—as were Julie Sze, Mike Ziser, and the wonderful graduate students and participating faculty of the Mellon "Environments and Societies" Colloquium hosted by the Humanities Center at the University of California, Davis. I want to thank my own graduate student colleagues—some of whom are now professors, including Ryan Boyd, Shannon Brennan, Kyle Bucy, Elizabeth Callaway, Kathryn Dolan, Brandon Fastman, Megan Fernandes, Timothy Gilmore, Sarah Hirsch, Zach Horton, Andrew Kalaidjian, Kelly Kawar, Judith Paltin, Shanna Salinas, Nicole Starosielski, and the dedicated members of my "Science Studies and Cultures of Environmentalism" seminar of winter 2011 and my doctoral colloquium of 2012–2013. All have made intellectual contributions to my recent thought and work. So have my former colleagues at the University of California, Santa Barbara, Stephanie Batiste, Ann Bermingham, Julie Carlson, Elizabeth Cook, Jeremy Douglass, John Foran, Aranye Fradenburg, Catherine Gautier, Bishnupriya Ghosh, Andrew Griffin, Carl Gutierrez-Jones, Ken Hiltner, Richard Hutton, Chris Newfield, Swati Rana, Josh Schimel, Candace Waid, and Janet Walker. From Harvard University, site of my own development as a graduate student, I've continued to receive support, intellectual prodding, and sound advice from Philip Fisher, Elaine Scarry, and, again, Larry Buell. Larry's retirement party in 2011 reminded me of the excellent graduate cohort that nudged me into professionalism, and I'd like to give special thanks to Rebecca Kneale Gould and Nathaniel Lewis for their ongoing friendship and support.

When you get older, there are, in fact, too many people to thank. My coeditor of the journal *Resilience*, Stephanie Foote, earns my gratitude for her imagination, humor, sound organizational skills, and wonderful, out-of-the-box ideas. Allison Carruth, Julia Christensen, Megan Condis, Janet Fiskio, and the journal's many board members have generated vibrant intellectual contexts for the environmental humanities and for my own scholarship within that relatively new interdisciplinary field. Barron Bixler, who created the photograph of the Los Angeles River that is the visual flag of the journal, has been an inspirational colleague in that venture and in the Los Angeles arts collective *Project 51*, of which I became a member in 2012 and all of whose members (Jenny Price, Catherine Gudis, John Arroyo, Allison Carruth, Barron Bixler, and Amanda Evans) got me thinking harder about the interrelationship of community, play, and place. Russ Castronovo has been an excellent editor and colleague for many years, and I thank him. Gordon Hutner, my series editor at Oxford University Press, is a longtime mentor of the highest order, nurturing my good ideas and mercifully killing off my bad ones since at least 2000—no doubt very hard work, for which I am deeply grateful. Brendan O'Neill at Oxford has been in every respect a generous and efficient editor for this book, adding his savvy, creative input to crucial decisions along the way. General thanks to Oxford for keeping me involved at every stage of the process of bringing the book to print.

Let me end with a gesture toward friends old and new, without whom I couldn't get through a day, let alone write a book. For kindness, wit, and constancy, I thank Sally Dermody, Kathy Richman, Nancy Cook, Barbara Hirsch, Anne Lounsbery, Laurie Monahan, Jenny Price, Stephanie Batiste, Ernest Prescott, and Louque Batiste-Prescott, the latter being the only one of my friends whom I got to hold when he was two days old. (Sally Dermody, my mother, could make a similarly striking counterclaim.) Molly Westling, Karen Ford, Mary Wood, Grace Phelan, Julee Raiskin, Gordon Sayre, Bill Rossi, Alan Dickman, Elizabeth Reis, and Ted Toadvine of the University of Oregon already have proven to be colleagues in the best sense of the word—a sense close to friendship if not identical to it, by making my transition to a new position as the Moore Professor of English and University of Oregon "Duck" thoroughly joyous.

Finally, thanks to California, the best and worst friend a girl could have for twenty-eight years. This book is ultimately for you, my love letter and my farewell.

Earlier versions of this book have been published as "Petro-Melancholia: The BP Blowout and the Arts of Grief," in *Qui Parle: Critical Humanities and Social Sciences* 19 (Spring-Summer 2011): 25-56; "The Aesthetics of Petroleum, after Oil!" in *American Literary History* 24 (Spring 2012): 59-86; and "Fossil, Fuel: Manifesto for the Post-Oil Museum," *Journal of American Studies* 46 (May 2012) 375-94.

Living Oil

Prologue

Mark Twain wrote that his life was shadowed by prospective wealth. His family imagined that their Tennessee lands would someday bring them fortune. Year after year, the fortune failed to appear. Meanwhile, Twain sought it elsewhere, making terrible investments, like his famous gamble on the Paige typesetter machine, and then getting himself out of debt, by writing and lecturing. Even for those of us who are not great writers, thinking in print, whether on paper or on screen, compensates for what doesn't happen elsewhere.

My father is an oil man. Let me rephrase that. My life has been shadowed by his retrospective wealth, oil money. When I was about eight years old, I first heard of the family oil property, about twenty miles northeast of Houston. It was invoked in the car, with Loretta Lynn on the tape deck as the family toured around a small strip mall my father owned in northern Illinois. From the first, connection to it excited. I felt like we owned part of a race horse. After my parents' divorce, the oil fantasy died. It was my father's, and I went with my mother to California. Even before that time, before my transcontinental journey, the family oil lands had largely stopped producing oil. Now they aspire to be timberlands. Before that, there were futures in sand and gravel. What with the new recovery techniques that have revitalized the oil industry in the last decade or so, perhaps my father's lands will be oil lands again.

As an academic, feminist, and about as far to the left as one can reasonably live in the United States, I spend a good deal of time disagreeing with my father. He waxes poetic about the Tea Party. Yet he's the only member of the family who reads my work, eager to criticize and debate. Certainly I couldn't think of oil without him. My last stop on the research trip that brought this book to conclusion was Houston. My father and I drove up to the old family oil property from there, after promising that neither of us would tune to a partisan radio station. Muzak only.

Sheets of rain fell on the oil country, which looked to me like a woodsy sand patch, transected by a rushing creek. Walking across the sandy soil to get to managerial headquarters, in a tin-roofed shed about the size of a tract home, my shoes flooded. Rain pounded the tin roof. Drainage, my father said, is what he thinks about. "Drainage, drainage, drainage!" he laughed. Knowing me, he talked about stewardship. We didn't mention subsidence, an inevitable by-product of sucking out the innards of earth, pumping water in and taking oil out, decade upon decade. "It's sinking here," my father said finally, when we weren't on the land anymore, sitting at a restaurant in Houston. He put out his two hands flat, slowly lowering them. "In many respects, it's not a desirable place." "But there's synergy here," he continued, "There's intelligence. Energy brings intelligence, and that makes synergy. When you're here, it's like the center of the world." The tin-roofed building that houses his company, more explicitly the company that he's had a small share in since birth, sports a door sign that reads, "World Headquarters." It's a modest sign, the sort you make at the hardware store.

When my father was twenty-one, he first came to the oil lands, visiting from college. His maternal grandfather, a Virginian called "Old Top," had gotten a hand in back in the Thirties. My father had been living on family charity since he was a small child. His father left his mother and him when he was six months old. He had a room at the grandparents' home in San Antonio, where in the local movie theater he played matinee shows as a magician to make spending money. Once in college, he saw his mother's situation grow precarious, as family circumstances changed. Oil became the next magic trick. According to him, his collaboration as a young man with other shareholders got the land producing again in the early 1960s, making money just long enough to give my grandmother a "pension." If oil hadn't come through, my father says, he might have had to live with his mother, to support her. "Maybe you wouldn't be here," he said. I am an oil man.

Every book has precedents outside of its apparent archive. Even academic books often grow, if circuitously, from the heart. My personal investments as an environmentalist and as a person grown up in oil shape what happens in this book and in the life lived around it. Before the educational opportunities that I've had, there was father and mother. Texas and California. After a fashion, this book honors both.

Introduction

ULTRADEEP, PETROLEUM CULTURE IN THE AMERICAN CENTURY

In terms of calendar years, we stepped into the twenty-first century about
ten years ago, but in all other ways we have continued to live the life of
the twentieth century, with our ongoing love affair with coal and oil.

—SUBHANKAR BANERJEE (2010)

I. Living in Oil

Reports of oil's death have been exaggerated. From the front lines of oil exploration, the photographer Subhankar Banerjee, writing about Arctic drilling for
his "climatestorytellers" blog, and the nonfiction writer Rowan Jacobsen, writing
about the Gulf of Mexico, warn that the problem isn't that we're running out of oil,
but that we're not.[1] The activist and scholar Michael T. Klare names our current era
"Tough Oil World," riffing on the oil industry's term for conventional oil resources,
which it calls "easy oil."[2] Tough oil is tough not just because it's hard to get, but
because of the devastating scale of its externalities. The world's oceans promise
"more than a trillion barrels of oil reserves," according to Jacobsen—many of
them only available by ultradeep drilling through salt formations that befuddle
our seismic imaging technologies.[3] To drill "ultradeep" is to go down 5,000 feet or
more, an extension of the once space-age ambition of deepwater drilling: to go as
far as 1,000 feet. Klare notes that Brazil's offshore discoveries, including the Tupi
field in the South Atlantic, lie "beneath 1.5 miles of water and another 2.5 miles
of compressed salt, sand, and rock."[4] These deposits promise 100 billion barrels
of oil and an inter-American alliance that could loosen U.S. dependency upon
the Middle East. They also present huge technological challenges, including how
to drill the salt dome and how to handle the high concentrations of natural gas
believed to pocket the pre-salt field. The challenges of ultradeepwater oil rapidly
are being met, but without much consideration for external costs.[5] On land, the
23 percent of the world's oil reserves open to private development include tough
oil sand and shale formations like the tar sands of northern Alberta and Venezuela
and the Bakken shale formation that underlies Montana, North Dakota, and
Saskatchewan.[6] Releasing the hydrocarbons from dense rock like shale and from
gummy bitumen requires water-and-chemical-intensive methods like fracking

and cyclic steam injection. The oil business always courted significant and sometimes catastrophic risk. Yet going ultradeep implies an unprecedented potential
for destruction because of where these last reserves are and the violence of the
experiments necessary to get them. Ultradeep implies a disregard for climate security and for the world's oceans, fundamentals of ecological health. Ultradeep also
implies an unprecedented devotion, even love.

How much do we love American modernity? Assume that "we" are residents
of the United States, or even just people identified with the idea of America,
its ideological, stylistic, military, and economic expression of modernity for
the past century or so. The continuation of this American century is what's at
stake in the "race for what's left," as Klare puts it, from the deepwater fields of
the South Atlantic to offshore West Africa to the Arctic seabed to the North
American oil and gas shales that underlie even my hometown of Ventura,
California. Energy systems are shot through with largely unexamined cultural values, with ethical and ecological consequences. The science journalist
Charles C. Mann recently raised the question of how the world will change if
another so-called unconventional resource, the crystalline natural gas buried
beneath the sea floor called methane hydrate, becomes more attractive than
oil, undermining the oil revenues of Russia, Iran, Venezuela, Iraq, Kuwait,
Saudi Arabia, and the United States.[7] The continuation of American modernity might depend on unconventional petroleum resources or falter because of
them, depending on what those resources are, who owns them, who benefits
from them, and how they play out. As a literature professor, I'm aware that
the narrative of petroleum is an unstable one, constantly shifting. I am not a
political scientist, economist, or engineer, and my point is not to prophesy the
future of fossil fuels, but rather to consider how the story of petroleum has
come to play a foundational role in the American imagination and therefore
in the future of life on earth.

It's helpful to begin this broad project by considering the charisma of energy,
as an American idea and a force. Years ago, the historian Richard White wrote
about energy, specifically the hydropower derived from the Columbia River,
as a means of talking about how work "involves human beings with the world
so thoroughly that they can never be disentangled."[8] White's point was, first,
that environmentalists miss the crucial ways in which work, not leisure, forms
our relationship with nonhuman life and force. "Energy" becomes a way to
talk about how both humans and nonhumans do work—and avoid it.[9] The
efficiency of the river as it rearranges the world to accommodate the variability
of its flow models efficient spatial arrangements that humans bring into being
as we learn to use the energy of water and wood, and of coal, gas, and oil.

White describes as an Emersonian insight the recognition that Americans
crave the rewards of work, riches and arguably a relationship with the world,
without actual labor. "They buy slaves," Ralph Waldo Emerson wrote in the late
1840s, "where the women will permit"—a tart dig at southern femininity, the

favored target of New England abolitionists.[10] Emerson also mentions steam and water power, which take the place of slaves in the quest to avoid labor in the North. The Canadian cultural critic Andrew Nikiforuk writes about how oil literally was conceived as a replacement for slave labor, a complement to abolitionism.[11] The nineteenth-century petroleum booster John McLaurin described oil as a solution to class warfare and gender inequity, in his 1896 *Sketches in Crude Oil*: "It saves wear and tear of muscle and disposition, lessens the production of domestic quarrels, adds to the pleasure and satisfaction of living.... If it not be a blessing to humanity, the fault lies with the folks and not the stuff."[12] It's easy to recognize McLaurin as a variant of the snake-oil sales-man, yet some of his rhetoric proves prophetic. The American middle class bloomed in a "bower" of natural gas and petroleum, to borrow McLaurin's antique phrase. The expansion of the U.S. middle class in the mid-twentieth century into a mass culture, inclusive of working-class arrivistes, the cul-tivation of the world's greatest system of public education, and essentially middle-class movements like feminism, antiwar activism, and environmental-ism presumed access to cheap energy. As Frederick Buell argues, oil replaced coal's "back-breaking labor" and widening of social caste with an energy infra-structure that seemed to support entrepreneurial individualism.[13] Coal fictions emphasize labor struggles, the potential power of the strike, and solidification of a working class, rather than the materialization of the liberal tradition in middle-class self-possession. The perceived benefits of oil for the sake of cul-tural progressivism are as important to consider as the more well-known tri-umphalist narratives of petroleum's critical role in World War I, when Winston Churchill decided to float the British Navy on petroleum fuel—or the huge contribution of U.S. oil to the Allies in World War II.

Suspended within a culture of oil, middle-class environmental culture would confront the single greatest difficulty of the ecological project—and its own potential hypocrisy—in fossil fuels. A crucial component of that hypoc-risy was the separation of labor from the definition of American "work," and thus of labor from our relationship, as Americans, to the nonhuman world. Consider a classic film moment from Hollywood. In *Giant* (George Stevens, 1956), Lesley Benedict as played by Elizabeth Taylor asks Jett Rink, played by James Dean, what it's like to be a "working man" in Texas, living alongside her cattle baron husband, "Bic" (Rock Hudson). "Well, that's something I'm gonna try to fix," Rink replies. The something that fixes Rink's status as a work-ing man sure enough proves to be oil, which makes him fabulously rich and infinitely less sympathetic. American popular culture both loves and hates the lucky strike that ushers in modernity with its derricks and airports, so much less romantic than a Wild West built on real animal horsepower. An Emersonian might conceive of modern energy without too much disapproval as the operant metaphor for modern social nature, by which I mean the ecol-ogy of modernity that we humans make, with nonhuman partners, through evolving and increasingly efficient technologies. While he disdained slavery, Emerson generally admired railroads and labor-saving machines. Mark Twain, as a southerner reared with slavery and toughened in the mining camps of Nevada, conceived the American aversion to labor in grittier terms. Twain described our propensity for gambling in earth—for the sudden and violent extraction of earth's ore that promised a forever after without labor. The prospective riches of the Tennessee lands that Twain's family hoped to sell offer a sweeter, nostalgic iteration of a brutal mining dream that included racism and magnificent destruction, like the fire near Lake Tahoe that Sam Clemens himself inadvertently set on a lumber claim. Energy as idea and as force nurtures the poetry of an Emerson and the realism of a Twain, high culture and low, an America to admire, to consume, to loathe.

The modern energy that focuses my efforts is petroleum energy, and in the word "petroleum" I intend a diversity of nonsolid hydrocarbon resources, including natural gas and, more consistently, oil. This is a book about contradictory emotions because it is a book about petroleum culture, by which I mean petroleum media, by which I mean the objects derived from petroleum that mediate our relationship, as humans, to other humans, to other life, and to things. It is a book of environmental cultural studies, driven by a fascination with petroleum aesthetics. Here the word "aesthetic" derives meaning from its most basic etymological root in how we sense and perceive, and from what have been called ideologies of the aesthetic, forms of representation and value expressed by means of display, spectacle, concealment, and stealth. We experience ourselves, as moderns and most especially as modern Americans, every day in oil, living within oil, breathing it and registering it with our senses. The relationship is, without question, ultradeep. There can be no "liveness" without mediation, as Philip Auslander has argued passionately and convincingly, making both the historical point that "mediatization is now explicitly and implicitly embedded within the live experience"—for example, we experience only "miked" voices as natural in the theater—and the ontological point that "liveness" has always been a relative term, not a pristine category.[14] Let me particularize Auslander's argument to say that liveness, as in seeming to be alive, now relies heavily upon oil. Oil itself is a medium that fundamentally supports all modern media forms concerned with what counts as culture—from film to recorded music, novels, magazines, photographs, sports, and the wikis, blogs, and videography of the Internet. Many more cultural forms indebted to oil can be named, and they will be throughout this book. Can the category of the human persist, practically speaking, without such forms indebted to fossil fuels?

Oil challenges liveness from another ontological perspective, as a substance that was, once, live matter and that acts with a force suggestive of a form of life. Just as anthropologists like Stefan Helmreich are looking to the microbial oceans "to explore shifting limits of the category of *life*," the microbial life in oil, in addition to oil's deep geologic history as life-through-time, forces questions of how biology, geology, and culture come together to define what counts as living matter.[15] When the concept of nature animates petroleum aesthetics, in oil museums where, for example, fossils are prominently displayed, the category confusion of life or oil powerfully disarranges the historic role of petroleum in the materials economy. It might seem that my task would be one of unconcealment in such cases. But often I find the confusion of oil and life more interesting than their segregation. To invoke Richard White once again, I think that the centuries of work we've done as modern humans to immerse ourselves in oil means that, in fact, we are loathe to disentangle ourselves or our definition of life from it. This does not mean, of course, that Tough Oil World is inevitable. Germany, for example, demonstrates a different way forward through its increasing reliance upon renewable energy sources. Germany currently thrums on 25 percent renewable power, and it has reduced its carbon emissions by 26.5 percent, making a more significant effort to mitigate climate change than any other nation.[16] The German Renewable Energy Act (2000) has become a model; promisingly, Germany's environment minister recently signed an agreement with China to expand solar and wind technologies in that country.[17] (Although it also should be noted that Germany has increased its coal usage, even as China struggles to combat "black carbon" air pollution).[18] The question of who the world leaders in efficient and clean energy production will be remains open. But clearly we have the technological intelligence to move beyond oil, given the political will. We had the technology to limit oil consumption even in the 1910s, when Thomas Edison and Henry Ford collaborated to invent lightweight batteries and lightweight, electric vehicles.[19] A conspiracy of lead-battery producers and the advent of World War I destroyed that possible world of energy efficiency, but its legacy continues, if unevenly, in sexy alternatives to internal combustion like the Tesla Electric Roadster. Even those nations that have banned the use of plastic bags, one of the most environmentally damaging consumer items made from petroleum feedstock, suggest the possibility of living more productively with oil, if not moving beyond it.

For me, thinking and writing about oil began as a fin de siècle affair, one that anticipated, as it happens falsely, that the turn of the twenty-first century would mean a new energy regime—an end of the American century as we knew it. I was inspired by the concept of "peak oil." The peak oil movement that grew up in the first decade of the twenty-first century foregrounded the prediction that Hubbert's peak, the point of maximum global oil supply prior to its dwindling, had either already occurred or was scheduled to occur around 2010. In terms of access to easy oil, peak oilers were surely prescient. More important, theirs was a future-project. They pointed to a "long emergency" in which the demands of extreme climate conditions confronted limited energy resources. The movement cited scientific modeling of global climate collapse and fossil fuel depletion in the new century, and experiential evidence of the same in weather freaks such as the European summer of 2003, Hurricane Katrina, and the fuel price spike of 2008. How to power the air conditioners of Europe, or of New York City, on a grid that we saw dramatically collapse in the northeastern United States and southern Canada, also in the early twenty-first century? Some predictions were dire, as the phrase "the long emergency" implies. Other peak oilers more optimistically focused on what Michael Ziser has called "the aesthetics of transition,"[20] the look and feel of newly localized economies that we find, say, in Bill McKibben's depiction of regionalized U.S. manufacturing sectors in *Eaarth: Making a Life on a Tough New Planet* (2010), or in James Howard Kunstler's community of unalienated (if exhausted) handworkers in the novel *World Made by Hand* (2008). The British director of the Transition Network, Rob Hopkins, started a worldwide series of community efforts to relocalize energy systems, often in gentrified small towns and hip urban enclaves such as Culver City, Los Angeles. Richard Heinberg of the Post Carbon Institute and Robert Thayer at the University of California, Davis, inspired design studios that came up with brilliant plans for the relocalization of resources in dense, well-knit communities. In 2007, my own city, Ventura, funded a remarkable "vision plan," a fully realized blueprint for a post–peak oil future. The combination of regionalized food and watersheds, local energy grids, and access to information technology— through "greened" grids—might remake the world in the image of Burlington, Vermont, or Portland, Oregon. Bring it on.

Of course, calculating conventional oil reserves is notoriously tricky, as, to cite only one problem, there are political incentives for oil-producing countries to misreport. So there must be some guesswork involved in locating a precise peak. The sexual politics of peak oilers, including Kunstler, can be disappointing, forecasting a bucolic return to traditional gender roles in the absence of cheap fuel. Some peak oilers prophesied a massive die-out of the human population, presumably in climate-imperiled regions of the Global South, as a precondition for the new (utopian) energy regime. An abrupt end to oil would devastate humans and other forms of social nature, such as domestic animals. Peak oil theory retains a hint of the elitist suspicion of the mass public that sponsored the biologist Paul Ehrlich's *Population Bomb* (1968) and Garrett Hardin's "Tragedy of the Commons" (1968), both of which became useful instruments for neoliberal policy makers, as Rob Nixon has shown.[21] Yet, again, peak oil imagines a future beyond neoliberalism. It posits an end to the energy infrastructure that sustains economic globalization in order to resolve the problem of the future for the majority of the world's citizens, who suffer from the privatization of resources and the dispossession of commons, sometimes through apparently natural processes such as coastal subsidence. More than thirty years ago, the environmentalist and renewable energy advocate Amory Lovins warned that "we must be wary of the danger of not being imaginative enough to see how undetermined the future is and how far we can shape it."[22] With conventional oil supplies dwindling, perhaps the future might again seem undetermined. At least "the future" might return as the primary project that it had been for much of the American twentieth century, through memes as diverse as "the space race" and "ecology."

In 2008, when the Texas oil entrepreneur T. Boone Pickens got serious about investing in wind and released the Pickens Plan while fuel prices at the pump in the United States hit an all-time high in July of that year, it seemed that energy regime change really could be on the way. Finally, there was a renewal of the "moral equivalent of war" on oil that President Jimmy Carter had called for as a response to the energy crises of the 1970s, just one year before the Reagans moved into the White House and took down the solar panels. The journalist Steve Coll has shown how Barack Obama used ExxonMobil to stand in for a widely unpopular Big Oil in the 2008 election, in an effort to build his presidential imaginary on green jobs and the disaggregation of government from corporate interests. "We must end the age of oil," candidate Obama had said in 2008.[23] During the first three years of the Obama presidency, Coll reports, ExxonMobil spent more than $52 million lobbying Washington and investing in congressional Republicans, acting like a political party, betting that if it could stock the House of Representatives, it could win the country.[24] From here, the historical trajectory gets familiar. Some highlights: In 2010, the U.S. Supreme Court, in *Citizens United v. Federal Election Commission*, used the First Amendment to uphold the rights of corporations to make unrestricted political expenditures. When BP's Deepwater Horizon rig blew out in April of that same year, federal response was, to say the least, disappointing.

Most poignant, in my view, was the state of Montana's 2012 challenge to *Citizens United*, which the Supreme Court summarily reversed. Justice Stephen Breyer's dissent points out that the Montana state law that the Court refused to consider reflected the state's unique history as a mining region. That 1912 Montana law banning direct political contributions by corporations had been created to stop the interference of the copper kings, who bought local and state elections. Montana now sits atop an oil shale formation and a new mining era, and it is over one hundred years behind its own history in terms of safeguards for its democracy. Another historical leap backward happened less publicly, when in 2005 what has become known as "the Halliburton loophole" in the Energy Policy Act of that year made fracking a form of oil recovery not subject to hard-won regulatory protections such as the Safe Drinking Water Act.[25] In *Oil: The Next Revolution*, a publication of Harvard University's Belfer Center for Science and International Affairs, author Leonardo Maugeri predicts a "glut of overproduction" of oil, largely because of what he calls the "high risk, high reward" U.S. "shale revolution."[26] The Belfer Center's research on shale oil was funded by British Petroleum and other energy companies.[27] Peak oilers failed to foretell the fierceness with which the oil industry would protect its assets, even the tough ones, regardless of the damage that "de-conventionalizing" oil, in Maugeri's euphemism, will do to the planetary climate, long-term economic stability, and human and nonhuman lives. Bill McKibben has named Exxon CEO Rex Tillerson the most "reckless man on the planet" in honor of Tillerson's assertion that, while global climate change is "real," it is merely an "engineering problem" with "engineering solutions."[28] Meanwhile, the oceans have become 30 percent more acidic, the temperature has risen .8 degrees Celsius, one-third of the summer sea ice in the Arctic has disappeared, the atmosphere over the oceans is 5 percent wetter, promising superstorms, and in the United States we're nowhere near a political commitment to create a carbon budget that essentially enforces "post-peak" measures.[29] Welcome to Tough Oil World.

Last year, the hills directly above my small, largely working-class neighborhood in Ventura, California, were fracked. Apparently this isn't news to the oil industry, as varying forms of secondary recovery, including fracking, have been going on in my area for about sixty years. Ventura and Santa Barbara counties sit atop the Monterey shale formation, which extends from coastal zones like the place where I live, about a mile from the beach, into the Pacific Ocean.[30] As a resident of a newly active frack zone and of one of the most auto-dependent regions in the world, I write from within the Tough Oil future. Yet I also write from one of the most progressive oil-industry regulating states in the United States, and one of the most privileged oil regions of the world in terms of per capita wealth and aesthetic resources, which are prized by real estate developers—a powerful lobby. Ventura, which is about an hour's drive from Los Angeles, has played the role of working oil town to its northern neighbor Santa Barbara's resort sanctuary. Yet neither place has escaped what industry might call its geological destiny in the ocean seeps and (now) shale deposits that have made the oil business prominent here since the 1890s. The world's first offshore wells were installed in Summerland, California, a small beach town just south of Santa Barbara. Neither a pristine nature hub that offloads the externalities of modern living onto outlying industrial deserts nor the Death Star of nature purported to be Los Angeles, my regional home holds dual investments in nature and oil. This complexity supports my contention that regions are vital intellectual frameworks for thinking about energy.

As one of the few people who have tried to write about the floating world of oil, I can bear witness to its slipperiness, to the ways in which it tends to trip fiction into incoherence. In the end, perhaps, it is the craft of writing itself—or rather writing as we know it today—that is responsible for the muteness of the Oil Encounter.[31]

—AMITAV GHOSH, "PETROFICTION" (1992)

II. Writing Oil

In the 1990s, Amitav Ghosh offered what has turned out to be the most influential first critique of "petrofiction," fiction about oil. In a review of the book *Trench* by the Saudi writer Abdelrahman Munif, who is known for the quintet of oil novels *Cities of Salt*, Ghosh laments that literary writing, in particular the novel, balks at the oil encounter. He notes the novel's preference for monolingual speech communities, its attachment to place, and its interest in separate "societies." According to Ghosh, these genre tendencies are unsuited to the "bafflingly multilingual" and "intrinsically displaced, heterogeneous, and international" world of oil.[32] Following Ghosh, the cultural critic Imre Szeman provides a more comprehensive explanation of why literature hasn't dismantled our self-subjection to oil capital. "Instead of challenging the fiction of surplus—as we might have hoped or expected— literature participates in it just as surely as every other social narrative in the contemporary era,"[33] Szeman argues. The question of how to write about the oil encounter has plagued novelists and critics, particularly those frustrated by what Szeman describes as the Left's failure to generate alternatives to oil capital at a moment when the dwindling of conventional oil reserves might tip us toward Tough Oil or toward a more sustainable future. I share this frustration. It is an unsurprising representational and critical morass, given the ultradeep relationship between we moderns and oil. As will become clear, I'm not seeking a literary ace in the hole or novel that writes oil as it is, "intrinsically displaced, heterogeneous, and international." Szeman and a dynamic group of self-named "petrocritics" have begun to archive potential candidates for this best, most representationally astute oil novel.[34] But compelling oil media are everywhere. Films, books, cars, foods, museums, even towns are oil media. The world itself writes oil, you and I write it. Petrofiction provides one route to understanding our entanglement. So does everything else. As a critical essayist, my challenge has been to find a point of view from which to frame the *everything* of oil. Each chapter of this book tries out (*essayer*) our investments, *my* investments, in a profoundly unsustainable and charismatic energy system. This is a short cultural history of, essentially, destructive attachment, bad love.

The question of how to discuss an unsustainable attachment to nearly every-thing sent me looking for models in environmental writing. The environmental historian Jenny Price's manifesto on how to write about another sprawling topic, Los Angeles, describes a narrative method that she calls, with characteristic humor, "mango body whip stories." The phrase originates in an anecdote. In a Los Angeles parking lot, Price found a note on her windshield—an irate note—that turned out to be, also, a receipt for something called "mango body whip." Her essay takes this as an excuse for an investigative foray to the store that sells the product, and then a brief description of its components, where they came from, and the labor and resource inputs required to bring "mango body whip" to the Beverly Center shopping mall. She elaborates that "mango body whip stories" look for and "follow the nature we use and watch it move in and out of the city, to track very specifically how we transform nature into the mountains of stuff with which we literally lead and sustain our lives."[35] I practice a variant of this narrative—and critical—method, which I call commodity regionalism. The critical genealogy of commodity regionalism moves through Price to her fellow environmental historians William Cronon and Richard White, and in environmental cultural studies through the unique career of Andrew Ross, whose recent study of Phoenix gives the term "sustainability"—at last—an explicit material context. Finally, commodity regionalism grows out of the interdisciplinary entanglements of cultural geography, arts practice, and architectural history in the work of Allan Sekula, Mike Davis, Kenneth Frampton, and Matt Coolidge, founder of the Center for Land Use Interpretation (CLUI), a research hub for cultural geographers, infrastructure geeks, and conceptual artists. Throughout the course of writing this book, I enjoyed the CLUI's tours and exhibits of petroleum environments, and I made use of its Internet archive, the Land Use Database, to locate oil sites. The journalist Lisa Margonelli's popular treatment of "petroleum's long, strange trip to your tank" in *Oil on the Brain* (2007) also models a way of thinking about oil through specific places and histories. Other populist versions of commodity regionalism appear in Annie Leonard's video shorts about the devastating externalities of our modern materials economy, for instance "The Story of Stuff" (2007), and in Alan Thein Durning and John C. Ryan's exposés of globalization-come-home in *Stuff: The Secret Lives of Everyday Things* (1997).

Much has been written about the ineluctably transnational character of oil stories since Ghosh's "Petrofiction." But literary and cultural critics often ignore how the national frame obscures the regional impacts of oil. There are key exceptions, such as a beautiful photographic essay on the Alberta tar sands by Imre Szeman and Maria Whiteman, the Swiss artist Ursula Biemann's videographic tour-de-force *Black Sea Files* (2005), Edward Burtynsky's "app" version of his monumental photo essay *Oil* (2012), which includes his informative and moving glosses on the sites that inspired his images, Warren Cariou's creative nonfiction storytelling of indigenous Canadians living in the tar sands, and the CLUI's ongoing exploration of oil and water in Los Angeles and Houston—all, tellingly, hybrid works of critical/creative performance.

As in my first book about charismatic and unsustainable commodities, *Manifest and Other Destinies* (2005), here I argue that the transnational, as the fundamental if elusive space of economic globalization, tends to be most visible in regional sites of capital production and transshipment. Commodity regionalism activates vital historical and ecological frames, opening an explicit point of view onto global-scale forces and flows, such that we can see and sense them. The regional frame assists, too, in the pursuit of the psychologically ultradeep, the affects and emotions lodged in gasoline fuel, cars, and in the thousands of everyday items made from petroleum feedstock, from lip balms to tampon applicators, dental polymers, and aspirin tablets. As Stacy Alaimo writes in a criticism of sustainability rhetoric that focuses on maintaining modern lifestyles, "rather than approach this world as a warehouse of inert things we wish to pile up for later use, we must hold ourselves accountable to a materiality that is never merely an external, blank, or inert space but an active, emergent substance of ourselves and others."[37] What Alaimo calls "an ethics of mattering" becomes particularly complex, sticky, when it comes to petroleum. We wear and eat it. Our bodies write it.

Regions became more socially and economically significant—in some respects more so than nations—when globalization assumed its mature form in the late twentieth century. Of course the term "region" signifies place at a variety of scales, but it specifically gestures toward the human scale that has allowed for planning efforts we associate with the aspiration of sustainable development. Arts practitioners, as I've noted, have seemed less anxious than cultural critics about evoking the scale of the human, what used to be conceived as vernacular "place" in the cultural geography of John Brinkerhoff Jackson. This may simply be because art often, if not always, presents something to the human senses. The photographer, artist, and critic Allan Sekula made economic globalization visible from within a discourse about containerization and the decentralization of commercial ports in his photographic essay, *Fish Story*. "A certain stubborn and pessimistic insistence on the primacy of material forces is part of a common culture of harbor residents," Sekula remarks, speaking of his resistance to the dematerializing rhetoric of the global as a legacy of his childhood in San Pedro, the port of Los Angeles. "This crude materialism is underwritten by disaster. Ships explode, leak, sink, collide. Accidents happen every day."[38] Couldn't the same be said of any site of the transshipment or refining of capital, such as the Gulf Coast of Texas, whose petroleum refineries process approximately 2.3 million barrels of oil per day?[39] Visiting such places, and living in them, makes clear that oil is a form of capital that bulks out and inhabits place, changing the quality of air, water, noise, views, and light.

Martin V. Melosi, a social historian based in Houston, makes a strong case for conceiving of "energy capitals" as physical regions rather than "centers for capital accumulation" in an abstract global field. "Energy-led development has transformed many cities and regions physically, influencing metropolitan growth, shaping infrastructure, determining land use, changing patterns of energy consumption, and increasing pollution."[40] In short, the material impacts oil makes on places *matter* in ecological, cultural, and aesthetic terms. When the architectural theorist Kenneth Frampton made "critical regionalism" a charismatic idea in the early 1980s, he saw it as a means of retaining an "adversary culture" against the technocratic modernism that threatened both architecture and critique.[41] Critical regionalism pursued the place-form "in its public mode" as a means of insuring "legitimate" power, by which Frampton meant that it cultivated a scale of place that could support genuine democracy, in Hannah Arendt's sense of a "space of human appearance" where we still might recognize one another as fellow citizens.[42] Critical regionalism was a "cultural strategy" in which elements of world culture were placed in conversation with the region, so as to mark the interpenetration of spatial scales and avoid provincial "populism."[43] It invested itself in local ecologies and materials, taking into account phenomenological questions of light, density, and "tactile resilience" against the dumbing down of place consciousness by weather-killing technologies like the air conditioner.[44] Invested in rematerializing capital and making explicit modernity's spatial logics, critical regionalism suggests a strong counterweight to oil's supposed elusiveness.[45] The method of critical regionalism has been complemented, for me, by developments in ecocriticism or environmental criticism, specifically Ursula Heise's recognition of scale as a primary critical problem and Joni Adamson's innovation of a style of academic writing that foregrounds the explicit material contexts of the critic's voice and those of her intellectual collaborators, be they persons, non-human beings, or texts.[46] Exquisitely analyzed regional studies of Nigerian oil culture by Michael Watts, Rob Nixon, and Jennifer Wenzel also point a way forward for commodity regionalism.[47]

The regional consciousness that I ascribe to my own critical practice exists and flourishes in fictions, nonfictions, poetry, performance, and testimony from within cultures of oil. No oil culture can exist without the self-consciousness of the world energy markets and foreign wars that oil sustains, and so, as the literary critic Graeme Macdonald suggests, there can be no "American" oil novel.[48] Or no national oil novel per se. However, there can be Louisianan and Californian and Texas oil novels, films, poems, and blogs that spill into the world—while at the same time offering scrupulous accounts of material effects and aesthetics, the feeling of petroleum stench in the bayou and the look of prison laborers on a California beach, raking up oil-soaked hay. I chose the coasts of California, Louisiana, and Texas as primary sites of study, because of the regionalist sympathies outlined above and because of the way that the West Coast plays against the Gulf Coast in the intertwined histories of environmentalism and fossil fuels.

For me, the dialectic of environmentalism and oil develops locally, but it ultimately delivers a strong national narrative of the twentieth-century United States, the so-called American Century. This narrative drifts to the nation's edges, to the oil coasts with their dual significance as markets and commons.[49] United States environmentalism with its potential to radicalize the middle class might have stalled neoliberal policies of enclosure and dispossession that now seem inevitable. Environmentalism has carried the potential to radically reconceive the meaning of progress. The first flourishing of American "ecology" in the late 1960s and 1970s included the seeds of movements that later developed in a more segregated fashion under the rubric of environmental justice, nurtured by the often nonwhite, rural, or poor members of so-called sacrifice communities that seemed to have been left behind by mainstream environmentalists. I would like to see the kind of strong recuperative work that has been done on U.S. discourses of environmental justice by activist-critics performed on what we might conceive as "mainstream" and middle-class U.S. environmentalism, a movement that is typically oversimplified by recourse to pat phrases such as NIMBY-ism.[50] California and Louisiana play crucial roles in the development of environmentalism as a force of culture in some respects divided against itself, a persistent and complicated national structure of feeling. American environmentalism grew up in conversation with oil in the bayous and oil on the California coast. Although in this book and in the broad American imaginary California might play the role of "environmentalism" to the Gulf Coast's "oil," it's worth noting that California ranks second only to Texas among the United States in terms of greenhouse gas emissions.[51] No place explored here stands apart from modernity, from the cultures of petroleum. To fully appreciate the potential radicalism of the ecology idea as it grew into a social movement in the United States, it is necessary to revisit that movement's relationship to oil and to reconsider oil itself as at least a conceptually public resource and aspect of cultural memory.

This book participates in an abashed nostalgia for the American twentieth century, a fondness that chokes on the recognition that the old ways drag on and that Tough Oil isn't the same resource as so-called easy oil, in terms of its economic, social, and biological costs. The specter of global climate change, perhaps finally made visible to Wall Street with the disaster of Hurricane Sandy, accompanies the Tough Oil future. Moreover, the oil and natural gas reserves locked in tar sands, shales, and the deep ocean have produced a return, in some North American regions, to local environmental and labor exploitation reminiscent of the frontier mining towns of the nineteenth century. Where populations long beset by failing regional economies embrace the new realities of Tough Oil, inadequate regulations and inadequately low taxes on industry promise to make the much hoped for re-industrialization of rural America "lousy for rural Americans," Lisa Margonelli concludes.[52] For example, without reasonable taxes on industry, who will pay for the millions of dollars in road damage that results from hundreds—if not thousands—of tractor-trailers hauling away wastewater at frack sites? The number of jobs coming to rural Americans from the shale revolution has been, so far, significantly over-estimated, though of course any new jobs for North Dakotans or rural Ohioans might look better, in those places, than none.[53] Conditions in oil and gas mining regions of the Global South are exponentially worse. As a point of contrast, this book ventures briefly into the Niger Delta. Oil's virtual war on Nigeria's ethnic minorities and on the indigenous First Nations of northern Alberta, who suffer from rare cancers linked to tar sands pollution, recalls resource conflicts foundational to modernity as we know it, such as the colonization of the Americas by Europeans—where genocide worked powerfully through ecological and microbial phenomena.

My research on the U.S. Gulf Coast in the wake of the BP blowout and Hurricane Katrina made clear that the state of feeling that I call petromelancholia, by which I mean an unresolved grieving of conventional fossil fuel reserves, has not been healed by more intensive extractive processes such as ultradeep drilling. The subsidence or sinking of Gulf coastal territories at a rate of approximately one football field's worth of land every thirty-eight minutes—or every fifteen minutes, according to one scholar—figures as geological melancholia, chronic land loss.[54] Some locals compare this land attrition to territorial thefts in war. The Gulf's commercial fishermen are keenly aware of nonhuman casualties—deaths, injuries, and genetic mutation—comparable to modern war tallies. At a recent screening of the film *Dirty Energy* (Bryan Hopkins, 2011), a fisherman's wife who was present and also interviewed in the film stood up and testified to the poverty and horror of the post-BP catch, describing crabs with lungs growing on the outside of their shells and harbor seals born without eyes.

As if to reassert the presence of bodies in a region where so many disappear and are disregarded, Gulf Coast residents have turned to performance genres, including poetry, videography, and blogging. In different ways, these genres create effects of bodily presence, as well as a virtual space of appearance, a place in which to recognize each other, again, as citizens deserving of protection and rights. In the Niger Delta, where over a half century of oil mining has almost entirely destroyed the marine commons, poetry has been conceived as "aggressive realism" because of its long-standing relation to political protest.[55] Nigeria also suffers coastal subsidence. The so-called delta blues of Nigerians offer a powerful counterpoint to the blues originating on the sinking edge of the Gulf of Mexico. The performance genres of these transatlantic subsidence cultures inspire deep sensory mimicry even in a distant reader like myself, situated in a privileged and relatively well-regulated oil region of southern California.

From the poetry of coastal Louisianans to interviews with southern Californians and Newfoundlanders working the tar sands in Alberta, the genre of testimony surfaces throughout this book as a reminder that its subject lies near to trauma as well as desire. Living in oil, through injury and pleasure, is personal, not easily transmissible as story. This is an aspect of the difficulty of writing about oil that Amitav Ghosh and his critical legatees haven't addressed. As Jacques Derrida argues, testimony and poetry are alike in their resistance to translation. What we do with testimony is enter into a contract with it, taking it on faith rather than as information that might be conveyed for itself, apart from the presence of the witness.[56] The transmissibility or resistance to translation of diverse oil narratives and the effectiveness of distinct media as a means of conveying evidence—say, of the decimation of more than 10,000 sea otters as a result of the Exxon *Valdez* spill—figure in this book as major topics. The social problem of forgetting the risks of oil extraction implies the aesthetic problem of how media incites or fails to incite protest, policy making, and other redemptive action. Debates that have raged in cultural criticism for decades, entering what now appears as a classic phase in Susan Sontag's and John Berger's writings on photography in the 1970s, resurface in chapter 1 in close examinations of oil spill media—including photography, magazines, film, blogs, and print books.

Like contemporary critics such as Maggie Nelson, I am skeptical about the relay of media → empathy → action that some of my fellow defenders of the arts and humanities would like to take for granted.[57] When the director of a documentary film stated to a live audience that he had done his job by depicting the decimation of Gulf Coast fishing one year after the BP spill so as to create empathy, and the rest was left to us, the theater emptied. His film *is* important, and the effort to create it on a shoestring budget heroic. Yet empathy attaches to no particular plan of action, as Sontag acknowledged, and it may even paralyze us in a shameful realization of the inaccessibility of political power, as Berger noted from the depths of the Vietnam War. Nonetheless, like Sontag in *Regarding the Pain of Others*, I want the images to keep coming.[58] Environmental media plays a crucial role in archiving, which is a means of measuring loss. As Lawrence Buell has argued, without environmental media we might not know either the extent of modern ecological injury or the baseline of ecological health by which to measure the damage. These media also generate sociability, by which I mean association for the sake of being together, a social form related to art and to play.[59] Both survivors and spectators of ecological crisis have been made excruciatingly aware of their exclusion from managed resource commons that, as the historian Peter Linebaugh argues, ought to exist as a fundamental right of modern citizenship from the time of the second charter of the Magna Carta.[60] The social has proven more difficult to privatize than situated resources, as has been shown, for example, by Internet protest communities responding to the BP spill or creating the Occupy movement in the United States, with its debts to the Egyptian protestors who staged a revolution on Facebook and in Tahrir Square.

Living Oil was remade, many times over, by communities beyond the academy and by modes of writing, speaking, and performing often distant from academic convention. It's a spilled book, flowing from literary criticism and cultural history into travel narrative and fragments of memoir. This stylistic hybridity speaks to my personal imbrication in oil and works to answer oil's complicity in privatization and dispossession with what I hope is an accessible humanist scholarship. When the public universities of Pennsylvania agreed to allow fracking on their campuses in an attempt to offset student tuition increases and other symptoms of drastic statewide cuts to public education, the fact that universities are in no sense "protected" from Tough Oil World became impossible to ignore.[61] Offshore fracking near my campus and onshore fracking in the agricultural region to the north of it leaves some of my colleagues nervous about what's in the water.[62] While studies haven't found that the drilling chemicals associated with fracking necessarily result in groundwater contamination, it's unclear what the seismic effects of fracturing near naturally occurring faults (say, in a seismically troubled seabed) might be. Moreover, natural gas escaping near the surface of some frack wells has been found to contaminate drinking water, and it contributes to global climate change.[63] These are strange concerns to consider within the conventionally pastoral frame of the North American university campus. The future of public higher education literally sits atop the shale revolution, with its extravagant risks. The global movements of these fossil fuels and their imbrication in all aspects of social and economic endeavor, let alone the personal nature of their effects in our bodies, demand the collaborative efforts of academics, artists, scientists, industry, and everyone—which means *everyone*—living in Tough Oil World. Without such collaboration, there can be no narrative intelligence capacious enough to approach oil's cultural and ecological legacies. This book invites conversation.

Living Oil presents four distinct windows onto our persistent twentieth century as North Americans, living within oil primarily in the United States of America. In chapter 1, the Santa Barbara oil spill of 1969 generates a set of critical problems in oil culture that will resurface throughout the book, including the temporal limitations of radicalism, the relationship of media to action, and the forgetting of risk. Chapter 2 considers the aesthetics of petroleum in California and in the United States as the freeway-suburban complex develops through the mid-twentieth century, producing as many reasons for loving oil as for fearing it. In chapter 3, contemporary petromelancholia—the grieving of conventional oil resources and the pleasures they sustained—answers twentieth-century petroleum aesthetics with testimony from a disappearing world, from a World War III, in one author's phrase, that pits the ecologies of the Global South against oil extraction. Chapter 4 moves beyond the end of the world to visit three potential archives of the future, oil museums in Los Angeles, Alberta, and Texas that commemorate distinct genealogies of energy and diverse ways forward. In my epilogue, I offer a speculative nonfiction gloss on my own neighborhood as a vital energy district and some thoughts about future genres of protest. In my appendix, I outline the energy costs of producing this book as print media, with suggestions about the relative ecological weight of products meant for immediate disposal, like fast-food hamburgers, versus thought.

Origins, Spills

On February 7, 1969, one week after a massive oil spill in the Santa Barbara Channel, the *Santa Barbara News-Press* ran an image by a local photographer named Wally Stein. In the photo, a young woman stands in her living room, holding a toddler in her arms. She looks out of a picture window toward the ocean. Black smears stain the window—they are evidence of an afternoon's high tide, which, prior to the spill, would have splashed the beach cottage with translucent spray. The young woman, her oceanward gaze, the child, the beachside home, and the visual surprise of the stains tell a story of middle-class happiness and the ecological compromises made to assure it in the twentieth century. The woman has the allegorical fortune of being named "Mrs. Parent." The house has the symbolic luck of being beside the Pacific Ocean, a contributor to several theories of American fulfillment, beginning with the continental designs of Manifest Destiny. The newspaper caption asks us to consider the practical, implicitly moral, limits of oil spills: "Oil on beaches, birds, and boats—*but on picture windows?*" Picturing the future, as a parent, at the edge of the United States of America in 1969, we see the ocean, with its connotations of mother and eternity, through a lens stained by oil waste. Whether oil or ocean will determine the view remains an open question.

From the point of view of the future, oil can be seen to mediate such questions, making possible the printing and distribution of newspaper photographs, for instance, and the beach cottage off the frontage road, habitable because of freeways and cars. When I came to southern California twelve years ago from Massachusetts, I did not place petroleum at the center of environmental imagination, nor did I see the world through a lens bespattered with fossil fuel. The night of my arrival in Santa Barbara for a job interview, I walked onto the patio of my beachside motel and gazed oceanward at what turned out to be the flickering lights of platforms Hillhouse, A, and B, three operational derricks in the Santa Barbara Channel. The derricks stand at the edge of one of the world's biologically richest marine sanctuaries. In the dark, their lights showed me where to assume the ocean, and I appreciated them as indexes of a rich habitat that I could not see for myself. I found the lit platforms almost beautiful, regardless of my knowledge that on January 28th, 1969, a massive oil spill had occurred at Platform A. The spill befouled beaches, and it killed or sickened hundreds of seafowl and marine animals. In what the environmentalist and political scientist David Orr calls "the dialogue between oil and water"[1] which structures the modern world, Santa Barbara sounded the possibility of choosing: either oil and modernity, or water and a speculative world known vaguely under the sign of ecology. Santa Barbara in the cultural moment of the spill makes a fleeting appearance in Mike Nichols's *The Graduate* (1967), as the leafy, pastoral place without a freeway—for years, the town's stoplight frustrated coastal through traffic—where Benjamin Braddock claims his bride and, we imagine, eludes a future in plastics.

My own ambivalence about what I could and could not see in the Santa Barbara Channel that fateful night proved to be the start of a long conversation about how petroleum intervenes in environmental history and in imagining ecological facts. It also led me to consider what kind of origin story the Santa Barbara blowout of 1969 offers. The blowout of the well at Platform A began at about noon on January 28th, in the form of gas, as Union Oil workers were retrieving drilling pipe from a slant-drilling operation six miles off the coast of the tony enclave of Montecito. The drilling extended approximately 3,500 feet under the ocean floor. Gas shot up through the drill pipe, and the pipe was dropped back down into the hole. Then the top of the well was capped. But gas forced its way up through breaks near the bottom of the well hole, and then through cracks in the seabed. At that point, the accident began in earnest. For ten days crude foamed in a 150- to 200-mile-long slick off the coast, and it washed up on the beaches, bringing with it the dead and dying bodies of seabirds, fish, and occasional seals and porpoises. More than 450 species of seabirds frequent the Santa Barbara Channel, and local photographers documented dead and dying gulls, godwits, curlews, black-bellied plover, grebes, and California murres. The body counts offered by local media reminded readers of exactly what they stood to lose. This spill was not a discrete event but a seeping injury that would continue for over a year, since the Santa Barbara Channel is an unstable, seismically sensitive area. Without a bedrock cap, its porous ocean bottom fissured easily. Small earthquakes or tremors continually opened new fissures.

In standard environmental histories of the United States and the planet, the Santa Barbara spill figures as an incident of grievous pollution, comparable to the famous fire on the Cuyahoga River, also in 1969. For Santa Barbara residents who lived through the spill, it was "an explosion in consciousness," "a world-changing event," and a trauma. Paul Relis, an environmentalist who has become an entrepreneur in recycling and post-landfill waste systems, recalls first seeing the spill from the vantage point of a small plane. "It was a transformative experience, because I'm literally looking down into the upwelling of oil, oil surging in the ocean. I was mesmerized: I had never seen anything like it. And it hit me that this is a world-changing event. It was not going to be the same after this, whatever 'after' is."[2] Relis acknowledges that the innovations spawned by the spill event, in Santa Barbara and beyond, have become "old hat" for people who were born after the spill and even for many who lived through it. Forgetting, he suggests, comes about in part because a new consciousness succeeds in popularizing its goals. Under the aegis of the Community Environmental Council, which Relis cofounded with a dozen or so students back in 1969, Santa Barbara became a national leader in recycling, community gardening, green building, and domestic solar technologies. Places less fortunate than Santa Barbara, less wealthy and less identified with a coastline well-known in Hollywood films, give other reasons for why their spills have been forgotten. This chapter considers the strange transience in public culture of oil spills that have had effects on nonhuman life comparable to human death tolls in wars.

In 2012, the Santa Barbara Film Festival premiered *Dirty Energy*, Bryan D. Hopkins's documentary about the decimation of Louisiana fisheries in the year following the blowout on British Petroleum's Deepwater Horizon drilling platform. After the film, a fisherman and his wife who were featured in it talked with the Santa Barbara audience. I at least felt the expectation of intercoastal bonding in the air. This being the film's third showing at the festival, only about twenty-five people lounged throughout the theater. "We heard you all had an oil spill here in the 1960s," the fisherman from Louisiana began. "You are lucky, your coast isn't ruined. Sounds like your community has been strong."[3] Without belaboring the point, the fisherman and his wife indicated the difference between Santa Barbara and their town in Plaquemines Parish, Louisiana, which is working class and situated in a region heavily reliant on oil industry jobs. "We're one of the last places in America that has a culture, and it's being wiped out," said the fisherman's wife, as she spoke of crabs "being caught with their lungs on the outside of their shells," harbor seals born "without eyes"—victims of an ongoing story of poisoning that a television news anchor told this Louisiana couple cannot make the news unless she has something "positive" to say about being married to a fisherman in the wake of the BP spill.[4]

As our post-screening conversation progressed, Riki Ott, the marine toxicologist and activist who played a crucial role in responding to Exxon after the *Valdez* spill, joined the others at the front of the stage. When an audience member wondered aloud whether "starting a riot" might be the best response to the atrocities committed upon the ocean that the film presents, Ott joked that starting a revolution might be more fitting. Hopkins, the director, jumped in to explain his thoughts about action. "My job is to make you feel empathy," he said bluntly. "If you care at all about these people"—indicating the fisherman—"I'm going to let you find the answers."[5] Shortly afterward, the theater started emptying. As we filed out, I realized that what I had conceived as flawed about Hopkins's admirable film was also integral to its subject: It lacks structure. The postfilm conversation was also "about" the irresolution and unease that comes when narrative trajectories—the directional idea of revolution, for instance—fail to cohere. Hopkins later described his directorial ambitions to me in terms of "shattering" habitual ways of knowing: "My goal as a filmmaker is to crack, break and sometimes destroy ideas through giving people a life experience that they cannot UN experience."[6] If we conceive of plots, after Peter Brooks, as predominantly expressions of our desires for order, oil spills fiercely resist plotting. But what to *do* with a cracking, breaking, and leaking event, one that can neither be plotted effectively nor un-experienced? The filmmaker's valorization of empathy raises a host of other questions about what art can accomplish in regard to oil pollution, questions that will run the course of this book.

Spill stories swarm with agents, human and nonhuman, organic and machinic. They involve corporations, workers, remediating actors like the Coast Guard and chemical surfactants and polyurethane booms, human and nonhuman victims, activists, and the competing scales of a local site of injury and the vast global infrastructures of energy derived from fossil fuel. Oil spills have been conceived as international-scale "disasters" since the wreck of the supertanker *Torrey Canyon* off the coast of Cornwall, England, in 1967, which resulted in the death of upward of 15,000 seabirds. The *Torrey Canyon* wreck revealed the unpreparedness of both industry and government for major spills. David Orr's semiparodic argument that "oil has undermined [human] intelligence" includes the caveat that "it requires technologies that we are smart enough to build but not smart enough to use safely."[7] The *Torrey Canyon* spill was brought to a so-called end when the Royal Air Force bombed the ship with napalm, to ignite the crude. Terminating a spill is often synonymous with making it less visible. In Santa Barbara in 1969, dispersant hawkers lined up like snake-oil salesmen on the local pier, while frantic citizens poured kitty litter and talcum powder into the harbor in hopes of stemming the flow. As in the narcopolitics of the late twentieth and twenty-first centuries, in oil disasters blame ricochets among producers, distributors, and consumers who often describe themselves, guiltily, as "oil addicts." Coastal communities in the developed world have been forced toward an awareness of their implication in ecological injury. A 1969 cartoon from the *Santa Barbara News-Press* emphasizes the double-bind of affluent coastal living by picturing an anti-oil protestor jumping into his car to drive out for a day at the beach.

Because of their coastal location and proximity to offshore drilling and oil shipping, Santa Barbara's environmentalists came to recognize themselves as related to residents of Cornwall, England, later to coastal South Africans and Mexicans, and still later to the inhabitants of Prince William Sound and Louisiana. The "fundamentally somatic" intelligence that Orr recognizes as given to humans by our relationship to water has run up against oil culture's manipulation of images and—what is related—the image's distortion of time, its easy severance from context.[8] The coastal perspective worked out by Californians affected by the 1969 spill offers a still useable model of ecological thinking about the ocean as a damaged commons and the kind of sociality that living next door to such a commons might entail. In the United States, national ecological narratives have tended to be coastal, at least since the discovery of the ocean's "frailty" in the 1950s, through figures such as Rachel Carson, Jacques Cousteau, and Wesley Marx. As an originary incident, the Santa Barbara oil spill also points to the weaknesses of mainstream environmentalism as a movement in the United States. For instance, its attraction to middle-class rhetorics of rights, consumption, and sacrifice forecloses structural critique, and its overinvestment in spectatorship troubles its relationship to action.

Was Ecology Radical?

In one of many speeches delivered by Californians on the first Earth Day on April 22, 1970, Harriet Miller, a young woman destined to become one of Santa Barbara's longest-term mayors, prophesied that environmentalism would fail to become a "movement" because it was opposed to the values of the U.S. middle-class. "Pollution and destruction are by-products of our way of life," she noted, adding sarcastically that "public planning" and its enforcement at the federal level are "indulged in by godless communists but unthinkable for any right-minded American."[9] In lieu of planning, U.S. environmentalists would seize upon a discourse of rights. This would prove to be a dead-end, too, since the assertion of an "inalienable right to a decent environment," as stated in a 1969 constitutional amendment proposed by Wisconsin senator Gaylord Nelson, implies the curtailment of other rights, like driving your car. Miller could not imagine that "older" people would give up driving. She also could not yet imagine the string of legislative victories environmentalists won in the 1970s, including the National Environmental Policy Act of 1969, the Clean Air Act (1970), and the Coastal Zone Management Act (1972), all relevant to if not directly inspired by the Santa Barbara spill. Mainstream environmental writers, activists, lawyers, and lobbyists changed the culture of Washington, D.C. At a more intimate level, they reimagined what it might mean to make a good life in the United States, challenging core middle-class values.

Harriet Miller knew what we've come to see more starkly in the twenty-first century, that the U.S. Capitol floated on oil money—and middle-class environmental culture, too, would be suspended within a culture of oil. If the environment were a middle- or upper-class value, as it appeared to be in wealthy Santa Barbara, then actions to protect it would also sustain lifestyles run on petroleum, natural gas, and coal. Disneyland's House of the Future exhibit, opened in 1957, offered nuclear energy as a virtually "free" alternative to fossil fuels, prophesying an all-electric home that would thrum on nuclear power; the exhibit was sponsored by General Electric. The logic that cheaper nuclear energy equals more happiness replicated what the twentieth century already had proven through petroleum. Miller concluded her Earth Day speech with an ugly image: "As I watched a helpless, oil-soaked bird on the beach of Santa Barbara struggling for its last breath, I wondered if it might be a symbol—if it might be an indication of what man's last moments on earth would be like."[10] This young woman really had seen an oil-soaked bird gasping for breath, and many in her audience also had seen such suffering. The Santa Barbara spill occurred in waters only six miles off the coast, so a majority of affected animals washed up on local beaches. Birds, whose oil-damaged feathers inhibited flight, fell dead into the town. Privileged people, conscious of their happiness, witnessed the violence of the cheap energy that made it possible. They were traumatized. Oil, on the one hand, and beaches, on the other, struck at the heart of middle-class aspiration. Santa Barbara–style environmentalism promised an internal remaking of the global gold standard of living that southern California represented in the 1960s. But oil more than any other resource signaled the difficulty and potential hypocrisy of the ecological project.

The 1960s counterculture had dipped into the "ecology movement" prior to the Santa Barbara spill, making oil and energy primary examples of wrongful consumption. As the Beat poet Diane di Prima writes in "Revolutionary Letter #16," from the late 1960s:

> for our children's children, we will have to
> look carefully, i.e., do we really want/
> need
> electricity and at what cost in natural resource
> human resource
> do we need cars, when petroleum
> pumped from the earth poisons the land around
> for 100 years, pumped from the car
> poisons the hard-pressed cities....[11]

The stilted rhythms of this poem ("i.e., do we really want/need electricity and at what cost in natural resource") make it sound like deliberative thought, as well as a renunciation of the rhythmic pleasures of lyric poetry and song. An abstinence aesthetic is at work in di Prima. Her alliterative "p" sets up a fine short poem within the long poem—"petroleum...pumped...poisons...pumped...poisons...pressed"—that captures the relentlessness of the oil economy, inevitability as repetition. Di Prima traces a causal arc between "pumping" and the urban unease that, beginning with the Watts riots of 1964, betrayed sharp economic inequities beneath the civil rights discourse of liberals. The soft punch of the aspirated "p" as it leaves the mouth makes the spoken poem a soft threat. Of course the "pressed" cities di Prima mentions suffered environmental burdens explicitly linked to petroleum, such as air pollution that claimed urban lives, with record smog deaths in Los Angeles in 1967. But could di Prima, who looks so much like the young Bob Dylan in the cover photo for *Revolutionary Letters* (which she dedicated to Dylan), *really* renounce electricity? Long-playing records and FM radio are among the petroleum-supported media that generated the counterculture, with its political commitments to ending the Vietnam War and to "human interdependence," as the Port Huron Statement promised.[12]

Ecology might have been charismatic for the New Left, insofar as it indicated an alternative social structure that foregrounds the interdependence of beings. When I think of ecology in the United States circa 1969, I imagine social ecology movements that have emphasized questions of human health and potential and critiqued a more mainstream "environmentalism," whose key ethical problem became how humans *act upon* nonhuman life—as opposed to the reciprocal relations of humans and others.[13] Somewhat ironically, social ecology now lives at the margins of American history, shunted off to the back-to-the-land movement, communes, and Europeans. I use the terms "ecology" and "environmentalism" in this section loosely, in a way that is not meant to comprehend all aspects of either complex term. Of course both have changed significantly over time. As the historian Donald Worster reminds us, "ecology" grew up as a movement in response to atomic bomb testing, suggesting a life-centered, holistic science operating outside of the military-industrial complex.[14] In the late 1960s and early 1970s, "ecology" became a rallying cry both for those who sought radical social change and those now more easily identified with liberal tactics like lobbying, litigation, and boycotts. Back when self-declared ecologists and environmentalists might be the same people, they spent a good deal of time circling around the question of whether their emergent movement was radical. That question, whose stakes still feel high, often returns to oil.

The automobile, symbol of middle-class self-definition, served as a primary fetish-scapegoat for burgeoning environmentalists. At a Survival Faire in San Jose, California, in 1970, organizers bought a new car and buried it as a symbol of the task they saw confronting ecology action groups—essentially the task of creating an entirely new energy and transportation infrastructure, getting the country off of oil and cars. In his fine history of the first Earth Day in 1970, Adam Rome recalls that "the automobile was public enemy number one...target of much of the day's guerilla theater."[15] Numbers of youth killed by the internal combustion engine rivaled the horrifying tallies coming out of Vietnam. Kenneth P. Cantor's contribution to *The Environmental Handbook* (1970), which was prepared for the Earth Day "teach-in" and imagined as a movement Bible, begins with an anecdote about Chuck Herrick, co-founder of the group Ecology Action in Berkeley. "Chuck was killed in an automobile crash on the way to a Peace and Freedom party convention in Ann Arbor in May, 1968...He joined over more than 50,000 Americans who that year sacrificed their lives to the great god of American culture, the Private Motorcar."[16] Cantor's referendum on the car culture of the 1950s and early 1960s dips into memoir, as he recalls his visit to Santa Barbara after the oil spill: "A stench extending for miles....A dead bird is carried off in a plastic bag. I try to take a picture of it. Its guardian shields it from my lens. Birds are now no longer waterproof....Most die....Somehow, millions of years of evolution haven't prepared them for a six-month incarceration in sheds at the Ventura County Fairgrounds. How unkind nature has been to Union Oil."[17] Cantor's riff on "nature's" unkindness to the oil company recognizes the impact of images of dying birds to a culture not yet used to them. Demonstrators smashing an automobile at the first Earth Day in 1970 recalled antiwar protestors and urban rioters attacking police cars. But their target wasn't the Establishment so much as the self. The same kids who invented the custom car scene around Los Angeles to assert a subculture distinct from their (metaphorically) "plastic" parents turned against the car as the 1960s ended, initiating a strain of market-based piety that would be summed up in the counter-consumerist slogan "save the Earth."

An editorialist for *Ramparts*, the slick New Left magazine out of Berkeley, picked up on the protestors' sadonarcissism and indicted the car burial at the Survival Faire as a symptom of political naïveté. "To buy the car in the first place was to pay the criminal and strengthen him....In opposition to this misdirected gesture of revolt, San Jose's black students angrily demanded that the car be raffled to provide defense funds for their brothers on trial."[18] Referring to the Chicago Seven—Abbie Hoffman, Jerry Rubin, David Dellinger, Tom Hayden, Rennie Davis, John Froines, and Lee Weiner, who were charged with conspiracy and inciting to riot at Chicago's 1968 Democratic National Convention—the editorialist draws a distinction between *radicalism* and ecology. The white middle class, who imagine action through consumerism, should take a lesson from politically astute African Americans. The editorialist in turn praises the students who burned the Bank of America building in Isla Vista, a student community adjacent to the University of California at Santa Barbara. Interestingly, this was to be the only bank burning in the United States during the heady period of anti–Vietnam War protest.[19]

A now-famous photograph of young people silhouetted against the burning bank—as its "America" sign falls apart—serves as the bright orange and gold, literally incendiary image for the May 1970 "Ecology" special issue of *Ramparts*, which was released almost concurrently with the first celebration of Earth Day. [FIGURE 1. 1] In the deep-orange left corner of the cover photo, we're offered the following preview from the magazine's editorial: "The students who burned the Bank of America in Santa Barbara may have done more towards saving the environment than all the Teach-ins put together."[20]

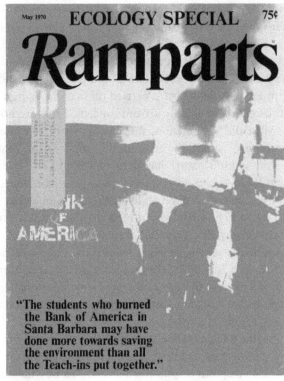

May 1970   ECOLOGY SPECIAL   75¢

Ramparts

"The students who burned the Bank of America in Santa Barbara may have done more towards saving the environment than all the Teach-ins put together."

FIGURE 1.1 Ramparts *Ecology Special Issue, May 1970*. Photo courtesy Guy Stilson and Greg Stilson.

Burning the bank is *radical* because it combines anti–Vietnam War protest, given the bank's ties to the U.S. occupation of Southeast Asia (it had branches in Saigon and Bangkok), with ecological consciousness. Two members of the bank's board of directors sat on the board of Union Oil. The point of the editorial's references to Chicago, blacks, Vietnam, Saigon, Bangkok, and the Bank of America is clear. If ecology isn't thought out on an international scale, if it isn't multiracial, if it isn't connected to larger structures of capital and war, then it's what *Ramparts* coauthors Katherine Barkley and Steve Weissman call the "Eco-Establishment." Barkley and Weissman bitterly noted that Atlantic Richfield and the Ford Foundation's Resources for the Future, Inc. (RFF), had given the environmentalist David Brower $200,000 to set up Friends of the Earth, the organization that published (with Ballantine Books) Earth Day's teach-in manual, *The Environmental Handbook*.[21]

Ramparts dismisses the first Earth Day of April 22, 1970, as a symptom of the "media's daydream of the co-optive potential of ecology," a distraction of student energies from more explosive matters in Vietnam. When the Santa Barbara Declaration of Environmental Rights, written by historian Roderick Nash, was presented to the U.S. House of Representatives on January 20, 1970, nearly one year after the oil spill, its emphasis on "heritage," "quality of life," "beauty," and "happiness"—not to mention "rights"—defined environmentalism within a constellation of middle-class values. The declaration proposed "a revolution in conduct towards an environment which is rising in revolt against us," suggesting a Franklinian ethic of right behavior, implicitly linked to how, or what, we consume. That the movement might be conceived as a reaction to "an environment rising in revolt against us," though the rhetoric intends to target out-of-control industrial pollution, places environmentalists in the place of counterrevolutionaries.[22] *Ramparts* caricatures them as "the conservation elite," with James Ridgeway quipping that "serious 'conservation' begins for *them* with the appearance of multitudes of the lower classes on their beaches; that's when they become aware of 'our imperiled environment' and the need for population control."[23] Ridgeway did not make mention of oil on the beaches, a more immediate stain in the minds of many Americans because of recent national coverage of the Santa Barbara spill.

What *Ramparts* fails to see in its special issue on ecology is the possibility that a middle-class, middle-aged ecological awakening might be in some respects more "revolutionary" than the cultural critique of self-declared radicals. Yet their suspicions are borne out, to an extent, in the work of contemporary popular environmentalists such as Garrett Hardin, a University of California–Santa Barbara professor whose now famous essay "The Tragedy of the Commons" (1968) essentially laments the presence of too many people on the beach. Actually, the national parks serve Hardin as a prime example of public space ruined by the public.[24] He imagines a lottery to restrict entrants. Hardin also praises inheritance and the maintenance of private property as stays against the "alternative of the commons, [which] is too horrifying to contemplate."[25] Although Hardin's analysis of why English agricultural commons failed as ecological and political systems is now known to be historically inaccurate, he picked up on the anxieties of Americans who had seen rural or semirural communities develop into dense suburbs from the 1930s to the 1960s. Set free of Hardin's explicit arguments, "The Tragedy of the Commons" has worked as a sharp warning about the difficulty of governing, and developing, shared environments like wetlands and forests. Yet his explicit arguments betray the links in the U.S. environmentalism of the late 1960s to elitist preservationist efforts of nineteenth-century "nature lovers" and to a wilderness aesthetic that the Indian historian Ramachandra Guha has dismissed as entirely misattuned to the ecologies of the poor and the Global South.[26]

When Hardin wrote about the commons, California in particular had become a poster child for overcrowding and aesthetic blight, in books like Raymond F. Dasmann's *The Destruction of California* (1965). Both Hardin and the biologist Paul Ehrlich are featured in *The Environmental Handbook*, putting population control at the center of the Earth Day teach-in, with "the right to limit the size of our families" at the top of Ehrlich's list.[27] The first edition of the *Handbook* in 1970 features a mail-in petition to "Mr. Nixon," meant to be signed and cut out of the book, which makes the claim that "the population problem is more serious than any other problem, therefore, at least 10% of the defense budget must be allocated to birth control and abortion in the US and abroad."[28] Whatever one's views on birth control, the idea that the defense department might be put in charge of it at home and abroad complements more flamboyant conspiratorial claims from environmentalism's early critics that, for instance, the aerospace industry stood to profit from pollution abatement.

Reading *Ramparts* and counterculture publications like the journal of the Students for a Democratic Society (SDS) against *The Environmental Handbook* and other works by those authors contributing to it, I see "ecology" and "environmentalism" being worked out by a youth culture destined to splinter as the Vietnam War wears on and the first oil shock of the 1970s puts a finer point on consumer responsibility. The similarities of the self-proclaimed radicals and the accused mainstream are in some regards more interesting than their differences. They share a print culture. *The Environmental Handbook* and Ehrlich's *Population Bomb* are advertised on the back cover of the *Ramparts* "Ecology" special issue, creating an off rhyme with the front cover's sharp dismissal of Earth Day and photo of the burning bank. "Survival in the Seventies Depends upon You Being Informed," the advertisement blasts, above a photograph of the two paperback books. Belief in the power of print to motivate action grounds the investigative reportage and hortatory style of *Ramparts*, while the admonition to "read" and "research" appears throughout *The Environmental Handbook* as a first line of defense.[29] The ecology movement is bookish, circa 1970. It also is gently prurient. Ads for the Swedish cult novel *Curious Yellow*, for the "sociological" foray *White Woman, Black Man,* and a "60-Second Sex Test" interrupt the gravitas of *Ramparts*. *The Environmental Handbook* half-jokes that Dow Chemical be repurposed as a maker of "pornographic products," since good sex acts as population control—a fragile logic.[30] What seems to be a predominantly male fear of pleasure, captured in repeated images of unwanted pregnancy, complements ecological desire.

Ecology as a worldview intends to shift the psychic and material infrastructures of modernity, for both self-proclaimed radicals and for those whom they critiqued as elites. Katherine Barkley and Steve Weissman write in *Ramparts* that, if aptly conceived, "ecology...would point the finger not simply at profit-making polluters or greedy consumers, but at the great garbage-creation system itself—the corporate capitalist economy."[31] Similar structural criticism frames *The Environmental Handbook*, which advocates a slow-growth economy, renewable energy systems, and a retooled family unit. The "Smokey the Bear Sutra," a chant-poem that opens the *Handbook*, uses the famous symbol of the U.S. national parks to soften a cry for "trampling underfoot wasteful freeways and needless suburbs; smashing the worms of capitalism and totalitarianism."[32] Smokey's doing the trampling in the poem, a teddy-bear icon of anarchy. The *Handbook* assumes that its readers will identify with the national parks, broadly conceiving them as middle-class aspirants who've visited the parks, perhaps on family vacations. "We are aware of racial tensions that could tear the nation apart," Earth Day organizers acknowledge: "We understand that oppressive poverty in the midst of affluence is intolerable."[33] Both *Ramparts* and the Earth Day *Handbook* draw rhetoric from Black Power, even as they rhetorically locate themselves to the side of it. Angela Davis and Bobby Seale were contributors to *Ramparts*, and Earth Day organizers looked to "black studies demonstrators" for models of "re-education."[34] Mixing up the symbolism of middle-class outdoor leisure, urban street protest, and South Asian sacred texts, *The Environmental Handbook* promises: "If anyone is threatened by advertising, air pollution, or the police, they should chant SMOKEY THE BEAR'S SPELL....And SMOKEY THE BEAR will surely appear to put the enemy out with his vajra-shovel."[35] Earth Day's virtual Bible indulged the profound silliness that had been a hallmark of the counterculture since Ken Kesey's critical pranksterism.

The "enemy" is perhaps the most coherent aspect of the nascent ecology movements. The enemy, for all, includes advertisers, utility companies, Big Oil, the automobile, and old-timers, meaning those stuck in "the industrial revolution phase of history."[36] Technology had proven in some respects good—and historians have shown the links between techie environmentalists like Buckminster Fuller and Stewart Brand and the development of the personal computer—but "technology at its best cannot save the whole scene."[37] Radicals differed from the new environmentalists in terms of how to confront the enemy. *Ramparts* thought the "ecology movement will really have to pull the big plug at the other end of the TV transmitter, or, better, at the production line itself" to make change in a world where consumers no longer influence production or media.[38] In contrast, Earth Day organizers trusted in the influence of "the public," in "public opinion" that might be expressed through consumer boycotts or in "public service advertisements" that describe "our common problems" in "public" venues, like trains and buses.[39] The word *public* sounds the bass note of Earth Day rhetoric, and it inspired a kind of political action that defines mainstream environmentalism's success. In the wake of the Santa Barbara spill, Californians organized a People's Lobby to pressure Sacramento about corporate polluters, an effort that was echoed in other states and through federal entities such as the Natural Resources Defense Council (NRDC), founded in 1970 for citizens interested in drafting environmental laws and lobbying or litigating for them.

Fourteen new federal environmental laws were developed after the Santa Barbara spill of 1969.[40] Similar local and state laws proliferated. The California Coastal Commission, founded in 1972, was tasked to keep beaches unpolluted by oil and gas development, among other things. The Commission took its place in a growing slate of regulatory policies and agencies, most notably the Environmental Protection Agency, which had been created two years earlier. The largely middle-class public summoned by mainstream environmentalism hadn't been as toothless as some New Left media imagined. Adam Rome reminds us that Earth Day, which erupted into more than 12,000 separate events on the day of its debut in 1970, created a lasting eco-infrastructure.[41] Yet certain New Left doubts prophesy the emphases of the U.S. environmental justice movement of the later twentieth century, such as whether regulatory agencies might be tools of corporations, whether interest group politics lead to compromise with polluters, and whether mainstream environmentalism is too "parochial" to attract underrepresented minorities. Rob Nixon has pointed out that only in the United States did a separate environmental movement (environmental justice) evolve to treat questions of social justice. One wonders what might have happened if more *Ramparts*-style critique had stayed with "ecology" into the 1980s. Such questions have long since worked free of New Left conspiracy theories that the ecology movement was engineered as a distraction from the Vietnam War by President Richard Nixon or by the more benign Gaylord Nelson of Wisconsin—the senator who sponsored Earth Day. Nelson claims to have dreamed up the Earth Day idea while reading *Ramparts* on a plane ride from Santa Barbara.[42]

By the time of Earth Day's creation, the New Left recognized itself as alienated from the popular base it might have expected in a country where an overwhelming majority had come to disapprove of the Vietnam War. In his classic study of the media and the movement, *The Whole World Was Watching*, Todd Gitlin chronicles the New Left's chaotic descent into a "decontextualized revolutionary symbol world."[43] Paul Relis, an antiwar activist and conscientious objector in Santa Barbara, recalls his own development from anti-war activism toward the promise of ecology. "I needed to be involved in the creative building side," he notes. In the wake of the Santa Barbara spill, Relis and his friends learned "how to be tactical" in new ways, combining the backyard engineering associated with the *Whole Earth Catalog* with savvy coalitional politics.[44] Santa Barbara's Community Environmental Council convinced the city's art museum to donate unused land for El Mirasol Polyculture Farm, which became an un-self-conscious public art exhibit on organic gardening and build-it-yourself solar technology. While still a student, Relis collaborated with an architecture firm to design a shoreline park to stave off commercial development of the Santa Barbara pier. His design, which cribbed from a 1922 city plan by Frederick Olmsted, Jr., made it onto the cover of the local newspaper and, with a few alterations, became public space that curtailed the proliferation of hotels. "There were dark times," Relis concedes, but he recalls a "symbiotic" attraction between activists and "bluebloods" in a town whose image and economy rested on beauty and coastal access.[45] In 1969, Santa Barbara was small, with approximately 60,000 people, and conservative, a stronghold for the John Birch Society.

Santa Barbara offers an ideal lab for questioning the relative conservatism—and radicalism—of the multifaceted movement that came to be known as American environmentalism. Harvey Molotch, a sociologist at the University of California–Santa Barbara at the time of the oil spill, first applied the term "radical" to what was happening in the wake of it. Radicals, argued Molotch (in, again, *Ramparts*), "are persons who live in conditions where injustice is apparent, and who have access to more complete information about their plight than the average man, giving them a perspective that allows them to become angry in a socially meaningful way."[46] In Santa Barbara, Molotch observed the radicalization of affluent people whose notion of safety—deeply connected to an ideal of natural beauty—had been destroyed. Protests against oil after the spill were mostly raised by town members, not students. By virtue of the injury done them, Santa Barbarans "have gained insights into the structure of power in America not possessed by similarly situated persons in other parts of the country," Molotch concludes, in what remains the most insightful social analysis of the Santa Barbara blowout.[47] Some of the particular lessons that Santa Barbarans learned: That the oil industry had no means of remediating spills; that industry had long been aware of the dangers of drilling in the seismically unstable channel; that Corexit, the dispersant favored by Union Oil, was toxic to marine life (a lesson tragically replayed forty years later, in coastal Louisiana); that events were sometimes "pseudo-events," as when President Nixon enjoyed a photo-op on a beach "cleaned" by workmen hired for the occasion of his visit. It seemed that government and Big Oil actually worked against "the public"—and the fundamental hopes for democracy suggested in that term—when a presidential commission recommended that the only sure method of spill remediation was drilling fifty new wells under Platform A. That process would take twenty years and enrich federal coffers.

In short, Santa Barbarans found themselves saddled with more complete information than could support complacency, to paraphrase Molotch. A complementary gloss on the cultural effects of the spill comes from Ross MacDonald, the hard-boiled crime writer who lived in Santa Barbara at the time of the spill and participated in the protests. MacDonald includes the oil spill in *Sleeping Beauty* (1973), a novel relocated to the fictional enclave of Pacific Point, a coastal community just south of Los Angeles. Here he describes Lew Archer, his detective protagonist, making his first foray onto an oil-soaked beach:

> I made my way down to the public beach and along it to the sandy point which partly enclosed the harbor. A few people, mostly women and girls, were standing at the edge of the water, facing out to sea. They looked as if

they were waiting for the end of the world, or as if the end of the world had come and they would never move again.

The surf was rising sluggishly. A black bird with a sharp beak was struggling in it. The bird had orange-red eyes, which seemed to be burning with anger, but it was so fouled with oil that at first I didn't recognize it as a western grebe.

A woman in a white shirt and slacks waded in thigh-deep and picked it up, holding its head so that it wouldn't peck her. I could see as she came back toward me that she was a handsome young woman with dark eyes as angry as the bird's. Her narrow feet left beautifully shaped prints in the wet sand.[48]

As it turns out, this handsome woman is the granddaughter of an oil magnate. Throughout *Sleeping Beauty*, wealthy people, many of them women, grieve birds, recognizing in the oil spill the mismanagement of men and the emptiness of their supposed security. *Sleeping Beauty* makes a weird hybrid of crime genre formulae and naive feminism. "Like the ghost of a woman who had already died," Lew Archer says of the young woman at the beach, when he fears she might have killed herself, "Or the ghost of a bird."[49]

MacDonald's evocations of an affluent community in shock express a historical moment that is representationally challenging, almost paradoxical. My interviews with locals similarly retrieved images of people standing at the waterline, frozen. The radicalization of an elite frames Santa Barbara's oil disaster. Some of the most privileged people on earth at the middle of the so-called American century were exposed to the knowledge that their world was not safe, not even theirs. What such a paradox would produce for environmentalism was an open question as of 1970. While not so open today, it is still a question worth asking.

To pursue what it means for the middle class or the affluent to experience radical insight, I first turn to a consideration of the relationship of visual and print media to the development of environmental sensibilities in the aftermath of the Santa Barbara spill.

Oil Spill Media, Parts I–III

I. THE LOCAL PHOTOGRAPHER

In 1969 the newspaper photographer and naturalist Dick Smith accompanied photojournalists from *Life* magazine to San Miguel Island to survey the damage of the Santa Barbara spill. The island, a "no man's land" within a U.S. Navy gunnery range, is a birthing ground for California and Stellar sea lions and elephant seals. Smith brought his teenaged daughter on the trip, who delivers one of the most memorable quotations in the *Life* article that followed it. "I feel as if I had just gone into someone's house where everyone was murdered, for no reason at all," she says, referring to the oil-soaked carcasses of sea lions at San Miguel, many of them pups.[50] Smith's photographs of oil-soaked mainland beaches were published in the *Santa Barbara News-Press* and other papers, and there are about two hundred Smith photographs archived at the University of California. Following his daughter's metaphor of unprovoked "murder," Smith's photos suggest the need to establish the evidentiary basis of a crime. The photos betray what taking pictures of dying animals might mean to someone who is not anticipating wide publication. Smith's photos occupy the line between private and public use that art historian John Berger recognizes as the site of personal history, redeeming photographic images from decontextualization and commodification. "If the living take the past upon themselves, if the past becomes an integral part of the process of people making their own history, then all photographs would reacquire a living context"—through personal usage Berger imagines how photographs might become genuine social memory, rather than a substitute for it.[51] In Smith's photos, we see both the journalistic tendency to punctuate an argument with an image and one man's grief-work. The personal loss of the image maker tends to get short shrift in discussions of photographs of injury, which have been targets of strong criticism since the 1970s.

Before returning to Dick Smith, I want briefly to situate oil spill photography within the rich critical conversation about images as witnesses to atrocity. Susan Sontag, Jacques Rancière, and others, recently Maggie Nelson, theorize the deficiencies of "the image" as a route to action—with images figuring as "our normal condition," in Rancière's words, rather than a special prompt to social change.[52] The photograph is assumed, understandably, to work for an effect upon an audience, and in that regard it often falls short of expectations. Writing of the Seattle-based photographer Natalie Fobes's images of animals affected by the 1989 Exxon *Valdez* spill, John Keeble laments "a studied element of romance in the face of inescapable horror."[53] For Keeble, an investigative reporter, the olfactory and tactile surprise of a carcass under one's shoe on a littered beach defines the experience of mass death in Prince William Sound. I think what Keeble is after is, like Berger, the artistic transmission of a more personal and contextualized memory, and his concern is that photographs of the *Valdez* spill make it abstract—therefore fungible. Also in play is what the cultural historian Alan Trachtenberg remarks as the challenge to photography generated by the "extreme" gap "between sense experience and mental comprehension" in the case of war—or, I would argue, in the case of an equivalent ecological trauma.[54] Keeble chooses a texturally rich photograph by Fobes of oil-soaked carcasses in a heap, birds and otters awaiting cold storage, for inclusion in his excellent book about the *Valdez* spill, *Out of the Channel*. The production of bodies as garbage, chaotic matter out of place, grounds this image. In contrast to the conceptual surprise of such a photo, images crafted to be readable, for instance dead otters with "paws crossed near their chests" echoing human mortuary conventions, might disappear into established memory scripts, blurring the particularity of the *Valdez* spill and the more than 10,000 otters who perished in the Sound.[55] Keeble's book begins with the inscription "In Memoriam" and a list of the Latin names of species afflicted by the *Valdez*.[56] This writing challenges photography and the kind of forgetting that Walter Benjamin and Susan Sontag, among others, have recognized as a result of modernity's turn against narrative toward "information." As Berger writes in dialogue with Sontag, whose words appear here in single quotes, photos "offer appearances...prised away from their meaning. Meaning is the result of functioning. 'And functioning takes place in time, and must be explained in time.'"[57]

The criticism directed at the political ineffectiveness and even violence of the atrocity photograph in the era of the Vietnam War made sense in the context of foreign combat that seemed, for the first time, to betray the consent of the American citizenry. Berger's concern was that such images dissipated political engagement. Yet when it comes to use, the argument between prose and photography for prominence in the documentation of atrocity often falls to the photograph. Photographs make their way into courts and congresses as witnesses. Natalie Fobes's images of the fallout left by the Exxon *Valdez* were used in both state and federal hearings as witnesses for Alaskan fishermen, while Subhankar Banerjee's photographs of the Arctic National Wildlife Refuge provided Senator Barbara Boxer with evidence to display on the floor of Congress against oil drilling on Alaska's North Slope. Ironically, this latter evidentiary performance devalued Banerjee's photographs as "art," causing their exhibit to be relegated to the basement of the Smithsonian national museum, with their descriptive tags removed.[58] The Smithsonian's curators saw a threat in the art form that has elsewhere been deemed merely a means of "stimulat[ing] buying and anaesthetiz[ing] the injuries of race, class, and sex."[59] The photographer and critic Allan Sekula will stand in here for a powerful counterargument for photographic realism, noting that photography complements the work of critical realism by making visible the persons and things that tend to disappear in cultures of capitalism.[60] *Fish Story*, Sekula's photo-essay about the postindustrial port, argues that "a certain stubborn and pessimistic insistence on the primacy of material forces is part of a common culture of harbor residents," such as himself.[61] He could be writing broadly of coastal communities adjacent to shipping channels and maritime industry like offshore drilling. "This crude materialism is underwritten by disaster.... Ships explode, leak, sink, collide.... Gravity is recognized as a force."[62] *Fish Story* asks us to think about how commodities move through space, rematerializing globalization by placing the iconic container in contexts of labor or disuse and degradation. Sekula's close-up images of an oil spill off Galicia, Spain, in the exhibit *Black Tide/Marea negra*, also offer the possibility that images might reveal material contexts indicative of obscured social relations.

Of course Roland Barthes makes the now widely criticized argument that photographs are thing-y, literally emanations of objects, light that has known the densities of bodies. The desire for this to be true gets wound up in the one image Barthes refuses to show in his classic *Camera Lucida*, an image of his dead mother as a child. That photography might be primarily grief-work, a means for both photographer and viewer to hold the dead, is at the bottom of Barthes's boldest claims. Jay Prosser argues that "it is the trauma of losing his mother that suspends the connotation procedures of photography" for Barthes.[63] In some respects, Barthes's melancholic theory of the photograph as a trace of the once-alive reiterates the photograph's earliest uses in the nineteenth century, when parents coveted photographs of dead children, dying Civil War soldiers clutched at photos of distant wives, and "spirit photography" promised proof of the persistence of individuals as light, photography's own medium. Long before images of dying soldiers dispersed our shock or the oil-soaked bird became easily assimilated by viewers as what the cultural critic Andrew Ross describes as a "de rigueur" victim,[64] photography was identified as pragmatic grief-work, because accounting for the dead figures, as a means of survey, into the project of mourning them.[65] Here again we return to Berger's admiration for the "personal photograph" as an image that incorporates history because it isn't dissociated from its originary circumstance—say, a child's death.[66] With this rich critical context in mind, I read Dick Smith's photographs of oil-soaked animals on the beaches of Santa Barbara through the traditions of memorial photography.

The Smith archive bristles with visible frustration and grief. As I rummaged through it, it felt to me like the disassembled memoir of a prisoner of war or some other disappeared person, although what literally slips away from Smith (into a future that the archive touches) are the lives of marine animals. In a folder labeled "Dead Porpoise Incident," Smith offers a typewritten report, crime-scene style. The subject is a pregnant porpoise that washed up on a Santa Barbara beach after the spill, thick crude clogging her blowhole. The California Fish and Game Department, camped out at a makeshift office in a beachside motel after the spill, attempts to cover up the porpoise death, at first refusing to examine the corpse, then refusing to attribute the cause of her death to oil. Smith's photographs are not included in the file that he assembled. He apparently was invited to photograph the death scene by a university biologist who feared that Fish and Game might dispose of the pregnant carcass—itself a kind of feminist grotesque. Fish and Game refused the biologist's offer to autopsy the animal and handed it to an official who did not know how to perform autopsies. In the file labeled "Dead Porpoise Incident," Smith comments on cover-ups of other marine mammal deaths, as well as on the poor death counts of birds and the misattribution of the causes of their deaths to sources other than oil. This seems to be a moment when neither government nor industry quite knew how to turn events into rhetoric, as the floundering of Fish and Game attests. In the idiosyncratic prose of testimony, Smith writes: "In general as it is not known what caused the death of the birds even though completely covered with oil, yet all are accounted for and tagged [T]hen why are not the mammals which have been washing up on the shores been given the dignity of the same accounting [*sic*]."[67] In fact only the birds that died at Santa Barbara's two designated bird rescue centers were counted, a small percentage of the whole.[68] Smith's photographs don't give better numbers, but they speak to the shared witnessing of death by a community of afflicted animals and the humans for whom they held meaning.

Smith's multiple exposures and experimental cropping of images of dead shore birds, combined with his sometimes taxonomic, sometimes anecdotal labeling of these images, recall photography as itself memory practice—a means of taking something into the self, repurposing it for the self, giving it story and place. Cognitive scientists have verified the fragmentary, reconstructed nature of memory and therefore the philosophical musing of Jacques Derrida, who wrote in an early essay that "memory is finite by nature…[and] always needs signs in order to recall the non-present."[69] Smith exposes his film of one long-necked California murre so as to pick up the context of a gritty, oiled beach. He overexposes the same image to obliterate the beach, as a wash of light. He again exposes the same image, flipped and in the negative, creating what appears as a psychedelic poster image

FIGURE 1.2 *California Murre. Photograph by Dick Smith. Courtesy of Dick Smith Estate, Dick Smith Collection, 1969–1971. SBHC Mss 56 Department of Special Collections, Davidson Library, University of California, Santa Barbara.*

FIGURE 1.3 *California Murre Reverse Negative Image. Photograph by Dick Smith. Courtesy Dick Smith Estate, Dick Smith Collection, 1969–1971. SBHC Mss 56, Department of Special Collections, Davidson Library, University of California, Santa Barbara.*

of the murre and a tribute to Victorian-era spirit photography. [FIGURES 1.2 and 1.3] I can't see this cynically, as a creepy aestheticization of suffering. The multiple exposures and croppings defamiliarize the bird, and they hold it. Taken straight, the murre standing weakly against the familiar sand backdrop of a local beach is impossible to look at for any length of time. As it lists under a thick coating of toxic crude, its eyes are still open, staring into the near distance. In the abstract, sans backdrop in either positive or negative exposure, those haunting eyes and the consciousness of pain they suggest disappear, and the bird becomes a shape of injury. The point of making the image seems to be the transcendence of the bird, the restoration of its dignity available to the camera by literally taking the essence of it.

Clearly these losses are close to Smith. The labels on the back of his photos indicate his irritability and disbelief. The writing on the back of one image of a young man dumping something off of the Santa Barbara pier asks the future archivist, "Are you ready for this! Kitty litter was poured on water."[70] The photo itself lacks drama, as the dead-black quality of the water in the harbor fails to register in the black-and-white image. The man pouring the kitty litter wears an ambivalent, unreadable expression. Perhaps what is most important about this photograph is that Smith anticipates its persistence into a future where such apparent ephemera will be relevant. In a gesture that has come to be associated with Derrida's argument for the forward-orientation of the archive, Dick Smith makes a bid for the future.

II. NATIONAL PRINT

As Susan Sontag remarked, magazines and newspapers "come to" us, or they used to, before the eras of self-selected micropublics and digital media.[71] A reader of *Life* magazine in 1969 might come upon Harry Benson's photograph of a sea lion pup drowned in oil without reading *Life's* cover story, "The *Life* Poll: Science and Sex." Taken as montage—as Sally Stein suggests we consider the format of the popular magazine—this issue of *Life* works through a series of visual and rhetorical puns to comment upon the ways in which life, in America, is moving away from natural arrangements.[72] A flip-through might raise questions about the future of parenting, it might stimulate desire for a Polaroid camera ("almost as easy as opening your eyes," the ad says), or the camera might set me thinking of a day trip to a windswept island in the Santa Barbara Channel, when oil isn't there. *Life's* photo-essay about the Santa Barbara oil spill, "Iridescent Gift of Death," exposes the spill's unreported damage to marine life in locations not easily accessible to the general public—such as San Miguel Island.[73] But since there's no directionality to a magazine, its images functioning as mix-and-match "elements of narrative," it is unclear how this story acts.[74] Arguments against the relation of spectatorship to outrage or action—such as Berger's that the photograph of agony actually disperses the viewer's shock—are supported by the magazine experience. A magazine might show me something I didn't expect, but it also distracts me, tempting me to skim, to linger over ads. Of course *Life* was financed not by its sales but by advertising from the time of its launch in 1936. Within the marketplace definition of personal freedom that magazines suggest—their popularity soared in the 1930s with the popularity of film, as readers longed for the commoditized "private life" of movie stars—atrocity images have an uncertain valence. They might offer "moments of discontinuity," as Berger says, with the viewer blaming herself for her inability to produce narrative from the image, thus rendering her unable to criticize the political structures that generate agony. After too many viewings, the oil-covered bird might seem "de riguerur," a tactical icon. Or it might be an effective image that still doesn't cause me to act.

Life's coverage of the Santa Barbara spill offers more muckraking than might be expected from a magazine designed to "to edit pictures into a coherent story" of U.S. middle-class experience, to paraphrase the mission statement of the magazine's first editor, Henry Booth Luce.[75] By the time of the Santa Barbara spill, atrocity had found a niche within *Life's* "corporate modernism," its synthesis of nationalism, consumerism, and a twentieth-century visual culture that was not easily contained by ideology.[76] The war photography that showed up in *Life* after 1943, and the pictorial representation of civilian deaths in Vietnam that marked the magazine's final years as a weekly, prepared the American public for some of the first glossy, full-color images of environmental injury, among which are those of the Santa Barbara spill. The

June 13, 1969, issue of *Life* arrived at more than six million U.S. homes while oil was still seeping on to Santa Barbara's beaches, reminding the nation of a story no longer "newsworthy" because it already had dragged on for five months. "As the oil leak off Santa Barbara keeps right on killing wildlife, the proposal is for all-out drilling," blasts the article's subheading.[77] This refers to the Nixon presidential commission's recommendation to drill out the channel in order to "save" it. The *Life* essay foregrounds the trickiness of picturing ecological damage. Iridescence reads beautifully in the lead image of the oily waters around Platform A—the subtle blues, golds, and browns of the spill emphatically support the medium of color print. Yet author David Snell reminds us that this unnatural iridescence means "a sea gone dead" and the end of a subtler beauty—the "fiery wake of phosphorescence in waters alive with microscopic marine life."[78]

Remembering this story probably will begin in Harry Benson's photographs and may end there. Surely someone saw the horrific photos and chose not to read David Snell's text. An infant sea lion who is not visibly stained by oil but apparently starving looks out at the viewer from beneath the article heading, while two pages later another infant cuddles its oil-splotched, toxic mother. Still another adult sea lion, apparently dead, lolls in a pool of crude. We see oil-covered rocks on San Miguel Island and immediately below that a smaller photo of a Union Oil worker steam cleaning rocks on a mainland tourist beach—a pairing meant to ironize "public relations," which only pays attention to damage that can be seen by many people. In the final image of the essay, a dead infant sea lion lies amidst oil-soaked refuse, its corpse coming as an unpleasant surprise in an intriguing jumble of glossy black shapes—black rocks and what appears to be an industrial wheel. The closed eyes of the pup are what Barthes might call the photo's *punctum*, the incidental detail that makes it resonate.[79] Because the eyes are closed, they suggest that the pup is merely sleeping, giving it the peaceful look of an animal that might open her eyes at any moment, although we recognize that this will not happen.

The eyes of these animals, when they are open, look at us and away from us, the mere fact of their being able to look suggesting pain. Looking at these photos forty years on is still upsetting, raising again for me the question of what such photos actually *do*—although wiser critics might warn me to let that go. As Sontag acknowledged late in her career, nuancing so many of her earlier remarks about the image as a mode of forgetting, atrocity photographs have garnered so much criticism in part because "we" viewers, and critics, feel that we cannot do anything about atrocity: "Moral indignation, like compassion, cannot dictate a course of action."[80] This ethical disappointment is not the fault of images. Berger would frankly argue that it underlines our lack of political freedom—the same problem that consumers control neither production nor media, which *Ramparts* identified for environmentalists. "That we can turn away, turn the page, switch the channel, does not impugn the ethical value of an assault by images," Sontag concludes, arguing that the image still offers a primary means of knowledge.[81] Her emphasis on whether or not atrocity images are given in a space conducive to "being serious" is worth pursuing here, insofar as *Life* magazine initiates the imaging of the modern oil spill for a mass public.

The first context for Harry Benson's photographs in *Life* is David Snell's text, and it is dead serious. If I read it, I will know more about the spill and probably remember more. Snell emphasizes that the spill is not over, as Nixon suggested as early as March. He indicates its duration by making note of an affected animal: "He was an infant sea lion on the 118th day of the Santa Barbara oil spill."[82] The first to announce large numbers of dead mammals in the wake of the event, Snell also offers readers what cannot be seen in the pages of a glossy magazine—the animals' unnatural smell. Infant sea lions that drag themselves through oil no longer smell like themselves to their mothers and will be abandoned. The ocean smells of "high-grade crude." Dead sea lions stink "sickeningly." Snell and his crew count more than one hundred corpses before "we became weary and sick of the tally."[83] After local media noted what appeared to be mass sea lion death on the island after flying over it in helicopters, the U.S. Navy assured the public that the apparently dead animals were "sleeping." Accurate numbers for dead mammals and birds never have been reported, nor was the amount of oil spilled in the channel ever accurately estimated. Snell describes some quarter of a million gallons of crude blackening waters and shores as seepage continues into June. The caving of the national media to Union Oil's public relations serves as the villain of this essay, probably because Snell, as a journalist, can do something about it. Yet the essay concludes in futility. Its last line, as the crew leaves the island: "Behind us was the black vision of the dead world which may come."[84] Common to atomic-bomb imagery in science fiction, this image of a nonfuture essentially concedes the ephemerality and self-reflexivity of the magazine experience. There's nothing left but to turn the page.

Most *Life* subscribers probably remember the June 13th issue, as does a friend of mine who was eight at the time of its publication, for its cover image of a fetus, made to appear as if in a test tube against the larger backdrop of outer space, twinkling with stars. Stanley Kubrick's *2001*, with its lush imagery of existential doubt, would be released in a matter of months. In *Life*'s cover story "poll" on science and sex, only 3 percent of participants had heard of artificial insemination before registering their opinions about it. In sum, women were more favorably inclined toward reproductive technologies than men. The story that frames the poll is a book excerpt from *Second Genesis* by *Life*'s science editor, Albert Rosenfeld. It delivers an amped-up diatribe about the death of the family, of mothering, and of heterosexuality. In "in vitro world," as Rosenfeld calls it, women "can begin to have their babies without carrying them, thus freeing them from their ancient bondage."[85] Competing for a dwindling supply of males—who will be sexually exhausted—women may accept "polyandry" or "turn to each other."[86] It strikes me as remarkable that *Life*'s typically mainstream and middle-aged readership could share, even for a moment, Rosenfeld's hysterical, radical imagining. "Could society devise adequate substitutes [for mothers]?" he asks. "Could the trans-humans of post-civilization survive without love as we have known it in the institutions of marriage and the family?"[87] Similar questions were being asked by counter-culture communards. In Ernest Callenbach's *Ecotopia* (1975), the "disappear-ance of the nuclear family as we know it" complements other structural shifts in production, from an ecological emphasis on slow growth to specific and even prophetic innovations, like a prediction of on-demand publishing.[88] With some anxiety, Callenbach's first-person narrator, Weston, notes that "because women have absolute control over their own bodies," they "openly exert" the "right to select the fathers of their children."[89] *Ecotopia* recognizes the most challenging aspect of ecology as the emotional authenticity that grows out of gender equality and the de-reification of labor.

The sexual revolution complemented middle-class environmentalism insofar as it generated a nostalgia for the nature idea, yet feminist women and men had to recognize how nature could be tactically deployed. *Life* yearns for capital-N Nature. The magazine's rhyming images of infant sea lions robbed of their mothers by toxic oil and "helpless" human infants, motherless "in vitro," suggest that we all have gotten in too deep—tech-nology runs out of control, with mothers as the first casualties. A photo of a mother cradling an infant appears in the upper-right corner of *Life*'s cover, offsetting the psychedelic and lonely world of the in vitro fetus. Compensation for the sexual liberation of women, which more than any-thing else in the middle-class playbook signifies the death of nature, might be the twinkling outer space visible from within the test tube. The Apollo 8 pops up in a two-page spread on the Paris Air Show, next to a color spread assuring readers that peace has returned to Berkeley's People's Park. Given space, and the billions of pounds of fuel required to get there, "trans-man" might escape "trans-woman" *and* unruly youth, if not himself. To get into space and back to natural(ized) gender, we need a great deal of fuel. NASA would have relied on kerosene in the 1960s, whereas today shuttles use cleaner hydrogen systems. Throughout *Life*, the fossil fuel regime that had supported American masculinity through car culture and solid indus-trial jobs shares ad space with liquor and appliances. The simulacra of the ads, promising to meet impossible expectations, as Daniel J. Boorstin complained in *The Image: A Guide to Pseudo-Events in America*, compen-sate for a nature proven too fragile.[90] To love life, love *Life*, the "in vitro" world of the magazine, the disembodied masculinity of the astronaut, the mechanical maternity of refrigerators. How might the dying sea lion act within this circular logic?

III. THE INTERNET AND GLOBAL SCALE

Internet media "comes to us" in somewhat the same way that a magazine image might befall our browsing eye, but it also foregrounds the idea, perhaps the fantasy, of choice. For instance, when I search for *Life* magazine's treatment of the BP oil blowout and spill of 2010, I am served a menu of hyperlinks to distinct magazine features. One link leads me to the spill's animal victims. Choosing to click on that link places me in an ethical bind.[91] Atrocity images are not befalling me as I flip through pages of text and ad copy, but rather I am seeking out images of injured animals, much as I might pursue a discounted pair of shoes. Maggie Nelson argues in a similar vein about the human rights organization the Hub's Witness project, a website that intends to raise awareness about human rights atrocities by archiving images of them. Nelson writes that "for better or for worse, one's experience of surfing the Hub is shaped by the do-I-or-don't-I-want-to-watch question."[92] The so-called eco-pornographic impulse has to be enacted, when, for instance, one clicks on the link for animal victims and, at the site, chooses to scroll through a slide show—images only accessible if I move my finger—of oil-drenched pelicans and burning turtles. To me, this is not a good "place" to be seriously thinking, albeit at a necessary distance, about the suffering of animals. As a person who is old enough not to have grown up with the Internet, I can't stand the feeling of choosing to look at the pain of others (human or not), especially when it is coupled with the realization that my "click" will be archived by Google and become part of a consumer profile more indestructible, to my regret, than even the most expensively produced imagery in a Sierra Club exhibit-format book. When David Brower led the Sierra Club into publishing and advertising in the 1960s, he imagined print media as a means of either speedily attracting attention to an environmental problem or preserving an endangered place, like Glen Canyon, in a monumental book.[93] Either way, environmental media reached toward things outside itself, rather than back to the consumer's profile.

My classroom experience with young people suggests to me that they are no more inured to images of environmental atrocity than were twenty year olds paging through *Life* magazine in 1969—and in fact the one comment offered below *Life*'s 2010 photo archive of BP's animal victims when I first visited the site came from a youngish-appearing viewer who says simply, in the spirit of Sontag, "I feel so bad. I wish I could do something." My concern isn't that animals coated with oil have become a variety of titillation merely, but rather that no one might ever choose to look at such injury, if choose we must in the media environment of libertarian market sense that we inhabit. Without looking at animals dying in oil, through the happenstance of print media intended for middle-class leisure, thinking about such victims, and about, say, the regulation of offshore oil drilling, may also be less likely.[94] Which could leave the act of witnessing and knowing such things through seeing them even more exclusively to those affected by industrial accident—often working-class and otherwise disenfranchised communities that, like many in and around New Orleans after Hurricane Katrina, will be pressed to disseminate images of their personal disasters, through Internet videography that may or may not be picked up by national outlets. While there is much to be said for so-called victims speaking for themselves, such "self-mediating" also strikes me as a symptom of the curtailment of American social services since the 1980s (coinciding with the privatization of the news via cable television) and the diminished possibility of a national public.

That diminished possibility isn't entirely new, and in fact transitions between mass media platforms have coincided with innovations in environmental action and even philosophy. The formation of Greenpeace in 1970 signified, among many other important facts, that the Sierra Club's strategic uses of print media now failed to meet the needs of the times. The times, for Greenpeace activists, were televisual. In 1969, 59 percent of U.S. television owners said that they received their primary sense of the world from television. As Kevin DeLuca describes it, Greenpeace organizers were Canadians who felt indebted to Marshall McLuhan. Greenpeace founder Robert Hunter called McLuhan "our greatest prophet,"[95] arguing that the importance of image events "is not whether they immediately stop the evil—they seldom do. Success comes in reducing a complex set of issues to symbols that break people's comfortable equilibrium, get them asking whether there are better ways to do things."[96] Greenpeace sought an international viewership, with North America's television owners—a broad middle class—as a primary audience. Their direct-action tactics were from the beginning also about the footage that might be created about them: In an inflatable Zodiac boat, an activist holding a video camera confronts the Soviet whaling ship the *Vlastny*, on June 27, 1975, fifty miles off the coast of California. The films of Soviet harpooning that these activists took and passed on to U.S. news networks essentially created the "Save the Whales" campaign that is still identified as a centerpiece of American environmentalism.

Equally significantly, Greenpeace agitprop filmmakers depended upon the structure of television news, which, as Todd Gitlin notes, compresses even the highly economical style of the newsprint story. From the perspective of the 1960s and early 1970s, Gitlin saw television news as a perpetrator of media framing that was biased in part because of its format.[97] Rapidly produced and disseminated televisual "events" were woven into the discontinuous flow of advertising breaks and station announcements. This deliberately interruptive flow, as Raymond Williams describes it, destroys the meaningful contexts that could communicate more complex political goals, such as the New Left ideal of participatory democracy. Williams's argument about television echoes Berger's about the photograph severed from historical intimacy and time. Since cable news outlets have dominated television since the introduction of

CNN's twenty-four-hour news in the 1980s, more aspects of an event might be displayed on television, to change up the continuous reportage, but media frames are unashamedly tied to corporatist goals.

It is arguable as to whether now there are more opportunities for in-depth reportage across all media news platforms, where the contexts of events might exceed or shift conventional media frames. If more such opportunities do exist, they can expect a niche audience, in contrast to the more representative, national audiences of the network news of the 1960s and 1970s. On the other hand, Josh Fox's remarkable documentary about hydraulic fracturing, *Gasland*, offers a fine example of how a documentary that airs on a cable television channel such as HBO can snowball into a national *and* grassroots phenomenon through Internet citation and social networking. Where niches collide—in this case environmentalists, working-class communities victimized by corporate landgrabs, and film buffs impressed by Fox's Sundance debut—a "media bomb" still might detonate. Anxiety about the disposability of film experience also dissipates in a digital environment that supports an endless proliferation of video. Of course, seeing these virtual bombs requires a dedication to looking at screens that in themselves have changed the meaning of "the environment," making seeing (and knowing) congruent with what you summon or with what deliberately finds you as an addressee.[98]

When *Life* magazine debuted its oil spill photographs in 1969, the idea of a national middle class did not yet seem tired, nor did it seem incredible that a magazine directed primarily by Ivy League–educated white men might dictate the terms of the U.S. middle class. In 1972, when *Life* ceased to operate as a weekly magazine, the reason cited for its demise was the splintering of the United States into two markets, where the division was conceived as generational. Now historians understand what happened to *Life* in terms of poor management decisions—*Life* bought the *Saturday Evening Post*'s subscription list, which drove up costs more than revenue—and the birth of niche markets in the early 1970s.[99] Today it is hard to imagine a magazine designed to produce a national middle class. It is even hard to imagine what a magazine is for, period. Magazines affiliate with quaint cultural terms, like "lifestyles" and "self-image." They function as marketing kits for other media, like soap operas or cable television networks. Magazines also suggest tremendous ecological waste, reflecting huge water and energy inputs necessary to make paper and glossy color prints.

Perhaps as a tribute to the cultural obsolescence and ecological impact of the magazine, the photographer Steven Meisel ran a fashion essay titled "Water and Oil" in the August 2010 issue of Italian *Vogue*, which featured twenty-four images of the model Kristen McMenamy dressed in couture drenched in fake crude oil.[100] McMenamy wears birdlike feathers in two of the images, lies about on rocks in positions emulating toxic fatigue and—in what is Meisel's most putatively daring shot—coughs up what appears to be seawater, like a dying bird.[101] Most viewers of Meisel's editorial did not see it on paper, in *Vogue Italia*. The editorial is all over the Internet, as are other Meisel spreads, including one from 2006 featuring models playacting as terrorists and airport security. Because so much viewing of Meisel's "oil spill" pastiche happened via the Internet, from comments sections to blogging, it is easy to enter a boisterous conversation about whether the photos are exploitation or art, whether they denigrate animals or women, whether they comment on anorexia, whether they sell clothing (prices are listed) or sell a notion of glamour that always has been wedded to death. Clearly, these photographs made people feel and think something, at least in passing. They also "happened" to people, insofar as regular readers of *Vogue Italia*, on paper or online, didn't tune in expecting a visual discourse on ecocide. Fashion journalists who write about the photographs note the waste involved—the airplane fuel required to ship the clothing and models to Europe, the ruin of the clothing by the fake crude, the waste of ad paper to sell clothing that is rendered barely visible by an overwrought mise-en-scène. The fashion industry's reflection on the industry's own ecological footprint may be Meisel's most significant intervention. In a sense, what he has done is simply expose the material infrastructure that supports the glossy magazine. Water and oil are preconditions of fashion, whose waste is inextricably linked to its elements of style.

Water and Oil

"The meaning of water might be best approached in comparison with that other liquid to which we in the twentieth century are beholden: oil," wrote David Orr in *Earth in Mind*, a polemic on environmental education. "Water as rain, ice, lakes, rivers, and seas has shaped our landscape. But oil has shaped our modern mindscape, with its fascination and addiction to speed and accumulation."[102] Orr's interest in water as embodied human memory points to our literal embodiment as ocean insofar as the evolution of human life begins in the sea. Human blood, chemically speaking, bears a strong resemblance to sea water. "Water has inspired great poetry and literature," Orr continues, making "water" indicative of an aesthetic, sensory intelligence. "Our language is full of allusions to springs, depths, currents, rivers, seas, rain, mist, dew, and snowfall. To a great extent our language is about water and people in relation to water. We think of time flowing like a river. We cry oceans of tears. We ponder wellsprings of thought. Oil, on the contrary, has had no such effect on our language."[103] I would have to disagree with Orr's conclusion that oil "has given rise to no poetry, hymns, or great literature, and probably no flights of imagination."[104] Moreover, those who study oceans might follow the literary critic Patricia Yaeger's insightful concern that the world's seas have been exploited by metaphor, set up for plundering by aesthetic categories such as the sublime, which make it difficult to recognize the ocean as

vulnerable habitat even after the shift toward ocean conservation in the ecological thought of the twentieth century.[105] Between the sublime kitsch of the
eternal sea and the plastic nightmare of the North Pacific Garbage Gyre, there
are what I'll call "working aesthetics" of oceans. This term implies the sensory
knowledge of ordinary people who utilize oceans and coasts, for work and
pleasure, and who at times have marshaled their everyday coastal aesthetic
against pollution, industrial fishing, and oil. Santa Barbara offers an interesting case study of how aesthetics operate on the ground to protect, and undermine, the right to an ocean commons.

From 1955 into the months following the Santa Barbara oil spill, someone compiled a scrapbook about oil's incursions into southern California's
coasts. The compiler is nameless, an anonymous donor to the University of
California. The book itself presents a collage of Union Oil press releases and
clippings from Santa Barbara papers, clippings from the *Los Angeles Times*
and other national and international papers and magazines, and oil company memorabilia, such as a Union Oil matchbox. Photographs of oil-soaked
birds, of tankers, and of greasy waves compete for visual attention on the
huge pages, many of which are yellowing with glue. It was in this scrapbook that I found the image of Mrs. Parent staring out of her oil-bespattered
window. In it I also recognize a rough narrative of a community positioned
staunchly against industrial aesthetics and, by extension, corporate intru-
sions into local governance.

Who, I wonder, created this scrapbook? Was it an oil worker or oil company executive, a reporter, an elderly "blueblood" who read the papers? Given
the number of Union Oil press releases in the scrapbook, and the wry inclusion of the matchbook, I imagine it was someone either close to the oil industry or the press. Personal accounts of spill-related injuries, mostly published
letters, jar against newsprint announcements of industry innovations, including the drillship the *Glomar Challenger*, which was "the first major drilling
unit equipped with anchorless, dynamic positioning for unlimited water
depths, developed by the General Motors AC-Electronics Defense Research
Laboratories of Santa Barbara."[106] The person who made this book lived in a
culture of oil and of accident, and the scrapbook intends to lift both out of the
ordinariness that might normalize a spill. Practically every news day brings
new invention and new risk. This scrapbook's chronology overlaps with what
California's eminent historian and state librarian emeritus, Kevin Starr, has
named California's "golden age," the long decade from 1950 to 1963 when
the state garnered more than $50 billion in U.S. defense contracts, twice the
amount received by any other state.[107] One of Santa Barbara's most outspoken
future environmentalists worked for General Electric's local TEMPO think
tank, reporting to a man who later became the administrator of NASA. The
acidification of the scrapbook's paper testifies to the material inevitability of

forgetting the conflicted desires (e.g., for oil and water) that birthed main-stream environmental sensibility.

First, I consider the desire to be near to water. Living on a pristine coast is a privilege denied most Americans, and the coasts of the mid-twentieth century were not necessarily more pristine than today's, sometimes less so. The national fantasy of coastal living as an acme of middle-class happiness grew up with the popular media of southern California surf culture in the 1950s, although coastal romanticism does not begin or end in any particular place. As the historian Alain Corbin reminds us in his magisterial history *The Lure of the Sea*, "the sea-shore began to develop its appeal in the middle of the eighteenth century"—after centuries of being associated with the cha-otic physical ruins of the biblical flood. Still, one can find nineteenth- and even twentieth-century accounts of American beaches used essentially as waste dumps. Rachel Carson's immensely popular publications on the sea, including *The Sea around Us* (1951), parts of which were serialized in the *New Yorker*, reintroduced the ocean to middle-class and affluent Americans as the materialization of the world, the space that contains all time and all places. What the ocean offers, Carson tells us from the first, is an opportu-nity to get close to origins, understood geologically, biologically, and also metaphysically, in the Romantic mode: "Beginnings are apt to be shadowy, and so it is with the beginnings of that great mother of life, the sea."[108] I say Carson "reintroduced" this notion of the originary sea because it can be seen as Romantic or ancient, in the Western tradition, and also indicative of the philosophical imagining of non-Western, island peoples whose use of the ocean as an everyday road does not lessen its metaphysical force as a site of eternity.[109] To readers of the *New Yorker* in the 1950s, Carson linked the time-less "mother sea" to a more scientific idea, that in the ocean we can readily see the interdependencies of life forms. Again, ecology figures as the sociable science in the Cold War era.

In the background of midcentury ecological thought lurked the menace of atomic bomb testing and the persistence of radioactive isotopes like Strontium 90 in baby teeth and mother's milk. For Carson, the ocean offered a gentler parable of systemic effects than nuclear fallout. "What happens to a diatom in the upper, sunlit strata of the sea may well determine what happens to a cod lying on a ledge of some rocky canyon a hundred fathoms below, or to a bed of multicolored, gloriously plumed seaworms carpeting the underlying shoal, or to a prawn creeping over the soft oozes of the sea floor in the blackness of mile-deep water," Carson muses.[110] Her sea is eternal and fragile, transcen-dental and swarming with explicit, vulnerable bodies. With its insistence on the cornucopian abundance of the sea, this prose does not adequately prepare us for the garbage gyres. Yet Carson recognizes that the oceans will become more transparent and exploitable. The penultimate chapter of *The Sea around*

Us, "Wealth from the Salt Seas," previews an era of ocean mining with no less poetry than Carson offers the seaworms. Apparently unperturbed by "active exploration" in the Gulf of Mexico, Carson explains the geology of ocean deposits ("on the continental shelf, also, the salt domes may mark large oil deposits") and writes wistfully, so it seems, of a coming time when "we shall depend less on the stored wealth of prehistoric seas and shall go more and more directly to the ocean" for oil.[111] Carson reports on seismic testing for oil deposits using dynamite charges without questioning how such activity might "well determine what happens to a cod lying on a ledge." In her rhetoric, which seems at once prescient and terrifically blind, ocean encompasses oil, belittling human history and the age of fossil fuel, "for all at last return to the sea."[112] The project of researching *Silent Spring* would alert Carson to the far-reaching consequences of industrial pollution of the oceans.[113]

In the figurative and imaginatively probing media of literature, Carson previewed the actual plumbing of ocean depths through "deep water photography" and "television"—promises soon to be realized for the entertainment of the mass public by Jacques Cousteau. Cousteau's 1950 book *The Silent World* prepared the way for the film he would release with a young Louis Malle in 1956, and it reminded readers that the development of underwater technologies had been largely a military venture. During World War II Cousteau worked in a naval intelligence unit in Marseilles, where he was encouraged to conduct diving experiments. Diving during the Nazi occupation of France, he imagines himself flying, and he wriggles into sea caves to collect lobsters. The book makes of subsea technology a kind of deep play. Risks that may be life-threatening are nonetheless taken for pleasure. "Their heads and antennae were pointed toward the cave entrance," Cousteau writes of the cave lobster. "I breathed lesser lungsful to keep my chest from touching them. Above water was occupied, ill-fed France."[114] Cousteau's celebration of scuba-diving "menfish" in the early 1950s helped create an emergent ecological masculinity associated with both the solitary reflection of philosophers and the ocean's maternal fertility—in opposition to the bomb and the intimate brutality of world war in Europe. The symbolic work done in the name of "the ocean" has never been unmixed in its attunement both to interspecies relationships and to the military and industrial technologies that assist human knowledge of ocean depths.

Stewart Brand has argued that the ocean formed a lively counterpart to outer space for mid-twentieth-century Americans.[115] Cousteau's "aquanauts" offered this imperfect ocean–space analogy to television viewers as a pun. Both space and ocean were environments hostile to human habitation and knowable only through prostheses. Both spurred high-tech industry. The anthropologist Stefan Helmreich recently coined the term "alien ocean" to "flag the space-age imagery that informs scientific invocations" of the ocean, particularly in light of new developments in genomics and biotechnology.[116] However, as Susan Faludi suggests, in the middle of the twentieth century space seemed "a sterile environment...a void man moved through only passively, in a state of almost infantile regression."[117] Faludi argues that the space race failed as "masculinity insurance" for American men, from what she conceives as the nonexperience of astronauts in space to the collapse of defense industry jobs in the 1980s. Later, Joan Didion would invoke the masculinity crisis in former aerospace hubs like Lakewood, California, naming the crisis as fallout of the industry's symbolic creation of "an artificial ownership class" to do skilled handwork in the plants.[118] Unlike outer space, the ocean could be entered by anyone, and it was teeming with life that—if alien—also functioned as a fundamental resource. American men who worked in defense industry jobs in coastal southern California could go home after work and dive for abalone, scallops, and fish. This was a different kind of masculinity insurance than that proffered by the Cold War and aerospace jobs.

"I was so angry," recalls James "Bud" Bottoms, referring to the Santa Barbara oil spill.

> Because I had lived off the ocean, scallops and fish, raised my kids on lobster. And there was my icebox—it was destroyed. We stood there and looked at this beautiful ocean that was now black, quiet, still. Dead birds floating in. We stood there and cried, because there was our life. I'd grown up in West L.A. and Santa Monica, then came up here in '48 for college, after the war. So I just lived out of the sea.[119]

Bottoms was working as art director for General Electric's TEMPO think tank when the blowout happened. It is important to him to refer to the event as a "blowout" rather than a "spill," to mark its violence. He recalls his boss warning him not to use the company's Xerox machine to create protest documents, since board members from General Motors were touchy. He also recalls the painful realization that his top-flight industry job might be pointless. The ocean, not space, seemed to promise the long future. But suddenly the ocean seemed completely vulnerable, on the brink of ruin.

"Who cares about space?" Bottoms asked himself shortly after the oil spill of 1969, recognizing that earth's environment must be his primary concern.[120] He later asked the same question of Thomas Paine, his former boss, who became head of NASA. Paine's response was to invite him to the Apollo 13 launch in April 1970—an ironic reintroduction to the high purpose of space exploration, given that this failed mission is most popularly associated with the phrase, "Houston, we've got a problem." The launch took place just weeks before the first Earth Day, for which Bottoms created green-and-blue "ecology" flags similar to the well-known Earth Day flag designed by John McConnell. Knowing that Bottoms liked dolphins, Paine told him that dolphins had gone to space. What he meant was that he had given Neil Armstrong World War II submariners' emblems, which picture dolphins, to take to the moon. "He was a far-out guy," Bottoms recalls of Paine. "He'd speculate about a basketball game or ballet on the moon. Weightless!"[121] Bottoms eventually left General Electric and devoted himself to sculpture, the arts practice most indebted to gravity. His first piece, a naked woman embracing a leaping dolphin, is called *Survival*. His most famous sculpture, Santa Barbara's Friendship Fountain, showcases three leaping porpoises in the near-exact location at the base of the Santa Barbara pier where Bottoms stood with a placard reading "Get Oil Out" back in 1969.

When Bud Bottoms talks about dolphins, he mentions his Malibu friend John Lilly, the controversial neurophysiologist who brought dolphins into U.S. environmental culture in the 1960s, touting them as a type of extraterrestrial intelligence and "mental health expert" that might teach humans how to have good conversations, more meaningful jobs, and better sex.[122] The anthropologist Loren Eiseley, following on Lilly and on Gregory Bateson's belief that dolphins valued social relationships over "things" because they didn't have hands, dreamed of handless menfish confined to the world's oceans in penitence for their near-destruction of earth. In his classic 1960 essay "The Long Loneliness," Eiseley writes, "If man had sacrificed his hands for flukes, the moral might run, he would still be a philosopher, but there would have been taken from him the devastating power to wreak his thought upon the body of the world.... Perhaps such a transformation would bring him once more into that mood of childhood innocence in which he talked successfully to all things living but had no power and no urge to harm."[123] The dolphin offered refuge, a new site of manhood, for men alienated and shamed by the atomic bomb. The promise of a post-frontier manhood indebted to some of the communalist values of social ecology runs throughout popular culture about dolphins, even today.

Recent discoveries by neuroscientists about the brain of the common dolphin (*Tursiops truncatus*) have been seized as evidence of dolphins' advanced emotional intelligence. For instance, the dolphin's limbic system may be stretched out over more of the brain, so limbic information—emotional information—is more integrated into dolphin brain function. Dolphins have a higher ratio of association neurons in the neocortex to neurons in the limbic system and brain stem than humans, suggesting the possibility that they have a greater capacity for abstract thought, creativity, and emotional self-control. Male dolphins choose to have erections.[124] Lilly and company's glosses on the near-constant sexual expression of dolphins—including pleasantly "buzzing" each other's genitals with sonar—lay at the core of what they imagined as dolphins' superior sociality. With pointed irony, the historian D. Graham Burnett has described Lilly's imbrication in Cold War sensory deprivation experiments that featured cruel animal experimentation.[125] Burnett also reveals the complementarity of Lilly's project to U.S. Navy propaganda and the navy's militarization of the ocean, in competition with NASA, as Earth's "deep space." For nascent environmentalists like Bud Bottoms, though, dolphins meant simply a better kind of personhood. They were a transitional object to hold on to as the twentieth century hurtled into space and men lost their bearings in aerospace companies whose social purpose seemed vague.[126] Bottoms recalls leaving his job with GE after sixteen years, and in the same year getting divorced, exploring Jungian psychology, and dreaming of dolphins. In his dreams, women embraced the smiling, breaching animals. Going to the beach became a way to rethink the orthodoxies.[127]

Eight out of the current ten U.S. national seashores would be created in the 1960s, spurred by earlier ideas of a public right to ocean access. The same year that saw the publication of the National Park Service's argument for federal protection of coastal commons, *Our National Shorelines*—1955— also marked the passage of the Cunningham-Shell Act, which created an "oil sanctuary" or no-drill zone in the tidelands off Santa Barbara and in a one-mile buffer zone around the Santa Barbara Channel Islands.[128] The jurisdictional complications of coastal zones and the hunger of state and federal governments for oil revenues caused the Santa Barbara City Council to take the unusual step in the mid-1960s of trying to augment the sanctuary protection by annexing the ocean adjacent to the city, in hopes that the tidelands could become part of the city proper. This annexation attempt intended to dilute the power of the State Lands Commission, which controlled state oil leases. The tidelands sanctuary off of Santa Barbara often has been in dispute, recognized as potential revenue by the state and by city leaders when they are faced with budget problems. Local news archives record bickering about the sanctuary. Yet repeatedly the city acted to maintain the sanctuary status of its coast, with legislators, citizens, and journalists citing the "unique beauty" of their shoreline as an amenity more valuable than oil. When the spill of 1969 happened, locals lamented that despite their extraordinary efforts they had not been spared. Why should Santa Barbara be spared? *Life* magazine asked, characterizing the response of a Senate committee assembled to address the oil spill. Like the rest of the country, Santa Barbara ran on oil.[129] The sanctuary idea suggests elitist exceptionalism linked to privilege and, more explicitly, to high-end real estate. Yet Santa Barbara also was home to practices of ocean "commoning"—the everyday fishing, surfing, and diving of residents—that cut across class divisions. The city always has supported a large population of renters attracted to its beaches and ocean.

The word "sanctuary," with its medieval connotations of "a holy place," a site of "refuge" from punishment, and even "heaven," implicitly acknowledges the earthly reign of something else. In this case, the something else was, and is, oil. For the largely working-class industrial city of Long Beach, about one hundred and twenty miles south of Santa Barbara and twenty miles south of Los Angeles, the necessity of living with the oil business suggested a different kind of legacy. Long Beach would not promote itself as a sanctuary from industry, but as the site of the world's most beautiful oil field. This now famous field of oil islands in Long Beach harbor was proposed for the city by the same Los Angeles firm that created Houston's AstroWorld. The project's lead architect, Joseph Linesch, vowed to make Long Beach the place that proved "oil and people *do* mix."[130] Linesch's drawings for the city of Long Beach open industrial aesthetics to almost surreal improbabilities—the sort of thing you might see in theme parks.[131] A joint venture by Texaco, Humble (now Exxon), Union, Mobil, and Shell, known colloquially as THUMS, negotiated the right to drill within Long Beach city limits by proposing a beautification clause. At Long Beach harbor, four oil drilling islands were made with dredged sand and granite barged in from Catalina Island. Strong colors, full-grown trees and shrubs, and modernist concrete forms decorate each island. Some of the islands have waterfalls that empty into the ocean and can be lit by floodlights at night. Terra cotta and steel shells ringed with balconies encase the islands' 180-foot drilling rigs to make them look like high-rise structures, or "beauty spots harmonizing with the urban development of our coastline," as a Long Beach newspaper crowed.[132]

Here was a beauty linked not to the geological time of the ocean and its millions-year-old denizens, like the common dolphin, but to a community's "futuristic" image, as one journalist put it.[133] When the Long Beach City Council voted to name the drilling islands "The Astronaut Islands," with each island taking the name of a dead astronaut (Grissom, White, Chaffee, and Freeman), the city signed onto a Cold War future-complex far from ideas of ecology, the sociable science. [FIGURE 1.4] D. J. Waldie, who wrote the fine 1997 *Holy Land: A Suburban Memoir* about Lakewood, the same town near Long Beach that Didion recognizes as a casualty of aerospace, argues compellingly that "the aesthetically privileged" fail to see the charisma of forms expressing economic aspiration, like tract homes and—more spectacularly—oil islands.[134] In response to a negative commentary about the oil islands that appeared in the *Los Angeles Times*, the architect Linesch sent the *Times* an essay by a Long Beach high school senior who named the islands as her favorite art object.[135] In Long Beach, oil allied itself with art, conventional bearer of the beautiful, while the advocates of oceans, postspill environmentalists, reconsidered beauty in terms of life.

In the days following the Santa Barbara blowout, Bottoms and the former California state senator Alvin Weingand co-founded the activist group Get Oil Out (GOO), which launched a series of demonstrations. They burned Union Oil credit cards at Santa Barbara's Stearns Wharf and staged a "sail-in" during which fishing and leisure craft surrounded the seeping

FIGURE 1.4 *"The World's Most Beautiful Oil Fields," Long Beach, California. Collection of the author.*

Platform A.[136] Men and women in the boats hoisted signs warning the oil industry out of the channel. In speeches, press releases, demonstration slogans, and mimeographed pamphlets, GOO described the blight that struck the Santa Barbara coastline in terms of a failure, by government and industry, to recognize "a living ocean" as a public right.[137] In these documents, beauty has multiple meanings, from the wealthy property holder's right to an ocean view to the city council's right to a tourist industry to the more radical and even posthumanist "right" of regular people to live near to other life, in a kind of interspecies sociability. The aesthetic philosopher and literary critic Elaine Scarry makes a suggestive argument about beauty as a state of "opiated adjacency" in which we put ourselves aside to appreciate some other, in such a way that being adjacent, not central, results in our intense pleasure. In dialogue with Iris Murdoch, Scarry writes: "A beautiful thing is not the only thing in the world that can make us feel adjacent; nor is it the only thing in the world that brings a state of acute pleasure. But it appears to be one of the few phenomena in the world that brings about both simultaneously... thereby creating the sense that it is our own adjacency that is pleasure-bearing."[138] I cannot follow Scarry to the conclusion that beauty becomes a "prelude to or precondition of enjoying fair relations with others."[139] However, I recognize her emphases on the "decentering" of self in the ambit of beauty as relevant to an ecological rethinking of beauty in terms of being near to other life.

Santa Barbarans writing to local newspapers worked over the beauty idea to give shape to their grief. For instance, a woman named Jenny Perry complains to the *Santa Barbara News-Press* in an alliterative style reminiscent of Rachel Carson's sea prose: "The harbor smells. It always did, of course. But a foul foundry smell has done in the whiffs of fish and salt and kelp that let a working girl play outdoor type with wind in her hair. Rocks are black. No starfish will dot their sides for kids to count on any summer Sunday soon. The water swirling about the rocks, and slapping the sides of boats and slips, is brown and gray and dead and rank. Rainbow rivulets do not help."[140] As John Keeble has said in regard to the Exxon *Valdez* spill, ecological grief responds to the "removal of a presence" from the beach and near-shore waters.[141] That presence amounts to other lives. In the *Valdez* incident, the loss included hundreds of thousands of marine animals. Activists in Santa Barbara realized fairly quickly that the loss of so much life, as the spill leaked for nearly a year, was difficult to represent to each other, let alone as a news event.

Bottoms created the drawings for his first children's book in the immediate wake of the spill. He published the book only recently as *Davey and the GOM* (2008), with "GOM" standing for "Giant Oil Monster." In Bottoms's book—which is enthusiastically blurbed by Patagonia founder Yvon Chouinard—the story of David and Goliath meets another ancient story, that of the physicist Archimedes in the Second Punic War. Archimedes instructed the soldiers of Syracuse to use their shields as reflecting mirrors to burn invading Roman ships with the rays of the sun. As *Davey and the GOM* concludes, the lone little man, Davey, assembles a crowd with hand mirrors pointed at the oil slick. "The power of the sun's reflection was more than the GOM could bear," we're told.[142] A rare burst of color in the largely black-and-white book—yellows, reds—underlines the quite literal victory of solar power. Bottoms's oil slick spirals upward, toward the sun itself, imploding in a black heap like the Wicked Witch of the West. What the book does not convey is that its large cast of helper animals—harbor seals, dolphins, pelicans, and seagulls sullied with oil—could not have been resurrected by Davey, or anyone. Their flourishing in the book is wishful resurrection, really an iteration of the trauma that Bottoms and others experienced back in 1969.

As the 1970s began, GOO leaders became increasingly vocal about the global scale of the battle that their slogan implied. Some left the group precisely because of the breadth of its aspiration (one former member told me, "C'mon, what's the likelihood of *really* getting oil out?"), while others assumed the role of publicly remembering their disaster as part of an ongoing, international history. Spill stories lack continuity—particularly given the geographical distances that separate spill events. Yet there is significant continuity in how spill remediation fails, down to the use of the same toxic surfactant, Corexit, in the 1969 Santa Barbara spill (where the Sierra Club demanded its discontinuance) and in multiple spills up through the BP blowout in the Gulf of Mexico of 2010. GOO's leaders traveled in the 1970s, and they began keeping accounts of spills off of distant coasts, such as Japan's inland sea and that of Chile, Singapore, and Portugal. The GOO archives reflect the gradual globalization of the cause, as local activists follow oil itself into the world.

An annotated copy of Noel Mostert's 1974 short series "Supertankers" for the *New Yorker* sits in the GOO archives, accompanied by typewritten notes that someone made about Mostert's book of the same year, *Supership*. The issue of tanker and barge traffic in the Santa Barbara Channel both predates and postdates the spill of 1969. The Exxon *Valdez* accident would make clear the magnitude of risk that tankers posed, and it would initiate regulatory measures that forced oil tankers and barges to carry insurance for unlimited damage. Fifteen years prior to the *Valdez* spill, Mostert's polemic about oil tankers might have sparked the sort of national conversation jumpstarted by *Silent Spring*, given his publication venue and the scope of his environmental thinking. Yet his is largely a forgotten prophecy, long overshadowed by the *Valdez* spill. That this is so speaks to the difficulty of pre-empting Big Oil's ordinary "accidents." Mostert forecast that the long-term effects of oil shortages in the 1970s would lead to the construction of more tankers, larger tankers, deepwater ports ruining the gorgeous scenery of northern European inlets, wrecked tankers, massive spills from tankers, massive bird and marine mammal deaths, and increasing beach pollution. He pointed to a heavily capitalized, apparently unstoppable global trend: Entrepreneurs such as Aristotle Onassis pushed the oil business into supertankers after the closing of the Suez Canal during the 1967 Six-Day War in the Middle East; the Japanese built tankers to unprecedented scale and were doing feasibility studies for a million-tonner; the oil-dependent countries had dwindling oil resources or none at all; they would barter and fight for foreign reserves and ship internationally, ecology be damned. During the winters of the Global South, fully loaded oil tankers rounded the Cape of Good Hope, where huge waves are endemic. The operation of these tankers in the southern winters violated the most common rule of marine safety, which is that a ship should be loaded according to the climate of the seas.

The long routes of oil tankers and the fact that they were too expensive to keep in the ports that could hold them changed applications of maritime law. Most tankers sailed under flags of convenience, commonly Liberian, which meant that it was difficult to prosecute violators. Mostert saw the supertanker as a superbomb, almost as dangerous and undervisualized as the Ohio-class nuclear submarines that still patrol the world's seas.[143] The cartoonish images that frame his *New Yorker* piece illustrate the dangerously low visibility of the tanker threat, showing just the outline of a ship barely discernible above water. Supertankers typically sit with their hulls about 80 percent submerged. As a South African, Mostert expressed particular alarm about massive damage by tanker pollution to the rich bird life of the African coasts, and he predicted that northern Europeans and North Americans would neither be aware of nor concerned by such southern tragedies. It is interesting to consider what American environmentalism would look like now if *Supership* had been as widely read, argued about, and lauded as *Silent Spring*. Though tankers have become subject to regulation and tanker spills greatly reduced, fulfilling Mostert's most pragmatic goal after the fact of the *Valdez* spill, still his global ecological vision would have been useful for the late twentieth century.

The imagination of world oil may have complemented the dynamic litigation scene that became the Santa Barbara oil spill's most concrete legacy—but this global thinking is difficult to see in the public culture that remains in the archives. Like many U.S. communities, Santa Barbara mobilized in the 1980s against the appointment of James Watt as secretary of the Interior and the Ronald Reagan administration's attempts to weaken or cancel environmental gains of the 1970s. Historian Robert Sollen describes Reagan's first term as president as "open season on offshore California," recounting seven years of legal battles to restore state authority over federal leasing.[144] Californians won repeated stays against oil leasing throughout the 1980s and 1990s, with the Santa Barbara "sanctuary" effort transformed into state policy by the Coastal Sanctuary Act of 1994. The establishment of the Channel Islands National Park in 1980, after nearly fifty years of advocacy, extended the sanctuary concept, with its connotations of a regional resort, into the larger ideal of a national commons. The waters surrounding the islands became a National Marine Sanctuary in 1980, in accordance with the National Marine Sanctuaries Act of 1972.[145] Because the Santa Barbara Channel is an ecotone or transition zone, where warm waters from the southern California Countercurrent mix with the colder waters of the California Current, it nurtures biodiversity. Within the channel 481 species of fish, 220 plant species, up to 610 invertebrate species, 18 species of whales and dolphins, and the largest concentration of blue whales in the world can be found.[146]

Since containerized shipping increased traffic in the port of Los Angeles by 150 percent in the early 1990s, the Santa Barbara Channel also has become a primary route to the busiest port in the United States.[147] In the early 2000s, a series of unexplained whale deaths in the channel were attributed to collision with tankers, which have since been mandated to slow down when they enter these waters. The presence of this volume of shipping means not only more ballast introduction of nonnative species but also the introduction of oil, mixed in the ballast of emptied tanks, as cargo coming down the coast from Alaska, or as leaked gasoline fuel. The sociologist Thomas D. Beamish refers to such incremental and cumulative ecological injuries almost poetically, as "crescive troubles."[148] Finally, there can be no *sanctuary* from oil here, at least not in the strictest sense of "sanctuary" as a place of refuge, a place where animals might disport and breed without the inadvertent penalties—or externalities—associated with oil drilling and transport. The political scientist and marine activist Michael McGinnis suggests that the marine sanctuary idea needs to be redesigned to reflect the multiple sites and species that sustain ocean ecosystems. Concerned primarily with commercial fishing, McGinnis recommends a system of linked, "no-take" Marine Protected Areas (MPAs) rather than larger sanctuaries whose boundaries are arbitrary to ocean life. Recent wins of MPAs off California's central coast are more evidence of the civic engagement with marine ecologies that marks this part of the world.

In the wake of the Santa Barbara spill, an entire state fashioned an image of itself as "environmental." Yet images always are in danger of being captured. A short walk on the University of California at Santa Barbara's Coal Oil Point Reserve will lead you to oil storage tanks owned by the Venoco corporation, which stopped using its nearby marine terminal for oil barging operations in 2012. Today Venoco ships oil via an onshore pipeline, and its tanks abutting the campus reserve and state-protected Snowy Plover habitat are in the process of being decommissioned.[149] But Venoco is now fracking in the waters off of campus point, where university land extends farthest toward the ocean.[150] Local oil presents a constantly moving target. Narratives, which require time to tell and take time into account in their telling, remain more resistant to misappropriation or misreading than images. What has become evident in my effort to construct a narrative of Santa Barbara's 1969 spill is how much of the experiential dimension of it has been consigned to library collections rarely visited, dismissed as a case of affluent NIMBY-ism, trivialized or forgotten. Tourism, wealth, Oprah—the constellation of values most readily recalled by "Santa Barbara"—have little to do with the shock of that flat, black water, or the litter of bird carcasses at the waterline, or the public at the beach, witnessing.

The print media that carried the spill, such as newspapers, glossy magazines, mimeographs, speeches, and photographs that might prompt memory, are scattered in public and private places—recently Bottoms made a "memory box" for an exhibit on the 1960s at the Oakland Museum. Meanwhile tar balls borne from oil drilling and from the natural oil seepage in the channel gum up the feet of walkers on Santa Barbara's beaches, every day. A 2003 study by the U.S. Geological Survey using biochemical techniques to "fingerprint" the crude on local beaches found that most came from natural seeps but that some of the oil could not be distinguished from that being pumped at two rig platforms, one of which is the notorious platform A. The seepage of oil from the Santa Barbara Channel adds up to about 4,000 gallons per day.[151] A colleague of mine commissioned a fabulously textural, smelly painting made out of the oil tar, because, she says, its pungent odor reminds her of the local coastline, the ocean, days when the children ran in from the beach. Like me, she wasn't here at the time of the oil spill, or in its aftermath. It's unclear if "beach tar" would seem less sensuously evocative if she had.

Epilogue

After the BP blowout of 2010, Santa Barbarans organized a nonprofit organization called Stand in the Sand to offer support to their sister coastal communities along the Gulf of Mexico. This fund for the Gulf is still augmented by donors, both within and beyond California, and it offers another kind of memorial for not only Santa Barbara's spill but also for the fragility of all coastal ecologies. The rally hosted by Stand in the Sand in the fall of 2010 included a diverse array of speakers, from Jean-Michel Cousteau (whose Cousteau Foundation now has headquarters in Santa Barbara), then Santa Barbara mayor Helene Schneider, a Native elder representing the area's Chumash nation, and a small group of Bolivians who spoke, in impeccable Spanish, about the destruction of the territories of indigenous peoples in South America by neoliberal policies dating back to the early 1970s. As no translators were on hand for the Spanish-speaking guests and a woman who spontaneously volunteered to translate became shy, only portions of the crowd could hear the international history that they brought to what was an otherwise interregional North American event. The Stand in the Sand rally was a performance against forgetting, a bid for thinking ecologically from within the long-term contest between the values of oil and water. Yet even in the moment of this earnest performance, some forgetting occurred, in the inability to translate.

In the fall of 2010, California's poet laureate emeritus, Al Young, posted a brief dialogue on the "lessons" from the Santa Barbara spill of 1969 in his blog. In this entry, Young offered the most resonant literary legacy of the Santa Barbara oil spill, a poem by Conyus, "The Santa Barbara Oil Disaster; or, A Diary."[152] Dated February 1969, the month that prison crews from San Luis Obispo, Santa Clara, and San Diego counties were brought to Santa Barbara by Union Oil to clean up the oil-soaked beaches, the poem has been twice revised, once in the wake of the BP blowout. In it, Conyus comments explicitly on efforts of memory such as the poem itself, and in turn upon the forgetting of people like him—a prisoner and beach clean-up

FIGURE 1.5 *Richard Nixon Photo Op with Beach Crew. Photograph by Dick Smith.*
Courtesy Dick Smith Estate, Dick Smith Collection, 1969–1971. SBHC Mss 56, Department of
Special Collections, Davidson Library, University of California, Santa Barbara.

worker. [FIGURE 1.5] In an email correspondence with me, Conyus verified that the poem arose from his own experience: "I am indeed the protagonist in the poem. I was there and lived the moment as it was, from
day to day, but not as a poem then, but a poem, much, much, later. I have
had many experiences in my life, and this one I shall always remember,
and never forget."[153] He added that he was happy to hear that his poem was
being taught at the university, because he feared that "most people know
nothing" about what it felt like to live through the weeks and months after
the spill. Certainly the role of prison labor in clean-up efforts has been
underrepresented.

On "Day Twenty," the last entry in the "diary" that structures the poem, the
speaker concludes:

> Some of us get stored
> in cardboard & canvas,
> others in cells
> & dungeons, until the next time,
> when the fires come,
> the earthquake hits,
> or the Great Santa Barbara Oil Disaster/ Or:

The colon that emphatically fails to end the poem reinforces the paratactic structure of "fires...earthquake...or...." The point is that there will be more disasters, in California and in a world built around risk. In each of these apparently new crises the same persons will be called upon to clean up and to do the even dirtier work of intimate witnessing. It will be important that these witnesses are put away or "stored" when their labor is done.

Early in this narrative poem, in the section titled "Day Three," the poet recognizes his efforts as those of a field slave, watched closely by other African-American service workers in Santa Barbara's affluent, "island" plantation:

> On the beach,
> in the window
> of the Santa Barbara Yacht Club,
> Black servants watch us,
> swing picks & shovels
> in the wet sand
> like machetes
> clearing a cane field
> on their small island
> in the Caribbean.

The reference to the Caribbean calls up the Gulf of Mexico, reassembling disparate spills and disparate acts of burdening the disenfranchised with remediation labor. This prisoners' work is also the work of poets, as Conyus describes it. Their "cleanup" both defamiliarizes and restores the mundane, a therapeutic practice that draws an eager audience. "The people/came to watch us work," the poetic speaker recounts. Repeatedly, the poem notes such watching. "Some said, 'my! Don't they look almost human!'/Others said 'a convict is a crime, don't forget that.'" Bearing the shame of a country "lowered...in Vietnam," these "almost-human" prisoners on the beach allow "the people" to continue being "people" by keeping themselves apart from the killing that is evident on the oil-soaked sand, and in Vietnam, and in "the gas chamber at San Quentin"—a surprising image that erupts on Day Four as the destination of "driftwood," which the prisoners drag across the beach for burning. "The women of Santa Barbara/watch us drag driftwood/across the rocky beach/to the gas chamber at San Quentin." The awkwardness of such imagery betrays the discomfort of those watching the prisoners destroy evidence of the spill, "the women of Santa Barbara," as well as an identification of the spill with other kinds of atrocity. The women of Santa Barbara will reappear on the beach a little later in the poem, as a kind of battlefield sanitary commission, who "brought rags/for us to wipe/our oily/black hands on."

Quite late in the poem, on Day Sixteen, these rags resurface, and we learn that they impart a striking color to the scene: red. The rags have become flags of a tenuous promise offered by "citizens" to "prisoners" who enact the vulnerability, guilt, and lack of freedom that the citizens themselves feel in the presence of their death-stained beach. Of the black ocean, Conyus writes:

> All night you can hear
> the ocean cough
> & spit up oil,
> like a young child
> lying on its back
> with pneumonia.
> We clear as much phlegm
> & muck from its throat as we can,
> & mop his sweaty head
> with oily red rags.

This ocean that is a child lying on her back calls up the asthmatic, urban children who have become the twentieth century's most wrenching symptom of industrial pollution. The atmospheric scale of "ocean" dwindles in this image of its frailty, while the prisoners' kindness brings back an age-old and patronizing American story of national healing come by way of black hands, brown hands—the fundamental humanness (in "hands") of the dispossessed, those not powerful enough to be world-destroyers. This ocean will belong to the men with the oily red rags, the "convicts," so long as it is hurt and black. The black waters speak of "suffocation," literally of "baby seals/that have suffocated/in the thick water"—an image reminiscent of the *Life* magazine spread that would follow the composition of Conyus's poem by four months. The black water also invokes the figurative suffocation of an affluent people, "Santa Barbarans," by what they had imagined to be the good life. Speaking of "caskets of beautiful Cadillacs," the poem calls to mind those car burials and smashings that took place during the first Earth Day and in the immediate wake of the Santa Barbara oil spill. From the point of view of the prisoner raking the beach, the elements of the modern speed-fix—cars, freeways—are memento mori.

As Day Nineteen brings the speaker back north, to the Morgan Hill correctional facility and into a redwood forest work camp in San Mateo, he will imagine himself "Free of oil,/free of tar,/& free"—*free at last*, to echo Martin Luther King, Jr.'s famous anaphora, itself an echo of a traditional African-American spiritual. On the beach at Santa Barbara, the speaker and his fellow prisoners brought "freedom" to the oil dead in a gesture that speaks of the value of these dead to those who had to touch them and throw them away like garbage:

> For thirty miles along the beach
> dead bodies of sea mammals
> float up & beach themselves like dominoes.
> We cut the larger ones up
> with chain saws & axes,
> & loaded them into the
> jaw of the skip loader for the cat skinner.
> The rest, left bloated & stinking,
> we burn with gasoline & torches
> to let the fire free them.
> High in the sky turkey vultures soar
> above the spiraling smoke
> of sweet crude oil clouds,
> looking for baby seals
> that have suffocated
> in the thick water.

The speaker will reflect upon the sharks who tear apart the carcasses that float back to sea and then die "from petroleum poison/along the shore/of Oregon,/& Washington." His bonfire of the dead recalls a bonfire of 676 oil-soaked birds that was filmed at Gore Point, Alaska, by a clean-up crew in the aftermath of the Exxon *Valdez* spill. The crew was frustrated by the lack of direction from highers-up about how to get the toxic animals out of the food chain. A boat skipper employed by the Alaska Fish and Wildlife Service, Drew Scalzi, made the film of the burning carcasses so as to prove that he wasn't destroying evidence against Exxon. The film then became a kind of "underground classic," in John Keeble's words.[154] In it, the birds are laid out in a long line on the beach and photographed. The crew builds a seven-foot-high pile of driftwood and ignites it, carrying the birds, one by one, to the fire. As Keeble describes it, in the Gore Point film "the movement is toward complete involvement, an emotional sinking in. The line between the disengaged bureaucratic view of the world and being in the world is inescapably crossed."[155] I couldn't find the film on the Internet, or anywhere. For some of the same reasons that Scalzi made his video monument to 676 dead shorebirds, Conyus recounts the dismembering and burning of marine mammals in "The Santa Barbara Oil Spill Disaster; or, A Diary." The poem accounts for work well done, for rage, for love, and to assert self-respect from within a job that is ethically dirty. The Alaska crew probably did not read Conyus, although they are predicted and remembered in his words. Every oil spill remembers every other, from the mid-twentieth century onward. These iterative events spill across history to happen again as if they are happening for the first time. The intimate miseries of oil spills, archived in poetry and narrative, in photography and film, cannot remain public for long. What Derrida has described as the poetic and therefore untranslatable, untransmissible quality of witness testimony meets extra resistance from complicit cultural memory, a national imaginary saturated in oil.

The Aesthetics of Petroleum

Forgetting the trauma of an oil spill or the death toll of sea otters in Prince William Sound to resume modern life as usual implies not only the vagaries of memory and the cognitive paralysis of despair, but also something terribly compelling about modern life as usual. This chapter answers the last with an exploration of why oil has been allied with happiness for North Americans, particularly those who most benefited from oil revenues and infrastructures—many in the United States, many Californians, the parents and grandparents of the 1960s radical ecologists. Loving oil has a great deal to do with loving media dependent on fossil fuels or petroleum feedstock from the early to mid-twentieth century, when oil became an expressive form, although often hidden as such, in plain sight. This chapter looks most closely at the paper-back print book, television, and the twentieth-century Hollywood movie as expressions of the modern fossil fuel complex. The twenty-first-century peak oil movement offers insights into the petroleum aesthetics that enlivened the twentieth-century United States, and with it much of the world. Imagining an epochal break with the old pleasures, the old infrastructures, peak oilers remind us of what precisely the "old" pleasures are.

In an early twenty-first-century comic book that might be titled *Style Guide for the Long Emergency*, but is instead titled *Fashion 2012*, cartoon characters ponder the role of aesthetics in a near future that delivers the convergence of peak oil and global climate change.[1] The peak oil movement gathered intensity in the first decade of the twenty-first century, as environmentalists and even some industry leaders worried publicly that the peak in global production of conventional oil resources either had already occurred or was about to. At the same time, the extreme new weather of global climate change promised intensive energy use—a long emergency, indeed. Though 2012 marks the supposed end of the world by the Mayan Long Count Calendar, *Fashion 2012* posits not apocalypse but rather "people living, global warming, economic change." "I just don't know how to dress anymore," one character muses. "They used to say 'dress for success.' With the new reality, what is success when no one is get-ting rich?" Another thinks, "I can't afford to drive my car anymore...am I a failure?" The small book pivots upon the brighter assertion of a third character that "there are other things I can be." But, as we turn the page, the cartoonist, Marc Herbst, introduces his own primary question, "What does that look like?... That is a question for artists."[2]

Imagination is a cornerstone of peak oil media, which emphasizes the importance of narrative and art in moving beyond the Age of Oil. In their attempt to liberate the modern world from oil dependency, peak oilers have excelled in delineating the philosophy of taste that complements the fossil fuel regime. They bring to light the aesthetics of petroleum in their attempts to create new structures of feeling. On YouTube, Rob Hopkins, founder of the Transition Network for a sustainable post-oil future, urges us to remember that, although oil may be running out, imagination is not. "There's no reason that the imagination and ingenuity that got us up to the top of the peak in the first place is going to disappear when we have to start figuring out how we're going to get down the other side."[3] Peak oiler James Howard Kunstler vividly represents modes of fabrication not reliant on petroleum infrastructures in his post-oil novel *World Made by Hand* (2008). For example: "Larry Prager was our dentist. With the electricity off most of the time, he did not have the high speed drill anymore. He got ahold of a 1920s pulley drill in Glens Falls, and Andrew Pendergast helped him rig it up to a foot treadle which Sharon could operate like a pump organ as she assisted her husband."[4] Kunstler's *bricoleurs* animate a sentiment of hope within a future of diminished resources, just as Hopkins's "transition tales," which he tells to adults on YouTube and to children in public libraries, intend to create feasible, if imaginary, infrastructures for worlds powered by renewable energy.

As Frank Kaminski argues in the first critique of post-oil fiction, post-oil authors recognize that people need "to be moved emotionally, as well as through their senses."[5] I concur that the narrative arts will be key actors in establishing the ecological resilience of the human species. By Rob Hopkins's definition, the resilient community must be flexible enough to reinvent its fundamental infrastructures, releasing itself from oil dependency to produce, largely by hand, all that it consumes. Holding a liter of petroleum, Hopkins gestures toward us with it from the visually dense YouTube screen. The pale brown contents of the glass liter bob up and down: "This liter of petroleum contains the same amount of energy that would be generated by my working hard physically for about five weeks.... The best place for this is to stay in the ground."[6] What might *that* look like? The specificity of Hopkins's "five weeks" of hard labor generates muscle memory and an emotional drag on his salutary call for post-oil environmental imagination.

This chapter offers a historical treatment of the aesthetics of petroleum, recognizing the American twentieth century as a high point of petromodernity, by which I mean modern life based in the cheap energy systems made possible by oil. Literature and film have recorded sensory and emotional values associated with the oil cultures of the twentieth century. To explore how social affects might be shifted toward a different-looking and -feeling post-petroleum future, I read physical infrastructure against artistic forms such as the novel, keeping in mind that almost every media available to us today is materially and even philosophically indebted to oil. In a sense, what I'm doing is the cultural project implied but left unfinished by peak oil activism, whose insights have turned out to be less telling about the near future—where Tough Oil reigns— than about the emotional power of twentieth-century material cultures. The persistence of the 1920s–1950s as defining periods of American fashion and style contributes to the difficulty of addressing global ecological problems such as anthropogenic climate change.

The sociologist Mimi Sheller has written about how the "kinesthetic" and "aesthetic" dispositions created by acts of driving, which she sketches within the larger "emotional geography" of automobility, must be taken into account as we confront the convergence of peak oil and global warming. Citing feminist and queer theorists' calls to recognize the body's investments in material culture, Sheller contends that any environmental argument against car culture must take into account the "affective contexts that are also deeply materialized in particular types of vehicles, homes, neighborhoods, and cities."[7] In brief, we have to consider the consequences of loving sprawl. One example of how ignoring such affective matters can backfire appears in a psychological study cited by the geographer and climate change consultant Susanne Moser, in which people who had been educated about anthropogenic climate change said that they were more likely to purchase SUVs in order to protect themselves from the extreme new weather.[8]

While both Sheller and Moser are interested in emotions as indices of feasible environmental policy, the philosopher Kate Soper has asked, more fundamentally, if there can be a "new erotics of consumption or hedonist 'imaginary'" that complements sustainability, in other words an affective intensity attached to limited growth, or no growth, that might rival, say, the embodied intensities of petromodern consumer culture, with its pimped autos, supple plastics, and diverse hard, soft, and wet "wares."[9] Soper's foundational query is echoed by the cartoonist Herbst, who—in addition to raising the dilemma of dressing for success in a failing or (optimistically) relocalizing economy—asks simply, "How does today's community gardener dress? How can we imagine what that acts like?"[10] Rather than give away the ending of Herbst's Fashion 2012, in which a post-petrol style does begin to materialize, I'd like to press his question upon history. I ask why petromodernity has enveloped the Euro-American imagination to the extent that "oil" has become synonymous with the world, in a large, Heideggerian sense of the human enframing and revealing of earth, thus the world we know.

As a recent Wikipedia entry begins, with unintentionally absurd poignancy: "Why is oil so bad?" This query will be my refrain. What interests me is why the world that oil makes remains so beloved, rather than the more obvious problem of why it is difficult to build an entirely new energy infrastructure. Following Lawrence Buell's investigation of "toxic discourse" in the late 1990s, I want to remain cognizant of pragmatic concerns but not focus upon them.[11] My questions are for artists, broadly speaking, rather than physicists or engineers.

As I've noted, one of the most truly revolutionary, in the sense of world-upturning, aspects of late twentieth-century environmentalism was its primary focus on the oil spill, which jumpstarted the U.S. ecology movement in California in 1969 and offered a reinterpretation of oil extraction as death-making, rather than as a realization of modern life. Yet most human survivors of the twentieth century, including a good number of self-identified environmentalists, are driving cars, using petroleum-based plastics, walking on asphalt, filling our teeth with complex polymers, and otherwise living oil. Peak oil thinkers like Hopkins may be the deliverers of twentieth-century environmentalism's most revolutionary promises. Yet the success of translocal movements such as the Transition Network relies implicitly on actual apocalypse and a drastic diminution of human population—prospects rather cheerily expected by some peak oilers. Perhaps the insight here is that the human body has become, in the wealthier parts of the world, a petroleum *natureculture*, to use Bruno Latour's term for the inevitable intermixture of the self-generating (organic) and the made.[12] Moreover, larger petroleum naturecultures envelop many of us as seamless atmosphere. We live the trope "oil weather," which was coined by early twentieth-century oil workers to describe the persistent fires so common to oil fields that they became naturalized as climate.[13]

The United States has experienced the natureculture of petromodernity since roughly the 1920s, when, ironically, some labored to imagine living oil just as now others labor to imagine living without it. For example, Upton Sinclair's novel *Oil!* (1927), the basis for the Academy Award–winning film *There Will Be Blood* (dir. Paul Thomas Anderson, 2007), is committed to international socialism, equating the oil business with the technophilic horrors of World War I and a global economic restructuring that denies human-scale values. Yet this "committed" book also generates a series of aesthetic images and environmental emotions that valorize driving and even the process of oil extraction, showing both of these industrial-era activities as modes of facilitating the body's capacity for self-extension toward other life.

Early in *Oil!*, Sinclair writes of a father and son stopping by the roadside to put chains on their tires: "Dad wiped his hands on the fog-laden plants by the roadside; the boy did the same, liking the coldness of the shining globes of water."[14] Roadsides are prominent landscapes in *Oil!* In the preceding scene we have an example of literature doing what Elaine Scarry has described as "directing" the imagination's peculiar powers of virtual perception. Images of gauziness and transparency (fog, water) are overlaid upon another depicted surface (plants) to render the latter (plants) an apparent solidity.[15] Sinclair's image feels lifelike. He transforms the roadside into a vivid imaginary place— one more capable of generating affective investment than sites of higher politi- cal value in his novel, such as his communitarian college, "Mt. Hope." Even for one of the most ideologically driven American novelists, the aesthetic plea- sures of petroleum undermine political solutions.

Why is oil so bad? 1.) Because it has supported overlapping media envi- ronments to which there is no apparent "outside" that might be materialized through imagination and affect as palpable hope.

Sinclair's *Oil!* is a type of peak oil fiction, since it was written as a warning against global petromodernity from around the moment of peak oil *discovery* in the United States—again, the late 1920s. The novel strives to imagine cur- tailing petromodern development in a manner complementary to the fictional post-petrol futures offered by twenty-first-century peak oilers. In both cases, imaginative thinkers struggle to break out of media environments already sus- tained by petroleum infrastructure. Cut to a scene rather late in *Oil!*, when Sinclair's radical hero, Paul Watkins, lies dying in a Los Angeles hospital. The reader has been directed to feel outrage over Watkins's injury. He was beaten at an Industrial Workers of the World rally by Red-baiting so-called patriots. As Watkins loses consciousness, Sinclair, in a rare nod to modernist technique, intercuts the absurdly pleasant song playing on a neighbor's radio with his manifest plot. The controlling voice of the novel, at this point an earnest social- ist youth, is silenced by popular lyrics: "What do I do?/I toodle-doodle-doo,/I toodle-doodle-doodle, doodle-doo!" Given that Sinclair was not a playful prose stylist, this rare instance of heteroglossic *frisson* points archly to the manner in which the comic potential of a modern consumer culture already founded on cheap energy challenges the intention of "doing"—as in acting in a manner truly counter to petrocapitalism.

The novel itself is a media environment that refers to (and is referred by) other media environments supported by petroleum, from the fictional auto dealerships that Sinclair tells us sponsor the fictional neighbor's radio broadcast to the petroleum involved in the manufacture and transport of the novel. In the late 1920s, commercial book manufacturers might have relied on coal-generated electricity, perhaps even older steam or hydropower tech- nologies. One could still find commercial presses operated by treadles, like Kunstler's vintage dental drill. These probably would be printing small-town newspapers.[16] However, it is likely that petroleum-based fuel was used in the transportation of Sinclair's book, even in the late 1920s.

The total distance for book shipment then could not have approached the approximately 1.25 billion miles that books travel today, primarily in trucks and container ships. The 2007 edition of *Oil!* that I refer to here is heavily indebted to petroleum. A mixture of petroleum-based resins and oils make up the ink that creates the words on the page of my edition of *Oil!*, words that direct my imagination and activate my senses. I literally enter an immersive, virtual environment through petroleum language. Petroleum in the form of diesel fuel supports my book's travel, and the travel of its component parts, namely its paper. Then there are the electricity, fuel oil, and natural gas required to keep press equipment running, to heat and light buildings that house the equipment. The book occupies many sites, some of which exist solely for it, such as its place of manufacture, storage warehouses, retail stores, libraries, private homes. Ultimately my edition of *Oil!*—well, not mine, but one like it, could be thrown away and driven to a landfill. Imagine, then, more diesel.[17] To step outside of petromodernity would require a step outside of media, including the modern printed book. *What does that act like?*

The inescapability of petroleum infrastructures has entered fiction as both dystopian and utopian space. These spatial imaginaries were of particular literary interest in the 1950s and early 1960s, when petromodernity reached its classic form within the U.S.-built environment and—not coincidentally—North American media theory began to develop under the influence of Marshall McLuhan. In both petrodystopias and petro-utopias, spatial representation defies realism insofar as space appears closed to history, to changes over time. There are few if any temporal paths out of the conceptually whole *ou-topos* of perfection and disaster. For Ray Bradbury, writing in the 1950s in Los Angeles, which I conceive as the "it" city of twentieth-century petromodernity, the saturation of human life by petromedia in *Fahrenheit 451* (1950) takes the form of a city soaked in kerosene, which is a highly flammable distillation of crude oil. The smell of kerosene pervades the novel, as do the results of its work—namely the burning of books and, metonymically, the end of critical thinking. Here we have an exploration of oil infrastructure as a mode of censorship, inflecting people's most intimate lives.

Bradbury's alarm about the domination of wraparound media such as television sounds today a bit shortsighted and panicky, a pop version of the philosophical indictments of mass culture's complementarity to fascism associated with Theodor Adorno and Max Horkheimer. What I find interesting about Bradbury is the explicit connection he makes between the totalitarian thought police, the "firemen," and fossil fuel. "Kerosene...is nothing but perfume to me," the conflicted fireman Guy Montag quips at the start of the novel.[18] As *Fahrenheit 451* draws to a conclusion, Montag has fallen in love with books and has been forced to watch his own small collection "leap and dance like roasted birds, their wings ablaze with red and yellow feathers."[19] The dream of fire voiced by the novel's evil fire chief, Beatty, as "the thing man wanted to invent but never did...perpetual motion,"[20] reverberates throughout the novel in (petrol-fueled) automobiles on (petroleum-based) asphalt streets and in the perpetual flicker of television, screening (through predominantly fossil-fueled electricity) the fictive city's denizens from the world resource war that sustains their totalitarian regime. Fire, whether contained within an internal combustion engine, an electrical wire, or loosed in "a great nuzzling gout" upon books, fulfills the human desire for perpetual motion. Beatty is wrong. The long-sought invention of perpetual motion *has* been achieved. The varied channels of fire (TV, freeways, radio) are, at best, carriers for the human senses and surrogates for political agency.

What is impossible in Bradbury's petrodystopia of the 2050s is what we might call self-generated motion, the body techniques that humans and animals originate without prostheses. The fireman experiences his "hands" as depersonalized, part of the kerosene hose, and the birds we see in flight are never birds, but flapping, exploding books. The fire engine appears as a "salamander," the "hound" as a cybernetic organism. Metaphorical equivalence and substitution, where automated life gets called up to take the place of self-generating life, indicate an ecological aphasia. Meanwhile humans walking or even slowly driving, so as to utilize their senses in real time, can be classified as criminals.

The media theorist Friedrich Kittler suggests that depersonalization, the loss of the timebound body, becomes the human condition beginning in the Victorian period, when predigital media appeared that could record and store sense data. "Once the technological differentiation of optics, acoustics, and writing exploded Gutenberg's writing monopoly around 1880," Kittler writes, "the fabrication of so-called Man became possible. His essence escapes into apparatuses. Machines take over functions of the central nervous system, and no longer, as in times past, merely those of muscles."[21] Kittler recognizes early sound media in particular—like the phonograph or the radio playing in the background of the novel *Oil!*—as remaking the real from the outside in. "Were the phonograph able to hear itself, it would be far less mystifying in the final analysis than the idea of our hearing it. But indeed we do: its vibrations really turn into impressions and thoughts. We therefore have to concede the transformation of movement into thought that is always possible—a transformation that appears more likely when it is a matter of internal brain movement than when it comes from the outside."[22] One need not recognize media in terms of the deep, neurological automation of the human as a remembering and narrating (time-ordering) subject. Kittler even does not indulge such totalizing critique.

For Ray Bradbury, writing in the early 1950s, when the Cold War produced a continual simulation of ultimate endings, public culture seemed to have been robbed of vitality by the immediate reactivity of the radio and television programming broadcast into private homes. Thoughts and feelings were beginning to be prompted by these machines. Meanwhile, the "sensuality and memory" incited by books, where one still can imagine between the lines, as Kittler suggests, lost out to the "physical precision" of "a reproduction authenticated by the object itself" in film and sound media.[23] Was there no more time for human memory, called up by the sensations we might have while reading a novel? Kittler illuminates a cultural anxiety that often accompanies transitions among media platforms, such as those to radio and then television in the early and mid-twentieth century. Television expanded its persuasive power a thousandfold between 1945 and 1975.[24]

Bradbury's injured public culture stands in close relationship to what we might call nature, or life. Nature, always defined primarily by what it is not, figures here as antithetical to the speed of cars and the reactivity of the screen. Human association in actual or material space can only be had on the outskirts of cities in *Fahrenheit 451*, by criminalized intellectuals dissenting from the margins of the kerosene apocalypse. In a prophetic gesture toward peak oil speculations about "post-oil" American futures, here the collapse of the petrol infrastructure in cleansing fire signals the possibility of real political engagement and a self-directed cultivation of the senses. The rebellious uncle who is arrested "for being a pedestrian" in *Fahrenheit 451* uncannily reappears in Bradbury's short story "The Pedestrian" (1953), where he attempts to pursue an education of the senses in material, embodied time by leaving his air conditioner and TV and walking around the city at night.

Bradbury apparently wrote "The Pedestrian" after he was stopped by the Los Angeles police on Wilshire Boulevard in 1947, for being a pedestrian.[25] In the short story, an agent of state power in the form of a driverless police car arrests and incarcerates the man who refuses automobility, the home "viewing screen," and the air conditioner, in order to go out "walking to see."[26] Similar refusals of mass culture for the practice of reanimating public space by walking are imagined in mid-twentieth-century critical arts practices such as the Situationist dérive, rambling, self-directed walks reflecting the unique psychogeographic narratives of practitioners.[27] Recall, too, the exploratory walking, biking, and motorcycling associated with a lived appreciation of vernacular landscapes in the humanist geography of John Brinckerhoff Jackson, much of it recorded in his breakthrough journal *Landscape* (1951–1968). Pedestrianism as a means of enacting the commons has strong roots in the mid-twentieth century, at a time when varied technologies seemed to be moving the public domain inside.

At the conclusion of Bradbury's "The Pedestrian," the driverless car whisks the walker away to a psychiatric clinic "for Research on Regressive tendencies."[28] From the back of the car, the pedestrian continues to look around him, making meaningful notation of "the empty river-bed streets" in metaphors that recall the concrete and steel refashioning of the Los Angeles River as a type of street.[29] The historian Jenny Price has described the transformation of the Los Angeles River as "the greatest disappearing act in environmental history."[30] The concrete channeling of the river began in the 1930s as part of a comprehensive flood control plan and quickly became symbolic of post–World War II technological optimism as well as the potential revenge of the *bios* that the river-engineering repressed, destroying rich wetlands. In the film *Them!* (Gordon Douglas, 1954), giant ants engorged on nuclear waste nest in the Los Angeles River's concretized channels, emerging at night to forage for children in the city's manicured neighborhoods. The science fiction classic *The War of the Worlds* (Byron Haskin, 1953) also makes Los Angeles the home of a modern technocratic invasion by "aliens" who can only be mastered with a persistent bacteria that testifies to the value of even the most degraded life forms as copartners in human species survival.

These films mark the relationship of the military-industrial complex to petroleum infrastructures like highways and suburbs, which were imagined in part as a means of dispersing population targets in the event of nuclear war. Soon enough, southern California's suburbia would be seen, worldwide, as a gold standard of middle-class lifestyle. The filmic monsters of these 1950s science fiction films, "ants," "bacteria," and the like, play the counterhegemonic role of environmental prophets. Donna Haraway calls them "protean embodiments of a world as witty agent and actor."[31]

In the years following 1950s science fiction responses to nuclear panic, when the environmental author and poet Gary Snyder would name bacterial microorganisms in our intestines as evidence that "wildness" still thrives among us, the nightmare-mutation version of environmental awareness available in the Cold War era reached a gentle maturity. Yet the pests, dirt, disorder, and chaos theory that still energizes the U.S. environmental movement and its 1960s counterculture base never fully triumphed over the technocratic petrol dreamscape whose total environment can be read as a realization of perpetual motion. It's instructive to recall that Ray Bradbury himself became a consultant for Disneyworld's Epcot Center, and that Bradbury quipped that Walt Disney was the only man in Los Angeles who could popularize public transit, due to the popularity of the trams, trains, and steamboats available for public use in Disneyland.[32] Disneyland also offered the centerpiece "autopia" ride, which allowed children to assume the happy risks of driving miniature, gas-fueled cars. Bradbury and Disney both assisted the imagination of a civic landscape of total mediation based in cheap energy.

I use the term "petrotopia" here, signifying petroleum-utopia, to refer to the now ordinary U.S. landscape of highways, low-density suburbs, strip malls, fast food and gasoline service islands, and shopping centers ringed by parking lots or parking towers. My inclusion of the term "utopia" in a description of a far-from-ideal environment draws upon David Harvey's critical assessment of utopianism as a hegemonic "spatial ordering." Harvey recognizes the implementation of utopianism as resulting in political systems that "strictly regulate a stable and unchanging social process," such that "the dialectic of social process is repressed" and "no future needs to be envisaged because the desired state is already achieved."[33] The building of the auto-highway-sprawl complex has been a utopian project. We can recognize its origins in the Radiant City of Le Corbusier or the massive highway projects of Robert Moses—disasters on the human scale, for the most part, born of what Corbu called the "rapture of power...and speed," racially inflected schemes to eliminate urban "blight," and more broadly the potential of traffic, né commerce, to expand the bandwidth of information and pleasure.[34]

As utopia, petrotopia represents itself as an ideal end-state, the service economy made flesh, repressing the violence that it has performed upon South Bronx neighborhoods leveled for freeway development or the wetlands below New Orleans, which were filled to build suburban homes. While petrotopia represses the dialectics of social and ecological process, it foregrounds a temporal schema that serves its goals. Sprawl and spread suggest movement outward, in time, but minus an ethical imperative that ascribes notions of consequence to time. In its amoral, monstrous reproduction of itself in its own image, petrotopia resembles the species of utopia Harvey describes as the processual utopia of free-market ideology, which, when it "comes to ground," produces space to restlessly destroy and reorganize it in the service of capital.[35] This relentless production of space creates problems of scale that, in turn, invite the return of repressed consequences, irreversible damage.

The points at which utopian imagining, "the infinite work of the imagination's power of figuration," in theorist Louis Marin's terms, meet a discrete unit of narrative time, something that happened and can't be undone, can be instructive of how petrotopia betrays itself, tipping back into the more solid proposition of socioecological disaster.[36] Temporally discrete event produces rents in the petrol screen. This essentially formal problem of narrative structure challenging an ideology reliant upon iconicity and image has been discussed in philosophical terms as the bad faith of technocratic modernity. The social theorist Barbara Adam names the fantasy of temporal reversibility as a fundamental principle of the technoscientific optimism growing out of the Cold War.[37] The damage wrought by technoscience can be undone—that is the fantasy. It is my purpose here to consider a few events in the cultural history of oil where the specter of the irreversible interrupts such ebullience, and the media environments sustained by the petroleum infrastructure break to static.

In the early 1970s, on the verge of the world oil crisis that would throw the sustainability of U.S. fossil fuel dependency in doubt, the British architect Reyner Banham experienced a conversion. After years of reviling the decadence of U.S. car culture, Banham fell in love with Los Angeles. For him, the fact that Los Angeles seemed to have been built for the purpose of "direct personal gratification," with its robust public "architecture of commercial fantasy" served by ubiquitous freeways, signified a savage "innocence."[38] His Romantic, distinctly European exoticization of American frontierism in *Los Angeles: An Architecture of Four Ecologies* (1971) makes it a distant cousin to Chateaubriand's *Atala* (1801), the early European invocation of the American noble savage that inspired James Fenimore Cooper. Banham named Los

Angeles's auto-infrastructure "autopia," after the ride Walt Disney designed for the Tomorrowland section of his California theme park, the one where children drove miniature cars. For Banham, Los Angeles's autopia becomes a virtual network of organisms (humans, cars, signage, freeways) engaged in mutual, sustaining relations as a "fourth ecology" within the urban region.

Banham naturalizes the urban petroscape by explicitly comparing it to Los Angeles's coastal ecology, which he recognizes as a "surfurbia" sustained by human practice and copartnership. Place, ecologically speaking, becomes a system of use, of living. This is the vernacular reading of the built environment also evident in *Learning from Las Vegas* (1972) and in the work of J. B. Jackson and Jane Jacobs. Both "the freeway system in its totality" and the "seventy-odd miles" of "white sand running from Malibu to Balboa" suggest to Banham democratic access and "transcendental values," "a state of mind" that remakes humans living in the Los Angeles basin as "Angelenos."[39] Banham's likening of the Los Angeles highway system to the beach as civic commons falters at only one point within his poetic analogizing, and that is in the discrete historical moment when smog "came" to Los Angeles, in the mid-1940s. In the midst of asserting (in one of his most polemical claims) that traffic does not have a negative social effect in Los Angeles, Banham concedes that smog, emanating from traffic, does: "It is the psychological impact of smog that matters in Los Angeles. The communal trauma of Black Wednesday (8 September 1943), when the first great smog zapped the city in solid, has left permanent scars, because it broke the legend of the land of eternal sunshine.... To make matters worse, analysis showed that a large part of the smog...is due to effluents from the automobile."[40] That cars could make a black city figures for Banham as an eclipse of the utopian imaginary of California in much the same way that Bill McKibben, in the late 1980s, recognized anthropogenic climate change as the end of nature. Southern California, with its sunshine and endless opportunities for self-extension via gadgetry, was, for the twentieth century, the location of the Nature of the Modern.

When this paradise of modernity met smog, the *Los Angeles Times* initially reported the city besieged by a "gas attack." The event at first appeared mysterious, linked to "industrial stacks and vehicle traffic," but inexplicably severe.[41] The southern California press offers an archive of shock and at times absurd efforts to indict the atmosphere for, it seems, breach of contract. "One municipal judge threatened to adjourn court this morning if the condition persists."[42] It took years for the oil refineries and smelters in the industrial grid south of Los Angeles to curtail emissions, and automobiles weren't recognized as the major cause of the problem until the 1950s. The Air Quality Act of 1967 gave California the right to enforce antipollution measures stricter than those required by the federal government—an exceptional right that was recently reanimated by proponents of higher CAFE standards for the state.[43] Smog threatened to change California's literary genre, from a paradisiacal allegory to a cause-and-effect driven narrative shaken by contingencies, concluding, at best, in the treatment of unexpected effects, remediation. Climate-amenity migrants were scared by southern California's "atmospheric freaks," and both tourism and the real estate business suffered.[44]

Personal means of remediation, such as the "smog mask," the "smog suit," and even smog-proof makeup, suggested a smog lifestyle that was both ironic and earnest, insofar as it connected Los Angeles's maturation as a city to the pollution crises of other great industrial metropolises.[45] London's Great Smog of 1952, caused by sulfur dioxide emissions from coal fires, originated the smog mask that became both solution and joke for Angelenos. The artist Claes Oldenburg's drawing *Smog Mask* (1966) now hangs in the Los Angeles Museum of Contemporary Art. [FIGURE 2.1] A profile of a woman wearing a mask that appears as a giant penis and scrotum, the drawing in its current context comments on the history of Los Angeles, suggesting southern California's self-realization as a natureculture in which genetic mutation or at best cyborgism will replace the naive "delights of out-door life" touted by turn-of-the-century boosters. In 1886 it was possible for a *Los Angeles Times* columnist operating under the nom de plume "Susan Sunshine" to state

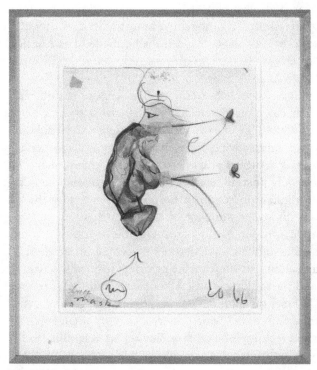

FIGURE 2.1 *Claes Oldenburg, Smog Mask, 1966, Museum of Contemporary Art, Los Angeles. Partial and promised gift of Blake Byrne.*

that "our houses may be flooded with fresh air and sunshine three hundred days a year."[46] In 1956, the *Long Beach Press-Telegram* recommended enclosing oneself in a personal climate: "Want to Beat the Smog and Heat? Put on a Mask and Start a Fan." A photograph of one Carl Bishop of Long Beach illustrates the technique of creating personal weather, warning that Mr. Bishop, looking elephantine rather than penile in his smog gear, might scare off "the door-to-door salesman." The effects of smog on Los Angeles sociality are implicit.[47]

When the complexity of an effective smog abatement treatment became clear, smog grew from the status of an "attack" or "atmospheric freak" to a regular "season." The season was September, southern California's late, hot summer. In fact, smog is oil weather, like the industrial fires that were originally named as such by oil-field roughnecks. Initially the industries targeted by antismog activism (primarily the oil, gas, and automobile industries) argued that smog could not be a legal matter precisely *because* it was weather, a self-generating atmosphere attributable as much to the Los Angeles basin's temperature inversions as to smelters, refineries, incinerators, and tailpipes.[48] The weather argument, ecologically unsound, helped polluters evade restrictions, while on a conceptual level, for advocates of modern social nature, it also proved devastating. This oil weather, unlike oil-field fires, is amorphous, unspectacular, and persistent. It does not aid and abet the proliferation of images of progress. In fact, smog drove away traffic, the material proof of petromodern success. Airplanes avoided the beclouded Los Angeles basin until low-visibility landing technologies were developed, which happened largely in response to Los Angeles smog.[49]

From the 1940s smog crisis onward, Los Angeles has offered a front line in the ongoing battle for the meaning of the environment, whether this term means nonproduced life or a broader designation of the lifelike objects, infrastructures, and screens that humans make, sometimes in concert with nonhumans. In sum, Los Angeles poses the question: Is "environment" life or media?

The seemingly postmodern idea of the environment as screen, specifically, may originate in southern California well before the smog era. In the peak oil discovery moment of the late 1920s and early 1930s, when California was producing 20 percent of the world's oil, numerous derricks and other industrial structures presented an aesthetic problem to Californians almost as inescapable as smog. In 1930 the firms of Olmsted Brothers and Bartholomew and Associates submitted a report to the Los Angeles Chamber of Commerce titled "Parks, Playgrounds, and Beaches in the Los Angeles Region," which offers a curious amalgamation of conservationism and technophilic fantasy. The report is familiar to historians for being a ghost in the archives, a much-written-over layer of the city palimpsest that represents an alternative to contemporary Los Angeles's freeways and strip malls. Olmsted and Bartholomew offer a gentler petroscape in which highways, which the planners termed "pleasure parkways," justify their existence by providing exemplary views.[50]

The word "parkway" indicates a history of auto usage that predates the 1930s, in which cars were imagined as touring vehicles rather than simple means of getting from one place to another. Roads, in turn, were conceived as scenic drives. As Kenneth T. Jackson notes, "Extraordinarily wide, these elaborate roads [parkways] were seen as extensions of the developing park system, intended to provide a pleasant pathway from one open space to another."[51] Curvilinear, planted avenues created the picturesque look of early twentieth-century suburbs. What is significant about the Olmsted and Bartholomew plan for Los Angeles County is that it proposes a road system made up almost entirely of parkways for an intensively industrializing urban region. This plan, again, pivots upon the idea of screens. "Screens" for Olmsted and Bartholomew mean landscape features that can be allocated generously to hide ecological wounds.[52] Their screening strategy suggests what McLuhan called the "puny and peripheral efforts of artists" to register adjustments to new scales of technological development that were bound to change human sociality.[53] McLuhan always essentially interpreted media as environment. The architects' generous plantings and carefully constructed views are attempts at a faux "atmosphericity" that covers the sights and sounds of industries producing biochemical effluents already building toward the smog crisis.

The genealogy of Los Angeles's car culture from the production of cheap petroleum coming out of California does not figure in the Olmsted and Bartholomew plan at all. This is odd, given that the spread of derricks into southern California beaches and residential suburbs constituted a huge problem in this period for regional planners, who were torn between promoting industry and real estate. Derricks blocked ocean views and made surrounding communities ugly. Because oil deposits were often located just offshore, derricks tended to mass along the coasts on the most valuable beach properties. The Olmsted and Bartholomew report includes one photograph of Signal Hill, the Long Beach neighborhood that Upton Sinclair uses as a model for his fictional town of Prospect Hill in *Oil!* and that came to be called "Porcupine Hill" due to the massing of oil derricks upon it. Under the report's grainy photo of Signal Hill a caption suggests that "along the ridge among the oil wells a parkway is needed."[54] This caption and photograph, not at all elaborated in the body of the text, seem stunningly incongruent. Would the insertion of a pleasure parkway for leisurely driving amongst the oil derricks reframe them as an aesthetic good? Or is the point to screen this massive development along a parkway corridor that walls out the preconditions of its own presence with plantings? The intentions of the urban planners' single assay at oil-field design cannot be recovered. Their indication that "form" might be achieved against the historical and ecological problems of irreversibility makes their plan for Los Angeles recognizably modern.

The industrial practice of diffusing the aura of a thing by "bringing it close," as Walter Benjamin describes the achievement of reproducible images, shows up here in the possibility of making a roadway into the surreal landscape of the derricks, a landscape that the road would then remake as screen experience—visual "interest" without the symptoms of threat or power that might be implied by keeping such things as oil derricks at a distance.[55] Olmsted and Bartholomew's plan for Los Angeles participates in the tight-cropping of devastated landscapes that has been attributed to the recent monumental images of industrial waste made famous by the Canadian photographer Edward Burtynsky, in his series *Manufactured Landscapes* (2003). In both cases a kind of media game replaces the notion of a messy material world, tenuously held by social and ecological relationship. Such media tactics might obscure ecological injury, but they also make genuine bids for agency in the face of oil's self-referential and apparently total world. Writing of (petroleum-derived) plastics at midcentury, Roland Barthes described the prominence of such oil media as "ubiquity made visible."[56]

2.) *Why is oil so bad?* Because of the mystified ecological unconscious of modern car culture, which allows for a persistent association of driving with being alive.

When the firms of Olmsted Brothers and Bartholomew and Associates submitted their regional planning report to the Los Angeles Chamber of Commerce in 1930, they argued that road-building would be a primary means of conservationism for southern California. This equivalence of conservationism with roads predicted, in an oblique manner, Aldo Leopold's dictum that conservationism relies upon the altering of point of view, in his essay "Conservation Esthetic" (1949). Roads were to be designed to confer value upon natural amenities, like lights shone upon paintings in a museum. They also could direct attention away from industrial development. The planning report focuses its aesthetically inflected conservation on the rehabilitation of "unsightly commercialized streets," because "much of the joy of the day's outing will depend upon their condition."[57] As noted, Olmsted and Bartholomew wanted to frame Los Angeles County in its entirety within a system of so-called pleasure parkways. They even proposed that a parkway be extended into the Pacific Ocean at Santa Monica Bay, for unimpeded sea gazing "absolutely away from buildings and concessions."[58]

The massive environmental degradation built into this idealistic plan, which intended to allow democratic access to California's natural amenities by placing a highway loop in the ocean, speaks to the problem of thinking in terms of consuming rather than producing environment that Mike Davis has recognized as plaguing southern California developers since the 1880s.[59] I think it important to remark that what was sought by Olmsted and Bartholomew was, at bottom, a reiteration of human-scale values, among which they recognized something like biophilia, E. O. Wilson's romantic sociobiological concept of human attraction to other life. To drive into the ocean was to touch other life, without the dangers attendant upon actual submersion in an atmosphere hostile to human physiology. The 1930 Olmsted and Bartholomew report proposes the car and road system as potentially positive ecological actors.

This ecological reading of the American road correlates with Upton Sinclair's naive prophecy of road culture in *Oil!* and predicts the climax of a U.S. road-pleasure complex in Jack Kerouac's *On the Road* (1957), Vladimir Nabokov's *Lolita* (1955), and the Route 66 touring of the early 1960s. Included in the rich *bios* invited by the road is the proliferation of human language through the ingenious device of the road sign. Sinclair's narrator makes note of these "funny signs" and "endless puns" and "jollity rampaging" in pre–billboard era road text scrawled onto rocks, house-siding, and even trees.[60] The abundance of this crude signage predicts a more sinister proliferation of double entendre and puns in the late 1940s road culture of *Lolita*. We might also note that it predicts the proliferation of twentieth-century road fiction. The emergent U.S. road narratives of the 1920s shed light on the road genre in its classic phase. In comparison, we might parse the ecological aspirations of car culture from its ecological effects, including habitat loss, human death, and the racial segregation performed by suburbs and freeways.

The first chapter of *Oil!* reminds contemporary readers why Olmsted, Jr., who was the son of the architect of Central Park, might assume driving to be a means of environmental education. What the car suggests in *Oil!* is not the speed/power complex associated with modernity but rather a series of encounters with rich ecologies supported by the automobile's prosthetic body and a rhizomatic network of fourteen-foot-wide roads that figure as openings rather than disciplinary paths. Sinclair's boy-narrator, Bunny, son of the oil magnate Dad Ross, who drives the car, identifies "jackrabbit" and "butcher bird" and "road-runners" from the passenger seat. He notes the manner in which the automobile "unrolls" "new vistas...deep gorges, towering old pine trees, gnarled by storms."[61] The novel indicates that Bunny's passenger-side viewing facilitates an activity of imagination and virtual vitality not available to his father, who drives. Taken together, auto, highway, and scenery act as a moist media, to borrow Roy Astor's term for media that is at least partially organic. The road and car make the child's experience more lifelike.[62]

In the same historical moment that Sinclair writes, Frederick Olmsted, Jr., was designing the infrastructure for passenger-side fancies like Bunny Ross's, creating the now familiar features of state and federal park roads, such as turnouts, spurs, and loops, in a report he completed prior to his plan for Los Angeles, the *State Parks Survey of California* (1929). Unlike the Olmsted plan for Los Angeles County, much of *State Parks* has come to fruition in today's built environment. Commissioned by the Save-the-Redwoods League, this report emphasized the importance of state control over what Olmsted terms "foregrounds of more notable and valuable landscapes enjoyable from the road."[63] Here is another version of environmental screening that set real limitations on industrial forestry.

Up through the 1920s, when California voters approved a road-accessible state park system, the car was conceived as a means of achieving a premodern vision of nature that had been lost to the railroad.[64] Like preindustrial transport by horse, cars allowed closer, slower viewing than had been possible in trains. Auto tourism captured the U.S. middle class in the early twentieth century and was boosted by auto club campaigns to "See America First,"[65] before visiting Europe. By the 1950s, the fact that automobiles could reach speeds up to one hundred miles per hour and that more than forty thousand miles of freeways were in the making shifted the ecological significance of cars. The car "problem" received articulation in the Wilderness Act of 1964, which prohibits motorized vehicles from federally designated wilderness—a promise not clearly met, as Edward Abbey famously notes in his manifesto on industrial tourism. Abbey chides the park system for road-building that caters to "the indolent millions born on wheels and suckled on gasoline."[66] In the scenic loops that Olmsted had designed in the 1920s to bring people into the woods, Abbey saw a conspiracy to return parkgoers to the modern eyesore where their journeys began, the gasoline station. Cars began to suggest moral flabbiness as well as pollution and, given the plausible new speeds, acute danger.

A primary critical emphasis from within road culture has grown up around the concept—and the ordinary experience—of roadkill, which indexes the habitat loss and damage to nonhuman life exercised by cars. Roadkill testifies to the car's power to bring the organic excess of living and dying bodies into the sphere of the "privatized mobility" that Raymond Williams recognizes as the modern media complex.[67] Marshall McLuhan described automobiles as "hot media," meaning media that so completely stimulates the human senses that it obviates the need of thinking or the perception of distance from the pleasure-giving object.[68] Yet how many family road trips have been rudely interrupted by the vision of a domestic pet mangled on the side of the road? Or, still worse, by a potentially fatal collision with a wild animal such as a deer? Roadkill speaks of the animal, in the broad sense of the mortality that even modern media cannot resolve. For the cultural historian Brian Ladd, "roadkill" indicates whatever gets in the way of the modern progress narrative of creative destruction, where capital moves rapidly to new sites of cheap and efficient production, leaving a trail of defunct manufacturing sites and regional laborers in its wake.[69] Roadkill speaks to externalities and friction, to hidden costs and unexpected impediments.

The artist Stephen Paternite has based his career in roadkill photography, which he has practiced since the early 1970s as a means of emphasizing the "strong imagery going on along the side of the road," in his words. "During the summer months of 1973, I began working on a series of road-kill animal sculptures, which depicted the confrontation between animals and massive industrialization."[70] In early 1975, Paternite produced a portfolio of handcolored black-and-white photographs, entitled *Thirty-Six Road-Kills*, in perverse homage to Ed Ruscha's *Twentysix Gasoline Stations* (1963), which will be discussed later in this chapter.

Paternite's images foreground death as a primary effect of speed. He also points up the intimate knowledge of nonhuman life that results from everyday highway accidents. The photographer's shoes sometimes appear just at the margins of his images to indicate his witnessing position inches from an animal corpse, reminding the viewer of just how close roadkill brings us to the otherness of nonhuman bodies. Think Elizabeth Bishop's "The Moose," with its emphasis on the ecological epiphany produced by a chance encounter between a looming animal and a bus—yet with the encounter deadly and too close for the essentially aesthetic insight indicated by the word "epiphany." Paternite's photos present the uncanny, the sticky-organic, the defamiliarized materiality of the grotesque. "Roadkill" under the scrutiny of his lens is *us*, the fragility of our own bodies in the shadow of the internal combustion engine and the tons of steel that define everyday movement in cars.

Anticar activists who recognize the car as a key contributor to greenhouse gas emissions, climate change, and habitat decline have politicized such considerations of roadkill as a rich metaphor. The planet itself might be analogous to roadkill, in such a view. We don't see such pointed environmentalism in road fiction. Yet in both early road novels like *Oil!* and the classic 1950s road novels, the likelihood of accident challenges the assumption of road pleasure and the truism offered by Jean Baudrillard, in his assessment of modern car culture, that "movement alone is the basis of a sort of happiness."[71]

In Nabokov's *Lolita*, Lo identifies a "squashed squirrel" on the road with an interest usually disallowed her in Humbert's solipsistic narrative.[72] In the same scene, she hurls an epithet at Humbert as "we almost ran over some little animal or other that was crossing the road"—and then she tells Humbert, bluntly, "you raped me."[73] Like car accidents, sex comes about in *Lolita* as a violent mistake. "Car men" such as Humbert extend the incidental violence of sex, open its possibilities, through the privilege of cars and roads. The 1956 Interstate and Defense Highway Act, authorizing the building of 41,000 miles of interstate roads, came into being one year after *Lolita*'s publication. Set in the late 1940s, *Lolita* predicts the continental access promised by this federal freeway system, which had been on the planning table since 1944. The freeways create an ultimate privacy, facilitating social forgetting that might assist psychosis, as in Joan Didion's freeway novel *Play It as It Lays* (1971), or sex crime, as in *Lolita*. Consider Lionel Trilling's reading of the "curious moral mobility [*Lolita*] forces upon us" as if it applied not to our reacquaintance with the shocking aspects of romantic love through pedophilia, as Trilling attests, but also to our acquiescence to the petrophilia that makes the novel's 27,000 miles of driving imaginable.[74]

Lo, not old enough to drive, remains an accessory to HH's transcontinental drive. She's a stylish extra, like the bulbous front bumpers (nicknamed "Dagmars" in the auto industry) that were added to cars in the 1950s so that they might appear to have protruding breasts. Lolita and HH almost personify the schizophrenic sexiness and heaviness of the 1950s automobile, with its bulbous body and rocketlike tail.[75] Their actual car, a dumpy Buick LaSalle, suggests the aesthetic rationing of the 1940s during the Second World War, when auto plants converted to make munitions. Car culture in the 1950s grew, in part, from the perception that wartime sacrifice must be answered by production for style and pleasure. The tension between these contradictory schema of pleasure, an aesthetic of renunciation and an aesthetic of luxury, shadows *Lolita*. Stanley Kubrick's film adaptation of the novel (1962) plays up the winking styles of the 1950s, while the French-American production directed by Adrian Lyne (1997) imagines a bucolic road culture, with strong visual emphasis on the awkwardness of Humbert's vehicle—an analogue to his "humiliating, sordid, taciturn love life," as he describes it in the novel.[76]

In HH's doggerel, he refers to Lo as his "car pet," an endearment that suggests her abject status (pet, carpet) as well as her relationship, as an accoutrement, to the sexy new "makes" of the postwar years. From prison, Humbert writes to Lolita:

> Where are you riding, Dolores Haze?
> What make is the magic carpet?
> Is a Cream Cougar the present craze?
> And where are you parked, my car pet?[77]

These lines are penned after HH has lost Lo to Clare Quilty in a crosscountry car chase that inadvertently educates him in the variety of sexy car models that Quilty borrows or owns. Humbert's consumerism isn't so successful as Quilty's, as is made clear by his failure with Lolita. The literary critic Dana Brand argues that HH's fall into an actual sexual relationship with Lolita indicates a transition from idealistic aestheticism to consumerism that renders him "guilty," according to the value schema endorsed by the novel. "Consumerism is a false double of aestheticism in that it involves a dependence upon the actual rather than the merely imaginative possession of objects," Brand concludes.[78] HH's incestuous dream of impregnating Lolita in order to produce Lolita the Second and then, from that offspring, Lolita the Third provides a radical example of his movement away from nympholepsy as rarified art toward an obsession with productivity and gratification through a kind of sexual Fordism.

The auto industry's marketing philosophy institutionalized the fickleness of consumer desire in opposition to the utilitarianism that had originated with the Ford Model T. The industry's still dominant philosophy of "Sloanism" is named for Alfred P. Sloan, a president of General Motors in the 1920s. In the late 1920s, Sloan recognized that the Model T, the dependable industrial product that grew cheaper every year and came in one color, offered a bad business model. Sloan created the profession of auto "stylist." Auto stylists were fashion designers set upon the auto industry to help turn cars into virtual apparel, "creating a certain amount of dissatisfaction with past [still functional] models."[79] Their reign wasn't secured until the 1950s, after the economic upheavals of the Depression and the Second World War. Then the car became the first industrial object to privilege style over engineering—expanding the criteria for obsolescence. The style-driven economy of the mid-twentieth century affected social relations, art, and desire itself. David Riesman's sociological classic *The Lonely Crowd* (1961) betrays the insecure "other-directedness" of Americans at midcentury, as middle-class work shifts from a basis in "craft skills" toward salesmanship, advertising, and media.[80] In its broodings on sex and death, road fiction complicates the emphases on obsolescence encouraged by the auto industry, with its confident reliance on cheap fuel.

Classic road novels of the 1950s, *Lolita* and *On the Road* measure sharp grief ("O sad American night!"), drawn from their solipsistic tendencies fed by speedy driving and language play, against a craving for the genuine sociability ("real straight talk about souls") that could be found, as both pain and pleasure, in the diverse public spaces of the 1940s.[81] As Louis Menand has written of *On the Road*, "Nostalgia... was part of its appeal in 1957. It is not a book about the nineteen-fifties. It's a book about the nineteen-forties.... The interstates [had] changed the phenomenology of driving."[82] The nostalgia for the 1940s that Menand identifies as an inspiration for Kerouac can be recognized in both novels as a specific longing for the residual infrastructures—and social possibilities—associated with outmoded cultures of public transit and the urban heterogeneity that precede the era of suburbs and freeways.

Lolita and *On the Road* offer premonitions and parodies of white flight, where the segregation implied by this phrase is foreshadowed in the transition that the historian Eric Avila describes as a transfer "from the heterosocial spaces of streetcars [and pre–World War II cities] to the insular, privatized cell of the automobile."[83] At the end of the Second World War, Americans, who accounted for six percent of the world's population, owned three-quarters of its cars. Suburbia sprawled, thanks to the 1949 Federal Housing Act, which facilitated low-cost financing of suburban tract developments. Many of these developments implicitly or explicitly banned nonwhites. The Highway Act consecrated the geography of segregation that had been set up by the Home Owner's Loan Corporation, the Housing Finance Agency, and tactics of redlining, blockbusting, restrictive covenants, and municipal incorporation.[84] Avila argues that the innovations of 1950s infrastructure materialized "a set of spatial fantasies that asserted what city life should (and should not) be and upheld traditional models of social order after an extended duration of economic turmoil and global conflict."[85] United States literary history records these moments of white spatial incorporation through sensory memory. For example, consider the feel and smell of new asphalt that assaults Latino/as whose Los Angeles neighborhood is violently divided by the construction of a highway loop, in the first pages of Helena María Villamontes's *Their Dogs Came with Them* (2007).

A convergence of some of the sociological facts of suburbia in *Lolita* claims the life of Charlotte Haze, the health-conscious and grimly sophisticated suburban mother whose sacrifice to the suburban street lands her in an "eternal heaven among an eternal alchemy of asphalt and rubber and stone."[86] This is *Lolita*'s foundational car wreck. Significantly, heaven takes form here as car parts and petroleum products, save "stone," which perhaps refers to Charlotte's grave. Or maybe HH inserts this naturalistic word for the sake of resonance and "prose style." Charlotte's eternity is aptly conceived as the petroleum-rubber-steel infrastructure that allows the exquisite privacy that HH exploits to molest her daughter. That infrastructure shrinks the "gigantic" America of HH's European imagination to "a measly suburban lawn and a smoking garbage incinerator,"[87] a fantastic image of ecological diminishment. It also facilitates Humbert's miles and miles of driving, away from the suburban lawns of New England. His queer inversion of white flight still depends on its kit of media, privacy, and access. Late in HH's journey with Lolita, when he begins to long for the "plausible impersonation" that he recognizes as the suburban family, he identifies "guilty locomotion" as "vitiating our powers of impersonation."[88] Road living denaturalizes what for HH appears as the everyday incest of the nuclear family, its privatized production, laying bare "a hard, twisted teleological growth,"[89] the family itself as criminal's itinerary.

The difference between an itinerary—requested by HH's lawyer and, he anticipates, by his juror-readers—and a "joyride,"[90] the word HH uses to describe what he does with Lolita, goes to the heart of Nabokov's own teasing resistance of ideological or moral readings in favor of aesthetic bliss. The bliss-versus-ideology conflict generally troubles the road novel because it is a genre, like nature writing, explicitly interested in recording phenomenological experience. "Voraciously we consumed those long highways, in rapt silence we glided over their glossy black dance floors," HH muses, attesting to the kinesthetic thrills of good roads and, implicitly, to the state and federal subsidies that prioritized good roads as an American project. "Not only had Lo no eye for scenery but she furiously resented my calling her attention to this or that enchanting detail."[91] Lo doesn't voice the visually stunning observations of landscape that Humbert bequeaths upon the novel. For example, he notes: "a passing glimpse of some mummy-necked farmer, and all around alternating strips of quick-silverish water and harsh green corn, the whole arrangement opening up like a fan, somewhere in Kansas."[92] To Humbert, "unfastidious Lo" appears to be "charmed by toilet-signs—Guys-Gals, John-Jane, Jack-Jill, and even Buck's-Doe's."[93] To follow Humbert's logic, imagine Lolita possessed of a pop sensibility, anticipating the wry sanctification of commercial signage in the work of a Warhol or Ruscha. Suspicious of HH's mnemonic designs, we also might recall Lo's visits to gasoline station toilets back on the morning after her first "strenuous" sex with Humbert, when she demands a bathroom to repair her hurts. These gas station toilets, buoyant pop icons, offer a nearly infinite referral to rape. As the second section of the novel wanes, Lo's toilet stops allow rendezvous with HH's tormentor, Quilty. Gas stations become potential switchpoints in the novel, almost ekphrastic moments when the narrative stops to reorganize itself around the architectural information of what pop theorists and artists would recognize as the most universal structure of the mid-twentieth century.

We have no narrative access to the intention that attracts Lolita to gas station toilets or their mischievous signs. She is filtered through HH and the language-play that cocoons his narration from "an outside world that was real to her" but proves only reluctantly real to him through the dumb witnessing of homely objects, such as gas pumps, "whitewalled tires," "bright cans of motor oil," and "that red icebox with assorted drinks" in front of the typical filling station. "Those stationary trivialities," HH avers, "look almost surprised, like staring rustics, to find themselves stranded in the traveler's field of vision."[94] The accoutrements of the gas station, especially toilets and telephones, suggest to HH "the points where my destiny was liable to catch."[95] The gas station itself marks a halt and an exchange, cash for fuel, that complicates automobility conceived as happiness and freedom. Ed Ruscha would turn the heroic version of Route 66 touring that Humbert apes on its head with his small pop art book *Twentysix Gasoline Stations*, in which twenty-six gas stations along Route 66 appear in an arbitrary sequence, out of chronological and geographical order, as exemplars of the "non statement with a non style" that Ruscha elsewhere identifies as "contemporary decadence."[96] The gas stations offer constellations of signs, not narrative. Clusters of repeating figures, prices, fluttering flags, words such as "regular," "Standard," "service," occasional icons of movement, like the brand *Pegasus*, and subtler architectural references to flight—these make up not a story per se but a configuration that implies mobility, banality, money. Ruscha's small book zaps travel of affect, which inheres in the strong choices that constitute style. Yet the gas stations, each shot from the same angle at an impersonal middle-distance from across a road, inadvertently develop a mood—of isolation, even loneliness.

Ruscha and Humbert Humbert both wed banality to alienation, anxiety, and the uncompensatory prosperity of postwar America. The cash nexus that supports HH's exploitation of Lolita—increasingly visible as she becomes a fierce negotiator for money—similarly sustains "old Melmoth," as HH calls the purple-gilled La Salle that he views as a coconspirator and externalization of his overheated desire insofar as the car holds remnants of Lolita (bobby pin, sock) long after she has escaped. As the road trip with Lolita drags on, HH complains of its drain on his wallet. The car finally forms part of Humbert's dowry for the grown-up Lolita, Mrs. Richard Schiller. The dirty secret of *Lolita* and of the road novel more broadly is that its bliss, whether felt in response to a sunbathing nymphet or the textures of an asphalt road, bears relation to fundamental economic acts. Even the "durable pigments" that sustain the "aurochs" of Lascaux in the last paragraph of *Lolita*, emblems of the persistence of beauty, rely on a spent earth.[97]

In *On the Road*, bliss likewise inheres in primarily kinesthetic and visual sensation that *seems* to be divorced from resource consumption, whether in the hitchhiking that allows Sal his "greatest ride of my life" in the flatbed of a Minnesota farmer or the feel of coasting with Dean "down to the San Joaquin valley…thirty miles without gas."[98] Frequent theft and hijinks in hired cars and as a parking attendant in New York City make Dean an eccentric advocate of ride-sharing, while Sal favors hitchhiking and public transportation because he hates to drive. The trouble these guys have holding onto cars shows how "beat" they are and establishes a working-class or deliberately down-mobile white identity consonant with the carny slang meaning of "beat" as exhausted, poor, and beaten down. Kerouac explained the origins of "beat" in the argot of Herbert Huncke, the gay street hustler who seduced the movement's godfather, William F. Burroughs. "We learned the word from [Huncke]," Kerouac told Al Aronowitz in 1959. "To me it meant being poor…like sleeping on subways, like Huncke used to do, and yet being illuminated and having illuminated ideas about apocalypse and all that."[99] Much of the movement that happens in *On the Road* actually does not take place in cars.

The novel indexes sore feet, Sal's "silly huaraches," his immigrant-Italian peasantry, his lack of ability to end up where he wants to be—the relationship of this passive movement to Buddhism will only make sense in light of Kerouac's later writing.[100] "Who did they think they were, yaahing at somebody on the road just because they were little high school punks and their parents carved the roast beef on Sunday afternoons?" Sal asks of some California kids in cars who heckle him and his girlfriend, Terry, as they hitchhike.[101] Terry is Chicana, and the scene helps legitimate Sal's pious assertion that "in a way I am" Mexican, too.[102] A premonition and parodic inversion of white flight, *On the Road* describes flight from whiteness conceived as a set of stultifying social conventions ("roast beef on Sunday").[103] At the same time, the novel emphasizes that the Beats, beaten down as they are, still move around more easily than the superlatively "joyous" African Americans and Latinos who represent a life apart from what Sal vaguely identifies as "white sorrows." The discrepancy between white guys with mobility but no money, and "colored" people who can't go anywhere, previews a freeway ideology that would make the immediately accessible world 41,000 miles larger for persons with cars, while those in inner cities continued to perceive their livable space as limited to a few neighborhood streets and public transit routes.[104]

Despite its areas of blindness, *On the Road* cannot be dismissed as uncritical fodder for "teenage cretins and stealthy masturbators," as the literary critic Morris Dickstein argues Humbert Humbert might see it. There are keen evocations of longing for the North American land here that make palpable a frustrated relationship to ecological knowledge in the era of mass media and the bomb: "Soon it got dusk, a grapy dusk, a purple dusk over tangerine groves and long melon fields; the sun the color of pressed grapes, slashed with burgundy red, the fields the color of love and Spanish mysteries. I stuck my head out the window and took deep breaths of the fragrant air."[105] On a bus heading toward Salinas, Sal's "out the window" observations are tinged by the high-color graphics of fruit ads, which he might have seen on boxes in market stalls or on billboards or on the siding of railcars and trucks. His vision also reflects what Carey McWilliams has labeled the California Spanish Fantasy Past, which was disseminated primarily through print media beginning in the 1890s.[106] Almost nothing about Sal's "most beautiful of all moments"[107] suggests an ability to read the land beyond the iconography of "ads and fads," to borrow one of HH's expressions. Any scenic passage from *On the Road* reveals a similarly mediated approach—which does not diminish the book's beauty but rather signals the divorce, even for many working-class kids, of nature from labor, from concrete knowledge of partnership with the nonhuman. Sal's stint as a cotton picker only underlines the absurdity of his self-description as "man of the earth."[108] Ironically, the diminishment of U.S. farming communities brought about by the automobile, hence the relatively new strangeness of their native land to most Euro-Americans circa 1947, when this novel is set, translates into a nostalgia satisfied by driving.

The longing to really see the land, that sharp desire to be more alive through its life, is an important twentieth-century environmental emotion connected to automobility, and Kerouac eloquently expresses it. Putting on a moving vehicle allows for a sort of ecological minstrelsy, a being and not being *out there* similar to Sal's "digging" the black jazz scene of New Orleans or the "Mex chicks" in the California farming town of Sabinal.[109] Such indulgent passing achieves a note of poignancy because of a single environmental fact that Kerouac buries near the end of *On the Road* and that links his "white sorrows" to the countercultural environmentalism that would develop in the wake of the 1950s. Kerouac's buried fact is the bomb, a key cause of Beat disillusionment. Driving amongst indigenous Mexican villagers in the Sierra Madres, Sal comments: "They didn't know that a bomb had come that could crack all our bridges and roads and reduce them to jumbles, and we would be as poor as they someday, and stretching out our hands in the same, same way. Our broken Ford, old thirties upgoing American Ford, rattled through them."[110] In

Kerouac's hands, the car becomes a broken piece of unthinkable American power that the novel utilizes for thinking about American power.

While nuclear annihilation haunts the road novel in its classic period of the 1950s, from the inception of road fiction as a genre it has focused on accident, rather than the incalculable total threat of nuclear modernity.[111] Road novels of the 1920s, such as *The Great Gatsby* (1925) and even *Oil!*, are as interested in car accidents as are the road novels of the 1950s and the 1970s, when the oil crisis coincided with postmodern meditations on grisly road death such as J. G. Ballard's *Crash* (1973).[112] The twentieth-century road novel's use of car accidents to define social threat that is survivable by humans as a species but not by individuals can be seen as a tentative exploration of the basic premises of environmental justice, such as how the vernacular landscape might be regulated to ensure a baseline of human health.

The highway has been described, with an edge of irony, as modernity's most resilient civic space. The speed at which complex social negotiations have to take place on highways, along with the literally explosive potential of the internal combustion engine, reminds drivers and riders of the physical limitations of human agency. Liberal notions of citizenship as noninterference with others' rights are also materially evident on the road. Cognitive psychologists interested in the psychology of accident repeatedly cite the task of driving a car as exemplary of skill- and rule-based processing that can be interrupted by common performance errors such as the diversion of attention or the misapplication of good rules in unexpected situations. Modern sociality and modern thinking have been shaped by driving.

In folk wisdom, the fundamental rule of the road is to drive defensively, in other words, to get out of the way. This is not always possible for humans, even with the help of painted lines, safety cones, and other paraphernalia of social avoidance. Brian Ladd reminds us that "autophobia" literally means a fear of the self, and that cars have been feared in large part because they betray the weaknesses of the human organism.[113] On a day-to-day basis, cars prove that we are incapable of guaranteeing our safety as a species. In the immediate wake of the classic road novel, Ralph Nader offered his first strong analysis of why we should be afraid of ourselves in cars, living as we are within the clutches of an auto industry that lobbies for deregulation. In Nader's *Unsafe at Any Speed* (1965), the U.S. government's hands-off stance toward Detroit allows thousands of accidents caused by the faulty suspension-system design of the Chevrolet Corvair. Beginning his exposé with an anecdote about Rose Peirini, a housewife whose left arm was severed when her 1961 Corvair tipped over as she was driving at thirty miles per hour on a quiet suburban street, Nader offers an almost novelistic realization of the everyday risk served up by the internal combustion engine and its massive steel body.

While Nader's muckraking belongs to a different literary genre than, say, *On the Road*, road fiction offers a phenomenological rendering of some of the same modern problems that Nader presents. Road fiction asks what the risk of automobile death feels like, beyond the apparent consent-model that seems to be guaranteed by the presence of an auto insurance industry and reliable actuarial tables.

For Nabokov, the privatization and deregulation historically associated with automobiles are preconditions for a libertarian and self-consciously murderous art. That art seizes upon the car as one of its expressive media. The "diaphragmal melting" that Humbert experiences as he deliberately crosses the yellow line dividing traffic in the final chase scene of *Lolita* is his last pedophilic orgasm, a willful violation of the fundamental disciplinary infrastructure of modern culture.[114] Adrian Lyne's *Lolita* tellingly begins with an enactment of this scene. *On the Road* offers an ethically simpler reading of risk society, from the point of view of an average human intelligence with the internal combustion engine at the center of its fragile ecology. Dean Moriarity's extravagant weaving in traffic might be cast as machinic cocksmanship. Yet Sal narrates it as an enactment of anxiety, in Freud's sense of anxiety as the preperformance of something feared.

Dean's wreckless driving anticipates the auto wreck that apparently haunts all twentieth-century American boys:

> He passed the slow cars, swerved, and almost hit the left rail of the bridge, went head-on into the shadow of the unslowing truck, cut right sharply, just missed the truck's left front wheel, almost hit the first slow car, pulled out to pass, and then had to cut back in line when another car came out from behind the truck to look, all in a matter of two seconds, flashing by and leaving nothing more than a cloud of dust instead of a horrible five-way crash with cars lurching in every direction and the great truck humping its back in the fatal red afternoon of Illinois with its dreaming fields. I couldn't get it out of my mind, also, that a famous bop clarinetist had died in an Illinois car-crash recently, probably on a day like this.[115]

The sequential slow-time of literary prose, captured in the deliberate malapropism "unslowing," makes this passage feel more like a bad dream than the heartchoking entertainment that a similar scene might offer on film. The vast difference between the speed of literary prose and the speed of the automobile signals an opening, in the road novel, for a kind of critical reflection unavailable while driving.

The car wreck and the bomb are instantiations of otherwise vague white sorrows that link Kerouac's Beats to the white counterculture that made environmentalism hip in the late 1960s. Nader's *Unsafe at Any Speed* initiated a consumer movement against auto-industry deregulation that also assisted contemporary U.S. environmentalism, in its expression as regulatory activism. As media that allied human freedom to kinetic stimulation, cars made the mass death promised by the bomb more intolerable, more symbolic of what it might mean not to move or feel. Cars made the human body more valuable, pleasurable, and fun. They also caused, and still cause, more human deaths per day than any single agent, forcing questions about human consumption, the price of the mediated self, made possible by cheap fuel. For Americans, the car and the road enable the sense of radical materiality—feeling embodied—that has been theorized as ecological affect, implicitly in Bruno Latour's contribution to Actor-Network-Theory and more explicitly in corporeal feminism.[116] The U.S. road novel archives the human coming-to-knowledge of itself as volatile *matter*. Twentieth-century U.S. environmentalism holds phenomenological debts to car culture that entangles it in unhelpful body sensations and narrative emotions, like petrophilia and white flight.

3.) *Why is oil so bad?* Because its biophysical properties have caused it to be associated with the comic "lower bodily stratum," in Mikhail Bakhtin's phrase.[117] In brief: Oil has been shit and sex, the essence of entertainment.

The biophysical properties of oil made it difficult to demystify, especially in the 1920s when the United States approached peak oil discovery with the excitement attributable to other mining events, like the Gold Rush. Upton Sinclair's *Oil!* debuted at a moment of heightened public ambivalence about oil extraction. Of course, oil continues to generate ambivalence as we recognize the scarcity of the relatively accessible, conventional resources that Sinclair celebrated. Oil's "liquid mobility" and "subterranean" origin, as Michael Watts observes in regard to oil's symbolic resonance in contemporary Nigeria, continue to suggest "all manner of extraordinary magic events," including the contrary fantasies of "life without work" and the "power to tarnish and turn everything into shit."[118] While the extraction of oil cannot be performed without labor, the spectacle of its gushing from the earth suggests divine or Satanic origins, a givenness that confers upon it an inherent value disassociated from social relations. A former Venezuelan president poetically referred to oil as "the devil's excrement."[119] Oil's dirtiness and fecal qualities, as a "black and sticky fluid"[120] emerging in the wake of pressurized natural gas, have served to naturalize it and to place it within a comic, relatively open narrative frame. The representational problem oil presents to the committed artist, be he a socialist such as Sinclair or an environmentalist, has to do with oil's primal associations with earth's body, therefore with the permeability, excess, and multiplicity of all bodies deemed performed *and* given. While the documentary realist can present the immiseration of oil workers or the pollution of environments subjected to oil mining, oil itself retains the indeterminacy and openness to mystification of a living/performing spectacle.

The spectacular nature of the oil strike, in that it allows an audience to experience discovery with its own senses, confers an illusion of democratic access to such scenes, also an illusion that oil, and its profits, belong to everyone. While in many American countries oil has been recognized as the property of the nation, in the United States oil rights almost always have belonged to private owners.[121] Though recognized in certain environments such as city- or state-owned beaches as a public resource, oil has been used to defend private land ownership *as the basis of democratic access* to social goods within the United States. Yet the aesthetic properties of oil as sight, sound, and smell, especially in the "mysteriously thrilling" performance of the gusher, perpetuate the fantasy of public participation. Frederick Buell has described the "exuberance" in early twentieth-century reportage of oil accidents such as gushers in comparison to the mere squalidness of coal mining disasters.[122] In Upton Sinclair and nonfiction accounts from the 1920s, lines of cars show up to witness strikes and gushers, modern miracles.[123]

In the novel *Oil!*, oil itself returns, with almost every representation of its discovery, as an excessively embodied figure, the viscous medium of unregulated play. It is apparently more alive than its human witnesses. Paul Thomas Anderson's loose film adaptation of *Oil!*, *There Will Be Blood*, captures aspects of oil's liveliness in Daniel Plainview's (aka Dad Ross's) first oil discovery, when in the midst of the well's gush oil splashes onto the camera lens, leaping toward the viewer in what would be a marvelous 3-D effect had the filmmakers employed that technology. Plainview's turn toward the Satanic also bears relation to oil's power of self-propulsion. During the well fire in Little Boston that maims his son H. W., Plainview callously ignores the boy, standing spellbound before a (computer-generated) column of burning oil. That oil has a greater life-value than the human is signified by the film's scaling of Plainview and his roughnecks as small figures in silhouette against the brilliant column of oil and fire. In the novel *Oil!*, narrative point of view assists oil's capacity to stimulate excitement. Moments of oil discovery in the novel are filtered through the preadolescent consciousness of the oil magnate's son, Bunny. "There she came! The spectators went flying to avoid the oily spray blown by the wind. They let her shoot for awhile, until the water had been ejected, higher and higher... she made a lovely noise, hissing and splashing, bouncing up and down!" (78) For a thirteen-year-old male narrator, industrial-scale pollution and waste translate into arousal and premature ejaculation. In Bill Brown's philosophy of everyday things, "thing theory," such literary figuration might be construed as a revelation of the emotional history in oil, "the anxieties and aspirations that linger there in the material object."[124]

Early twentieth-century photographs from U.S. oil camps in California and northern Veracruz tend to be comic, emphasizing the spectacle of the gusher and its blackening of oil workers, local buildings, and landscapes. Such photographs suggest an industrial blackface whose secret joke is the multiform agency of money, rather than whiteness. But race played an important role in the early oil industry. California oil camps were segregated and predominantly white, while U.S. companies in Mexico maintained a rigid racial caste system amongst their "white," Chinese, Mexican, and indigenous

workers.[125] Robert Vitalis, writing of American production on the Saudi oil
frontier of the 1940s and 1950s, reminds us that U.S. oil companies learned
the value of dividing and segregating workers by ethnicity from the late
nineteenth-century copper mining industry of Arizona, in which U.S. miners
moved against Mexican labor.

The efficiencies of racialized labor management were reinforced through
early oil industry experience in California, Texas, Oklahoma, and Mexico.
"Texaco, Chevron, Exxon, and Mobil—Aramco's owners—accumulated
decades of experience in dozens of locales: Beaumont, Bakersfield, Coalinga,
Marcaibo, Oilville, and Tampico. And they laid out each field and camp everywhere in the same way, decade after decade."[126] For Aramco, the U.S. company in Saudi Arabia that had evolved out of the Standard Oil Company of
California, racial segregation took the form of distinct wage scales, employee
training, and separate housing—with Arab and Indian workers living in
thatched, floorless huts known as "barastis" well after American workers had
moved into air-conditioned homes. In Mexican oil camps, white employees
typically lived in hotels with electricity and modern plumbing, while Mexican
workers lived in company cottages without either water or toilets—or in
cheaper, crowded hotels. The growth of U.S. oil interests into Bahrain and
Saudi Arabia followed closely on Mexican oil development of the 1920s, and
racial lessons learned in Mexico carried into the Middle East. When Wallace
Stegner wrote an industry-sponsored history of American oil exploration in
Saudi Arabia in the 1950s, he was asked, by Aramco, to avoid using the term
"coolie" for Arab and Pakistani labor, although that slur was common par-
lance for industry workers.[127] Stegner instead bluntly compared Arabs to "the
Indians of North America"—he imagined both groups in awe of "the products
of the [American] tinkerers and gadgeteers" who essentially colonized them.[128]
Stegner's Saudi oil history, *Discovery*, would be published thirteen years after
its completion in an expurgated form through the company magazine *Aramco
World*.[129] Finally *Discovery* was released as a paperback, in the same year that
its author won the Pulitzer Prize for *Angle of Repose* (1971), a book that takes
significantly more interest in the labor hierarchies and ecological repercus-
sions of mining.

Yet the scale of the oil industry—again, not calibrated to human values—
made possible representational sleights of hand in which racialized bodies, and
labor itself, might be occluded through a mediated visibility. Such occlusions
became significant for the industry's promotion. Edward L. Doheny, the oil
baron whose life story Upton Sinclair drew on for *Oil!*, helped to create a genre
of pro-oil propaganda in the 1920s that has a recognizable legacy in U.S. popular culture through oil epics such as the film *Giant* (1956) and even the television series *Dallas* (1978–1991). Though Doheny lived in southern California,
his most extensive oil interests were in Mexico, along the Gulf Coast's so-called
Golden Lane, from the port city of Tampico to the indigenous town of Tuxpan.

THE MEN WHO CLOSED IN CERRO AZUL NO. 4.

FIGURE 2.2 *Petroleum Workers drenched in oil. W. J. Archer and Edward L. Doheny, Mexican Petroleum, ed. W. J. Archer (New York: Pan American Petroleum and Transport Company, 1922), 103.*

This essentially offshore location for early U.S. oil corporations allowed for less regulation and more strenuous manipulation of imagery.

In *Mexican Petroleum* (1922), a booklet issued by Doheny's Pan American Petroleum and Transport Company and cowritten by Doheny, a company clerk named W. J. Archer describes the oil-soaked workers who sealed off a notoriously wasteful gusher called Cerro Azul No. 4 at an oil camp in Veracruz: "No photograph could adequately portray the appearance of [these men]. Their clothes were drenched with oil until their weight became insupportable. Hands, faces, everything were [*sic*] a shining black. Every tool, every piece of equipment, every building within range of the well, glistened and dripped in the sun."[130] In the photograph that accompanies this description, we see the men standing in a receding arc like actors making a curtain call, with oil-soaked bodies turned to brilliant, reflecting surfaces. [FIGURE 2.2] They are metallic and stationary. In a text where the racial difference of ethnic Mexicans raises concerns—Doheny and Archer anxiously reiterate that the Mexicans are loyal to the U.S. company—here a group of workers becomes universalized, iconic. In fact, all of these workers were "foreign," in other words non-Mexican and theoretically white. The value of the photographic image inheres in its making this fact irrelevant, in its superimposition of mineral wealth upon multivalent skin. Blackness has nothing to do with race in this image, but rather with the emptying of the signifying potential of culturally particularized bodies toward a dazzling visual effect.

What is literally depicted in such images of oil-soaked men is industrial waste. The photographic image, with its relatively low narrativity and under-determined temporal dimension, "crops" pollution as a story that necessarily unfolds slowly over space and time. The industry pamphlet recasts the massive spillage of Doheny's poorly regulated gushers, which we now know caused extensive damage to local Mexican ecologies and food systems, in terms of a visual and stationary art: "Every leaf, every flower, every blade of grass now vivid with greens and brilliant colors...was converted as if by magic into the fantastic dream of some futuristic painter, all a glistening black as if fashioned of highly burnished metal."[131] *Mexican Petroleum* betrays a surprising interest in aesthetics. We can see in this early industry literature a working-through of the greenwashing associated with today's oil corporations. Compare Doheny's literary depiction of the gusher to that of Carleton Beals, a Left journalist and member of the Mexico City avant-garde, who wrote about Tampico in the novel *Black River* (1934). In the following scene, a self-sufficient indigenous farmer, José, contemplates the aftermath of a gusher on a neighboring drill site owned by CEMOC, a company meant to represent Doheny's PEMEX. "The blackish brown fluid was running over everything. The sump-hole had filled and overflowed. A black tide had crossed the barbed-wire fence, invading the yard. In a little while his mother's grave under the willow tree lay under a black pool, out of which stuck a tilted, clumsy cross. 'Drowned in oil,' he thought."[132] Emphasizing oil on the ground, invading vulnerable cavities such as sump-holes and graves, Beals divorces oil from aspiration, which so readily figures as vertical "spurting." He also makes clear that drilling threatened the economic and cultural autonomy of ordinary Mexicans.

In fact, Edward Doheny's Cerro Azul well cast miles-long blankets of crude on the Mexican countryside that surrounded it. The oil, acting as an efficient herbicide, killed flora within days of exposure—but this is the revisionary narrative of an environmental historian.[133] For Doheny, in 1922, it could all be conceived in terms of "marvels," special effects *avant* the apparatus of the green screen or computer-generated images. *Mexican Petroleum* points to the complementarity of the "youngest of industries," the film industry, and the oil industry. "No [still] photograph" can convey "the force" that Doheny unleashes, the pamphlet asserts.[134] Doheny insists that he must maintain a film crew on site at his Mexican camps. Film's capacity to capture time, and in effect to document the destruction wrought by the gushing wells, allows Doheny to ally himself with the power of both oil and time. Early on, filming oil was wedded to extracting it. As Rahman Badalov has written of the film industry in the oil-rich nation of Azerbaijan, "It was inevitable that the paths of oil and cinema would intersect....The struggle to harness this energy gushing forth has become our destiny."[135]

Oil fires, in particular, have been compelling to the film industry from the time of the Lumière brothers' short, *Oil Wells of Baku: Close View* (1896), which Robin L. Murray and Joseph K. Heumann analyze as a potentially environmentalist film. Depicting a small human figure moving back and forth in front of a raging oil-field fire, the film demonstrates an interest in establishing visual scale. Yet the apparent unconcern of the human actor erases the risks of pollution and loss of life. The actor's blasé attitude turns the fire into an everyday event, even as we recognize fire as the film's object of interest, an object much larger than the human actor. There is incongruity here that inspires wonder, the desire to figure out what we see for ourselves while believing ourselves, represented through the surrogate of the film's confident human figure, to be safe. Murray and Heumann recognize *Oil Wells of Baku* as the first in a series of films treating disastrous oil fires where "the notion of spectacle obscures or even erases ecological readings."[136]

The ambivalent relationship between film and the ecological history of oil again shows itself in the mid-twentieth-century Hollywood production *Tulsa* (Stuart Heisler, 1949), which garnered an Oscar nomination for special effects in 1950. The brilliant, Technicolor fire scene in *Tulsa* made it the most expensive film to be produced by the limping Eagle-Lion Company, a B-movie production outlet, in the late 1940s. This oil fire scene offers a rich texturing of hot colors along with morally inflected visual pleasures such as the slow crumbling of industrial structures, like derrick towers. The fire is set by a Native American character, Jim Redbird as played by Pedro Armendáriz, who has been outraged by the oil industry's devastation of Cherokee ranches. *Tulsa* attempts to tame the spectacular entertainment offered in its extended treatment of burning oil, which marks the high point of the film both in the sense of its diegetic climax and mimetic aspiration, by framing it within a didactic conservation narrative.

Drawing upon associations of fire with ritual cleansing, *Tulsa* invites an interpretation of the explosive oil-field fire as a moral lesson, on the scale of apocalypse, for its female lead, played by Susan Hayward. Hayward's red hair and sexual voracity as the character "Cherokee Lansing" index the entertainment values of fire itself while denigrating them, too, as illicit consumption. *Tulsa* is set in the 1920s, during Oklahoma's oil boom, and Hayward—portraying a greedy oil baroness who erases her modest Native American origins—performs the female overconsumption that would characterize the 1920s in popular history after the sacrifices of the Great Depression and the Second World War. Lansing's chastening by fire restores her, and the Oklahoma frontier of postwar nostalgia, to the patient discipline of the film's ideal husband, an ecologically sensitive oil geologist played by Robert Preston. Still, as Murray and Heumann quip, "It is the massive fire scene that sells the film."[137]

With an edgy, Vietnam-era cynicism, *Oklahoma Crude* (Stanley Kramer, 1973) reanimates the plot of *Tulsa*, gendering petrophilia as excessive female desire in the character "Lena Doyle," played by Faye Dunaway, in order to test the links between cheap energy and modern feminism. In this comedy on the brink of the first oil crisis of the 1970s, the female lead's will to produce is answered by scarcity, oil sands "dry as a popcorn fart" that realize her desire to become a "third sex" by "screwing herself" only too literally. Lena's father,

Cleon (John Mills), dies in the process of defending and working her rig; her own body is exhausted, half-starved, and humiliated by labor at the derrick and self-defense against the private army of an oil company that jumps her claim. As *Oklahoma Crude* concludes with Lena smeared in greasy crude and calling tentatively after her mercenary lover (Mase, played by George C. Scott), the humiliation of the feminist blurs into an indictment of Western boom mentalities, as if modern gender performance itself were a type of greed, and work, humiliated by ecological limits. The film's explicit critique of feminism is uninteresting, but its insight that some of the most apparently progressive aspects of modern selfhood stand to be humiliated by oil scarcity feels prophetic. Crouching with Lena in front of her spent well, the film audience was prepared, as of 1973, for the end of petromodernity as we knew it.

Yet the "energetic therapy" of the 1970s oil shocks did not produce the "taste for asceticism" imagined by Baudrillard and by diverse advocates of living small, convivial modernity, and the "autonomous house" movement, which taught Americans how to make their own solar-powered homes.[138] Film renewed its commitment to petroleum as spectacle, even in anti-imperialist documentaries such as Werner Herzog's *Lessons of Darkness* (1992), or with ambivalence in Anderson's *There Will Be Blood*. More needs to be said about *There Will Be Blood* as an "oil film," since it is not necessarily readable as a film about oil, at least not in the topical sense of the contemporaneous petro-thriller *Syriana* (Stephen Gaghan, 2005). The film's rich ambience and the exaggerated performance of Daniel Day-Lewis as oil magnate Daniel Plainview releases it, to an extent, from political contexts. Yet both filmic ambience and Day-Lewis's performance can be read as commentary about oil. Released on the eve of the oil price spike of 2008, *There Will Be Blood* offers a nested nostalgia, for oil production, first, and secondarily for the body effects made possible by petromodernity. The film's final shooting script suggests the rationale for what critic Kent Jones characterizes as its "sensorial bonanza."[139]

Anderson's script obsesses on the resistance of bodies, their heft, the friction of their interaction. He attributes strong agency to both organic and inorganic bodies: arms, mules, deserts, pulleys, trains. "Daniel is pushing a cart with the upper half of his body...then he drags himself to catch up with the cart—he does this over and over and over and over again across the desert floor."[140] This scene as written in Anderson's final shooting script describes Plainview's struggle out of the New Mexico desert after he breaks both ankles falling down his silver mine. The scene was never shot, and what we see in the film instead is Plainview, with one broken ankle, push-pulling himself across the desert. The physics of the enacted scene could not accommodate the gross humiliation of the body ("over and over and over and over") that Anderson wrote into the script. Similarly, the script version of the roughneck Joe Gundha's death overmatched what was materially practicable on set. In all caps, Anderson shouts his aspiration to replicate the sensorial intensity of a man falling into a well, slowly suffocating in oil mud:

VERY GRAPHIC. [Gundha's] HEAD LANDS IN THE MUD AND BEGINS
TO DROWN. THE HOLE IS VERY VERY THIN—BUT HIS WEIGHT
AND THE SLIDE KEEPS TAKING HIM DOWN...THE IMAGE AGAIN.
CAMERA UNDERNEATH THE MUD. WATCHING THIS MAN DIE
INSIDE THIS HORRIBLE DEATH.[141]

The audience will never see through this lens underneath the mud, the mud's
point of view of a drowning human face.

What a remarkable image that would have been, homage to the labor of the
roughneck through the most horrific possible imagining of his physical over-
coming by earth, his antagonist and rival. In a crude Marxian sense, Anderson
could be said to pursue the disalienation of labor, at sites where human physical energy learns of its own limitations through the resistance of other matter.
What we do get, in Gundha's death scene, even as it is filmed, with the actor
skewered by a fragment of the drill, or in the opening scenes of Plainview hit-
ting rock with pick axe in the silver mine, is the feeling of fabrication—what it
feels like to make, and to be remade by, the physical world. Here is essentially
the same affective investment in fabrication played up in peak oil novels such
as Kunstler's World Made by Hand, the "do-it-yourself" solar house models of
the 1970s, or, for that matter, Moby-Dick (1851), which previews the birth of
petroleum-derived energy in the later 1850s through a scrupulous accounting
of how humans make whales into oil. We hope that there will be blood in this
literature of fabrication, if only blood from an errant thumb subjected to a
hammer, so that we might see ourselves again in the world we make.

Fundamentally, There Will Be Blood enacts a mourning for production,
oil production specifically and manufacturing more broadly. It makes perfect sense that this mourning would take place in a U.S. film of the early
twenty-first century—and that this film itself should attempt to replace its
lost objects (physical labor, local production, oil) with body effects, the produced sensation that Linda Williams describes as film's "system of excess" and
a normative means of popular entertainment.[142] There Will Be Blood is a melodrama, one of the excessive, popular genres, insofar as the masculine emotions that it explores are not repressed and in fact explode in Plainview's verbal
tirades and extravagant gestural ticks—body techniques so flamboyant as to
place Day-Lewis himself in the category of "special effect" for one reviewer.[143]
Infantile emotion and self-conscious body work contradict what might be
called the empiricist, mineral realism of Daniel Plainview's character type, the
self-made tycoon we've also encountered, for example, in Chinatown's Noah
Cross. The excessive Plainview becomes a body double for oil, in all of its abject
impurity as me/not me, inside/outside, alive/dead.[144] Libidinous rage leaps out
of the man, machinic quirks overmaster him, his kin have "not a drop of me"
in them, granting an uncanny biological literalism to the betrayals of sons and
brothers that haunt less extravagant male melodrama, like classical westerns.

Every humiliation heaped onto the "oil women" of *Tulsa* and *Oklahoma Crude* appears hugely magnified in the humiliations of Plainview, the preacher Eli Sunday, the child-man H. W., and voiceless characters such as Joe Gundha.

Humiliations on-screen invite the viewer's masochistic pleasure, and the film effectively mixes up the registers of pleasure and pain by allying similar sensational effects with contradictory narratives of injury and triumph. The splice of the drill cleaving Gundha's upper body echoes the satisfying clank of Plainview's pick axe against silver and the heavy splat of bowling pin against skull in the final scene of Eli Sunday's murder. The rich aural dimension of *There Will Be Blood* invites deep mimicry in its audience, which Anderson heightens through H. W.'s deafness, producing an aural point of view for H. W. through which we hear only "internal" noise resonant of blood flow and heart-thump. Disability often works in fiction to provoke heightened awareness of sensory knowledge. But sound is by no means the only or even strongest body effect generated by *There Will Be Blood*. One could read the film through its visual investments in textural surface, from the porous human skin to the scratchy weave of pulley ropes, or through its precise, almost muted color palette, framed by the anomalies of bright-black oil and fire. My point is that the film gives almost too much sensory information, as if it mourns not only its earlier industrial setting, petroleum "made by hand" in southern California, but also the film medium itself, its dream of a virtuality in which body effects break free of actual, situated matter.

When Plainview delivers his final line, "I'm finished," at the scene of both a murder and an archetypal mode of twentieth-century industrial leisure, the bowling alley, we have to ask—with him, perhaps—what is finished. I do not see *There Will Be Blood* as a peak oil narrative, but as a signal of the tiredness of twentieth-century stories about modernity, particularly the U.S. frontier myth that explained modernity to the twentieth century. The film is "about" obsolescence as an excess of feeling, extravagant feeling that is the wake of spent stories and modes of production. In this sense, *There Will Be Blood* tells a story of peak oil and the peaking of the film medium itself insofar as it has been dependent upon petroleum.

Film stock, like the ink used in modern print media, is essentially petroleum. In recent years, polyester or PET film stock has been experimentally recycled into fuel.[145] To some extent digital technologies promise to liberate the physical bases of film from petroleum, though the intensive use of fuel oil, tires, and diesel generators for set lighting will keep the film industry an environmentally high-impact business for years to come. In the wry documentary *Greenlit* (2010), director Miranda Bailey discovers the near impossibility of making a truly carbon-neutral film, given a crew's most ordinary habits, like consuming huge amounts of water from plastic bottles. Many filmmakers, including Paul Thomas Anderson, now publicize the supposed "carbon neutrality" of their films. *There Will Be Blood* promotes itself as "100% carbon neutral" because its producers purchased carbon offsets from NativeEnergy, a nonprofit organization that helps finance the construction of Native American, family farm, and community renewable energy projects—primarily wind farms. Carbon offsets are the easiest way for the industry to earn green credentials, since its production technologies still rely heavily upon the burning of fossil fuels. Ironically, *There Will Be Blood* utilized film techniques of the 1930s and 1940s to achieve a cinematographic style particularly steeped in petroleum.

The film's on-location shooting in Marfa, Texas—at the same site where the oil epic *Giant* was shot a half-century earlier—has been touted by its director of photography, Robert Elswit, as a return to authentic filmmaking, "when truckloads of equipment went to the middle of nowhere and stayed there."[146] Location filming typically requires road building and asphalt paving to accommodate equipment-laden trucks. UCLA's *Report on Sustainability in the Motion Picture Industry* (2006) cites location filming as a major source of environmental degradation within the industry. Anderson eschewed the use of digital dailies for *There Will Be Blood*, which meant that film dailies had to be flown from Marfa to Deluxe Laboratories in Hollywood, to be developed and flown back to Marfa for viewing on site. A great deal of fuel enabled this film's sensory bonanza. "The color space of motion picture film is completely different from digital color space," Elswit notes. *There Will Be Blood* was designed to look like a twentieth-century film.[147] Elswit and Anderson created an authentically filmic style using twentieth-century photochemical processes rather than newer, arguably more sustainable digital technologies. Only two major sequences in *There Will Be Blood* had to be "digitally scaled up," according to Robert Stromberg of Digital Backlot: the massive blood flow from Eli Sunday's crushed head at the end of the film, and the leaping oil and flames from the film's gusher fire in the fictional town of Little Boston. The filmmakers built one derrick in Marfa, which they set on fire and filmed, but their petroleum-fueled fire failed to create a "feeling of power, of the pressure just underneath the surface of the ground" commensurate with what they imagined as viewer expectations of burning oil.[148] Industrial Light and Magic stepped in to meet the standards stoked by prior oil media, from the time of Edward L. Doheny's primitive reels. We have learned to expect of oil maximum motility and liveliness, as if it were blood.

The lines of cars that still congregate at wildfires surrounded by television film crews in the inland suburbs of San Diego and Los Angeles counties honor the spectacular legacy of the original oil gushers and the media that brought them to mass audiences. That legacy is our sprawl, the suburban strip malls and housing tracts dependent upon the automobile and asphalt roads, the normative American infrastructure that, when it intrudes into southern California's dry chaparral, makes an invitation to fire. Visual, kinesthetic, acoustic ("hissing"), tactile, olfactory—oil touches us intimately, and everywhere. That's entertainment.

4.) *Why is oil so bad?* We gather to watch.

Petromelancholia

Loving oil to the extent that we have done in the twentieth century sets up the conditions of grief as conventional oil resources dwindle. When expressed in terms of faith in oil futures, Tough Oil offers one response to such grief. Other responses include declarations of "the end of oil" and calls to treat ourselves for an unsustainable petroleum addiction. This rhetoric comes out of the peak oil activism and so-called postcarbon thinking introduced in the last chapter, which sometimes forgets that carbon is a basis of all life. The feeling of losing cheap energy that came relatively easily, without tar sands extraction, ultradeep ocean drilling, and fracking, has not been collected into one movement or even named in criticism. Provisionally, I will name it "petromelancholia," although melancholy, as psychoanalysts understand it, fails to fit, exactly, the twenty-first-century condition that remains my object of concern. Before ideologies harden into hegemony, there are structures of feeling that contain potential ideologies and not yet solidified, aspirant cultural norms. Raymond Williams made these structures of feeling a central archive for cultural studies, an archive that might be accessed, though never fully, through literature and other art forms, like pop music. The arts sometimes theorize inchoate cultural feelings before they become movements—and before critics impose interpretive frameworks on the arts.

On the Gulf Coasts of Texas and Louisiana, writers and filmmakers have been slowly working around the problem of subsidence, the sinking of these coasts that results from oil mining in wetlands and in the Gulf itself, and from the sea-level rise and new climate features, such as superstorms, that are related to the gaseous emissions of fossil fuel. Subsidence means the gradual sinking of the land, and it makes for a geological complement to melancholia when the latter is understood rather simply, as a grieving that has no foreseeable end. This chapter treats petromelancholia both as a mode of preserving the happier affects of the U.S. twentieth century and as an incitement to activism.

Glenn Blake, a southeast Texas fiction writer, portrays Gulf Coast subsidence through the figure of a beloved child who is lost to the water, in the short story "Chocolate Bay" (2001). Chocolate Bay branches off of Galveston Bay, southwest of Houston. In Blake's story it is a place where real estate prices reflect relative levels of subsidence. The peninsular property once claimed by "oil executives" and "country club" types sits atop grass browned by encroaching tides, and amidst skeletal, hurricane-wrecked houses.[1] Blake's protagonist, Drew, finds the poignant sign "Don't cry" scrawled above the mantel of one abandoned home.[2] Drew's own dream of learning about nature by living in a subsidence zone makes him somewhat of an academic, figuring loss as an analytic problem. "If I can understand the tide, I can understand what has happened," he hopes.[3] What has happened turns out to be not just the slow diminishment of the coast by subsidence but the sudden drowning of Drew's toddler, who walked into the creeping bay one evening while Drew watched a football game on television. Losing his son meant losing his wife, too, who had begged Drew to leave the subsidence zone. The dead child haunts Drew as a ghost who appears to him in another wrecked peninsular home, "baby bream kissing the tips of his fingers."[4] Meanwhile, Drew takes measurements of the tides: "Ascertain month by month variations in the depths of the tides for a forty-eight month period. How quickly are we sinking?"[5] The story "Chocolate Bay" recognizes intellectualism as itself a mode of melancholic attachment, the incorporation of loss, or failure, as a knowledge project. We should be wary of becoming too *interested* in subsidence. Ultimately, this chapter pursues transitional moments when petromelancholia tips forward into activism.

The title of a recent article in the satiric newspaper *The Onion* offers an ironic joke: "Millions of Barrels of Oil Safely Reach Port in Major Environmental Catastrophe." The article was published shortly after the 2010 BP blowout, and it makes fun of the fact that oil production in the Gulf of Mexico might ever be conceived as an environmental good. Describing the routine docking of an oil tanker at Port Fourchon, Louisiana, *The Onion* continues: "Experts are saying the oil tanker safely reaching port could lead to dire ecological consequences on multiple levels, including rising temperatures, disappearing shorelines, the eradication of countless species, extreme weather events, complete economic collapse."[6] As Rebecca Solnit notes in her blog memoir from New Orleans, the BP blowout is "a story that touches everything else."[7] I place Solnit's comment next to the title from *The Onion* because, in distinct tones, both point to the ordinariness of oil production, its enmeshment in the "everything else" that we know and do, including the consistent injury of our planetary habitat.

Mike Davis has written of the "dialectic of ordinary disaster" in relation to the apocalyptic rhetoric that defamiliarizes predictable geological events such as landslides in the poorly sited inland suburbs of Los Angeles.[8] Extending Davis's critique, Rob Nixon refers to the "slow violence" of neoliberalism as the occluded referent of "disaster," which in a modern risk society is often a misnomer.[9] From the Greek *astron*, or star, "disaster" refers to an unforeseen calamity arising from the unfavorable position of a planet. The BP blowout confirms disaster criticism's focus on the expectedness of the so-called unexpected while pointing to a different aspect of how ecological collapse can obscure human social and technological histories. Here the problem is proximity. The petroleum infrastructure has become embodied memory and habitus for modern humans, insofar as everyday events such as driving or feeling the summer heat of asphalt on the soles of one's feet are incorporating practices, in Paul Connerton's term for the repeated performances that become encoded in the body.[10] Decoupling human corporeal memory from the infrastructures that have sustained it may be the primary challenge for ecological narrative in the service of human species survival beyond the twenty-first century.

The BP blowout poses a unique representational challenge because it follows an unusual episode of dereification, a failure of the commodity form's abstraction. This "disaster" did not work as spectacle, in Guy Debord's sense of the mystification of modern means of production through screen imagery.[11] The continuous spill-cam video feed available on the Internet that depicted oil shooting out of the damaged well—however that might have been manipulated by BP—offered a humiliation of modernity as it was understood in the twentieth century, largely in terms of the human capacity to harness cheap energy. Unlike anthropogenic climate change, which resists narrative because of its global scale and its as-yet limited visibility, the Deepwater Horizon rig localized a plethora of visible data. Only later would marine scientists recognize the multitude of invisible victims of the blowout, the marine life destroyed by chemical dispersants used to "attack" the spill. The BP blowout resembles Hurricane Katrina in its manifestation of events that support predictions of environmental catastrophe (e.g., peak oil, global climate change) that otherwise might be dismissed as exaggerations of scientific modeling or Left fear-mongering. Yet, just as Katrina did not result in a changed national affect toward black, urban poverty, the BP explosion has not, it seems, spurred Americans to reconsider loving oil. "Even if they cap the well, hell it's just another oil spill," sang Drew Landry to the president's awkwardly sympathetic Oil Spill Commission in mid-July 2010.[12] Landry's briefly famous "BP Blues" predicts that the blowout will not have the effect on the Gulf Coast that the Santa Barbara oil spill of 1969 had on California.

What Katrina and the BP blowout foreground is a competition between emotional investments. The first investment inheres in modernity as we know it, through its fossil fuel infrastructure; the second, in ecology as the network of human–nonhuman relations that we theorize as given habitat. We learn from these two events on the Gulf Coast of the southern United States not only that modernity and ecology are entangled objects, to paraphrase the philosopher of science Bruno Latour, but also that the melancholia for a given nature that has characterized modern environmentalism might be eclipsed, in the twenty-first century, by an unresolvable grieving of modernity itself, as it begins to fail. Catriona Mortimer-Sandilands has written eloquently of "melancholy natures," the displaced affects and rituals such as "nature nostalgia" or "ecotourism" that stand in for lost objects, like extinct species, which cannot be properly grieved.[13] In a nod to queer scholarship on melancholia after AIDS, Sandilands makes the apt point that "melancholia is not only a denial of the loss of a beloved object but also a potentially politicized way of preserving that object in the midst of a culture that fails to recognize its significance."[14] The queer reading of melancholy as "socially located embodied memory" shadows my own interest in grieving oil, although obviously oil has an extremely high cultural value in the United States and elsewhere.

What impedes a productive grieving of oil, if we're to follow Freud in supposing that grief should be superseded by the taking of a new object, is that we, by which I mean myself and most moderns, refuse to acknowledge that conventional oil is running out and that Tough Oil isn't the same resource, in terms of economic, social, and biological costs. Denial inhibits mourning, a passage forward. This chapter explores petromelancholia through the cultural expressions of the U.S. Gulf Coast and, in brief contrast, the Niger Delta. These southern geographies are biologically rich deltas that either are or are becoming contaminated subsidence zones, and in distinct ways they perform a lively response to such loss.

Feeling Ecological

Of contemporary industrial "accidents," Latour writes, "the recent proliferation of 'risky' objects has multiplied the occasions to hear, see, and feel what objects may be doing when they break other actors down."[15] For Latour, all objects have agency, and the fundamentally ecological, relational materialism worked out through Actor-Network-Theory gets a boost from incidents that physically play it out, such as the BP blowout, where, for example, benzene and other volatile organic compounds associated with petroleum extraction entered the living cells of coastal clean-up crews.[16] Of course Latour's sort of ecological thinking, where humans mingle and are perhaps invaded by other "agents," does not necessarily feel good to the ordinary people enmeshed in these events. Feeling ecological need not be pleasant. I use the phrase "feeling ecological" as a gesture toward Timothy Morton's concept of a *dark ecology,* indicating the humiliating desire and dependency of the human upon non-human actors that have become a prominent theme in twenty-first-century environmental criticism.[17]

Ironically, "feeling ecological" in the positive sense of happy affect toward the nonhuman now may consist primarily in feeling at home in the obsolescent energy regime of the twentieth century. Artists responding to both Katrina and the BP spill locate the human, as an ontological category, within industrial-era infrastructures that may be not only in the throes of failure but also predetermined to destroy basic conditions of (human) living, such as water systems. That melancholia for modernity might eclipse environmental melancholia and activism in the context of the U.S. Deep South makes especial sense, because it could be said that U.S. modernity never assumed its fullest form there, so it still piques aspirational desire.[18] Rather than acting as pure counternarrative to the ecological violence of late capitalism, the stories that Katrina and the BP blowout produce tend to imagine modern infrastructure failure as tantamount to human species extinction. It is as if our species might be unthinkable without these increasingly obsolescent objects.

In President Barack Obama's June 2010 Oval Office speech on the Gulf oil spill, the words "catastrophe," "disaster," "assault," and "epidemic" touch the edges of what is happening in the Gulf, which the president describes as no less than the destruction of "an entire way of life," the loss of "home" for tens of thousands, perhaps hundreds of thousands, of people. Noting that "the oil spill represents just the latest blow to a place that has already suffered multiple economic disasters and decades of environmental degradation," Obama moves away from the idea of disaster as singular, connecting it, if vaguely, to past policies of deregulation and privatization.[19] But he cannot link this past to a tangible national future; the speech was widely criticized for its vague prescriptions. In the tradition of presidential rhetoric, Obama concludes within sacred, rather than historical, time, with a reference to the tradition of the Blessing of the Fleet, an annual event that takes place in predominantly Catholic Cajun fishing communities throughout Louisiana: "As a priest and former fisherman once said of the tradition: 'The blessing is not that God has promised to remove all obstacles and dangers. The blessing is that He is with us always... even in the midst of the storm.' "[20] The priest's words seem to refer back to Hurricane Katrina ("the storm") and were most likely spoken in reference to that event, as the president places them in that context.

Once we start talking of humanity in terms of the sacred, as Hannah Arendt pointed out in the wake of World War II, we essentially acknowledge the collapse of constitutional or civil rights—sacred humanity is humanity without citizenship, "raw" and unprotected. Giorgio Agamben has since revised Arendt, urging a consideration of *homo sacer* as the modern everyman, the man who can be killed, without legal retribution, but not sacrificed, in other words not inducted into the redemptive time of the sacred. The "naked human," in Arendt's words, or "bare life," in Agamben's, marks a modern dissociation from protective traditional statuses as well as the volatility of constitutional guarantees.[21] Similarly, humanity defined as ecological, in the sense of those whose "way of life" is conditioned by a regional ecosystem, may as well be recognized as humanity unprotected by rights or status—the human animal whose primary community is nonhuman. Obama's repeated invocation of Gulf Coast residents' threatened "way of life," which echoes and has been echoed by media accounts of the loss of "a way of life" or a "unique way of life," indicates that Gulf Coast people have fallen out of (or were never included within) the concept of modernity, where life practices are not clearly tied to place. The historian Ramachandra Guha recognizes "ecosystem people" as those enmeshed in nonhuman ecologies that feed and sustain them, and who are threatened by the omnivorous capitalization of their resources. Perhaps it is an exaggeration to describe parts of the southern United States as other than modern.[22] Yet when modernity evinces spectacular failure, as in the oil-soaked Niger Delta or even the significantly more privileged oil colony of the U.S. Gulf Coast, a revised definition of "ecosystem people," indicating humanity at the mercy of collapsing naturecultures, can be useful. The recognition by Gulf Coast residents of their deep entanglement with modernity's most risky objects has prompted a discourse of activism, the environmental justice movement (EJ), as well as a vernacular poetry of species failure.

The Gulf Coast materializes a twentieth-century U.S. history in which energy, perhaps the most essential quality of biological life, has supplanted personhood, the social "face" of the individual human body. Southern personhood has long been degraded in the U.S. national imaginary, in part as a legacy of slavery—southern blacks in particular continue to struggle with the imposition of social death—and in part because of the perceived backwardness of southern industrial development, which has figured as the lassitude of the South's poor whites. From the headquarters of the U.S. oil colony, Houston, Texas, the African-American sociologist Robert Bullard fostered the U.S. EJ movement in the 1980s as a direct response to the influx of polluting industries into southern states in the late twentieth century. What Bullard saw in the South of the 1970s and 1980s, in his self-described role of "researcher as detective," was the local trail of a global trend, the bargaining away of health— a baseline measure of human energy—for jobs.[23] EJ's well-known definition of the environment as the place where "we" (humans) "live, work, play, and pray" should be understood as, in part, an explicitly southern response to the trade-off of civil rights for corporate privileges in a region where humanity had historically been commoditized through chattel slavery.

EJ is now a vibrant international movement, and the Gulf Coast influences upon its North American theoretical framework are sometimes overlooked. The oil corridor from Houston to Mobile helped produce this second wave of environmental activism that resonated with other national and international protests on behalf of human health, "ecopopulist" revolts, in Andrew Szasz's terms, including Lois Gibbs's battle with the Hooker Chemical Company in the working-class suburb of Love Canal, New York, and the international response to Chernobyl.[24] African-American activists recognized that toxic pollution spelled the revision of a hard-won, racially inclusive concept of U.S. citizenship and the reintroduction of *homo sacer*, the man who can be killed without repercussion. Bare life has been a recurrent theme within southern U.S. history, an index of both racial and regional disenfranchisement. Bullard writes tersely of the vulnerability of southern poverty pockets to corporate exploitation: "Jobs were real; environmental risks were unknown."[25] The paper mills, waste disposal and treatment facilities, and chemical plants that made the South the last mecca of U.S. industrialization in the 1970s and 1980s—in 1980 Jimmy Carter famously intoned "Go South, young man," in response to a national recession in which only the South seemed to be growing industrial jobs—had of course been preceded by the oil industry, which set up shop in coastal Texas in the last decades of the nineteenth century. The bargaining away of southern health for jobs has a historical arc concurrent with that of U.S. modernity, though it is perhaps only now, after Hurricane Katrina and in the wake of the BP blowout, that the inclusion of U.S. southerners within the South as a *global* region has become clear.

When Robert Bullard notes the intangible quality of environmental risk, in comparison to the hard realism of jobs, he points out a problem that environmental advocates have long recognized as both representational and political: Environmental damage yet to come, without (current) aesthetic dimensions, does not stir up alarm or activate an ethic of care. This is one of the supposed pitfalls in trying to communicate the threat of global climate change—it still can't be seen or felt *enough*, the argument goes, at least not in the continental United States. Hurricane Sandy, washing away the environs of our nation's financial capital, may finally have resolved the "question" for Americans of whether coastal erosion and sea-level rise are planetary problems. Yet for decades, the Gulf Coast has been sinking, quite visibly manifesting a dramatic change in climate and geological structure. What was marsh is now open ocean—to the tune of 25 to 40 square miles of disappearing marsh per year, and that is *prior* to the BP spill. The strong aesthetic dimensions of this problem, whose geological name is subsidence, have been well documented by journalists, politicians, and even Shell Oil, which launched a media campaign to save the wetlands in the early 2000s. Loss at this scale of a nation's territorial state would normally be attributable to an act of war, which calls to mind the comedian Lewis Black's joke (again, incongruency that should not register as incongruency) that the United States might declare war on BP, since the corporation is "attacking us with oil."[26] Yet the sinking of the Gulf Coast has not stirred significant national outrage, even since BP's debacle. Mike Tidwell, the environmental journalist whose *Bayou Farewell: The Rich Life and Tragic Death of Louisiana's Cajun Coast* (2003) marks perhaps the best-known first chronicle of Gulf Coast subsidence, notes in that book his own struggles to garner attention for the crisis. Initially Tidwell's reportage was relegated to his newspaper's travel section, an editorial choice that underlines the perception of the loss of the Gulf wetlands as a regional peculiarity.[27]

Explicitly political iterations of the subsidence story linked it to human health and the survival of the city of New Orleans nearly a decade before Katrina. In 1998, the Louisiana governor's office, with the state's Department of Natural Resources, the U.S. Army Corps of Engineers, the Environmental

Protection Agency, the U.S. Fish and Wildlife Service, and all twenty of Louisiana's coastal parishes, published *Coast 2050*, the first comprehensive plan for restoring coastal Louisiana and a clarion call for federal remediation of the ecological "system collapse" wrecking the Gulf Coast.[28] Potential losses were listed then—lists we hear again, twenty years later—as 40 percent of the country's wetlands, one-third of its seafood, one-fifth of its oil, one-quarter of its natural gas, and a "historic" urban center of some 500,000 persons, e.g., New Orleans.[29] The price tag for coastal restoration at the time of *Coast 2050*'s publication, the late 1990s, was around $14 billion, modest in comparison to estimates of what restoration will cost in the wake of the BP blowout. Former Louisiana governor Mike Foster envisioned federal legislation akin to that which created Everglades National Park, and he hoped it would be passed into law by 2004. "Yet despite these efforts," Tidwell wrote in 2003, "the nation remains almost totally ignorant of Louisiana's plight" (*BF* 336). Tidwell's epilogue to *Bayou Farewell*, written in 2005, after Katrina, expresses the hope that the massive hurricane "finally awakened America to the fragility and importance of south Louisiana." But the book concludes in the fatal rhetoric of the sacred: "Either we are witnessing the death of something truly great in America or the start of something even better, something new and blessedly permanent" (*BF* 333, 334). *Bayou Farewell* prominently features the Cajun Blessing of the Fleet. Again, the sacred is invoked when social death has already occurred and civil rights suspended. Thinking through Gulf Coast subsidence as a narrative that has not become national despite its dissemination through national media raises the question of when, exactly, the Gulf Coast fell out of the U.S. territorial imaginary.

One might say—as anthropologist James Clifford suggests—that it becomes clear that a certain set of humans have lost civil rights and protections when scholars gather their oral history, with the archiving of the voices of a doomed community serving to memorialize their sacrifice. In the first year of George W. Bush's presidency, 2000, the now defamed and defunct Minerals Management Service (MMS) funded an oral history of southern Louisiana, *Bayou Lafourche—Oral Histories of the Oil and Gas Industry* (2008). Bayou Lafourche is the Gulf Coast region most intimately linked to the deepwater drilling that began in the 1990s, and it was chosen as the site of the oral history project in part to create an epochal break between the era of onshore oil drilling and "shelf" drilling for natural gas and the OCS (outer continental shelf) deepwater industry. In the prologue to *Bayou Lafourche*, author Tom McGuire acknowledges that "people who knew these communities prior to the oil and gas industry, people who orchestrated the technological innovations to explore, drill, and produce in the marshes and bays for the coastal wetlands, people who ventured out into the open Gulf in the risky pursuit of fossil fuel—they were passing away. A collective memory . . . was dying out."[30] Since "incorporated towns with municipal governments which might be expected to *was this because they were conducted orally?*

→ preserve community history" were few along the Gulf Coast, and "corporate memories have been erased through mergers, acquisitions…closures," and "blue-collar workers seldom write memoirs," the project solicits the federal government, the MMS, to support the transcription of voices that have no other representative (*BL* 2–3).

The result of the grant proposal would be some four hundred interviews, archived at several Gulf Coast universities, and a book-length report, *Bayou Lafourche*, that alternately could be titled *MMS: The Novel*. The report has "not been technically reviewed by MMS," and it is "exempt from review and compliance with MMS editorial standards" (*BL*, "Disclaimer," iii); it seems to be yet another object that slipped through MMS regulatory filters and, ironically, condemns the federal government's role in the industry history that it describes. A messy social panorama comprised of interwoven interviews, *Bayou Lafourche* predicts the rash of interwoven life stories that appeared in the aftermath of Hurricane Katrina, from Spike Lee's epic *When the Levees Broke* (2006) and journalist Dan Baum's nonfiction *Nine Lives* (2008) to Josh Neufeld's graphic novel *AD: New Orleans after the Deluge* (2008) and writer/producer David Simon's recent HBO series, *Treme* (2010–). To a certain extent, all of this post-Katrina art foregrounds the tension between the structure of the individual life, with its aspiration and its foreboding of death, and bodiless corporate structures that change form over durations longer than human life spans. Corporate temporality, like ecological time, is not strictly historical, insofar as it involves the duration of systems and "persons" neither human nor mortal. The larger conflict between human and corporate ecologies is played out more specifically in post-Katrina narrative when the wished-for triumphalism of art meets a limit-point in the collapse of naturecultures (techno-ecological systems) made vulnerable by the deregulation that feeds corporate entities.

Bayou Lafourche intends to offer an epic of oil-made-by-hand, of petroleum extraction as craft and embodied memory. Interviewees reflect a landscape where risky objects like deepwater rigs share real time and space with traditional extractive work such as shrimping, since the shrimpers' large boats have been used for years to service the offshore rigs. Oystermen, who don't enjoy the off-season compensation from Big Oil that shrimpers do because their smaller, flat-bottomed boats are not oceanworthy, emphasize the more purely ecological perspective of the oyster beds that they work, which are the natural filters of the wetlands. "Barataria Bay used to be full of oysters," Whitney Dardar, a Houma fisherman, complains, "Oysters don't grow like that anymore because there is too much salt.…I know a lot of places that oysters used to grow that they don't grow anymore. Now, it is like the Gulf; it is all open. They are trying to restore and all but I think they are about twenty years too late for that. They pump and pump all that oil and don't put nothing back. It sinks and sinks and sinks" (*BL* 118). Nearly every interviewee mentions the problem of subsidence;

all recognize that the profit their region has gained from the oil industry is balanced by geologic loss, salt water invading freshwater marshes due to shipping canals cut for oil transport, fresh water kept from replenishing marshlands because of the channeling of the Mississippi River, also for industry and development. Living on the line between earth and world, between ecological systems and the technologies that attempt to make them more accessible, the ordinary people of Bayou Lafourche live at the cutting edge of climate collapse. Theirs is, and has been for decades, a twenty-first-century ecology.

The oil industry picked up in southern Louisiana in the 1930s with the arrival of the Texas Oil Company, now known as Texaco. At first resented, the "Texiens," as Cajuns called them, began to hire locals for their skills as carpenters and sailors, bringing jobs to a poor, rural region made more desperate by the Great Depression. For the World War II generation in south Louisiana who became middle class as a result of Big Oil, the industry still appears, nostalgically, as a robust future. Subsidence fails to make sense within this historical boom narrative, even as it is being somatized. *Bayou Lafourche* only touches the U.S. oil industry downturn of the 1980s and the reinvention of the industry in the 1990s through deepwater play. With deepwater drilling came unprecedented technological experimentation, subcontracting to foreign rigs and crews, the perception of federal takeover, and less local love for Big Oil. As early as the Submerged Lands Act of 1953, the federal government claimed ownership of the continental shelf to three miles off the coast of Louisiana and other Gulf states, with the exception of Texas and Florida, which own the ocean bottom extending twelve miles out from their coasts. What this meant is that the United States would be in charge of leasing the OCS, and federal coffers would enjoy income from deepwater leases—if the technology ever got that sophisticated, which was scarcely imaginable in the 1950s.

Windell Curole, a Cajun radio personality and marine biologist who has a large voice in summing up *Bayou Lafourche*, dissociates the U.S. government from any image of a "country," representing its role in the Gulf region as that of an irresponsible corporate actor: "If you're a business man, CEO of government USA, and I see three billion dollars [from leases] coming into my treasury in my business...I'm going to make sure that things that protect that infrastructure are in good shape and yet government doesn't see it that way" (*BL* 164). Curole rejects both the ecological and the moral price that he feels has been levied on Louisiana, by the oil corporations and environmentalists, respectively. "We're human beings. It's us and the environment we live [*sic*] and the environment and every part of it, well, every part of it. We use up stuff just like every animal uses up stuff in the environment, but the point is don't use it up so that the reason you're living there isn't good anymore" (*BL* 163). The repetition of "the environment" and "every part of it," ticks duly transcribed by Curole's interviewer, indicate the anxiety of ecological compromise, a constant rehearsal of losing something not quite anticipated. Human aspirations toward incorporation as part of a privileged and potentially timeless entity such as Texaco falter when subsidence begins to indicate a new telos of infrastructure, infrastructure that serves itself. The MMS oral histories offer a template for art (as in innovating, creating, engineering) as a practice not intended to build or complement human culture.

The poet Martha Serpas, who has lived all her life in Bayou Lafourche, suggests a postscript to the MMS interviews that were conducted throughout her home parish. Serpas refers to the dialectic of petroleum and subsidence as "decreation," in a poem of that name and elsewhere in her collection *The Dirty Side of the Storm* (2007). Imagining herself in a coffin that has been unsettled and set afloat by the invading ocean, the poet writes, "Someone will lay a plaster vault for me to ride,/like long boxes children pull down flooded roads./In my plaster boat I'll ride Gulf shores/till I vanish like a rig in the sun."[31] The poem suggests the Leeville cemetery, one of many Cajun burial sites that have floated out to sea due to subsidence. Serpas's poetry invites an openness to personal extinction ("If only I could give the land my body…I would lie against the marsh grass and sink,…and welcome the eroding Gulf"), as if humans count primarily as matter, our corpses sandbagging the wetlands (DSS 79). To live in such a world is to be sculpted by subsidence, with that geological artist linked tenuously to the rigs, whose silhouettes against the sun make them appear as symptoms of distant intelligence. Serpas and the MMS interviewees offer a vernacular poetry of human species collapse: heroic, Catholic, melancholic. Feeling ecological means the discomfort of surrendering historical thinking, with its linearity that honors the perceived arc of human lives, and welcoming breakdown of the human into "marsh grass and sink." This organicist vision is not unfamiliar in environmental discourse, yet it takes on force, and threat, in a place where human bodies literally fight back the ocean because of the technologies meant to extend human energy and comfort. Feeling at home in a petrol "world" creates an affective drag on thinking through human survival.

THE SOCIAL PROMISE

In the weeks and months after the BP blowout, the people of the Gulf Coast reasserted their reasons for living in an efflorescence of regional sociality that has taken place largely on the Internet. Social networking on Facebook and in the blogosphere has kept the blowout alive, with emphases on human intelligence and empathy as ecological actors. Internet first responders to the BP blowout join a vibrant recent history of activist reappropriation of new media for the purposes of "culture jamming" or remaking corporate memes, such as the Greenpeace/Adbusters 2000 "Spotlight" campaign for Coca Cola, which published *subvertisements* of Coke's polar bear icons huddled on melting ice to protest the climate effects of the hydrofluorocarbons (HFCs) Coke used in its cooling and bottling processes.[32] Early uses of the Internet to protest BP focused less on brand hacking (which BP essentially performed for itself) than on foregrounding the capacity of the Web to provide a space of appearance, in Hannah Arendt's term, in which the potentiality of power—"whose only material condition is people living together"—might be fulfilled through collective speech.[33] Regardless of the Internet's embeddedness in corporate and state efforts to extend neoliberal economies, and its own petroleum footprint as media, its facilitation of cheap self-publication and its extension of public access offers the potentiality of rapid response by communities organized around issues not clearly associated with political rubrics (e.g., the nation) or ideologies.[34] Post-blowout Internet activists have been performing the gathering of marginal, invisible agencies that Latour recognizes as the essentially ecological promise of the social, to "assemble beings capable of speaking" (*PN* 53).

For example, Project Tantalus, a research proposal by three scientists to gather water samples from the Gulf region and beyond using Facebook, promised to perform a social definition of intelligence as collective experience.[35] As the title of Tantalus suggests, researchers' frustration about not being able to reach the water, in all of the locales where oil-tainted water might show up over time, inspired them to seize upon Facebook as a means of collecting 100,000 water samples from the Caribbean and the U.S. Atlantic coast. Rules for making samples were to appear on the Tantalus Facebook page in what amounted to both an admission that professional scientists were outmatched by the extent of the BP spill and an opportunity to reinvent public science along the lines of the Smithsonian Institution's nineteenth-century weather project, which mobilized hundreds of amateur weather observers to generate a "national" image of weather systems. "This is an opportunity, I think, for people to get involved and be part of the larger picture," said chemist Mark Olsen, one of the three creators of Tantalus, who believes social networking will be crucial to twenty-first-century environmental monitoring.[36] Along the same lines, the smart phone app Project NOAH, which stands for "networked organisms and habitat," allows "citizen scientists" to contribute photographs and notes to a database for wildlife siting. The NOAH app has been used by some Gulf Coast residents as a means of measuring habitat loss since the BP disaster.[37] As with the nineteenth-century weather project, these Internet archives open the hierarchical structures of science into hands-on practice for volunteers, who not only enjoy sample-gathering as a means of building the public knowledge base but also experience a sensory connection to the sites of environmental injury. What is on offer is an aesthetics of intelligence. In short, efforts such as Tantalus and Project NOAH promise "feeling scientific" among a plurality of researchers, amateur and professional, whose copresence on the Web seems to verify our capacity, as humans, to do something about even large-scale environmental tragedy.[38]

The personal blog offers a very different model of Internet speech, scarcely recognizable in terms of an idealized public sphere that fosters disinterested intelligence yet also viable as a space of appearance in which the political potential of living together might be realized. In the wake of the BP disaster, Poppy Z. "Doc" Brite's *Dispatches from Tanganyika*, hosted by LiveJournal, featured regular coverage of the BP blowout and its aftermath, of lingering post-Katrina trauma, of New Orleans food culture (Brite's partner is a chef), and of Brite's struggles to find compassionate care as a pre-op trans-man. In short, *Dispatches* eloquently addresses the problems of being human: Its deep themes include embodiment and its discontents, the ethical complexity of empathy, and the interruptive moments that constitute happiness. Brite cribbed the blog's name from a letter written to author John Gregory Dunne by an editor comparing New Orleans to Tanganyika and New Zealand as unthinkably off-center places. Tanganyika is a former European colony that ceased to exist in 1965, when it united with Zanzibar to become the independent nation-state of Tanzania. In the West, it has acquired the mythology of "the cradle of humanity," due to archeologist Louis Leakey's discoveries at the Olduvai Gorge. Doc Bright writes from Tanganyika/New Orleans as a queer humanist, upholding but also shifting the value of the human by emphasizing our (relational, socially enacted) materiality. Many of his/her readers have signed on because they are transsexual, or because they are New Orleanians—both queer statuses to the extent that New Orleans residents have, since Katrina, been regarded as a people not quite returned, deathbound subjects following their "historic" city.

One of Brite's entries on the blowout emphasizes the blog's capacity to memorialize subpolitical events, in Ulrich Beck's term for issues removed from national agendas.[39] At Shell Beach, which is the site of both the Katrina Memorial and a BP cleanup at the time of Brite's visit, Brite simply notes what s/he sees: "We saw pelicans and people fishing in Lake Borgne and, way out on a pier, guys in lifejackets messing with huge piles of fluorescent boom. As we walked back to my car, a St. Bernard Parish sheriff's deputy came by in a little golf cart and gave us a desultory warning about taking pictures. 'Go ahead and take pictures of the [Katrina] memorial and y'all hanging out, but be careful about them working over there, because BP will get pissed off.' He obviously didn't like saying it and was only trying to save us getting yelled at, so I didn't burden him with the knowledge that I had already committed a felony by snapping two or three crappy long-distance shots."[40] The Katrina Memorial follows Maya Lin's Vietnam Veterans Memorial in Washington, D.C.; it is a somber wall listing the names of those who died in the flood, those who could be identified. The memorial stands as a reminder that the realization of a war comes about through the destruction of human bodies and that here human bodies realized a racially inflected civil war, enacted in ordinary urban space. This memory, so devastating to the American ideals of democratic pluralism and federal citizenship, can be photographed, while the placement of absorbent polyurethane around New Orleans to combat oil invites a suspension of the normal privileges of citizenship in peacetime. BP's bans on photographing "clean-up" have inspired a great deal of amateur journalism. But Doc Brite lets the conspiracy speak for itself, showing merely by what s/he can see and say in the blogosphere the absurdity of BP's attempt to inhibit ordinary people from knowing that they are living together and once again suffering together. Noting the essential kindness of the policeman on his "little golf cart," Brite refuses not to recognize him/herself in even spokespersons for the corporation and state. Such acts of recognition assure the potentiality, at least, of social assemblage, and of politics.

This persistent effort of recognition touches the dynamic of empathy, of entering into the pain or simply the material place of others, and empathy raises ethical problems. Saidiya Hartman, writing of empathy as an excuse for somatic "enjoyment" of black suffering in abolitionist literature, is only one of the better-known cultural critics to remind us that empathy is kin to spectatorship, entertainment, cooptation.[41] Doc Brite's response to the filming of David Simon's HBO series *Treme* delivers a stark critique of empathic colonization: "I respect many of the locals hired as consultants by 'Treme' (mostly folks who were doing pretty well already, as far as I can tell) and I'm glad if the work has helped them, but I don't feel that Simon and company have done New Orleans any favors by bringing this show here. Let us keep our (fictional) selves in the public eye as we choose to. Don't come sniffing around from Hollywood and take it upon yourself to ~~exploit our pain~~ tell our story."[42] *Blogging Treme*, a promotional site for the HBO series, responds to Brite by implying that s/he is a hypocrite who ignores the cultural work of sentimental fiction, such as Charles Dickens's literary pleas for impoverished London.[43] HBO's "literary history defense" does not answer Brite's concern that filmmakers ought to compensate residents of Central City, one of New Orleans's poorest neighborhoods, for the inconvenience of filming in their streets and homes. But if sentimental fiction, with its implicit mandate to feel for and humanize those denied civil rights (children, prisoners, animals, slaves), can be invoked as a potential means of recuperating New Orleans, Brite's own performance of sentimentalism deserves further scrutiny. In *Dispatches*, s/he emphasizes the necessity of foregrounding one's own pleasure in feeling as motivation for what might appear to be an ethic of care.

The first documented BP-related suicide stirs Brite to question the effectiveness of the blog itself as a tool for generating sociability and political action:

On Saturday [June 23, 2010], the *Times-Picayune* printed the story of Captain William "Rookie" Kruse of Foley, Alabama, who appears to be the first BP-oil-disaster-related suicide. I became sort of obsessed with this man, not so much because of any particular thing about him as because

I know he will only be the first. We saw the wake of suicides after the federal
levees failed, and that was when most of the worst had already happened
and there were things we could do about it. Now there is nothing we can
do, and we know this has only begun to happen. My mind made a weird
cross-connection between Captain Rookie and Dylan Thomas's poem, "A
Refusal to Mourn the Death, by Fire, of a Child in London," and I spent a
couple of days obsessing on the poem, too, trying to figure out why I'd made
this connection.... Is it that the first death symbolizes all those to come?[44]

The comments section that follows this entry—which also includes a lengthy
discussion of Brite's search for a transfriendly doctor and desire to begin hor-
mone therapy—features a recurrent dialogue between Brite and "wanderingastray," a reader who knew "Rookie" Kruse. "Rookie was a family friend,"
wanderingastray remarks. "If you can, try to think of him as the man he
was—a friendly, loving soul so connected with the Gulf that he had seawater
in his veins. I hate that his death affected you the way it has, but at the same
time, there's a tiny part of me that is still at least a little glad that he is remembered."[45] Brite's response interrogates his/her motives for memorializing a
stranger's suicide: "I hope my post didn't seem to dishonor or diminish him
in any way. It absolutely wasn't my intention, but sometimes I'm afraid I come
off as making other people's tragedies all about MEEEEEEEE and OMG MY
FEEEEEEEEEEELINGS."[46] A reassurance from wanderingastray that there's
"nothing but respect and love in everything you do, darlin'" prompts Brite to
reflect upon how "one of the few things I appreciate about having been raised
and socialized as a female is that I can usually cry."[47] This is sentimentalism
disassembled into the constituent elements of its twentieth-century critique—
the feminization of feeling, the dangers of empathic cooptation, the dubious
cultural value of representing another's pain.

In the heyday of the sentimental novel, conversations "breaking down"
the effort of fellow feeling also occurred, for example those that inspired
Harriet Beecher Stowe to publish *A Key to Uncle Tom's Cabin* (1853) in
order to prove that she had not fabricated black suffering in slavery as a
means of advancing her own political position or literary career. But the
blog makes the critique co-extensive, in time and space, with the empathic
performance—it offers the possibility of immediate correction from those
closest to the injury, in addition to multiple perspectives upon the injury.
If nothing else can be said about the personal blog, I would suggest that it
has made possible the distribution of authority over feeling, particularly
pain and identification with injury, within the sentimental genre. In other
words, the problem that Hartman identifies of a single author or silent
reader acting as "proxy"[48] for the injured in sentimental texts that rely on
the imagination of shared sentience is troubled by the blog's interactivity,
which authorizes many potential witnesses as well as those perceived as

the injured to speak about, or author, human pain. Brite's hypertext links to a *Los Angeles Times* article on Kruse's suicide and to Dylan Thomas's poem offer counternarratives to her/his sentiment, in addition to an active trail of how that sentiment played itself out in her/his reading and physical movement—as Brite must have retrieved the obituary and the poem from a computer file or print archive. We have, in these fragments of "Rookie" Kruse, also a shimmering hologram of Doc Brite's mobile body, and this is important insofar as Brite, as author, fails to disappear into or stand *for* Kruse. A few lines down from Kruse's story, we can approach both Brite and Kruse from another context, through a hyperlink to the Thomas poem, "A Refusal to Mourn the Death, by Fire, of a Child in London" (1945). It is the last line of the poem, "After the first death, there is no other," that Brite asks us to consider.

Of course once we have linked to the poem, we can interact with it as we please, moving away from the specific phrase that Brite remembers. The interactivity of the blog makes the effort of grieving also an effort of collective intelligence, as inevitably readers work together to think through the meanings of Thomas, of Rookie Kruse, of Doc Brite. I, for one, read more of Thomas's poem. Throughout the poem, Thomas refuses mourning, in the Freudian sense of replacing the lost object or instigating a new attachment. "The shadow of a sound" of prayer, itself a surrogate for the dead child, will come forth from the poet "never," at least not until the end of all living, when "the still hour/Is come of the sea tumbling in harness." In the preceding line, which concludes the first stanza, and again in the penultimate image of the final stanza, we are asked to conceive of water as a figure of eternity, that which holds the cyclical time of all living and dying and has, by its essence, no end. What seems the poet's refusal of consolation is softened by his imaging of the dead child held in a mode of time figured predominantly as water: "Deep with the first dead lies London's daughter,/Robed in long friends,/The grains beyond age, the dark veins of her mother,/Secret by the unmourning water/Of the riding Thames." The comment I choose to add to Doc Brite's remarks on Rookie Kruse's suicide and Dylan Thomas's poem is that the BP blowout severed water from the traditional symbolism that has allowed oceans and rivers to stand for a temporality larger than any dying.

The still hour came to the Gulf of Mexico, but this hour looked like nothing we imagined, because it made the ocean visible as a collection of mortal bodies—waters "bleeding oil," in Alabama conservationist John Wathen's phrase, suffocating and burning animals, bubbling waves that signal damage to the water column by toxic dispersant.[49] What becomes of the human when the ocean is no good for metaphor? Where the blogosphere compensates for the bleak condition of being alone with mortality is in its interactive and therefore open-ended mourning. This is environmental melancholia enabled as an effective means of preserving lost objects (lost *lives*) through Internet sociality.

ENDURANCE THROUGH GENRE

The ecological value of artful expression as means of human endurance became a significant touchstone for discussion in the wake of Hurricane Katrina, and to an extent Katrina nurtured the regional arts community that still is responding to BP. In the film *Trouble the Water* (2008), for example, fifteen minutes of Kimberly Rivers Roberts's and Scott Roberts's amateur videography, a practice again gaining prominence since the BP media ban, makes possible the imaging of human biological resilience as something like enduring nausea. The viewer loses equilibrium in their dizzying footage, which creates deep mimicry, "communicating trauma as a visceral and cognitive experience," as Lauren Berlant describes the translation of intimacies made possible through testimonial rhetorics.[50] From videography to the blogosphere to the book, experimentation with what we might call lively genres, artistic forms in the service of human health and survival, began in earnest in Katrina's wake. "We are becoming aware that biocultural evolution is more tragic than comic," writes African-American poet and critic Jerry W. Ward, Jr., in *The Katrina Papers* (2008), "that battles with external nature eventually are transmuted into battles with ourselves."[51] Ward's project in TKP, his shorthand for the book subtitled *A Journal of Trauma and Recovery*, is nothing less than shoring up his, or our, contribution to the biocultural fate of the species. To this end, Ward advocates "creating what is not literature."[52] For him, this means pushing literature to become "interdependent," mingling in biological practices (eating, sleeping, sheltering) and the infrastructures that sustain them. Keeping in mind the material organizations that enable particular kinds of art, "interdependence" also could be a call to rethink genre in terms of the sustainability of media, from digital to print.[53]

Although Ward claims that he neither can nor will theorize the relationship of art and disaster, TKP gives philosophical heft to the conversation that shows up unselfconsciously in the proliferation of post-Katrina art about the interdependence of singular lives. In TKP, writing, as a means of making time conventional, serves as a weak surrogate for living. Living, in turn, figures as like water, insofar as "life" sympathizes with water's evasion of measurement and sequence. "Time knows what it is," Ward writes. "It is flowing past the hotel on the surface of the Mississippi River."[54] Water's instigation to enact time as something other than progressive sequence figures in "Hurricane Haiku," one of the many poems that interrupt TKP's narrative prose: "Aqua vitae heard/ Mad death massing in their throats:/Blues, disaster hymns."[55] The water of life, strong liquor, strangles the urban poor, the southern poor, Africans "in the slave ships," as Ward elsewhere refers to Katrina survivors. But after or even within the episode of human dying, in the collapsed time of haiku, "aqua vitae" returns, as rhythmic (time-conscious) language, the blues, "disaster hymns" that immerse Katrina in histories of flooding along the Mississippi delta, of racialized poverty, of pellagra and sharecropping. Sound, in "Hurricane Haiku," is voice *and* water, both standing for prelinguistic, elemental expression that cannot be parsed through Sausserian or calendrical systems of difference. If this implies a Romantic naturalization of voice, the poem's thrust is pragmatic. The storytelling arts, the blues, hymns, are heroic but not triumphant here, human biocultural rhythms that relive but do not resolve traumas of systemic disruption.

Throughout TKP Ward reminds us how the repetitive—and improvisational—rhythms that mark historical wounds also index diminished parameters of human health and energy that should not be obscured by the beauty of the rhythms. The lessons of African-American history include the contingency of culture and health, for all humans. "It is not about us," Ward writes, presumably referring to Katrina survivors and particularly to black Katrina survivors. "The sad condition of our planet is the damnation of all classes; it is a signal that the American empire shall gnash its teeth."[56] Ward ties African-American history to the tentative "pre-future" of "our planet" and the fate of humans more generally, again highlighting, in a lyrical echo of Bullard's EJ work, the relevance of the Gulf Coast, and the black South, to U.S. ecological futures. Updating Richard Wright's naturalism for the era of global climate change, Ward urges a consideration of global climate change in terms of war—race war in the sense of both warring racial factions and of *the human race* at war with the collateral effects of modern technologies, corporate greed, and political compromise. Ward writes: "Friends urge me to see the film that is based on Al Gore's lectures regarding global warming. If I don't ever see the film, cool. In either case, the weather in New Orleans can inform me about the progress of global warming. The film I really want to see pertains to the origins of World War Three. It has not yet been produced and edited to protect the guilty."[57] The weather in New Orleans stands for the vulnerability of that city, and many locales within the Global South, to climate collapse. That the U.S. Gulf Coast delivers an American environmental prophecy is central to Ward's critique.

With "World War Three," Ward offers a frame for global climate change that supersedes older environmental narratives. Turning repeatedly to poetic forms, Ward essentially jettisons story structure to display the unclosing wounds of New Orleans's black, Latino/a, Vietnamese, largely impoverished climate refugees; Doc Brite's *Dispatches from Tanganyika* similarly maintains an open narrative frame, inviting a collective response to local injury. In contrast, Josh Neufeld's graphic novel *A.D.: New Orleans after the Deluge* (2008) elicits a mass public, at the national rather than regional scale, through more conventional plotting. Neufeld's novel grew out of a comics blog hosted by the storytelling site *Smith* magazine and to some extent is about the art of telling a compelling story, crafting suspense and resolution. *Smith* offers a test run for comics authors, who can increase the market for print editions of their work by tens of thousands through preliminary web distribution.[58] Neufeld's popular audience shows up awkwardly on the *Smith* site, for instance when a comment praising his skillful plotting ("Looking forward to the rest!") is answered by another online reader: "I wonder if any of you jerkoffs are really from New Orleans…but yeah…looking forward for the rest…ha ha."[59] We can credit this correction to what I have described as the blog's capacity for distributing authority over feeling, such that sentiment is negotiated by multiple authors.

By making Katrina into comics, Neufeld takes sentimentalism to its representational limit, wherein actual persons become stripped-down icons to be "filled" by the viewer/reader. Following Marshall McLuhan, comics theorist Scott McCloud argues that because our "mind picture" of ourselves is "just a sketchy arrangement…a sense of shape…a general sense of placement," we see realistic drawings of faces as other persons but experience cartoon faces as *potentially* ourselves.[60] Similarly, Sean Cubitt recognizes comics as a precursor to simulation games, although the ludic possibility built into games with multiple outcomes cannot be realized through comics panels, or in a comic that treats a historical event (such as Katrina) whose outcome is known.[61]

A.D. marks a departure for Josh Neufeld from his first Katrina-related publication, *Katrina Came Calling: A Gulf Coast Deployment* (2006), which appeared as a LiveJournal blog and then as a printed book. The evolution of Neufeld's experiments with genre (blog, printed journal, comics) traces a struggle to find artistic forms relevant to ecological endurance. In *Katrina Came Calling*, Neufeld recounts his stint as a Red Cross volunteer in Biloxi, Mississippi, taking himself to task for his self-identified uselessness as a "culture-producer" ("what real good are comic book stories?"), theorizing his commitment to Katrina survivors as an effect of "scopophilic attraction," and wondering if the 9/11 bombings created an expectation of the scale of crisis that Katrina answers more fully than smaller disasters.[62] *Katrina Came Calling* digs around in the psychology of empathy, turning up an appeal to ecological crisis as, at best, a new kind of war that might encourage moral clarity. "For me, 'disaster relief' had a double meaning," Neufeld reflects. "It also meant relief from the doubt, confusion, and gnawing self-hatred of being an American in today's world."[63] *A.D.* also offers relief from the uncertainties of being an American insofar as it subverts the World War II–era origins of the comic superhero, that midcentury everyman with his anxieties about the bomb, who was expanded through larger-than-life avatars of exceptionalism and Cold War preparedness. In contrast, *A.D.* gives its reader-viewers the opportunity to become larger-than-life humans *in extremis*. The book plots a virtual tour of bare life, leading the viewer to enact closure by letting go, panel by panel, of all the privileges of U.S. modernity, including comics.

Chronicling seven "real" individuals' journeys through hurricane and flood, *A.D.* highlights the diversity, connectivity, and segregation of a modern city, suggesting the distinct odds of survival for an unemployed African-American woman (Denise), an Iranian shopkeeper and his black fishing buddy (Abbas and Darnell), a gay doctor who lives on the high ground of the French Quarter ("The Doctor"), a middle-class black student (Kwame), and two down-mobile white artists (Leo and Michelle). Neufeld presents almost an archeology of the private spaces of this varied cast, their homes and small businesses in New Orleans, as if sifting through Pompeian households and calculating class-based resilience based on which furnishings are unearthed from the ruins. In the comics tradition attributed to *Tintin* creator Hergé (Georges Rémi), Neufeld's settings are realistic in their meticulous accounting of material culture, while his characters are drawn loosely enough to evoke broad identification, even though we read them as variously ethnic or "white." Denise becomes our Dantean guide through the underworlds of the New Orleans Superdome and the Ernest N. Morial Convention Center, nightmare instantiations of the graphic novel's generic iconicity. Here there are no particular objects or persons. The ubiquitous male/female icons on the bathroom doors of these institutional spaces acquire a referential tie-in to filth and excrement, raising questions about how the iconicity of the comic genre might also enable depersonalization and disposability.

As a hand art that requires little translation, since it is not dependent upon language or culturally specific imaging, comics potentially could disseminate new global stories to normalize more sustainable energy regimes or defamiliarize obsolescent ones, as in Harriet Russell's post-petroleum short comic *An Endangered Species, Oil* (2007).[64] Yet the ecological fate of print comics is itself uncertain, betraying the lack of resilience of certain artistic genres within increasingly untenable systems of production. Neufeld queries the future of comics in *A.D.* through his character-double, Leo, who loses some 15,000 comic books in the post-Katrina flood. When Leo learns that his Mid-City neighborhood is under seven feet of water, his subsequent disaster fantasy earns a two-page panel, featuring Leo, starkly uncolored and therefore visually permeable, spinning with his erstwhile comics in a deep-red toxic sludge. The white, paper-colored bubbles from Leo's mouth suggest that he will survive, but his comics are already pink, taking on the expressionistic hue of the killing waters. Given the amount of water that it takes to make comics, newsprint, or any printed book, the fate of Leo's collection could be said to refer back to the material history of this popular art in some of the oldest and most ecologically damaging industrial practices.

The making of paper involves cooking wood chips until the tightly bound wood fibers separate into pulp, a process that consumes a tremendous amount of fresh water—which is why paper mills are often built next to rivers. According to Michael W. Toffel and Arpad Horvath, one year's worth of the *New York Times* (a single subscription) consumes about 22,700 liters of water.[65] Toxic effluents released back into rivers and streams by paper mills include cancer-causing dioxins. These effluents have been found to impair fish reproduction by interacting with fish neurotransmitter systems, and they are linked to human mercury-poisoning through consumption of contaminated fish.[66] About 76 percent of all pulpwood production for U.S. paper takes place in the U.S. South—the paper industry was an early target of Robert Bullard's analyses in the 1980s. The latest episode of ecocide inflicted upon the South by the paper industry involves genetically engineered pine plantations, some sterile and others allowed to propagate their seed, which will result in a huge falling off of biodiversity. Because the U.S. South has less public land than any other national region, it has been difficult for environmentalists to block the growth of so-called franken-forests through state or federal regulation.[67]

By virtue of their means of production, books like *A.D.* are looped into the regional ecosystem failure of which Katrina, and the BP blowout, represent dramatic examples. As a complex four-color work, *A.D.* was printed in China, where lack of environmental and labor regulation make possible cost-effective printing of books that require high levels of craftsmanship, including graphic novels.[68] The dissemination of visual art through printing is quite literally very bad for the environment, contributing to the poisoning of rivers (mostly in China and the U.S. South), the clear-cutting of forests (mostly in Southeast Asia, British Columbia, and the U.S. South), and global climate change. The book industry is the fourth-largest industrial emitter of greenhouse gases. Add to that the emissions generated by shipping art books back to the United States from China. The unsustainability of print has led writers and graphic artists to digital media, whose primary environmental advantage over print media is its elimination of paper.[69] Yet, as Neufeld suggests in contrasting his blog and book versions of *A.D.*, the book allows for a play of "aspects of timing, meter, and rhythm," due to the tiering of images on the page and to the physical act of turning pages, which our LED screens don't allow.[70] I would add that the power of the gutter, that blank space between comics panels that invites the reader/viewer to make conceptual bridges across time, is diminished by the digital format—particularly where a web host allows reader comments onto the page so that social noise interrupts the perceptual "filling in" that cartoon iconicity invites. To me, it is unclear whether the social potentiality enabled by interactive web features such as comments sections ought entirely to replace the empathic mimicry associated with conventions of silent reading. Neurobiological speculations about intersubjective relations suggest that recognition of the shared states that make us human requires "inner imitation," which might be reinforced in silent reading, by imagining other lives.[71]

To be human, to be southern, to imagine our own bare life within a twenty-first-century ecology, we need now more than ever representations, narratives, pictures, moving and still. The answer to Martin Heidegger's question in the lecture *On Origins of the Work of Art* (1935–1936), "is art still an essential and necessary way in which truth that is decisive for our historical existence happens?" seems now more than ever to be "yes." Understanding the

Gulf Coast as a diminished American future may be crucial both to national and species survival. Such understanding takes time, the sort of time handled well by the traditional arts of duration. But the printed arts require great quantities of water and trees. There may not be time enough, in terms of the endurance of human habitat, for print media or for commercial film production, which also relies heavily upon petroleum products and is a major emitter of greenhouse gasses. What this means for the endurance of genre remains to be seen.

The relentlessly social and interactive creativity of the blogosphere may be complemented by performance arts that are entirely off-grid, or Internet sites that refer out to embodied performances. Patricia Smith, a four-time National Poetry Slam winner and author of *Blood Dazzler* (2008), a print collection of searing poems about Hurricane Katrina, makes a strong case in her multiple modes of performance for poetry as a genre that will survive because it flourishes live, performed by body and voice—and now the Internet promises easy replication of its performance. Watch Smith speak the poem "34" on YouTube. The poem honors thirty-four people who were not rescued, who were found drowned in a nursing home in St. Bernard Parish, Louisiana. The thirty-four come back through Smith, in distinct voices, like somatic memory borne on the human body's own ample waters. "The underearth turns to face us," says number "34," the last to speak.[72] The words that follow in the print version of the poem, "*leave/them*"—referring to the abandonment of the dead, the evacuation not given, the letting go of earth—resonate in performance as both betrayal and consolation.

PLOTTING AGAINST OIL

The confrontation of oil and water in the compressed space-time of fiction offers the mingling of eternity and modernity, god-time and industrial time playing out against each other, often at the molecular level of "sensibility, intelligence, and desire," to quote Félix Guattari's description of the interior, fleshly sites of ecological revolution.[73] Marine habitats that bear the effects of energy production are often unhappy ones. The potentially devastating coupling of hydraulic systems and energy infrastructures has not been conceived clearly enough in terms of physical impacts, according to the historian Martin V. Melosi, who regrets that geographers tend to describe the footprint of energy production in terms of "transnational spaces" rather than local environments affected by processes such as the refining of crude oil.[74] Fiction can lend a strong material dimension to such local impacts, and to economic relationships that have been made deliberately abstract, like the relationship of gas prices at the neighborhood pump to international oil markets.

The concluding section of this chapter focuses on two incompletely resolved mysteries set in oil deltas, the Niger Delta and the bayous of Houston, Texas.

In distinct ways, Helon Habila's *Oil on Water* (2010) and Attica Locke's *Black Water Rising* (2009) plot against oil, if we conceive of "plot," after Peter Brooks, as the interpretive activity that constructs "a story of the crime" otherwise unavailable to the reader. Plotting is an act of detection that reconstructs the object it pursues, in this case an energy resource that seeks to hide itself, to dematerialize as capital.[75] Both novels perform variants of detective fiction, which in the twentieth-century United States has been conceived as an "oppositional discourse," a response to the decenteredness and privatization of modern life, where social relations, laboring bodies, and material infrastructures have become difficult to see.[76] Finally, both thematize water as a key to establishing an interpretive point of view and a medium through which modern enigmas might be resolved.[77]

Early in *Oil on Water*, Habila gives his first-person narrator, Rufus, a brief monologue about the Hollywood film *Waterworld* (Kevin Reynolds, 1995). The film dramatizes life after global climate change has done its worst, raising sea levels to the point where dry land all but disappears. "There are long and beautiful shots of endless ocean," Rufus recounts, "with only Kevin Costner's frail boat on it, dwarfed by the liquid blue vastness. I fell asleep with the movie still playing, thinking there was something sad about a people who were born and lived and died on water, on rusty ships and boats and fantastic balloons, their days and nights filled with the hope of someday finding dry earth, their wars and industries and relationships and culture all driven by the myth of dry land."[78] Habila's gloss lends poignancy to the Hollywood film, making it, in turn, into a gloss upon an actual world devastated by rising waters. In the Niger Delta, rivers rise in response to the subsidence caused by the intensive extraction of oil from the region since the 1960s. According to one source, "In combination with predicted sea level rise as a result of global warming, about a forty kilometers wide strip of the Niger Delta could be submerged in thirty years."[79] Villages, which are called by the watery appellation "creeks" when they are far from established cities, already have been wiped out by flooding.

This variant of global climate change is too subtle for *Waterworld*, although the film critiques the fossil fuel regime that complements sea-level rise. Dennis Hopper's arch-villain, the Deacon, rules a community of "smokers" (cigarette- and oil-burners) aboard the rusted hulk of the Exxon *Valdez*. The "smokers" don't make it to dry land, the desired and finally real destination of the film's protagonists, but they do provide the film's best action scenes, including sublime explosions that their oil reserves alone could furnish where stagecraft is otherwise dependent on wind power. *Waterworld* inadvertently suggests that action, in the sense of satisfying plot, depends upon oil. The film also misses the ways in which water functions as an actual world and habitat for coastal and river dwellers. Only the Costner character, with evolved gills and webbed feet, knows the way water "moves," as he says. He will leave the band of atoll-dwellers who are set to slowly rebuild modernity on dry land, once he helps them find it. The reversion in *Waterworld* to the heteronormative economy of a John Ford western—where wilderness and savages are vanquished to save the basic production unit of the family—makes for a good reason to doze "with the movie still playing," as Rufus does. As Timothy Morton riffs—after Fredric Jameson—it is easier to imagine ecocatastrophe than the end of capitalism.[80] From the perspective of an oil-ravaged delta, Habila recognizes that water can do imaginative work beyond conventional European–American cultural constructs such as the sublime and the frontier.

After the BP blowout, it was said that water, the Gulf of Mexico, had been sacrificed for the sake of the shore. At least this is how the journalist Antonia Juhasz explains the aggressive use of more than a million pounds of toxic dispersant by BP and the U.S. Coast Guard, sometimes delivered by airplanes that literally bombed the ocean under the cover of night. While both Corexit 9527A and the supposedly more benign Corexit 9500 contain ingredients toxic to humans and known animal carcinogens, they were applied to the Gulf in unprecedented quantities and at subsea levels—apparently for the purpose of reducing the quantity of tarballs on beaches and other visible evidence of the oil slick.[81] By comparison, fewer than four thousand gallons of Corexit were used in response to the Exxon *Valdez* spill. Scientist-activists Wilma Subra and Riki Ott publicly denounced the dispersant bombing, emphasizing how dispersant bioaccumulates up the food chain and actually works as a delivery mechanism for oil, enhancing the ways in which oil, itself a toxin, bioaccumulates.[82] The biological remediation of the spill by oil-eating microbes also carries unexpected ecological tolls. As marine scientist Samantha Joye discovered, the microbes native to the Gulf of Mexico that eat oil need oxygen in order to do it, and they also secrete long strings of mucus in the process. With so many microbes at work on such vast quantities of spilt oil, drippy slides of mucus multiplied in the ocean depths, literally providing "mucus highways" for oil molecules to travel more efficiently to the ocean floor.[83] Oil on the floor of the ocean affects the growth of ocean-bottom breeders such as shrimp. Moreover, "dead zones" of oxygen-depleted water appear where oil-digesting microorganisms are present in abundance. Juhasz's excellent journalistic account, *Black Tide: The Devastating Impact of the Gulf Oil Spill*, presents itself almost in the guise of detective narrative. Her investigative reporting elicits material evidence that exists largely at the molecular level, so far out of sight as to be "disappeared" by politically motivated rhetoric.

In contrast to the microscale victims central to the BP aftermath in the Gulf of Mexico, heaps of visible dead populate Helon Habila's fictive Niger Delta. Habila conceives of journalism in *Oil on Water* as a means of imposing narrative coherence on ecological and social conditions so chaotic as to be illegible even to those who ordinarily live with them. The journalist is ideally an expert plotter who assists the culture in creating comprehensible and transmissible narratives, hence cultural memory. As Jennifer Wenzel reminds us in her review of Habila's novel, the journalist is also a bit of an opportunist, equating the transmissible plot with personal promotion.[84] The first-person narrator of *Oil on Water*, the journalist Rufus, acts like a detective, or like a literary critic such as Peter Brooks, insofar as he understands his role as creating an interpretive map (a plot) that generates a larger story. But Rufus, of necessity, rejects the kind of plotting associated with classic detective fiction in the Conan Doyle vein, where narrative closure comes about when the detective's interpretation diagnoses, produces, and thus essentially exorcises the crime. Since the extent of the delta and the devastation that wracks it are vast, Rufus confronts difficult choices in order to fulfill the fundamental condition by which plot becomes an effective means of cultural transmission—namely, that it must "be of a length to be taken in by the memory," as Aristotle writes in the *Poetics*.

At approximately 75,000 square kilometers, the Niger Delta is the largest wetland in Africa. The vast coastal plain of southernmost Nigeria, where one of West Africa's longest rivers empties into the Atlantic Ocean, has suffered more than fifty years of oil spillage, air and light pollution from oil extraction, and the most continuous gas flaring to afflict any oil producing region.[85] Since Shell-BP discovered oil in commercial quantities in Oloibiri in the eastern Niger Delta in 1956, Nigeria achieved an independence from British colonial rule that was almost immediately compromised by state contracts with oil corporations that funneled wealth and power to a minority elite. As Rob Nixon asks, "Who could have dreamed in 1958 [when the first tanker bearing Nigerian crude left Port Harcourt] that four decades and $600 billion of oil revenues later, some 90 million Nigerians would be surviving on less than a dollar a day?"[86]

The country exemplifies the paradoxes of the so-called resource curse, where reliance upon a single resource for economic survival leads to corruption and a profoundly unequal distribution of wealth. The Petroleum Act of 1969 placed control of oil mining leases in the hands of the Nigerian state, and the Land Use Act of 1979 went further to federalize oil resources at the expense of the delta's ethnic minority states.[87] The activist-writer Ken Saro-Wiwa's campaign against Shell and on behalf of the Ogoni people, one of the smallest ethnic minorities in the Niger Delta, brought the exploitation of Nigeria's so-called e.m. (ethnic minority) communities and ecosystems to international attention in the early 1990s—only to end, infamously, with Saro-Wiwa's death by hanging in 1995.[88] The Nigerian government accused him of inciting the murder of four progovernment chiefs and hanged him, alongside eight supposed co-conspirators. The Ogoni Nine have since become martyrs and international symbols of the sickening exploitation of the "once lush delta of death," in Nixon's poetic phrase.[89]

Helon Habila's fictions emphasize the significance of journalists as "conservationists," by which he means creators and archivists of occluded histories, including ecological ones.[90] *Oil on Water* offers a stark distinction between "the perfect story," which the callow Rufus craves to secure his career, and the deeper "meaning of the story" touted by a veteran journalist, Zaq. Only five pages into the novel, Zaq cautions Rufus and ostensibly the reader to "remember, the story is not the final goal."[91] This distinction between "story" and "meaning" forgives the lack of structure that haunts *Oil on Water* as an atmosphere of rising "fog" while at the same time indicating that the weight of the reading experience will fall on the interpretive or hermeneutic register. The reader, like the journalist-detective, will be called upon to decide how to assemble meaning from an overburden of victims and crimes. The plot, here, will of necessity be more economical, smaller, than the crimes toward which it points. *Oil on Water* proceeds as a series of flashbacks treating Rufus's journey into the heart of the delta in search of Isabel Floode, the white wife of a British petroleum engineer who has been taken by militants both for ransom and to publicize the delta's exploitation. Rufus's flashbacks about his river journey in search of the kidnapped woman come to us from different moments in time, some reversing the progress of the journey. This zig-zagging temporality creates disorientation that weakens the satisfaction of the novel's apparent denouement—the discovery of the white woman. The perfect correspondence of plot and story—such that the detective's inquest constructs "a story of the crime which will offer just those features necessary to the thematic coherence we call a solution"—fails.[92] We are forced to recognize plot not as a mechanism that produces truth or a facsimile of it, but rather as a raw means of human survival, a way of carving out a point of view "in" the contemporary world— which in this case appears as a landscape of liquid super-capital and the dispossession of our common resources. Plot grants the world a significance to ourselves that makes it bearable. It doesn't create coherence, "a solution," or redemption, however. Plotting is a subsistence practice, a means of making *some* meaning, of getting by.

The aptly named Mrs. Floode brings to the surface numerous other victims, mostly nonwhite or nonhuman and dead. We see them caught in the roots of mangroves, hung over high tree branches, and rolling along on the rivers and creeks that are Rufus's conduits into the mystery that quickly becomes a secondary concern to his survival. Both militants and the military agree that Mrs. Floode should remain untouched, and she becomes a token of a disenfranchisement that neither group can directly address. As is well known, the Nigerian military and Nigerian police have been bankrolled by oil companies through a process that one former Shell scientist calls, bluntly, "the militarization of commerce."[93] Mrs. Floode remains secure while the rest of this fictive world flies apart. Scenes of torture by an army major who douses militants with gasoline invoke the feverish sadism of Joseph Conrad's Kurtz—within a newer extractive regime. Wenzel aptly critiques the novel for its "rote voice-overs" of militants and soldiers, who never materialize as fully expressive, as human.[94]

More effective than the novel's dialogue are Rufus's lyrical accounts of the everyday flotsam in the delta's rivers and creeks. Here we feel the effects of covert genocide, subsidence floods, and widespread pollution, the impossible harvest of tainted waters. "The swamps and the mist always returned, and strange objects would float past us: a piece of cloth, a rolling log, a dead fowl, a bloated dog belly-up with black birds perching on it.... Once we saw a human arm severed at the elbow."[95] These waters littered with the refuse of destroyed lives become a primary archive for Rufus as journalist-conservationist. The unmotivated, paratactic logic of the rising rivers offers a strong challenge to the ordering necessary to plotting, where pattern—even in the simplest form of repetition—assures some degree of transmissibility and potential for action.

One critic of Habila's earlier novel *Waiting for an Angel* (2002) points out his resistance to structural critique, meaning his apparent dismissal of Marxist or postcolonial readings of Nigerian history by earlier novelists.[96] This criticism calls to mind Kwame Anthony Appiah's polemical argument in favor of the "post-realism" of second- and now third-wave postcolonial fiction as against the supposedly more transparent political novels of authors who inaugurated postcolonial critique in the mid-twentieth century.[97] *Oil on Water* shares in the modernist distrust of plot—while still expressing a persistent desire for it— that Appiah identifies with postrealist African narrative. Habila foregrounds a broad problem of finding any discernible structure in a postmodernized, utterly irrational world that is collapsing and designed to be unreadable. Modernization surely does not equate with a rational "realism" here. The temporal jumps in Rufus's account correspond to a dissolving of spatial boundaries and identities that are actual, historical. Flooded, polluted delta villages appear as "ghosts," abandoned houses on stilts in a waterlogged region where the river has gone dead, and as "fragile flotillas" of riverboat people searching for still-living waters amidst a "sci-fi" landscape of pipelines and flares. "The meager landscape was covered in pipelines flying in all directions, sprouting from the evil-smelling, oil-fecund earth."[98] Such drifting communities recall the grief of human habitat loss less subtly performed to Hollywood standards in *Waterworld*. The rusted drilling fields Habila describes—which in reality often have not been revamped since their installation in the 1960s—indicate an increasingly corrosive and exhausted industrial modernity.

The Niger Delta enters the reader's consciousness as a lived region less as transmissible plot than as an atmosphere of feeling. Habila names this atmosphere "the same indefinable sadness." Included in his vague descriptor are quite specific sensory cues, such as the persistent "foul stench" that refers through the narrator back to the reader from the dead matter and leaked petroleum in the delta, an olfactory message voiced at the molecular level. This smell, and the ubiquitous "gas flares like distant malfunctioning stars" that differentiate villages that have allowed mineral leases from those that have not, emerge as luminous images, largely overriding the normative plot functions that the novel appears to pursue. Some of the best writing about Nigeria's "oil doom" has been poetry, and Habila participates in the associative logic of that genre in his pursuit of meaning.[99] The poet Ogaga Ifowodo's collection about the Delta, *The Oil Lamp* (2005), uses the resonance of poetic language to evoke human pain from within a narrative context that includes the political and physical infrastructures of petroleum. Ifowodo's poetry has a strong narrative element, and in terms of genre we might see him meeting Habila halfway— from the narrative poem to the lyric novel, associative logics generating emotional knowledge in and around the interpretive effort of plot. Ifowodo's poem "Jese," about a 1998 pipeline spill and gasoline fire in Jesse Town, Nigeria, creates sense memory through strong evocations of sound, sight, smell, and the terrible intimacy of touch to bodies burned raw.

In "Odiri's tale," a section of the long poem "Jese" that treats a mother's burning, Ifowodo writes of human bodies literally cooking in the fiery gasoline river:

> ...the sizzles of body fat melting to add oil to oil, the crackle
> of bones bursting alight,
> the gurgle
> in her throat. And she sank into it, burned
> till she woke in a bed gummed to her back.[100]

When the fire began at Jesse Town, the gasoline leak from the pipeline had become a river that filled a ditch that was fifty yards wide and chest deep in some places. Villagers, suffering chronic fuel shortages and accustomed to black market sales of petrol and natural gas, ventured into the oil river with buckets and jerrycans. A spokesman for the Jesse Town council of elders estimated that 1,000 people were wading through the gasoline-filled ditch or standing on its banks when the fire started—1,200 were reported dead by the time it ended.[101] In the voice of an elder woman, Madam Edoja, Ifowodo simply sings, "Oil is my curse, oil is our doom."[102]

Nigeria is one of the few major oil-producing countries that has to import gasoline, as a result of misguided subsidy programs, scarcity of refining facilities, and corruption that lands much of Nigeria's oil in neighboring countries such as Cameroon, which will pay more for oil than the price mandated in Nigeria. Lines at gas stations in Nigeria can be miles long, and people are used to buying—at great expense—on the black market. Ifowodo offers a popular translation of the acronym for the state utilities company, the Nigerian Electric Power Authority (NEPA), as "Never Expect Power Always."[103] Improvised gas burners make up for "the dimmed promise of *eletiriki*," as electricity is called by villagers who sacrificed their lifegiving rivers and even the comforting dark of night—due to continuous gas flaring—for the rotten promises of modernization.[104] The journalist Lisa Margonelli reports that "Nigeria's flares present themselves in a particularly hellish way," recalling horizontal, low-to-the-ground fires "the size of a truck" which she witnessed in the Delta.[105] Gas flaring has been illegal in Nigeria since 1984, but deadlines typically pass without action. It represents a human rights violation, a significant contribution to greenhouse gas emissions, and a missed opportunity. The natural gas lost to flaring could bring much needed power to Nigerians. According to the UK *Guardian*, "despite massive oil riches, Africa's most populous country produces barely enough energy to power one vacuum cleaner among 25 inhabitants."[106] In "Jese," Ifowodo asks us to feel what it is to stand at the edge of a modernity that never comes, save in the form of devastating accidents.

Oil on Water raises strong questions about the difference between novels and poems as means of creating cultural meaning within time. If what a novel produces is a set of lingering sensations tied to the reader's everyday memory through improvised situational analogies, perhaps it can be called a poem, too. For example, one summer afternoon I "remember" the Niger Delta that Habila evokes in the smell of spilt gasoline at my local service station in southern California. *Oil on Water* addresses topical, urgent crises: The social and environmental degradation of the Niger Delta by "petro-elites" in the federal government and by militarized, multinational corporations; the ongoing, grinding wars of militants against the state; the siphoning off of oil from company pipelines by locals who sometimes maim themselves in improvised industrial accidents, aspiring to self-help. Yet this is not a social or historical novel if we define those genres as efforts to reconcile the beguiling totality of industrial modernity to the felt experience of modern social life. Habila chooses a smaller scale and intimate treatment, which may be, again, why he has been criticized by readers interested in suturing "feeling," that seedbed of ideologies, to material history. Wenzel notes somewhat archly that Habila has won two Commonwealth Writers Prizes, the latest for *Oil on Water*, "without even getting arrested."[107] Habila's first-person narrator, Rufus, is admittedly too close to his subject to report its broadest social ramifications—a problem made manifest by his focus on his sister, whom he refers to as his "best story."

As *Oil on Water* moves toward its conclusion, the novel raises broad questions about the value of witnessing and writing of what is witnessed, either as a journalist, novelist, narrative-poet, or as an interpretive reader. The point of finding Isabel Floode proves not to be the satisfaction of the reader's expectations—because we find her fairly early in the novel, when we already care more for other characters—but rather the chance to follow Floode through the novel's collapsing geography, to see that broken world. Similarly, Rufus describes the meaning of the kidnapping for Floode herself: "I thought, what could fate possibly want with her on these oil-polluted waters? The forsaken villages, the gas flares, the stumps of pipes from exhausted wells.... Maybe fate wanted to show her firsthand the carcasses of the fish and crabs and waterbirds that floated on the deserted beaches of these tiny towns."[108] For the geographically distant reader, the novel itself acts as such a fate.

By novel's end, Rufus has heard the "truths" of the kidnapped woman, of the major who hunts militants for the government, and of a militant leader called "the professor" who earnestly hopes that his side of things will be known. Yet he imagines them all away, to an extent, pushing this story to the margins of a near future in what seems the distant city of Port Harcourt while he steers his plot toward an island shrine, dedicated to the solar cycle and preserved from the incursions of oil mining.

Rufus's sister has come to live among the worshippers who tend this almost impossible oasis, and his journalist-mentor Zaq chose to die here. Clearly, this is where "meaning" lies—significantly removed from the totality of a social history that includes multiple crimes. The last image in *Oil on Water* is the sister's face—we think—and the narrator descending toward it, seeking an intimacy in many respects irrelevant to the larger story he's inferred but also the only aspect of it that matters to him. Plotting against oil involves, for Rufus, a struggle to maintain family and interior life. More broadly, the author Habila's plot conceives a future aside from oil, rather than making the attempt to capture and exorcise its ubiquitous power. In two weeks, Rufus imagines, Mrs. Floode will have "nothing but a memory" of her ordeal, an "anecdote" for the dinner table—as if memory itself, like "anecdote" or story, may be nothing but a personal property.[109] The novel does not promise to make a difference, as journalism apparently aspires to do. *Can writing heal?* Habila doesn't presume so much. Yet it's impossible to exit *Oil on Water* without feeling that if it has not "mattered" in the sense of provoking the reader to action, it has acted upon us as matter. For instance, that recurrent, petrol-rot smell, mimicked by the reader while scanning the printed page, reactivated at the local gas station: it's a sensory cue that invokes the essence of a dying place in the nostrils and the neurons at the base of the brain. Through this molecular intimacy, Habila conveys a transmission of ecological effects that linger, like sickness, in the body. Habila treats the novel as a lively genre, by which I mean a text eliciting visceral knowledge.

This Nigerian novel may at first seem to have little in common with Attica Locke's *Black Water Rising*, a mystery set in the early 1980s in Houston, Texas. But Habila and Locke face similar challenges in plotting oil as both a local crisis and international business. In different ways, both demand something of readers beyond private reading—again, they ask for our lively performance. The twentieth century's world capital of oil corporate headquarters, Houston, signifies wealth, power, and entrepreneurial intelligence. Yet like the Niger Delta, parts of Houston slowly sink, at a rate of one and a half to two inches per year.[110] Rising water reminds the affluent American city of a near future of, if not "doom" per se, devastating floods and extreme storms coming from the Gulf of Mexico—both symptoms of the long-standing interplay of oil and climate. Across two oceans, the Gulf of Mexico and the Atlantic, distinct petroleum futures materialize at the meeting point of rivers and sea.

The black water rising in Locke's novel might be the water of Buffalo Bayou, the polluted urban river that winds through the city to end in the Houston Ship Channel, a global center for oil refining. The black water might also be oil mistaken for water, since oil in the novel rarely escapes the abstraction of metaphor. It certainly isn't a substance in which Houstonians wade and burn, as in Jesse Town, Nigeria. In the winner's circle of the global energy game, both oil and its casualties slip beneath what can be clearly represented or felt. If Locke's detective finds oil, he might also call up some of its victims. We learn that oil, when it can be detected, brings referrals to other, imbricated bodies. Set just four years prior to Enron, to Ken Lay's dream of an unfettered energy market operating out of Houston, *Black Water Rising* pursues the privatized, decentered objects that Jameson recognized as inspiring the hardboiled detective fictions of mid-twentieth-century Los Angeles. Locke's protagonist-detective, a struggling African American lawyer named Jay Porter, conceives a plot to remake neoliberal policies and the systems that sustain them back into public knowledge. The ultimate goal of his plot will be a rebuilding of civic space, for the sake of democracy.

"We were really doing something back then, man," Jay's friend Kwame reminds him, speaking of their work with the Student Nonviolent Coordinating Committee and Black Panthers in the 1960s.[111] Flashbacks of Jay's activist career intrude upon his present life, working hard and "living second hand" at the bottom of the middle class. Back in the day, before an FBI bust that was perhaps arranged by his former girlfriend, Jay "planned to call for a nationwide boycott of some of the biggest corporations in America, companies that were continuing to benefit from a history of colonial and economic oppression of brown people."[112] Jay's focus was to be "Shell and Gulf Oil" and "the big petroleum companies sucking the Congo dry."[113] This precocious critique of resource theft under globalization, particularly the plundering of African oil, suggests a nascent, pan-African movement against world oil culture. Might Jay have brought his protest to the Congo, or to Nigeria? That would require another genre, and a different American history. Here, Jay's girlfriend stops him in his tracks, inciting a riot at his Rally for Africa by seizing the microphone from him and declaring it "our fight, too"—referring to herself and other white students in Students for a Democratic Society (SDS).[114] It turns out she might be spying for COINTELPRO. In a single scene, the novel summarizes the end of counterculture radicalism in the United States, the coming era of identity politics, anticoalitional "race blindness" and dissipated structural analysis, and years of New Left burnout that gave way to Ronald Reagan and George H. W. Bush, Jeff Skilling, and Ken Lay.

Locke recognizes "energy" as not only a shell game in the financial markets but also as one of the most overdetermined American metaphors, ascribed to—and occluding—individuals, communities, and even oil itself. *Black Water Rising* presents its narrative problem as the search for structures by which to determine its actors and objects. In contrast to Habila in *Oil on Water*, Locke seeks that "abstract" totality of social and economic life that, as Jameson avers, is so difficult to make into "concrete," felt knowledge. Locke works on a broad, panoramic social scale. Jay's investigation into the "apparently inhuman institutions and things" that accidentally involve him in a murder one night in Houston figures as the difficult project of a critical realism intent upon making modernity "comprehensible in human terms."[115] No less than this ambitious imaginative project is needed to resurrect a Left that appears to have collapsed around the first oil shock of 1973, which was a huge financial boon for Houston. Jameson describes Georg Lukács's ambitions for critical realism with the conditional statement, "If the modern work of art were only able to enlarge its point of view far enough, if it were able to make enough connections between such widely disparate phenomena and facts."[116] To recall Amitav Ghosh, it takes a large plot, in fact strategy, to convey the wide-reaching entanglements of oil.

Locke grounds her plot—and the larger problem of knowledge in the neoliberal era—in the local cultures of Houston. Her omniscient narrator notes Houston's "curious habit of razing its own history," referring to the paucity of buildings in the city from the midcentury period "before the postwar explosion of American highways made gas the most coveted commodity...before 1973 and the embargo, before the crisis, before oil made Houston."[117] Reimagining a continuous cityscape through material traces of setting, such as an early twentieth-century police station that survives amidst corporate towers, *Black Water Rising* presents, first, an urban palimpsest. The novel's revelations, and Jay's inquest, begin with infrastructure. Specific sites of the oil economy, such as the Houston Ship Channel and the Strategic Petroleum Reserves in the salt domes of coastal Texas, become geographical markers of the missing bodies that Jay pursues. Those missing bodies include a murder victim, hoarded oil, and Jay's own father, whose killing decades before in a racist hate crime haunts Jay with grief and terror.

The final lines of the novel depict Jay imagining the embrace of his long-dead father and hearing the words *"I'm not gon' let you fall"*—the most basic promise of a functional sociality, of family.[118] Yet these words are a "dream" whose replotting into narrative realism takes the form of a coda to the novel proper, a narrative fragment evoking a possible sequel in which Jay Porter will sue a major oil company for fraud. Through a complex series of scalar transformations, from corporate politics to personal trauma to U.S. racial history, the novel suggests that the restoration of a man and his community to health depends on the capacity of plot to link the abstraction of social "totalities" to domestic intimacies. The more fundamental point is that oil makes critical realism necessary to human resilience. I define critical realism here rather modestly, though with a nod to Jameson, as the mapping of a functional human point of view within late capitalism. In the terms of my definition, Helon Habila and Attica Locke both practice critical realism.

Both Locke and Habila also invoke a densely textured region to maintain a critical realist point of view. Ambitious as it is, *Black Water Rising* feels almost homely as a reading experience. The novel reads a bit like a city historical museum, bus tour, or a thorough perusal of the Houston daily papers over a number of years. Some of Locke's most impassioned writing embraces the finer points of Houston's social geography with geeky connoisseurship, for instance her detailed accounts of the workings of the Port of Houston, from the fragile alliances among unions to the status of the Ship Channel as both public and private property, to the kinds of workers who enjoy air-conditioned trailers and the kinds who carry boxes of toys. Petroleum infrastructures unroll in scenic descriptions, through Jay's third-person limited omniscient narrative, and even in dialogue. Houston's mayor—who is Jay's treacherous ex-girlfriend from the SDS repurposed as a Reagan Democrat—tells him: "This is the second-biggest international port in the country. You know that? You got any idea how much money floats on that water? Not to mention the oil. The *oil*, Jay. Those petrochemical workers go on strike too, and this whole country's going to feel the effects of it."[119] The novel evokes wonderment at the degree to which we Americans—Houstonians all?—are determined by the oil business. Certainly oil influences the dynamics of specific places and the limits, in those places, of conviviality.

To negotiate the workings of oil in place, in Houston, Locke must move continually between backgrounds and foregrounds, using the microscale to materialize macro-scale experience. From the almost unthinkable fact of the second-biggest international port—also the largest U.S. port in *liquid* volume—we focus down to the conceivable category of "petrochemical workers," and then farther down to a small subset of African-American workers who are embroiled in the novel's foreground action. Houston's African-American community bears the primary burden of being human in a diegetic world largely disassociated from human-scale event. This community's represented liveliness—like the uncertain flow of the urban river—carries the reader through the more abstract mappings of social and geographical relationship that the novel also performs.

When a fragile coalition between black and white stevedore unions breaks near the end of the novel, it breaks around the promise of "race-blind" hiring, which only the African-American protagonists understand as a refusal of their value, since racial history will continue to be seen in them. "I think the hope has always been that you see what you see, and you take us anyway, for who we are," says Reverend Boykin, Jay's father-in-law,[120] to which the white vice president of the Oil, Chemical, and Atomic Workers' union responds with a dismissive sigh. The one kind of black water not set to rise in this novel is the African-American labor pool, which is not only silenced by the empty promise of race-blindness but also set to fall as the Port of Houston shifts to containerization technologies that will make many of the port's solid working-class jobs obsolete. Of course it was primarily black and brown labor that continued to carry bales of cotton and boxes of toys at the port in the 1980s, as whites were promoted to managerial positions and dematerialized, so to speak, in air-conditioned, mobile trailers.

Repeatedly, Locke moves from the novel's traditional scope of domestic intimacy, as Jay struggles to maintain his marriage, to global-scale plots that prove to be manipulating everyone. To bridge the chasm between human-scale and petrol-scale event and to follow the ingenious plot that Jay gradually realizes, the reader must learn a great deal. Like Jay, who ends up doing research at the library of the University of Houston, the reader who commits to this novel commits to it as a research project. Here is where the novel slides away from private reading into live acts. Now I must speak from personal experience. In order to complete this novel, I memorized the acronyms of relevant maritime unions, considered how the interests of port commissioners might be distinct from those of a city mayor, imagined the location of refineries and docks along the Houston Ship Channel. Finally, I continued my research by going to Houston (see below).

Enjoying the satisfaction of Locke's denouement depends upon the reader learning a good deal about how oil moves and who moves it. Jay's investigation will only incidentally touch on the murder that opened the novel, which is, like the ostensible "mystery" of the British abductee in *Oil on Water*, a compelling excuse to explore the political ecologies of oil. As *Black Water Rising* draws to a close, it turns out that the Cole Oil Company (a company owned by two diabolical brothers and perhaps a nod to Koch Industries) had been using an old salt mine on the Texas coast for the illegal hoarding of oil, to facilitate price manipulation. This is the crime we have waited for, the one that makes "historical and sociological" abstraction concrete, resonant of degraded social relations. Attica Locke wrote *Black Water Rising* in 2008, when the United States was experiencing a devastating hike in gas prices that seemed inexplicable to Americans—a dim echo of the situation in the 1980s, when the novel is set. The work that this novel demands of its detective and of its readers makes clear why the rise and fall of energy prices is rarely described accurately by politicians or even journalists. Locke proves that plotting the machinations of the oil business requires scholarly work. To read the novel, we essentially must learn how to write it.

While neither Habila nor Locke invokes global climate change explicitly, both link what Nigerian authors call "the oil doom" to rising waters, coastal ecologies, and the diminishment of nonwhite, southern humans. These mysteries cannot conclude without our determined engagement. They are postcolonial mysteries, in the terms of Stephen Tatum, who recognizes a variant of traumatic repetition—and the deliberate refusal of resolution—in the mystery and detective fictions of formerly colonized peoples.[121] They also are postmodernization fictions, to reinvoke Appiah's word for fictions that refuse the equation of modernity with rationality and realism, exposing the breakdown of technological optimism through fantastic elements or modernist, open plots.[122] While not speculative fictions, these imperfectly resolved mysteries gesture toward alternate possible worlds from within a genre that traditionally (in the Conan Doyle vein) promised closure, the coming together of the planes of action and interpretation. The novels pursue plot to leave it, but not in the sense of lingering anxiety that we might associate with the imperfectly finished plots of noir detective fiction by authors such as Raymond Chandler. Here the open or diminished plot invites the reader to a kind of production.

In a now famous essay, the poet Tanure Ojaide, the first Nigerian poet to extensively treat the "immeasurable wound" wrought upon the Niger Delta by oil mining, writes of wanting to be an oracle. "One cannot live outside one's time," Ojaide argues, "even if one projects oneself into times future and past. Attempting to see beneath the surface is what I strive to do. I want to be an oracle, a knower of hidden things, the knower of the other side of things; not a conventional oracle who foresees doom."[123] In his collection *Delta Blues and Home Songs* (1997), Ojaide indicts the world's blindness to what Nigeria has lost for the sake of oil:

> Barrels of alchemical draughts flow
> from this hurt to the unquestioning world
> that lights up its life in a blind trust.[124]

Since at least Hurricane Katrina, some U.S. Gulf Coast writers have been thinking about art as Nigerians have done since the discovery of oil in their delta, as a means of seeing "the other side of things" or even seeing beneath the surface, where oil itself resides.

To see differently "beneath the surface" or from "the other side" is to begin to perform an inquest, a plot, upon historical truisms such as "oil brings prosperity."[125] What the critic Sule E. Egya calls the "aggressive realism" of Nigerian poets is, for Ojaide, a realism that has lost any association with leisure and private reading.[126] Of course the novel as a form in the West has been deeply associated with privacy and leisure. In literary historian Ian Watt's words: "It is further paradoxical that the process of urbanization should, in the suburb, have led to a way of life that was more secluded and less social than ever before, and, at the same time, helped bring about a literary form which was less concerned with the public and more with the private side of life than any other previous one."[127] Nigerian writers do not share these affiliations with the suburb or the turn from public culture. Habila and Locke, writing across two oceans into the heart of what has been called by the oil industry the New Golden Triangle (West Africa–the Gulf of Mexico–Brazil), suggest that in the era of Tough Oil the U.S. novel may learn from Nigerian "aggressive realism." Meanwhile, the United States may continue to import oil from Nigeria, which has been our fifth-largest source of imported crude.[128] This raises the question of how to up the volume in the United States about the destruction of a sister delta with genealogical connections to our own best cultural innovations, like American delta blues. To liberate itself from privatized time and space, the Gulf Coast novel might exit the conventions of its genre, as Locke's novel seems to hope to do, into the "instrumental aesthetics" of activism.[129] Whatever the future genres of oil fiction, we need to keep looking to the waters that carry some of oil's worst external costs.

CODA: LIVE PLOTTING

The illegibility of Houston strikes not just novelists and their readers. With its securitized production and shipping zones, its outsized humidity and mosquitoes, and its vulnerability to hurricanes and floods, Houston has been compared unfavorably even to Los Angeles, with Reyner Banham declaring "Los Angeles in the era of *Chinatown* to be a socialist state" in contrast to Houston in the 1980s.[130] The city has many identities. First, it was "the Bayou City," a misnomer indicating Houston's site as a port at the confluence of two rivers—although that confluence actually occurs twenty miles from the city proper. As of 1964, Houston became "the Space City," when the NASA Manned Space Center arrived at nearby Clear Lake.[131] The cultural critic Philip Lopate calls Houston "a very hidden city," where "the interiorization of city life"—in air-conditioned malls like the Houston Galleria and underground, air-conditioned walking tunnels—"has led to a confusing, insufficiently inflected space."[132] A recent architectural anthology names Houston "the Ephemeral City," citing its resistance to rhetorics of a common place, familiar to all.[133] Lopate complains of the Astrodome as the seedy *stadtkröne* or "city crown" that brings together Houston's oil interests, NASA frontierism, and the realization of privatized climate, since the Astrodome was the world's first air-conditioned indoor baseball park.[134] Yet metaphors of "transformative liquidity"—indexing the coexistence of water and oil as Houston's antifoundational ground—evoke the city's symbolic wealth.[135] Houston has long been an energy capital and therefore a site of metamorphosis. Matt Coolidge of the Center for Land Use Interpretation (CLUI) calls Houston "a chaotic and beguiling incidental landscape."[136]

The arts and environmentalist cultures of Houston find meaning in the city's water. Despite the channelization of Houston's rivers and limited access to the Buffalo Bayou largely because of the security lockdown on the Shipping Channel, water here bears the conceptual resonance of public space. The movement to revitalize urban rivers that could be said to have begun with national media attention to the burning of the polluted Cuyahoga River in Cleveland picked up here in the 1980s, steered by nonprofit organizations like the Buffalo Bayou Partnership. The urban river has become the place within cities from which to establish a distinct point of view, for the sake of replotting increasingly decentered metropolises into perceivable communities. On Houston's free public boat tour of the Shipping Channel, aboard the *Sam Houston*, I was shocked to see not a single human working in the refineries or on the barges and tankers that line the channel, despite the reassuring imagery of a mural in the boat's cabin, in which men bustled along the channel carrying cotton, wood, and rice. The mural of the anachronistically peopled port dates from 1958 and was donated by the Rotary Club of Houston. Still, the Shipping Channel tour remains one of the most popular tourist attractions for locals, who no doubt seek in their own backyard the excitement long associated with trans-shipment points, from railroad hubs to cowtowns. Although photography was prohibited on the boat tour, I watched a man mug for his son's iPhone camera, saying with pride, "Here I am, in front of the big old Valero refinery!"

When the CLUI took up residence at Houston's Mitchell Center for the Arts in 2009, it headed to the river. The CLUI's Houston field station, in a mobile trailer, sits at the site of a former junkyard on the shore of the Buffalo Bayou and directly across from the largest scrap metal company in the world, J. Proler and Company. One could read this siting as an indication of the trajectory of industrial modernity toward chaotic, unsustainable accumulation, junk and scrap. But the CLUI's director, Matt Coolidge, recognizes the station as an ideologically neutral, if strategic, gesture toward seeing as much of the city's workings as might be seen. The CLUI's "vigorously unbiased method" falls in line with Robert Venturi and Denise Scott Brown's now famous dictum about industrial architecture: "Withholding judgment may be used as a tool to make later judgment more sensitive. This is a way of learning from everything."[137] Coolidge describes the Houston field station as a "portal, and a reorientation facility."[138] The CLUI heightened the visibility of what it calls Houston's "industrial aquatic environment" through an interpretive research platform attached to a pontoon boat.[139] The boat, named *TexHex*, projected recorded and live video from a folding screen, supplementing the flow of the river with its own play of images. In photographs of *TexHex* on the river at night, we see waves of electric light enlivening the water around the boat, turning a normally flat, utilitarian waterscape into an environment, a surround.

The CLUI project in Houston uses water as a means of intelligence, a way to get inside an oil economy whose scale edges on the inconceivable. "The full extent of our saturation in the oil economy can be seen, felt, smelled, and fathomed" in Houston, the CLUI's newsletter, *The Lay of the Land*, boasts.[140] But how so? Of the urban riverboat tours he planned for Houstonians, Coolidge notes that "the boat allows you to transect through a space obliquely—from what is often the back door, the drainage corridor, the industrial waterfront—providing a new view of a city or region."[141] This is live plotting, inviting the imposition of interpretive will upon a story that will become legible through that interpretative frame and yet appear to extend beyond it. The goal of the CLUI tours that I've taken in southern California has struck me as threefold: 1) phenomenological—to sense and to remember; 2) narrative—literally, structuring a point of view in industrial landscapes that obscure personhood; and 3) incidentally political, since the construction of a point of view or narrative path within, say, an energy capital functions as critical and even aggressive realism, the recovery of social relationship and of matter.

When I visited the CLUI's Houston field station, I was struck by its strategically blank face, beginning with the storage-facility beige of the mobile trailer exhibit space and the matching beige carport that houses *TexHex*. The interior of the trailer hums at a temperate sixty-eight degrees. Its polyvinyl "wood" paneled walls and beige fabric recliners, two of which are perched in front of a large flat-screen television as if anticipating the nuclear couple, suggest American middle-class aspiration—the barest evocation of the living room. My traveling companion took a seat in one of these chairs, whose fabric was scratchy and cheap. Meanwhile I followed the instructions on a black-and-white wall text for viewing the flamboyantly titled "Houston Petrochemicalscape Landscan Video" on the TV. This fourteen-minute repeating loop offers helicopter videography of the petrochemical industries on Houston's Shipping Channel. The almost overwhelming omniscient angle of the "petrochemicalscape" comes at the viewer complemented by an ominous sound track indebted, in the film credits, to the Sleep Research Facility. Humped into our recliners, my friend and I repeatedly asked each other where the monotonous ticking sound was coming from. We realized soon enough that it was part of the audio program. Two floor speakers complete the exhibit's modest, family-style entertainment center.

As the "petrochemicalscape" becomes more lunar—with rows upon rows of brilliant white oil drums giving way to what appears to be a massive tailings pond—the sound track grows nervy, building toward buzzing, cacophonous dissonance. How remarkable it would be if an American family sat down, one day, to watch this on television. An evocation of the petrol sublime, these moving images are less reassuring than the Romantic mountain or waterfall because their movement is both humanly motivated and illegible, completely undercutting the confidence that the sublime was supposed to produce—that we humans actually could glimpse the infinite, God's scale. My friend and I identified occasional trucks and trains crosscutting the industrial maze with glee, seeing in them a vague hint of plot. About seven minutes into the film, as the music began to build, I stood up and went to a series of wall photographs in which our orientation to the scene appears in satellite images with "You Are Here" signs indicating the location of the field station, and by a directional arrow indicating the Buffalo Bayou's flow. Again, the river plays the role of narratological intelligence. The point of the video and its exhibit space seems to be the very great difficulty of plotting a landscape such as this.

The narrative potential of the CLUI's intervention in Houston is deepened by an archival effort that suggests the CLUI's most famous exhibit, its online

Land Use Database. This online digital museum houses photographs and standard descriptions of significant sites of American land use, often hidden sites, such as the strategic petroleum reserves and nuclear test areas. The second gallery in the CLUI's mobile field station offers an archive of images that recalls the CLUI's online gallery. This second gallery in the exhibit trailer shows some forty images of petrochemical industry headquarters in Houston under the title "The Corporate Boardroom." Here we can escape for a facsimile of the museological collection, after the disorienting assault of the "landscan" video in the first gallery. The photographs on the walls are modestly framed 8 x 10 prints, following what Coolidge has described as a "standardized, institutional photographic methodology" that works as an extension of mapping—and of the geographic survey. Coolidge lists among his influences the 1970s New Topographics photography movement, which featured standard-sized prints of suburban tract homes and other apparently affect-less spaces—many of them in the American Sunbelt and the West. The name "New Topographics" makes reference to photography's traditional uses in mapping, to what Britt Salvesen calls "the medium's capacity to record landscape in a more or less passive, inexpressive, and non-conventional way; the idea of the survey, understood as an extended sequence with archival rather than narrative coherence."[142] Some of the CLUI's "corporate boardroom" images are almost absurdly distant from their apparent subjects, the physical buildings that house oil industry headquarters. For example, ExxonMobil's corporate headquarters can only be photographed from outside the corporation's security perimeters, so what we get is a photograph of a manned entrance gate.

Text boxes positioned underneath the CLUI's photographs invoke the international histories and global reach of these largely unphotogenic corporate campuses. Of Goodyear Tire and Rubber, the CLUI's text box tells us that the Japanese withdrawal of natural rubber during World War II led to the U.S. development of synthetic rubber from petrochemicals, with plants now extending all along the Gulf Coast. Such history contextualizes the photographs, to an extent highlighting their resistance to reading through the contrast of an "interesting" history to a pictorially dull, unyielding image. The gallery's introductory panel offers more rhetorical flourish than might be expected from the standardized curatorial method suggested by the artless arrangement of the photographs. Under the heading "The Business of Oil," we read: "From the oil exploration, drilling, and services companies in the 'upstream' realm, to the conveyance, storing, refining, and processing activities 'midstream' and 'downstream,' these corporations, their innovations, and the products they collectively bring into being, have shaped the earth, sea, sky, and humanity, forever." The text box concludes: "All have offices here."[143] The zigzag between *forever* and *here*, seemingly disjunctive points in time and space, makes for an awkward epiphany. The CLUI research station invokes the necessity of getting outside of the galleries, getting to the river and walking

Houston's streets, living the metropolis with a conscious intention of plotting it for yourself, so that you can feel and know it, as a geographically empowered resident, a citizen. Pedestrianism becomes political action and therapy, a means of moving (literally, physically) against the melancholy of oil dependence. What better way to begin plotting against oil in Houston, Alberta, or Los Angeles, than to get out and walk near the water?

The Petroleum Archive

Every museum makes a statement about the future, about what kind of past will sustain it. My turn to the museum in this final chapter signals an insistence on moving forward, even from within the feeling-state of melancholic attachment to conventional oil and the world it made. Archives signal futurities. Since Jacques Derrida explored the significance of the archive in *Archive Fever* (1998), pointing up the double purpose of archives as sites of storage and revelation, the future orientation of the archive has become a strong theme in cultural studies. Of course the word "archive" often indicates collections of data not quite or not yet public, unshelved and secreted collections between "the personal and the impersonal, the public and the private," in the words of the historian Jeffrey Wallen.[1] My interest here is in public collections, museums. Tess L. Takahashi has remarked on the extraordinary proliferation of conceptual archives made by artists for public use in the first decade of the twenty-first century, for example the Center for Land Use Interpretation's digital Land Use Database, which was noted in the preceding chapter.[2] To me, this boom in do-it-yourself and "fake" archives suggests an extension of the literary genre of speculative fiction into archival performance that also stimulates the imagination of possible worlds.

The economic and ecological convulsions of the twenty-first century, complemented by deadlocked political partisanship in the United States, intensify desires to remap cultural memory in order to generate a different present tense. In the age of Tough Oil, the future has been dragged into the past, literally mired in hard-to-crack deposits of shale. A future of deep ocean mining or fracking calls up the ugliest American memories of exploitation, for instance, the abuse of labor, institutionalized racism, and ecocide constellated around copper mining in Arizona around the turn of the twentieth century. Today oil itself lives at a worldwide set of current and historical extraction sites that might work as "lieux de mémoire," to use the plural form of Pierre Nora's term for places that call up memories that may or may not correspond to actual histories.[3] To inhabit the memory of oil, I went to some of the places where oil lives, archives and monuments that light up its potential to shape future cultural meanings. The linked essays that follow are at once personal records of travel and close readings of museums devoted to petroleum as an everyday object, a habitual practice, and a resource destiny. I recognize myself as a museum tourist, although I make scholarly forays into the interdisciplinary field of museum studies. Each museum and each essay invites collaborative predictions about the fate of North America, now in its second age of oil.

I. Los Angeles

"If the problem of death can be solved, the solutions to other problems cannot but follow."[4] These are the words of the Russian librarian and philosopher Nikolai Federov, as performed by David Wilson. Wilson is founder and curator of the Museum of Jurassic Technology, Los Angeles's ironic encomium to the Renaissance *Wunderkammern*, which preceded Enlightenment-era museums of natural history. The "resurrection and resuscitation" in full body of all the dead who have gone before is a "task that will be realized by the museum," Wilson intoned in a voice-over at a recent screening of his film mash-up about Federov, *The Common Task* (2008). By this point in the screening it was unclear exactly who—Wilson or Federov—was commenting on the museum's foundational desire. Natural history museums in particular have partaken in the desire to archive life itself, creating an exhibit space of "universal time," in the phrase of the sociologist Tony Bennett, through the display of representative species from across the globe and across historical and geological periods.[5] Methods of natural history, such as systematic biology and taxonomy, made possible the very notion of biodiversity, according to the historian Robert E. Kohler. The historian Steven Conn argues that "ecological research is an updated version of nineteenth-century natural history" and that such research grows urgent in the shadow of mass extinction.[6]

Recent studies of global biodiversity show the extinction of as many as 10,000 to 60,000 species per year. In museum literature, the possibility of resurrecting these dead appears dependent on both scientific methods like species inventories and their dissemination through new media. "Bio-informatics" signifies the digitization of museum collections such that global information sharing can keep scientists up to date about species loss.[7] "Interactives" or multimedia displays promise to generate creativity in museumgoers, fashioning a public primed for the flexible thinking demanded by ecological crisis.[8] The question of what endurance means for "nature," "history," and the natural history museum seems to break around what will continue to count as lifelike: information or object, media or bone.

Los Angeles offers a rich setting for a consideration of these questions, both because it is the world capital of entertainment media and because it hosts the world's largest archive of Pleistocene fossils, preserved in the asphaltum sinks that formed atop the Salt Lake Oil Field, itself the world's largest urban oil reserve. The La Brea tar pits serve up natural history in the raw, and they share kinship with the Renaissance curiosity cabinet and other "disreputable displays of objects," in Conn's words, such as those that might be found at fairs, freak shows, or circuses.[9] The sensory regime of these bubbling, odoriferous sinks exceeds the didactic visuality associated with nineteenth-century natural history, which Michel Foucault once described as "nothing more than the nomination of the visual."[10] In a way that may not be apparent to tourists, the tar pits represent a regional ecology. They are a petroleum archive within a city that exemplifies better than any other what oil could make of modernity. The effort to build a museum around the La Brea tar pits tells a story about Los Angeles's image of itself through the twentieth century, its desire to make history and the authenticity we associate with "nature" from within an immensely profitable pursuit of spectacle. One even can imagine the tar pits in terms of the ecomuseum, the *ensembles ecologiques* developed most extensively in France during the 1970s as a means of honoring regional cultures.[11]

Asphaltum, the semisolid form of petroleum that bubbles in the misnamed tar pits, refers out to Los Angeles's freeway culture and to its "electric media" culture, to riff on an old McLuhanite term for film and television media powered by electricity—and is indebted to fossil fuel. The apotheoses of automobility and electric media on display in Los Angeles spring from the peak of U.S. oil discovery in the 1930s. Oil played a foundational role in the making of two aspects of Los Angeles's four ecologies, in Reyner Banham's terms: the ecology of *autopia* (the freeways) and the architecture of *the fantastic*, namely the commercial storefronts designed to hail automobile drivers. Yet the La Brea tar pits indicate a petroleum reserve—again, the Salt Lake Oil Field—that has been removed from the "destructive circulation of commodities," in Andreas Huyssen's phrase, and from the transformative industrial work of the modern energy system.[12] In the midst of the world city whose infrastructure, architecture, and cultural production most bluntly express how fundamental oil has been to modern aspiration, the La Brea tar pits make oil visible as a material presence that cannot be easily reduced to the abstraction of "energy." Fences cordon off this dense petroleum that sits at the surface of the earth, displaying itself to the naked eye as an organic, irreducible treasure. In the shadow of the Los Angeles County Museum of Art (LACMA), the tar pits can be contemplated as land art, with the potential to effect self-transformation that art implies to a middle-class public accustomed to refining its sensibility in museums. The opportunity to think of oil as nature and/or art opens broad possibilities for thinking about how oil has expressed fundamental notions of humanness.

The tar pits share in the qualities of both carnival and museum. They are stinking, sticky objects indicative as much of the humiliations of embodiment as the transcendental notion of the human, which has been articulated through technological prostheses, like computers or cars, that extend the human body—at an increasingly unsustainable expense. Unlike the Oil Sands Discovery Centre in Fort McMurray, Alberta, where bitumen, a substance quite similar to asphaltum, stars in a multimedia narrative whose first premise is the "transformation" and "refinement" of humanity through the heavy industrial labor of making a tar-like solid into oil, at Rancho La Brea oil has been decoupled from any clear idea of progress. The Alberta museum also displays fossils found in the bitumen—which the Canadian oil industry anxiously refuses to call "tar"—but there the fossils are incidental to the curatorial line, which reinforces the pleasures of disembodiment, of losing oneself in the big trucks and diggers that make tar sands extraction possible.[13] In northern Alberta, tar ensures that the modern cultures and infrastructures that oil made possible in the twentieth century appear, improbably, as "the future." In contrast, Los Angeles's petroleum exhibit has been in the making since the early twentieth century, in a time and place where oil seeps were ordinary, frequent, and indicative of what looked like an endless supply of cheap energy. With this essential confidence in the fossil fuel system, one could take petroleum as it presented itself, at earth's surface, and consider it as bothersome tar, decaying microorganisms, or as media through which large mammals, including humans, might be preserved.

This manifesto considers the La Brea tar pits, which by the first decade of the twenty-first century have fallen far toward the disreputable status of the carnival, as the potential site of a post-oil museum. What I mean by "post-oil museum" is simply a place where the cultural meanings of petroleum and fossil fuel more generally are on display, as a reflection on the age of conventional oil that we are now exiting. What I mean by "manifesto" is simply an exploratory and even playful critique, from the point of view of a museumgoer rather than a practitioner or academic specialist. My argument draws upon Bennett's recognition of the natural history museum in particular as a "civic experiment" that reassembles objects in such a way as to create new entities "that can be mobilized...in social and civic programs."[14] In brief, I recognize museums as organizing material cultures that generate new civic narratives and behaviors. The La Brea tar pits offer a layered narrative about living with petroleum in petrotopia (e.g., Los Angeles, USA) and the possibility of thinking beyond the explicit uses of oil that have defined modern energy.

PETROLEUM MEDIA

At the George C. Page Museum of La Brea Discoveries, opened in 1977 amongst the tar pits in Los Angeles's tony Hancock Park district, visitors learn about the problem of dying, if you are a mammal, and about what it means to be petroleum, which never dies. The mammal/petroleum difference generates a key aspect of the museum's drama, a locus of tension and anticipated resolution within the museum space, which relies upon petroleum-based media, including film and its famous asphaltum pits, to create a sim-ecology where mammals, too, might live forever, in the half-light of dioramas and continuously looping reels. Jonathan Spaulding, former associate curator of the Natural History Museum of Los Angeles County (of which the Page Museum is a satellite), argues that the curatorial voice of scientific authority that once organized such museums by taxon and chronology is "dead," citing "emotion," "sensation," and "rhythm" as key curatorial goals, to be accomplished through the spatial, acoustic, and kinesthetic art of scenography.[15] Historian Alison Griffiths argues that such emphases on multisensory media in fact date back to the nineteenth century, citing museum features such as panoramas and the slightly later innovations of habitat groups and period rooms as examples of how "illusionistically re-created space can reinforce the sensory experience of space and time travel" that museums always promise.[16]

The Page Museum's natural advantage, its literally immersive scene over the fossil-rich Salt Lake field, may offer a rather low interactivity ratio in comparison to the new media pyrotechnics of younger and richer museums. But it is still the only museum famous for literally sticking to its visitors, forcing the issue of its oozy embodiment. In an era in which screen culture has become so ordinary as to make less of an impression on museum visitors than an apparently authentic experience, the tar pits present a discomfort that signals the "real."[17] On a recent tour, my docent, Gail, ended her introductory remarks with a promise to hand out recipes for tar removal at the end of our walk amongst the sumps.[18] As parents warned errant children to stay away from the museum's lawns and the distracted found their shoes sticking in place, it became clear that our clothing was at risk, and with it the social abstraction and status that distinguishes us from other mammals. At the Pit 91 excavation site, where some of the museum's most significant fossils have been discovered, the filthy T-shirts and jeans of volunteer excavators are on prominent display. Here nature presents itself quite viscerally, as stain.

If no single framing narrative can be derived from sticky shoes or blackened socks, such by-products of the La Brea experience at least suggest our vulnerability to and interrelationship with other life. The museum's displays reinforce the message of our vulnerability. Like modern "body genres" such as the horror film, exhibits invoke visceral mimicry in visitors by representing the distress of lone actors.[19] The first stop on the outdoor tour that is the highlight of the La Brea experience is "the Lake Pit," an asphaltum pit covered in water, the sort of mirage that the large mammals of the Pleistocene fatally ventured into for a drink. "The story of entrapment" that is the museum's leitmotif unfolds at the Lake Pit, according to a museum postcard: It is performed by "a fiberglass mammoth" (to scale) "struggling as she sinks into the large asphalt lake in front of...the museum. A father and baby mammoth watch from the shore."[20] Docents will add that the sinking imperial mammoth is "crying out," perhaps "in pain" or in "warning" to her appropriately nucleated family. [FIGURE 4.1]

FIGURE 4.1 *Father and Son Enjoy Family Drama at the Lake Pit. The George C. Page Museum of La Brea Discoveries, Los Angeles, California. Photograph by Author.*

At other points on the La Brea tour, and in the museum's story theater, visitors hear of the "screams" of entrapped mammals (the western horse, the Shasta ground sloth), most of which are now extinct. The museum's drama is discomfiting, all the more so because it is scaled to children. One of its few interactive displays consists of a child-height game wherein large metal pins might be pulled from asphaltum muck, although what we learn is that the muck relentlessly grips the pins and we cannot move them. In this low-tech game, entrapment—which can be conceived as little else than slow death—becomes corporeal knowledge. "Pull up on the handle,/Discover what it feels like to be trapped in tar," the exhibit beckons. While the single human skeleton at the Page, known as "La Brea Woman," has been retired to storage, there is little question that human death is on show. With a cloying ordinariness (e.g., it sticks to your shoe), personal extinction defines our "authentic experience," offering the downbeat to this museum's emotional rhythm.

Perhaps the museum's consistent reminder of the biological arc of singular lives (as Hannah Arendt tells us, the concept of mortality depends upon the elevation of the individual above species) makes the geological temporality represented in the tar pits more readable.[21] Imagining waves of extinctions that mark the edges of geological periods requires a shuttling back and forth between smaller- and larger-scale notions of loss. My docent at Rancho La

Brea offered a strong argument for the difficulty of perceiving time at geological scales, as she explained when the Pleistocene occurred, some 50,000 to 10,000 years ago, and how its now-foreign fauna reflect the fluctuations of Earth's climate resulting from the rotation of its axis closer or farther from the Sun. "There are other theories of climate change," Gail noted, dismissively raising an eyebrow.[22] For her, this was not the place to throw the autonomy of geological process into question by discussing anthropogenic climate, although the petroleum patch could be an ideal site in which to raise such environmental concerns. Geological time, as a concept, has long been the natural history museum's ally, granting these museums what William Pannapacker celebrates as the aura of "things that are real."[23] Andrea Witcomb writes more cynically of the ways in which concepts such as aura and authenticity derive from "a museological practice which emphasized the importance of classification systems and taxonomies which attributed meaning to the object according to its physical characteristics." The nineteenth-century natural history museum's taxonomic systems claimed to express an immanent divine order, and they supported "a narrative of Western society as the pinnacle of civilization."[24] Through the 1960s, natural history museums offered an image of time's passage segregated from social turbulence.

But when, among nature's things, a natural history exhibit displays asphaltum, a form of crude oil that is a product of the Miocene seas that once covered the Los Angeles basin, a question arises for me: *Are some things that are real more real than other things that are real?* My point is auratic, rather than biological or ontic. By "aura" I mean the feeling and ambience of authenticity, which, as Walter Benjamin taught us, cannot exist without the mechanical means of destroying "aura" by separating objects from their images in media such as photography. At Rancho La Brea, the tar pits are in situ ecological features and therefore unlike the displaced natural objects typically associated with museums and laboratories, to which museums often have been compared. Although one can photograph the tar pits, their low visual readability makes for bad images, and they work best as multisensory media. They generate a physical ambience through the olfactory dimension of odor—specifically, the smell of hydrogen sulfide, which, along with the odorless methane gas that bubbles to the surface of the pits, betrays the formation of crude. Of course, too, they are viscous, and their stickiness offers a kind of bad patina, literally tracking their use over time by human excavators and unlucky animals.

Yet the tar pits extend into their geographic frame in a way that troubles their status as "real things." One only has to venture to the edge of Hancock Park to recognize their entanglement in a complex social history. The La Brea exhibit depends upon the high real estate values of the surrounding neighborhood of Hancock Park, which made possible the preservation of this portion of the Salt Lake Oil Field from intensive drilling. Hancock Park, in turn, both derives value from and confers value upon Wilshire Boulevard, the historical shopping district that is known as Los Angeles's Miracle Mile. It was on the Miracle Mile that the parking lot was essentially invented, as planners in the 1920s recognized the convenience of auto parking behind department stores in a city already poised to enable the individualized mobility of the car. Asphalt, which used to be made from asphaltum (and is now made directly from petroleum), paves "the mile" and the parking lots behind it. In the late 1960s, the parking lots of Los Angeles demonstrated the end of art and other *real things* in a series of aerial photographs that Ed Ruscha commissioned from a commercial photographer. Without a connection to the artist's own hand or to the promise of self-transformation evident in aesthetic categories such as the beautiful, Ruscha's *Thirtyfour Parking Lots* (1967) humorously enshrined the most ubiquitous indication of capital's homogenization of place. An art book of parking lots, photographed by someone other than the artist, empties the "art" concept, the "exhibit" or museum concept of the art book, and the idea of sacred space. Thinking about the parking lot as itself a kind of museum of modernity makes the conceit of the museum at La Brea, the asphaltum preserve, seem precious if not duplicitous. Does petroleum *ever* remain in situ, and what might be the ideological effect of showing it that way?

The original plan for "Pleistocene Park," an earlier incarnation of the La Brea outdoor museum, offered a clear alternative to car culture. It called for the screening of automotive traffic by landscape features and a single footbridge entrance to guard against auto touring.[25] Hailing from the 1920s, the "Pleistocene Park" concept marks the same decade that a *Los Angeles Times* editorial noted that all horses in Los Angeles "belonged in the tar pits" because this would be the automobile city. It was thought that climate itself dictated that cars should dominate southern California, since horses were still recognized as more capable of negotiating the ice and snow of eastern winters.[26] In 1919, the first gas station in Los Angeles, run by the Gilmore family, opened near the current site of the Page museum. Now the Gilmores are known for *The Gilmore Collection*, photographs of early fossil excavations on the La Brea ranch that their descendants donated to the museum. At the intersection of modern media (automobiles, photographs) and the Pleistocene (via the Miocene), the La Brea petrol preserve manages to ally itself to both media time and geological time. Both are arguably forms of deep time, insofar as both involve a temporality irrelevant to the work of human memory. William L. Fox has written a fine essay about what the La Brea tar pits and a horror movie featuring them, *The Volcano* (1997), tell us of the human sense of time, the way in which time has been "speeded up" by film narratives to the extent that longer-duration problems, such as oil scarcity and the increasingly devastating methods of oil mining, are not only imperceptible but indifferent to us.[27]

I admire Fox's essay, and I would add to its treatment of time the suggestion that geological and media time both offer styles of temporal imagining that enable the making of petroleum as a spectacle and, therefore, as a commodity.

The Museum of La Brea Discoveries allows us to conceive of fossil fuel as fossil and fuel, and predominantly as fossil. We learn at the museum that what might have been an oil field became a paleontological site. Fossils and fuel are distinct forms of commodity whose value relies, in both cases, upon the occlusion of specific historical relationships—social and ecological histories—that confer value. The fossil is the unique object separated by museum display from other cultural meanings, while fuel offers an abstraction of matter, a dream of disembodied energy.[28] The dramatization of "fossil, fuel" at Rancho La Brea shows us how commodity values rely upon the segregation of the natural from history. In contrast, a natural history concept that places nature and history in dialogue has the potential to generate ecological action, as the methods of systematic biology now intervene in global habitat and species loss.

ECOLOGICAL DESIGNS

The making of the La Brea tar pits from a loosely defined exhibit into a museum coincides with the introduction of ecology into the design of the natural history museum in the 1960s. In New York City, the American Museum of Natural History's two-year exhibit *Can Man Survive?* opened in April 1969, marking a sea change in both the themes and presentation of natural history. The exhibit explored many of the ecological issues haunting North Americans at the time, including overpopulation and industrial pollution. *Can Man Survive?* employed cutting-edge mixed media, Alison Griffiths notes, offering an "immersive informational and experiential architecture" that turned visitors from mere viewers into active and uncomfortable participants.[29] Visitors walked through various stages of the show to be confronted by looping films of river pollution, bacteria, and other blight, without recourse other than to move deeper into the museum space. This premier exhibit on world ecological damage called for a total virtual environment in order to deliver its message, which—as the exhibit's title indicates—was that humanity was destroying itself.

Such doomsday ecological thinking, together with an amped-up commitment to making natural history into "hypermediated" space, introduces the moment when Pit 91 was reopened for excavation in 1969 at Rancho La Brea. It had been fifty-four years since the last major excavations at the site, and the events of 1969 signaled a civic commitment to reimaging the tar pits as a place of scientific inquiry. The reopening was coordinated by paleontologist George Miller, who shepherded a small army of volunteer excavators in what was billed by journalists as a quest for the origins of humankind in the Western hemisphere. Miller's team found evidence of human presence in California approximately 15,000 years ago. Humanity showed up as trace, through decorative cuts made by tools on the leg bones of saber-tooth cats. Perhaps in celebration of this discovery, in 1973 Governor Ronald Reagan would name the saber-tooth cat as California's state fossil. Volunteers came together from all over Los Angeles to search for the origins of human culture in their own city. The "dig-in," as it was called, expressed civic pride and the flamboyant humanism of the late 1960s, mixed up with the hermeneutics of suspicion that also characterized the Vietnam War era.

In a letter to the *Los Angeles Times* of May 1970, a self-described "concerned citizen," Max Poschin, counts himself among the more than one hundred volunteers "privileged to have the opportunity of helping uncover paleontological treasures from the Ice Age" at Rancho La Brea. But Poschin's note of gratitude sounds a shrill concern: "What has happened to our priorities? ... We have billions to prosecute an illegal war in Asia or to send men on perilous missions to the moon, but not even a tiny fraction of that amount to extend the knowledge of man here on earth."[30] Poschin explicitly condemns the lack of funding for public science, and he suggests more broadly that his participation in the search for human origins at the "dig-in" has not led him to imagine a long human future. Similar predictions that greater scientific knowledge of humanity would only reveal our near extinction appeared in U.S. popular culture in this period, blatantly in Paul Ehrlich's *The Population Bomb* (1968) and glancingly in popular fictions such as Franklin J. Schaffner's film *The Planet of the Apes* (1968). The *Planet of the Apes* series offers a wry commentary on the natural history endeavor. Like the American Museum of Natural History exhibit *Can Man Survive?* the first *Planet of the Apes* film places human social history at the center of the problem of natural history, turning the tables on our curatorial ambitions by depicting the study and museum display of human subjects at a sophisticated research center overseen by orangutans. The fear that inspires the American Museum of Natural History exhibit and the contemporary film, as well as Poschin's letter, is that humanity has written itself out of ecological relations, following the technologies of war into an inarticulate end-time. If we are lucky, evolved orangutans might someday tell the story of how we overstepped ourselves with weapons such as the hydrogen bomb. This moment of intense anxiety about human endurance on the planet generated some innovative attempts to remake the practice of natural history in such a way as to decenter Western cultures and human subjects.

More than 750,000 species, including many micro-fossils, were uncovered at Rancho La Brea on Miller's watch, testimony to his dedication in avoiding what he called the "stamp-collecting" of large mammal specimens that characterized the earlier twentieth-century excavations.[31] Following on the heels of the 1890s "dinomania," which was characterized by the investment of philanthropists like Andrew Carnegie in massive *sauropod* dinosaur skeletons for display in urban museums, early La Brea excavators focused on large Pleistocene specimens, namely Columbian mammoths, ground sloths, American bison, saber-tooth cats, and American camels.[32] In contrast, Miller foregrounded the value of the asphaltum matrix that encased these trophy specimens, as it was the matrix that was the key to Pleistocene climate. The matrix offered plant micro-fossils. This was, again, the age of ecology, and Miller's volunteers were made aware that even tiny specimens might be relevant to the human story. Sadly, the Pit 91 project was facing bankruptcy by 1970, a problem later blamed on Miller's ambitious attempt to reconstruct a complete Pleistocene environment. When Miller was fired by the Natural History Museum of Los Angeles in 1972, the museum's director, Dr. Mead, stressed the importance of generating "more scientific information at less cost," an objective vaguely related to his corollary plan of making the tar pits into a "museum-like display."[33] The dual commitment of public science to education and research evident in this conflict is not unique to the Natural History Museum of Los Angeles. The fine-tuned, relational thinking that Miller introduced to his field workers in the 1960s had little precedent in the history of designs intended for the La Brea site.

Let's consider, briefly, the various iterations of "museum" that have been imagined at Rancho La Brea since the early twentieth century, in order to return to the current museum via ecological thought. For most of its history, the La Brea site was unmoored from ecological concerns, hitched instead to the theatrical problem of presenting the tar pits as a "wonder of the world." This was an effortful project, given that the pits essentially smelled and looked like mines to Angelenos accustomed to oil leaks and derricks in their neighborhoods. The famous "Lake Pit" where the museum's fiberglass mammoth now cries to her distraught baby became so deep and large because it had been a regular asphaltum mine, used for caulking, waterproofing, and fuel from at least the eighteenth century. The open pit mine was filled with water in the early twentieth century in order to offer a natural history feature to visitors of Hancock Park. This early act of outdoor scenography already implies a contest of meanings for what counts as natural history. The real ecological relations of locals to the asphaltum sumps, the use of these resources, could not be shown as "natural" in the sense that Pleistocene mammals could. The fiberglass animals now present in the park are products of a similar effort to make nature available to the senses not through its local uses—or even through the motile presence of the asphaltum itself—but through the representation of ancient mammals. The animal statuary suggests the conventional pleasures of natural history, referring to the more showy vertebrate fossils found in the pits. In contrast to the staining tar, the "animals" also create user-friendly interactive surfaces for parkgoers to touch, sit on, lunch beside, and photograph.

One of the most ambitious designs for the La Brea museum and park, and the design in which animal statuary figures most dramatically, is a Works Progress Administration (WPA) project referred to as the "Garden of the Giants." Howard Kegley wrote about it for the Los Angeles Times in 1940. "This stupendous undertaking, as a circus press agent might express it, will be super-colossal. In real fact it should out-Barnum old Barnum himself, for it will bring into permanent existence here, within a stone's throw of the world-famous Miracle Mile...a monumental memorial in masonry to a gosh-awful galaxy of prehistoric animals and birds."[34] These "permanent animals," crafted "in enduring rock," would ground an immersive, virtual landscape, through which "visitors, traversing the jungle-flanked paths, would unexpectedly come upon sculptured groups."[35] Fifteen years before the opening of Disneyland, the tar pits were conceived as a natural history theme park. Although WPA project planners stressed the "educational value such a monumental menagerie might possess," the project goal was sensational, making the effect of time and space travel that has been associated with museums into pure entertainment. Coming from the shops on Wilshire Boulevard into this spectacular park, visitors would experience a near-absolute departure from Los Angeles proper. They would wander into an "extinct" space-time. The petrol pits themselves have almost no meaning—social, sensory, or scientific—in this preserve of giant mammals. They are merely low-lying indices of an exotic *other* life, discontinuous with the Miracle Mile and modern humans.

The WPA ultimately did not approve the midcentury Garden of the Giants sculptural project because of the high cost of building over the active geology of Hancock Park. Gases arising from the pits were recognized as a perpetual fire hazard. Such perpetual fire suggests enduring life in a manner quite different from sculptural animals. The effort to express geological agency through sculptures of extinct mammals betrays a lack of imagination about where petroleum might fit within the natural history concept. It also suggests a human wish to make animals, and by extension ourselves, permanent—a task that mid-twentieth-century Americans liked to imagine might be feasible, given the right technology. Fiberglass, the material used to craft the latest set of Pleistocene mammals in Hancock Park, represents a chemical bid for endurance that, like many developed during World War II, utilizes petroleum-based plastics. The wish to be "forever animal" gets monumentalized, in oil.

For ordinary Angelenos, the La Brea tar pits have been close collaborators in human histories in a manner that park and museum designers tend to overlook. Vernacular use of the pits betrays long-standing appreciation for asphaltum as both a practical and an expressive material. While everyday use of the sumps for chores such as caulking faded with the dedication of Hancock Park as a scientific preserve in the early twentieth century, locals continued to interact with the tar pits in ways that exceed the directed goals of education or staged entertainment. The relationship between the people and their "tar" was intimate and sociable, if not ecological per se. For locals, the pits were matter that could convey messages, media in the most basic sense. Los Angeles newspapers brim with cases of individuals using the tar pits to make statements or to preserve strong feelings, presumably forever.

One celebrated case involved Mary Alice Bernard, daughter of the county livestock inspector and a "society" girl in the small-town Los Angeles of 1935.

Newspapers report that Mary Alice suffered from "amnesia" and from "a nervous breakdown."[36] For months during her nineteenth year, she went missing. The Los Angeles County Sheriff's Department searched the tar pits for Mary Alice's body, using a special apparatus to heat the contents of the pools so that heavy asphalt could be pumped out, and employing grappling hooks to drag the depths. The county was literally mining for Mary Alice. The cost of this was considerable, news coverage sensational. The drama had begun when Mary Alice's mother remembered the young woman's parting hint: "Someday you will find me in the bottom of the La Brea pits." In fact, Mary Alice turned up several months later in Los Angeles, having gone to San Francisco to take a job as a domestic. The tar pits search closed, with newspaper photographs of sheriff's deputies bending over draglines. This young woman's flight from her family and her class did not grant her the permanence, as a local heroine, that she might have achieved had she really jumped into the pits. Countless others seized upon the tar pits as means of indelible self-expression. Three years after Mary Alice's vanishing, a man billed as the "Tar Pits Suicide Hoaxer" was jailed for making a false report of his own suicide in the tar pits in an embittered note to his ex-girlfriend.[37]

The tar pits present a handy means of preserving bad affects. They have served as local channels that broadcast sensory cues, such as smell, viscosity, and visual obscurity, which intimate human vulnerability. The story of the 10,000-year-old "La Brea Woman" found in the pits mimics the noir-ish dramas of the twentieth century tar pits insofar as paleontologists continue to speculate on whether this woman was murdered due to her insanity—her skeleton suggests a sinus infection serious enough to affect brain function. Regardless of the validity of these speculations, the tar pits generate a good deal of thinking about what aspects of the mammalian body might be preserved, from its bones to its somatized feelings. In popular use, they suggest a rather dark ecology. They have served as sites for speculation about what might be done with human mortality, how the fragility of our own bodies might be used to make larger stories about humanity's relationship to itself, to geological time, and to other life.

When the Page Museum was built in the 1970s, its design expressed a brighter ecological mission. George C. Page, a former fruit-packing entrepreneur who recognized the La Brea tar pits as evidence of Los Angeles's singular heritage, commissioned an architectural design for the museum that preserved its historical status as an outdoor park. Rising like an indigenous burial mound from exhibit rooms built largely below ground level, the museum's external walls are covered with grass, making for sloping hills that visitors can sit and play on. Page responded to the "green" parks initiative that was popular in the Los Angeles of the 1970s. Too, his designers recognized that the asphaltum itself should be treated as a main event, signaling not only the original storehouse of the museum's fossils but also Los Angeles's natural wealth as an oil town. The Page has been intended as an indoor-outdoor museum that combines some of the social ideals of the ecomuseum with the spectacular pleasures of earlier museum concepts, such as the erstwhile Garden of the Giants. The museum's mission speaks well to the twin ideals of ecology and entertainment that marked the moment of its completion. In the twilight of the fossil fuel regime and the shadow of climate change, it simply needs to reanimate its vision.

TOWARD THE POST-OIL MUSEUM

A tour of the Page today makes clear that "life in asphalt" is no longer about ancient mammals, not really. The slick, black drums stacked up around Project 23 (a recent dig opened as a result of the neighboring Los Angeles County Museum of Art's proposed expansion into fossiliferous ground) look like miniature oil drums, which essentially they are. "Is that the matrix?" one of my fellow visitors asked, a rising note of expectation in his voice. The blocks of shiny drums, and perhaps the popular film of the same name, grant this once obscure product of the pits an almost glamorous persona. Matrix was defended as a key to ecological knowledge of the Los Angeles basin by Miller back in the 1960s, but forty years after Earth Day it has taken on new significance as a source of living microorganisms with potential "applications" for biotech, particularly biofuels, enhanced oil recovery, and bioremediation of oil spills. The U.S. Department of Agriculture and the Environmental Protection Agency provided funding for a recent study of the living bacteria in the La Brea matrix, conducted by environmental scientists at the University of California, Riverside. "We were surprised to find these bacteria because asphalt is an extreme and hostile environment for life to survive," reports Jong-Shik Kim, a postdoctoral researcher. "It's clear, however, that these living organisms can survive in heavy oil mixtures containing many highly toxic chemicals."[38] Entirely new branches on the so-called tree of life have been opened by the more than two hundred species of microorganism that Kim and his fellow scientists discovered. While the specific applications of this new life drive the research, the project produces a broad rhetoric of hope that life itself will persist through the most toxic scenarios of "hydrocarbon contamination and radioactive environments."[39] La Brea's living bacteria, progeny of soil microorganisms trapped in the petrol sumps tens of thousands of years ago, are *prepared*—for a worst-case anthropogenic climate, for the end of conventional oil, even for the bomb. The conceptual "application" for La Brea's new petroleum species is, simply, the future.

For museumgoers who witness this microscale bid for a future natural history—and it is possible to miss it, to walk right past Project 23, for instance—there will be questions, at least implicit ones, about how such a downsized future might accommodate the natural history museum. Microscale natural history unfolds in the privatized space of research laboratories and requires more explicit context than even the old-fashioned cabinet-and-text–based natural history museums provide. Then again, Steven Conn suggests that natural history museums survived a similar crisis of representation as early as the 1860s, when Darwinian theory shifted biological research "from science that could be conducted with the naked eye toward science that needed a microscope."[40] The Page gestures toward an exhibit of the potentially human-life-saving bacteria in the tar pits, illustrating how the bacteria were discovered and what the discovery might mean for the long future. This display looks a bit like a drawing table and sits awkwardly against a wall, in the shadow of the fishbowl laboratory, the museum's public exhibit of paleontologists scraping and cleaning the recognizable bones (helpfully labeled "Zed's pelvis" and so on) of La Brea mammals. "What Does Bacteria Look Like?" asks a cartoonish laminated booklet. Potato-shaped figures of "bacteria" meant to enliven the laminated pages give us an easy answer: Bacteria doesn't look like much, please imagine. While imagination and daydreaming can be more valuable modes of interactivity in museums than playing with high-tech displays, this exhibit fails to evoke dreams. Bioartists and bioarchitects have proven that microscale life can look like something beautiful, often through computer simulation and digital media.[41] It would be fabulous to see microorganismic life in oil, perhaps on-screen, that rivals the beauty of the Pleistocene fossil. Perhaps the scarce funding that besets most natural history museums today, plus a traditional commitment to the sensual vertebrate skeleton, keeps a remarkably exciting aspect of the Page Museum—entirely new "branches of life" growing up in local petroleum—confined to marginal display.

The life forms that petroleum generates tell us something about how to live through oil scarcity and into an energy shift, about how to clean up our toxic spills, about living through the destruction that has complemented human creativity. The Page Museum could be a premier site of thinking through the limitations of petroleum culture with the North American public and the science community. Rancho La Brea has long been a "post-oil" museum insofar as it has considered its asphaltum as matter in excess of the transformative energy idea. Since its preservation as a public park, the La Brea site has challenged the meanings of oil and demonstrated how not to get stuck in any single logic of its value—consider, again, that the oil business that might have developed on the museum site was given over to "science" back in 1915, under the assumption that it was more profitable, here, to mine fossils than fuel. The museum might reconsider its framing narrative. Through the microorganismic life in the tar pits, the Page could rethink the definition of natural history or even life itself along the lines that the philosopher Bruno Latour has considered in his discussions of the agency of things, both "real" and fabricated, in the ongoing story of ecology.[42] Petroleum has bumped up against various forms of life at this site for millennia, generating death and treasure and a unique means of storing life's forms and the birth of new living species. The museum's most recent, Telly-award–winning film, *Ice Age Fossils of the La Brea Tar Pits* (2004), begins to consider the multiple vectors of ecological action and power by making a vial of petroleum its star.

Immediately outside the "Behind the Scenes" theater where the film *Ice Age Fossils* is shown, a weather-worn animatronic sloth creakily ducks up and down, attempting to free itself from an equally down-at-the-heels animatronic saber-tooth cat. These are not the new audio-animatronics of Disneyland, where a 2003 "Living Character Initiative" inspired engineers to create figures so lifelike that their speech appears spontaneous and they move autonomously through unregulated space.[43] At the Page, visitors press a red button to hear the ground sloth's simulated screams. Last summer, the fiberglass imperial mammoth sinking into the Lake Pit slipped off of her cement base, floating to the far end of the lake, where she appeared to be summoning her "husband" and "child" to a frolicsome swim. The Page Museum seems on its way to becoming a museum of obsolescent infrastructure, following its Pleistocene mammals into the tar. The asphaltum, for its part, entertains the saviors of a new geologic epoch, the Anthropocene, in which the Earth that humans damaged through our profligate use of fossil fuels just might be saved by microorganisms grown up in petroleum sludge. These organisms can survive and digest our spills, our toxicity. When petroleum becomes more important as habitat than as energy to simulate habitat, or preservative for our bones, then a new natural history concept is required. This one can't be scaled to children or even humans, perhaps, but it can offer us the opportunity to reimagine life without ourselves at the center, which is a conceptual starting point for any sustainable design.

II. Alberta

On descending from Air Canada's Jazz small-plane service into Fort McMurray, northern Alberta, the museum experience earnestly begins. Lit screens announcing "Fort McMurray: More Than *You* Know" aggressively indicate the visitor's ignorance and then relieve it with comforting facts, such as "There's a quality of life up here that gives people the *confidence* to raise a family." At the edge of the airport's single, tiny baggage conveyor, a flat-screen monitor showcases images of mine workers and the sublimely massive trucks and shovels used for bitumen extraction. "A Career You Can Dig," announces a brightly lit sign—picturing a digger—above the gate for arrivals. For a tiny airport, the scale of the signage is impressive. Fort McMurray hosts an award-winning oil museum, the Oil Sands Discovery Centre, which will be discussed in some detail below. While this and the town's Heritage Park—which boasts "a past as rich as the Oilsands"—are official museum sites, the town itself offers a deliberate assemblage of objects and screens meant to hail visitors and to generate an authentic civic experience. Perhaps the same could be said of any town, particularly any tourist destination. But Fort McMurray is a destination for global capital and labor, not for tourists. Called a "frontier carbon society" by its detractors, Fort McMurray sits amid North America's largest bitumen deposit. A mixture of water, sand, and petroleum, bitumen has been seized upon since as early as the 1890s as an oil resource. More intensive and rapid development of this deposit began in northern Alberta in the 1990s, due primarily to concerns in the United States about the scarcity and political volatility of global oil. Andrew Nikiforuk, an astute Canadian critic of Alberta tar sands development, recognizes the venture primarily as a means of serving "the empire," meaning the United States, and as an instance of Canadian self-deception in regard to sovereignty. "Canada now calls itself an 'emerging energy superpower," Nikiforuk writes. "It is nothing more than a Third World energy supermarket."[44] Try telling that to Alberta's boomers. My own small comment to a customs officer on exiting Calgary that "it seems hard to see how this will work, in the long term," produced an exuberant, "It's working. They're bussing hundreds up there every day, I see it!"

Seeing the future, here, has become a regional art form, one that Alberta exports along with bitumen-derived crude for refining, in neighboring Ontario and abroad. Since the 1970s, Fort McMurray's population has nearly quadrupled. In its hurry to build roads and accommodate new housing developments, the town has racked up an infrastructure debt topping a billion dollars.[45] It also has become a hub for crack cocaine dealers and prostitution, as it imports thousands of temporary miners who serve long hours in work camps with pastoral names like "Borealis." Natural gas and shale oil boomtowns in the United States are experiencing similar "boomtown blues"— a diagnosis coined by Alexandra Fuller, who writes about Sublette County, Wyoming, which is a major natural gas producer. In terms similar to sociological studies of Nigeria and other petrostates in the developing world, Fuller sees Wyoming as "a 'carbonocracy' indebted to minerals for its promise of an easy life, yet strangely impoverished by its own wealth."[46] Studies of Marcellus shale boomtowns in the northeastern United States reflect similar patterns of deforestation, air pollution, housing crises, and a decline in social services as populations swell beyond carrying capacities.[47] The term "Gillette Syndrome," coined by the psychologist Eldean Kohrs in the 1970s to describe cultural decline in the coal boomtown of Gillette, Wyoming, has been reanimated by Nikiforuk, Fuller, and others to describe conditions on the Tough Oil frontier. In western North Dakota today, residents of the newly exploited Bakken shale formation have an especially peculiar problem. Urine-filled soda bottles they call "trucker bombs" are multiplying along local highways, symptoms of the scarcity of public rest areas in this once isolated region of the Great Plains.[48] The bottles can explode in heat and pose an actual danger to locals. Poised to become pop culture icons, "trucker bombs" are an absurdist index of the lax federal regulations that have opened U.S. oil sands and shales to aggressive fracking and mining.

Fort McMurray is not unique among Tough Oil boomtowns, although of course every boomtown originates in a history with specific local and international resonance. Oil sands workers here come from the Canadian Maritimes and other depressed regions, including Mexico, Croatia, and China. "In Canada we can see the future," a visitor from near Shanghai told a fellow tourist and me at Fort McMurray's Heritage Park, as he snapped a photograph of a former commissary called the "Nistawoyou Friendship Center." In the old commissary, life-size cutouts of Cree traders stand awkwardly among hanging pelts. The visitor from Shanghai continued, putting a finer point on his observation: "In China we can't see the future, we just know it's coming." Of course the future that we can see in Alberta or elsewhere might be just another image of the past, given that the future is by definition what cannot be seen. Heritage Park evokes such philosophy, giving visitors a glimpse of the oil, uranium, and fur trading histories of Canada's north, which suggest a pattern of heavy resource extraction leading into the tar.

What is euphemistically dubbed the boom of "unconventional" oil here replicates the coming of the Canol pipeline from Alaska through this region during World War II—a huge job-creating venture for Canada in the service of U.S. interests. "The Radium Scout," a doughty little train on view in Heritage Park, refers back to mid-twentieth-century uranium mining and forward toward what may be Canada's "nuclear spring," if nuclear power is judged the cleanest way to fuel the energy-intensive process of bitumen extraction. Heritage Park, conceived in the 1960s, contains seventeen historic buildings that tell of the multiethnic, international, and fundamentally extractive character of Fort McMurray prior to the construction of the Suncor Corporation's Millennium plant in 1967, which marks the beginning of the contemporary tar sands era. The fur trade, with its British administrators, French voyageurs, and indigenous (later Métis) labor force, creates a plausible historic analog for Alberta's current oil business, helping along the "heritage" project, whose major thrust is to illustrate how the present evolves organically from the past, without irreversible shifts or damage. Historian Mike Wallace notes that heritage museums in the United States began in the mid-twentieth century as a means of naturalizing corporate power, with Henry Ford's Greenfield Village (1929) and John D. Rockefeller's colonial Williamsburg (1928) developing in the shadow of peak oil discovery in California, Oklahoma, and Texas. These early heritage museums "distorted the past, mystified the way the present had emerged, and thus helped inhibit effective political action."[49] For me, the oddity of Fort McMurray's Heritage Park inheres in the relative newness of its buildings, several of which were either built in the late twentieth century or operated into the early twenty-first century, such as the "Ice Cream Shack," which "up until 2007 housed an ice cream business in Fort McMurray." The shift of an older downtown into Heritage Park reflects both the time frame of the heritage idea here (the 1960s and 1970s) and a more recent set of jolting displacements. Heritage Park strains to make "a past as rich as the Oilsands" visible to a boomtown where the future threatens to become an isolated, antisocial value.

Both the man from Shanghai and his interlocutor, a Canadian construction worker, agreed that the U.S. loss of manufacturing jobs over the past forty years had weakened it irreparably. "One thing's certain," said the Canadian. "The future's not in the States." Then we all trailed into a historic drugstore, to snap photographs of a lonely mannequin dressed like the town druggist circa 1940, posed in front of a cabinet filled with the erstwhile products of Canadian regional economies, such as Pony Brand marshmallow candy. The exhibit's aura of authenticity had everything to do with the eclipse of those twentieth-century regional economies, mostly by U.S.-based corporate entities like Walmart. A Canadian witnessing this heritage of U.S. economic imperialism understandably might desire a future recentered here. A recent issue of the Alberta industry journal *Oilsands Review* promotes loosening immigration restrictions on U.S. workers,[50] noting that the need for skilled labor in the oil sands might be satisfied by the United States, "where a persistently weak housing and commercial construction market and a high unemployment rate make that country a prime target."[51] The industry journal bursts with excitement about how the United States could be annexed to Canada's "story." John Davies, described as "an American leader in public persuasion," counsels Canadians that the "environmental *industry*" in the United States [emphasis mine] "figure[s] that they really need to impugn the character of almost an entire nation"—meaning Canada—in order to protest the Keystone XL pipeline. To ease alleged U.S. hostility, "You've got to tell your story, and you've got to tell it very carefully and well," Davies continues, concluding that "the beauty is that the Internet has come out and everything is transparent and everyone can reach everything."[52] As Nikiforuk reports, the Internet's beauty as a tool of inter-American persuasion was lost on Syncrude, the largest corporate developer of the oil sands, when a West Virginia grandmother named Elizabeth Moore posted images of her tour of a Syncrude plant on the Web.[53]

Moore's site is still online, with red and yellow "censored" signs in the place of images that she was forced to remove by Syncrude, Suncor, and the Oil Sands Discovery Centre museum. Ingeniously, the site makes censorship into an interactive exhibit. Click on a red icon and learn who suppressed which image, and exactly what the suppressed image looked like. The benign character of many of Moore's censored images, not to mention the availability of similar pictures online, make clear that in the oil sands the fear of being seen overshadows optimism about being able to see the future. Even a simple photograph of someone holding bitumen in his hand—an image also available to tourists on the cover of Suncor's "Experience the Energy!" tour brochure—was banned from Internet reproduction. Bitumen sitting in a masculine hand looks like a greasy solid, like tar rather than oil. "It ain't oil," Nikiforuk blasts, echoing other critics of the quality of the resource.[54] Oil sands promoters recognize the power of visual culture.

My own travel to Fort McMurray included rigorous questioning by customs officers in Calgary, where I changed planes, and polite questioning by hotel, museum, and tour providers about why I thought I had to see the tar sands. The fact that I traveled alone—and from southern California—made me seem odd. While I was in Alberta, Bill McKibben and more than a thousand others were being arrested for protesting Keystone XL in Washington, D.C. Upon learning where I came from, one Edmonton woman volunteered that, for environmental blight, southern California compared unfavorably to Fort McMurray. This was one of the most astute observations on offer from a fellow tourist, echoing my own feeling that, as a resident of one of the most auto-dependent regions on earth, I had a special connection to Alberta. Those of us who had come north to see the tar sands, the Oil Sands Discovery Centre, and the Energy Tour, which is sponsored by Suncor, were on a similar pilgrimage. We came to contemplate oil, the future, and our complicity in it. The woman who knew about southern California's environmental history told me that her grandfather had invented one of the original "separators" to segregate petroleum from bitumen. She wanted to see Suncor's Millennium plant, the original model for the bitumen mining and processing operations that now thrive around Fort McMurray. For three and a half hours, we shared a seat on the Energy Tour bus. Many of our fellow tourists worked for Suncor, Syncrude, and Shell Oil. My reasons for being on the bus were as personal as theirs. I wanted to see where the United States might be getting 60 percent or more of its petroleum for the next half century, what the boreal forest looked like in the throes of intensive mining, and what kind of culture is growing up around North America's largest oil patch. Each of these questions pertains to what we in the United States imagine (and demand) as a North American future.

PETROLEUM SCREENS

What I discovered at Fort McMurray was a hypermediated experience unlike any I've known, insofar as this is not a place known for spectacles and screens, like Las Vegas, Disneyland, or the famous West Edmonton Mall with its diverse, simulated environments. When I call my experience of Fort McMurray a hypermediated one, I refer primarily to the high density of metaphor in the place, the constant slippage of verbal images away from conventional referents toward new, sometimes unfinished, concepts. Take the word "oil sands," for example. This is industry's term for bitumen, heavy oil trapped in a complex molecule of water and sand that appears to the naked eye as a solid, far removed from the thin, clear substances recognizable to North Americans as fuel. At the Oil Sands Discovery Centre, visitors are allowed to stir bitumen—or attempt to—and to smell it, as we watch it made into slurry by adding water. This process feels homey, somewhat like a chemistry experiment, as it is performed by a young woman in the museum's small theater. On the walls of the theater hang what appear to be handmade quilts picturing moments of industrial process, including the unlikely visual subject for a quilt of "SAG-D," an energy-intensive method of heating underground bitumen deposits with pressurized steam. The quilt picturing SAG-D says simply, "Future." Ultimately, each barrel of bitumen produced as oil requires the consumption of three barrels of water from the Athabasca River, which is part of the Mackenzie watershed—the world's third-largest watershed and a system that flows north, into the Arctic ocean. It takes between 750 and 1,500 cubic feet of natural gas—"enough to heat a house for up to a week in winter," according to historian David Finch—to heat the water used to separate the oil in bitumen from sand. Another 750–1500 cubic feet is needed to upgrade bitumen "oil" into fuel oil.[55] The intensive processing required to make fuel out of bitumen sands belies the happy nomenclature "oil sands," in other words. "Tar sands," the opposition's term, carries more descriptive accuracy.

While this rhetorical conflict names the crux of the ideological battle for Alberta's oil development—in brief, is this a resource worth intensive capitalization?—it is only one of many similar, ongoing struggles for metaphorical dominance. The guide on Suncor's Energy Tour offered a remarkable, richly metaphoric evocation of the reclamation of tailings ponds, which are both elevated and sunken pools that hold the toxic water left over after bitumen extraction. Positioned alongside the Athabasca River, seeping into groundwater, and large enough to be visible from space, the tailings ponds are the gravest embarrassment of the oil sands industry. The companies direct their strongest rhetorical efforts toward the ponds. Although no reclamation project has yet to be certified by the Canadian government, and in fact scientists disagree about whether or not the boreal wetlands that are destroyed by bitumen mining can ever be restored, nonetheless Suncor offers tourists a model "reclaimed" tailings pond. Nikiforuk has argued that the oil companies' ideas of reclamation tend toward the mechanical rather than the biological, as if ecologies are Rubik's cubes whose components can be clicked in and out of place until a just balance is achieved.[56] The signage at Suncor's reclaimed pond tells us: "When it comes to tailings ponds, *making ground* can be groundbreaking. Suncor is the first Alberta oil sands company to have created a 'trafficable' surface in a tailings pond—solid enough to be revegetated." We were encouraged to walk on the former pond to feel the relative density of its surface.

The reclamation site bears the allusive name of Wapisiw, "after the first aboriginal man to bring oil to the first white man," according to our guide. The Wapisiw meadow at the Millennium plant sprouts barley, which has been found to grow well on reclamation sites. Yet Suncor's story proves more vigorous than its light green meadow. After explaining how the corporation "stockpiles" muskeg, the peaty substance that typically overlays bitumen deposits, for reclamation, our guide offered us a parable about tar sands mining and reclamation efforts. "We remove everything, clean up the oil spill which Nature left us, and put everything back." This equation of intensive mining with cleaning "nature's mess" was offered without irony.[57] In fact, the Suncor tour seems to be about learning not just a story, but a language without irony or even inflection. Keeping language fastened tight to referents gets tricky, of course, when your language is so richly imagistic. Should we wish to explain the tailings ponds to "a person who doesn't know much about the oil sands," we are welcome, said our guide, "to use our coffee analogy." Here's the Suncor coffee analogy: The tailings—which contain carcinogenic pollutants including PAHs (polycyclic aromatic hydrocarbons) and naphthenic acids—are "coffee grounds" left over from the process of making bitumen into oil. Later, we were asked to think of the process of drying tailings, by spinning them to remove water so that they can be "stacked," "like a farming operation." Farming PAHs? Our guide assured us that these analogies made difficult engineering processes comprehensible to nonspecialists and urged us, again, to spread her metaphors to the uninformed: "Please, use our coffee analogy."

Back at the Oil Sands Discovery Centre, a video shows the museum's virtual guide, "Professor Nositall," slurrying bitumen with water in his home kitchen. The metaphorical echoes of the "coffee analogy" and other labored tropes from the bus tour spread out through the museum and even into Fort McMurray proper. When I was questioned by customs in Calgary, what finally dispelled concern about my visit was my job, which signaled harmlessness. "English professor?" sniffed the customs officer, adjusting his frames. "Well...I guess we need those." To sort out the metaphorical blitz up north, indeed. A series of turning placards in the playroom of the Oil Sands Discovery Centre performs a radical metaphoricity that must confound Alberta's children. Under the heading "Resource," one placard asks, "Oil sand is like the filling in a sandwich. True or false?" Turn the card to find the answer, "True. The top slice is overburden, oil sand is the gooey filling, and the bottom slice is limestone. Yummy!" I might question the utility of this lesson, but it reinforces the metaphorical concept of "overburden," the industry's trope for the topsoil, plant life, and muskeg (in other words, the biodiverse habitat) it removes in order to get to the sands. Given that it takes the excavation of two tons of earth to make one barrel of bitumen, turning earth into metaphor marks a fundamental, necessary shift of referential ground.

What gets created in the contest of meanings signified by this volley of metaphorical speech about "tar" and "oil" is, finally, an ideologically and even ontologically unstable ground, given the slippage toward alternate meanings that metaphor allows and that points up a similar instability in all language. The very first interactive display in the Oil Sands

Discovery Centre makes this museum's civic intervention blatantly clear. This display's theme is the "transformation machine," which refers in the video footage that the visitor summons by drag-and-click to a mechanism that transforms the museum's virtual docent, Professor Nositall, from his human body into "an upgraded, electronic version" of himself, which looks like a drop of crude wearing a lab coat. This desirable "refinement," the video tells us, mirrors the separation of bitumen from its molecularly complex body. In general, embodiment is a problem here, to be remedied or enhanced by technology, including figures of speech.

In Fort McMurray, we are summoned to be confused about the real. We quite literally are invited to question where we stand—on real topsoil, topsoil that was recently made from toxic tailings, or perhaps on the crusty bread of a sandwich that ought to be removed to get to "yummier" oil beneath. Touring the tar sands, I was reminded of how Ralph Waldo Emerson, in the essay "Nature" (1836), recognized what was in his day the new technology of the railroad as akin to the linguistic technology of metaphor. Riding in the moving cars, Emerson noted, made the world outside seem fantastic, like a shifting panorama. For Emerson, this destabilization of the "outside" only accentuated an idealist notion of the stability of the ego or eye. The perceptual disorientation caused by the train, he argued, teaches us that "something in ourselves is stable." For me, the shifts of perception afforded by tar sands' metaphors do not produce a similar confidence. However, the Oil Sands Discovery Centre effectively limits its rhetorical extravagance and the instability produced by it. To distract from the conceptual dissonance incited by its rhetorical play, the museum courts our senses.

BODY WORK

As Alison Griffiths notes, a museum's immersive environment can include background details, such as the texture of its walls and floors. Every surface of exhibit space influences how the visitor moves through the museum and obtains an affective knowledge of it.[58] The Oil Sands Discovery Centre's walls are the texture of tire tread, and the museum space is delineated by metal cages reminiscent of the skeletons at construction sites or the reinforced cages of vehicles. A rich sound track including grinding, shoveling, and engine noise fills the museum space, almost to the point of evoking an air of danger, except that the visitor is trained, early on, to identify herself as the driver of the massive machines that the museum labels as "historical land artifacts." Individual exhibits offer a gear-shift mechanism that we use in order to choose which machines or processes will appear on flat-screen televisions behind miniaturized models of machines. The pure physical satisfaction of feeling the heavy gear shaft in one's hand, pulling and pushing it hard, because it has the resistance of the shaft of a truck, in order to trigger an exhibit of, say, "the dragline"—that first step in the process of summoning a screen demonstration of machine work—feels simply fabulous.

As out of control as life may have spun, with synthetic oil in your tank and storehoused muskeg underfoot, the simulation of driving makes a simple, compensatory, multisensory counterstatement of certitude. To experience the museum's maximal driving entertainment, visitors ascend a small industrial staircase—also textural, like tire tread—in order to sit in the cab of a massive digger and look at film footage taken from the cabs of similar trucks, in operation at different times of day and night at the Suncor and Syncrude plants. The gear shaft in this exhibit can summon filmic "driving" forward and in reverse. A gear shaft next to the cab, for visitors waiting their turn to drive, offers choices between distinct time-and-place reels, like "Suncor—Dusk" or "Syncrude—Night." In the cab, an audiotape of radio dialogue among truck and shovel drivers immerses the visitor in the banter of men exchanging nicknames and private jokes.

Coming up from the United States in the wake of the recent assault on bargaining rights in Wisconsin, Ohio, and other states, I felt a keen nostalgia for labor after viewing this exhibit. It spoke to me about what labor is supposed to feel like. The good old jobs, in construction and industry, and the old idea of dignified labor have long gone out of style in the lower forty-eight, as my Canadian fellow-tourist at Heritage Park noted when he asserted that the weakness of the U.S. manufacturing sector meant the future would be somewhere else. The oil sands museum would like you to believe that labor's future is here. The children's section of the museum displays a closet full of child-size industrial work suits, hard hats, and boots. "What kind of hat does an oil worker wear?" asks a placard nearby to the more confusing one about the oil "sandwich." Answer: "Hard hat." All this, the story of jobs, feels as simple and intuitive as driving. Entering Fort McMurray, a large sign reading "This Is What a Union Town Looks Like"—sporting diverse union insignias—reiterates the point made through phenomenological means at the museum. Yet Syncrude, the region's largest company, is in fact not unionized. The importation of temporary "foreign workers" who live in substandard housing at "camps" marks this as a postmodern economy indicative of globalization's worst uses of human capital. The apparently stable social status evoked by sitting behind the wheel of a big truck, listening to brotherly chitchat in North American English at the museum, is, finally, mirage.

The visitor's pathway in the Oil Sands Discovery Centre is marked by a series of industrial arches, resembling large pipes, which spell out stages in the mining process. Once we get past mining, and past the indoor truck exhibit, the museum's narrative becomes more abstract and reliant upon interactive displays in which Professor Nositall explains concepts such as organic chemistry. We don't "drive" the latter stages of the exhibit, and their pleasures, such as a grocery cart full of "beaver lumber," rely more on gentle humor than sensory stimulation. The beaver lumber exhibit sits within the final museum segment, labeled simply "Environment." The museum's very last exhibit about habitat disturbance and fragmentation presents a button that, when pressed, prompts a statement by Métis elder Fred MacDonald. Beginning in the rather vague "web of life" rhetorical vein which characterizes the museum's environmental messaging, MacDonald steps out of frame for a moment to talk about water— and the threat to fresh water presented by oil sands mining. MacDonald says quietly, looking directly into the camera, that water is getting to be a very, very important thing now—that it's more important now than oil. What a compelling way to end the peripatetic lesson of the Oil Sands Discovery Centre, with a statement about oil's relative unimportance to water. This out-of-frame moment, spoken by a now deceased, revered elder, almost explodes the museum's curatorial line, prompting larger-scale questions than the museum otherwise encourages visitors to ask.

After a few hours at the Oil Sands Discovery Centre, I walked back across the highway to my hotel, which is owned by the Cree First Nations in partnership with "Alberta's oil and gas industry," as the hotel brochure reads, in crucial industry hubs such as Fort McMurray and the Peace River delta. I ate a pizza called the "Anzac," the name of a local oil company, and attempted to tie up the day's loose ends. My mind returned to Crane Lake, our final stop on the Suncor bus tour. On a site intended for a tailings pond, a "change in drainage" resulted in a hole that had been excavated to hold toxic water filling, accidentally, with fresh water. In Suncor's words, "soon, a new wetlands ecosystem was born." Touting Crane Lake as "a rich habitat for wildlife and a popular recreation area for the people of the Wood Buffalo region," Suncor's signage at the lake utilizes the Canadian toad—variously named as "Augustus" or "Drillbit"—as a personified spokesperson for the "healing power of nature." The toad's porous skin indicates an environmental sensitivity that makes its presence in places such as Crane Lake an index of ecosystem health. Images of the toad are everywhere, although no live toads made themselves visible during my visit. The "Crane Lake Interpretive Trail Map" at the head of the approximately one-mile loop around the pond maps signs, not sites, for the visitor to "explore." These signs range from explanations of wetlands filtration ("Nature's Lifeblood") to a billboard, courtesy of Canada Ducks Unlimited, featuring the many ducks and other birdlife one might see here. On the lake's still shore, a large duck blind sits like a mis-sized shoe. The day of my tour, which was a sunny, temperate Saturday, there were no water birds about, and the only visitors to Crane Lake were us tourists from the Suncor bus. "Bears have been sighted around here," our guide told us, explaining why no one else had come for recreation.

While there are familiar words for the sort of hocus-pocus put on for energy tourists at Alberta's oil patch, I think the project of mediating what happens here goes beyond the self-referential corporate rhetoric we normally conceive as greenwashing. Fort McMurray has been set up as a museum of the future, for the benefit of all North Americans. The metaphorical environment that so startled me in Alberta is just a fragment of the unreal world that thrives in the United States, the fevered postoil dream that made possible, for example, what in a common-sense world would be a politically suicidal move by Republican congressmen to stall the extension of a middle-class tax cut to promote building the Keystone XL pipeline without further environmental scrutiny. The corporate fictions of the oil industry have become deeply lived cultures in North America, perhaps most poignantly lived by oil and natural gas workers who feel the friction between what they know and the tightly-woven web of homely analogies for Tough Oil, fracking, and dirty fuels. Years ago, the literary historian Lawrence Buell noted that the "ground condition" of environmental perception is metaphoricity, that analogical dance of substitution and return that isn't only a characteristic of tar sands rhetoric but of any attempt to write or speak or think the places we live. Since Buell's writing, cognitive scientists have discovered the metaphoricity of perception as a neurobiological fact. Our health and that of the living systems that support us depend upon how we make this metaphoricity "subserve"—in Buell's words—"mutuality rather than a proprietary self-interest."[59] As Henry David Thoreau understood, at the bottom of language we find no bottom, but rather relationships—a social ecology fundamental to politics and to language itself. During my visit to Fort McMurray, I had many conversations with people who don't believe in the tar sands, who have come to take a job and who try to make another kind of sense. It was in their conversation that I heard the poetry of collaborative imagination. "What's good about a place like this," one young cab driver told me, "is that people are fairly open to each other because there's nothing much here." I asked him if he didn't think that the future were here. "No," he said, gently laughing at me as if I were a child. Why not? I asked him. "Simple. The future isn't dirty."

III. Texas

The energy museums of east Texas offer the future as it was imagined in the mid-twentieth-century United States, when Space Age technologies promised endless progress and abundance.[60] In search of both the intangible heritage of Texas oil culture and monuments to Texas oil, I toured the region known as Texas's Golden Triangle.[61] Located between the cities of Beaumont, Port Arthur, and Orange, the Triangle gets its name from the rich oil field that developed here after the Spindletop gusher blew in 1901, just south of Beaumont. Spindletop produced 100,000 barrels per day, opening the possibility of a constant supply of petroleum fuel and inviting the twentieth century. "This place made the world what it is," a volunteer quietly remarked in the gift shop of the Spindletop-Gladys City Boomtown Museum, an open-air exhibit that replicates life in east Texas around the turn of the last century. Outside the gift shop, a framed poster advertised the "Deck the Derrick Wildcatter Weekend" festival. Each spring, children decorate the museum's replica of the Spindletop derrick with murals and mobiles. The Triangle is now known less for its oil fields, which were largely played out by the 1950s, than for its dense concentration of refineries. Industry touts "the New Golden Triangle" of West Africa, the Gulf of Mexico, and Brazil, while in east Texas flares from the oil refineries burn so brightly at night that they look like a golden triangle to airplanes. Now this brilliant flaring explains the region's moniker. The coastal city of Port Arthur, which grew up with Spindletop as an oil port, has become famous for its high incidence of cancer and respiratory disease, health threats associated with the volatile organic compounds that are refinery by-products. Southwest of the Triangle, Galveston struggles to recover from damages caused by Hurricane Ike. High-water lines drawn on coastal buildings testify to the worsening of storm cycles in the shadow of global climate change. The east Texas energy museums, which are offshoots of the museums of science and industry that are the most popular American museums, challenge local symptoms of loss.

Museums of science and industry can be traced to seventeenth-century collections of mechanical models which were intended to instruct and to stimulate invention.[62] In colonial North America, Benjamin Franklin assembled a cabinet of models that eventually found its way into the American Philosophical Society. The 1876 International Centennial Exhibition in Philadelphia inaugurated the first modern American museum of science and technology, the U.S. National Museum in Washington, D.C. Exhibits from the fair founded the museum's collection. The roots of science and industry museums in expositions and fairs—a genealogy that holds true in Britain, too, as the 1851 Crystal Palace Exhibition in London grew into the London Science Museum—concerned George Brown Goode, the first director of the U.S. National Museum. "The exposition or exhibition and fair are primarily for the promotion of industry and commerce," Goode warned, "the museum for the advancement of learning."[63] At the Museum of Science and Industry in Chicago, which was built as a replica of the Fine Arts building from the Chicago World's Fair, Julius Rosenwald introduced "moving displays" meant to delight visitors. Such displays have been a feature of science and industry museums ever since, which compromises their educative goals, according to critics.[64] "The visitor is assaulted with a point of view that approaches perilously close to propaganda," T. R. Adam wrote of museums of science, industry, and commerce in *The Museum and Popular Culture* (1939).[65] Adam saw the necessity of such museums "in a deep social movement that is attempting to find the proper instruments to adapt men to their changing environment"—a sentiment reminiscent of Henry Adams's famous complaint about the difficulty of catching up to the twentieth century.[66] But, Adam complained, "A true history of the machine should explain the attitude of the Luddites, the machine smashers."[67] The "immensely popular—and largely vacuous" American "technical museums," in the words of another historian writing in the 1960s, accelerate the "undiscriminating mechanization" of the U.S. environment.[68] More recent critics emphasize these museums' compliance with corporate donors.

I came to east Texas because I wanted to see how Big Oil's American Story compared with life on the ground in a major oil producing region. Regardless of what historians think, or what I think, about bombastic museums of industry, they are staples of American popular culture and contributors to public history. The National Air and Space Museum remains the most visited museum on the Washington Mall, despite or perhaps because of its "propagandistic elements and mass cultural appeals," in the words of one reviewer.[69] On a smaller scale, the Texas Energy Museum in Beaumont and the Ocean Star Offshore Drilling Rig and Museum in Galveston are museums of petroleum science and industry with strong corporate sponsorship. The Texas Energy Museum began its life as exhibit space for the Western Service Oil Company in Fort Worth before it was purchased by the city of Beaumont in the 1980s, while the Ocean Star is an actual jack-up drill rig that was bought in the late 1990s by a nonprofit organization that sponsors the museum, largely thanks to corporate donors. What the public historian Mike Wallace has described as "the corporate roots movement" beginning after World War II, when Boeing, for instance, invested heavily in Seattle's Museum of History and Industry, is on show here, too.[70] These museums are a type of heritage site, participating in what became known as "industrial heritage tourism" at the height of the larger heritage movement in the United States, Britain, and Europe in the 1970s.[71] Given the increasing influence of oil and energy corporations in U.S. electoral politics, it is worth considering how these museums monumentalize the U.S. past and its possible futures.

A historical timeline that doubles as a pamphlet advertisement for the Ocean Star Offshore Drilling Rig and Museum in Galveston offers a quick introduction to what history looks like from the point of view of Big Oil. The timeline finds its most pertinent "roots" in and around the Second World War. Offshore industry "firsts" interrupt and frame World War II, following the rising arc of the U.S. aerospace industry. In 1940, the first barge-mounted drilling rigs were developed, and in 1947 the first "out of sight of land" oil well was drilled off of Morgan City, Louisiana. Interestingly, the timeline—which juxtaposes industry events to "Historical Events," "Technology in Our Lives," and "Transportation through the Years"—does not actually list the world wars. It brackets the Second World War with the premiere of *Gone with the Wind* (1939) and the introduction of the bikini swimsuit in Paris (1948).[72] The timeline offers a broad global and temporal reach, beginning with Egyptian drilling innovations in 2,000 BCE. Yet neither of the world wars nor the Vietnam War appears as autonomous historical events. What the timeline does find histori-cal includes: Barbie dolls (1959), color televisions (1951), Model Ts (1908), the DVD (1995), and diverse innovations in the space, personal computer, and medical industries, including the inventions of Prozac and Viagra. With few exceptions, the Offshore museum serves up history in a style that the historian Peder Anker identifies with Cold War–era American futurism. "History was driven by inventions," Anker writes. "Political activity was unnecessary, and the only important revolutions were those of design."[73] Anker's words refer explicitly to Buckminster Fuller's futurism, which he associates with U.S. naval managerial techniques and design, as those matured during the Second World War—when Fuller served in the Navy. The oil industry is also indebted to the U.S. Navy, since sonar and radio positioning devices developed by the Navy in response to German submarine power have proven indispensable to offshore drilling.

Those political events that do appear in the Offshore museum timeline tell us even more about what counts as American history, if you are looking at it from the point of view of Big Oil. The list of exceptional inclusions fea-tures: the September 11 attack on the World Trade Center towers, the fall of the Berlin Wall, the creation of OPEC, and the beginning of the (scare-quoted) "oil crisis" with the Iranian revolution. These exceptions help contextualize neoliberal ideologies, including policy chestnuts like deregulation, in a past that makes them appear desirable and inevitable. The Texas Energy Museum in Beaumont gives strong voice to the American liberal tradition in a series of quotations printed on a floor-to-ceiling octagonal glass case in the midst of its primary exhibit hall. The case houses a bald eagle, exquisitely carved in wood. Gazing through the glass, visitors encounter the wooden eagle, a lit-erally heavy symbol of freedom, through almost diaphanous white-lettered quotations by Ralph Waldo Emerson, Thomas Jefferson, Theodore Roosevelt, Thomas Edison, Abraham Lincoln, Dwight Eisenhower (quoted twice), Milton Friedman (quoted three times), and other great men, including William H. Chiles, former CEO of the Western Oil Service Company. Western Service was a pioneer in "acidizing"—an early form of fracking. "The public recog-nizes increasingly that it has been taken to the cleaners," Friedman intones in the glass sheltering the eagle. "That bigger government is not better govern-ment." Emerson agrees: "Wealth brings with it its own checks and balances. The basis of political economy is non-interference." Similarly, Jefferson: "I pre-dict future happiness for Americans if they can prevent the government from wasting the labors of the people under the pretense of taking care of them."[74] The libertarian clarion call that can be assembled from these quotes made for an ideal introduction to a less explicit subject of the Energy Museum, but one that is also tied to the free flow of capital away from costly "interferences," including labor. That subject is automation.

SCENES FROM AN AUTOMATIC INDUSTRY

What Buckminster Fuller promoted as "comprehensively commanded auto-mation"[75]—design without politics and, implicitly, without us—appears in the Texas Energy Museum as the realization of the modern energy system. Sometimes the roots of environmentalism appear strangely complementary to the movement's worst enemies, like Big Oil. "Where are the people?" an exhibit on refineries asks visitors to the Energy museum. The exhibit offers its own response: "Technicians operate the units [of the refinery] from state-of-the-art, computerized, central control rooms. Relatively few people are required."[76] The closed-system efficiency of the refineries makes them illegible to passersby. The museum strives not only to render these systems as readable but also to make them interesting, given their distance from human-centered narrative. "You've Driven Past Them, What's Going On?" another exhibit asks about the refineries. The exhibit breaks down the refinery by way of its explicit tasks—such as, for example, "hydrocracking." Visitors press buttons to light up different areas in a model refinery where such tasks are performed. The disaggregation of the refinery system into constituent parts takes the place of more traditional narrative, and we find agency through conceptually dismantling the system. The next major station on the Energy Museum's exhibit path offers a purer sensory pleasure. Here we enter a virtual pipeline—a large, cylindrical room—where a circular screen offers a film meant to take us through the refinery "as if" we were droplets of oil. With bright yet subtly shaded coloration and bold, clean lines, the film visually evokes the feeling of *being-oil* in such a way as to stabilize the viewer's sense of agency within a complex system. I found the film visually pleasing and the "pipe" exhibition space comforting, womb-like. Of course my immersion in it depended upon my assuming the point of view of something inhuman and, arguably, not alive.

The human body inevitably returns, as advocates of automation have discovered, in oppositional movements such as the Luddites or in the unemployment statistics that crop up in regions where technology "replaces" traditionally human jobs. Industry accidents also function as openings through which the repressed human agency within an automated system leaps out, like a ghost in the machine. The problem of industry safety takes up exhibit space in both Galveston and Beaumont, and here we recognize human-like bodies. The Offshore museum's Safety Exhibit features a blond mannequin sitting on a bench with a casual air, wearing a hard hat, safety glasses, mask (sportily hanging around his neck), and a jumpsuit whose flame-orange color suggests the possibility of its inflammability. Without the wall text announcing this as a safety exhibit, it wouldn't necessarily be legible as such. But safety and its complement, injury, appear in compelling ways elsewhere in the Offshore museum—for instance, in the spectacle of the UFO-shaped Escape Pod on the museum's outdoor pipe deck. The bright red pod promises cramped quarters for twenty-eight persons in the event of an explosion, "with a two-way radio, safety gear, first aid supplies, water and a cooling system that pumps seawater over the pod until the crew inside can be rescued."[77] The success of the pod implies time enough to assemble the crew, and to get inside it and lower it from where it is suspended, high out of water on the side of the rig. For many crew members on the Deepwater Horizon, there wasn't enough time for all that. Such contingencies are only dimly imaginable at the Offshore museum. The beauty of safety features like the Escape Pod and the capsule-shaped Hyperbaric Chamber, for reacclimating rig divers to surface conditions, is that these structures appear as what their names imply. They are capsules, pods, Space Age vehicles whose retro-sexy abstraction depersonalizes the experience of accident.

In stark contrast to the driver's seat immediacy of the Oil Sands museum in Alberta, in these museums virtually driving an oil rig or tanker does not invoke gravitational pull, friction, or anything reminiscent of body work. Just as General Motors's model kitchens at the midcentury World's Fairs promised an end to domestic labor—and General Electric's TEMPO think tank in Santa Barbara predicted, in the early 1960s, that by 1984 "work" as we know it would be obsolete—here progress inheres in the elimination of jobs that, assumedly, most Americans would rather not do.[78] As a public historian, Mike Wallace offers advice to museums about how to treat the topic of "deindustrialization," which he suggests should be broken down in exhibit space into the more substantive problems of automation, union-busting, and capital flight.[79] Wallace urges curators to present challenges to "traditional axioms [like] 'high tech jobs can replace departed manufacturing ones.'"[80] Of course we don't see that kind of debate in the energy museums of east Texas. Nor did Wallace manage to induce such a conversation in Paterson, New Jersey, where he consulted about a museum commemorating the silk industry. Oil still thrives in east Texas, so commemoration of the industry—or questioning its flight—are inappropriate museum goals. "De-industrialization" might also be a misnomer for what's happening here, although job figures for the local oil industry aren't as robust as one might assume. But automation is on display, and it implies an attitude toward labor that is too easily elided in museum exhibits that emphasize what Neil Harris has called "the operational aesthetic," meaning the pleasure of seeing how *things* (emphasis mine) work.[81]

It's worth remembering that while the oil industry accounts for over 60 percent of revenues for the Gulf region, lower-skilled tourism jobs employ about five times more people (approximately 524,000) than oil jobs (approximately 107,000). This region may need the oil industry, as Hilton Kelley, a celebrated environmental justice activist based in Port Arthur, argues. It would be foolish to ignore the value of oil revenues and jobs to east Texas or to any oil-producing place, although Big Oil's power to re-industrialize America, in light of the development of shale and other unconventional resources, has been wildly exaggerated.[82] A pragmatic activist, Kelley strives not to drive out Big Oil but to change its relationship to the communities where it lives, to towns like Port Arthur, where unemployment stands at over 15 percent despite the presence of the largest oil refining complex in the United States. The "stresses of toxic exposure, poverty, and the feeling of lack of control" impact the health of people living near to refineries, research suggests.[83] Yet regulation must be won largely through local efforts that further tax affected communities. As unskilled jobs at Port Arthur's port complex became obsolete, working-class people, particularly African Americans, lost their niche. The devaluation of labor shows up inadvertently at the east Texas energy museums, which monumentalize industry (in its multiple meanings as intelligence, diligence, labor) without people.

You *can* virtually "work" at the east Texas museums, but you are encouraged to see work as high tech and disembodied, even if you don a hard hat while doing it. Sit in a "Cyberbase Drilling Chair" at the Offshore museum, grasp hand rests equipped with buttons and dials, and become a deepwater Captain Kirk, controlling operations on the drill floor of an offshore rig. In the Texas Energy Museum, navigating an oil tanker through the narrow Sabine-Neches waterway to the refinery docks at Beaumont is a televisual experience that requires the assistance of "modern radar and satellite technology." The experience of wonder—the feeling of thought, as Descartes describes it, of having an intellectual epiphany—comes through imagining the design precision of the "closed system of pipelines and tanks" that carry the oil from the ship to shore.

In general, these museums are high on wonder as an intellectual emotion and low on resonance. Resonance, in the words of Stephen Greenblatt, is "the intimation" in an object or series of objects of "a larger community of voices and skills, an imagined ethnographic thickness."[84] Repeatedly I found myself asking the question that was posed to me at the Texas Energy Museum, "Where Are the People?" At the same time, I got caught up in the operational aesthetic, marveling at how complex systems come together. The Underwater Construction exhibit in the Offshore museum helps the visitor to make a conceptual transition from traditional construction labor into "remote" undersea labor, which is performed by computer prostheses. This exhibit traces the development of scuba technology into progressively more incredible cyborg extensions, like the WASP Atmospheric Diving System, a hard suit that resembles a giant, yellow insect, with "powerful manipulator claws" that can be plugged into specialized tools. WASP divers can work at 2,300 feet.[85] The museum path leads us from the WASP suit to a Remotely Operated Vehicle (ROV), a robotic device for monitoring and installing subsea equipment that can be "flown" underwater from a remote surface location, using lights and television cameras for visibility. (We might remember the helplessness of ROVs attempting to manipulate the gushing Macondo well during the 2010

BP disaster.) "Unlike divers, ROVs never tire nor suffer from cold, pressure or the bends," exhibit text reminds us.[86] Automation is supposed to be seamless.

The two DVDs on sale in the Offshore museum gift shop heavily feature underwater construction, which doesn't photograph well but provokes wonder even in dark, grainy images of divers manipulating huge undersea chain links.[87] Because they offer a shadow of humanness in the shape of the machinic "suit," these diving images deliver a strong sense of comparative scale, of the hugeness of subsea drill structures and the relative fragility if not inadequacy of human bodies in comparison.

THE JUMPING-OFF POINT

To imagine scale requires a comparative analysis beginning with ourselves, and "we" are hard to locate in an automated system. Ironically, given the high-tech goals of these museums, they contain enough low-tech, traditional media to clumsily recall us to ourselves, to the limitations of the human senses. The museum media makes you think about how it is that you perceive and feel, because it is so far from seamless. Perhaps my favorite exhibit in the Offshore museum—and one that, interestingly, is pictured in the official report to the president on the BP blowout—is a lenticular image in which various cities (New York, Dallas, or Houston) can be viewed as if "inside" the anchor chains of the Devil's Tower, a deepwater platform in the Gulf of Mexico.[88] The Devil's Tower is a spar platform, meaning that it rests on a huge cylindrical hull that temporarily stores oil and that has to be held in place by thousands of feet of chain. The individual links of this chain are huge, each one about six feet in length. In the case of the Devil's Tower the anchor chains are so long and so widely distributed that their circumference on the sea floor would contain much of the surface area of a major American city. The lenticular image enacts this scalar epiphany, as we walk back and forth in front of the picture in order to "have" that moment of wonder when one or another city appears inside the chains. The effort of walking brings off the visual trick with an image too large to manipulate with the hands. Lenticular images began to be printed in the United States in the 1940s, often for religious or advertising purposes. Most Americans have probably seen the lenticular card with the butterfly on it, which appears to beat its wings as you turn the card slowly from side to side. Lenticular images have a philosophical if not a technical genealogy in Victorian-era spirit photography and its revelations of the "soul" of matter. They are the visual equivalent of the "aha" moment.

Other creaky magic is on view at the Offshore museum, where a 3-D map with viewing glasses reveals the extent of underwater pipelines in the Gulf and a host of 3-D walkaround models depict rigs, undersea conditions, and processes such as slant drilling. The Offshore museum Tour Guide Book touts the 3-D models as testaments to "early engineering" before "computer drafting software became available."[89] While the Texas Energy Museum brings some newer media into play, its older second-floor exhibits include robotic mannequins and hologram projection, staples of predigital virtuality. The failure of such exhibits to induce second-life virtual perception casts a shadow of nostalgia over east Texas oil, as if to remind us that, again, this *was* futurism, before Vietnam, Iraq, and the cynicism about high tech that accompanied drone technologies. These older media effectively mark the jumping-off point where what the senses can grasp has to give way to the imagination, to use a phrase common to westward-bound U.S. settlers to indicate a place where civilization as they knew it met the wild frontier. By performing what really couldn't be seen prior to computer drafting software, media such as the 3-D model pay tribute to the imagination of engineers who first entered the deep ocean.

Some of the industry metaphors prevalent in these museums—such as the term "Christmas tree" for the assembly of chokes, valves, and pressure gauges at the top of a well or the term "pigs" for ("squeaking") rubber devices that pass through pipelines to clean them—also foreground the contrast between the developing rig technologies of the late 1950s and 1960s and the simpler technological set that preceded them.[90] An article in the *Saturday Evening Post* from 1955 testifies to the unexpectedness of oil industry innovations offshore by describing offshore rigs through awkward analogies to more traditional things, like a "modern set of rooms" with a 360-degree ocean view, or "a twenty-five-story skyscraper which someone has carelessly built in water that comes up to the ninth floor."[91] These metaphors, like those technical ones that have persisted in the industry, make clear the perceptual gap between what was happening in terms of oil engineering at midcentury and how most people lived. Advertisements in the *Post* for Douglas airplanes and automobile "seat covers woven of wonderful new Saran," a petroleum-derived plastic, emphasize the growing demand for oil products in the 1950s.[92] But the frenzy of drilling activity offshore leaves even insiders bemused. "Boats or seaplanes or helicopters are ordered, dispatched, sometimes cancelled. Last-minute pinpoint weather data is constantly in the air."[93] The *Post* gestures toward the rapid speed of cultural change around oil in a humorous anecdote about a Cajun dispatcher listening to an offshore rig boss's grocery order ("sixty pounds of T-bone, fifty pounds of roast beef...twenty gallons of ice cream")—to which the dispatcher replies, "The world is sure going to hell!"[94] As of 1955, it was "going to hell" on a tide of abundance—a sweet, if disconcerting, dream.

Offshore drilling platforms with names like the Devil's Tower and Brutus make anxious poetry of the first Tough Oil frontier, which is what the oceans are and have been. The report to the president on the BP blowout reminds readers of how blunt the oil industry can be about its limited control of more remote offshore fields. This report, published as *Deep Water: The Gulf Oil Disaster and the Future of Offshore Drilling* (2011), under the aegis of the National Commission on the BP Deepwater Horizon Oil Spill and Offshore

Drilling, presents a peculiarly confessional—at times anecdotal, emotional—analysis of offshore production. The report notes that BP named the Mississippi Canyon lease that the Deepwater Horizon was drilling in the Gulf of Mexico in approximately 5,000 feet of water "Macondo," after the fictional town in Gabriel García Márquez's *One Hundred Years of Solitude* (1967). The presidential commission even includes Márquez's description of Macondo as if it were an apt gloss on BP's failure. As Márquez writes, "It was as if God had decided to put to the test every capacity for surprise and was keeping the inhabitants of Macondo in a permanent alternation between excitement and disappointment, to such an extreme that no one knew for certain where the limits of reality lay."[95] Where the limits of reality lie at 5,000 feet, the depth that marks the *minimal* limit for ultradeep drilling, have been troubling BP since the early 2000s. The company made its name as an industry leader by taking huge risks in deep and ultradeep water. Deepwater drilling begins at 1,000 feet. It is a phase of industry production developed in the 1970s, inspired by that decade's oil shortages. Ultradeep offshore drilling began to take off in the 1990s.[96] Again, this is the Tough Oil frontier. Or, in the words of Kenny Lang, BP's vice president for Gulf production, "This is as close as we get to the space age on Earth."[97] The east Texas museums got that Space Age rhetoric right. Regardless of BP's embarrassment with the Macondo well, the ultra deepwater "space race" will continue, because the oil is there. As the environmental nonfiction writer Rowan Jacobsen laments in *Shadow over the Gulf*, the world's oceans give the lie to peak oil, promising "more than a trillion barrels of oil reserves" worldwide.[98]

Like all Tough Oil, the ultra-deepwater cache, "beneath ten thousand feet of water and five miles of salt and rock"—with salt, in particular, offering significant challenges to seismic imaging—presents extreme costs that throw the value of the oil into doubt. Ultra-deepwater oil from the Gulf of Mexico costs about twelve times as much as oil drilled in the Middle East, according to Jacobsen.[99] Even if improved technologies bring down economic risk, the risks ultradeep drilling poses to human life, ocean ecologies, and global climate are incompletely understood and potentially huge. Yet similar objections might have been raised in the 1950s, when offshore drilling began to take off in the Gulf of Mexico, or the 1970s, when deepwater play began to mature. The report to the president on the BP spill reminds readers that the oil industry, and in particular offshore oil, has long been a business with unacceptable risks, with inadequate industry watchdogs such as the American Petroleum Institute (essentially a lobbyist for Big Oil), and with a history of understaffed regulatory agencies. In 1969, for example, the Gulf region's lease management office had 12 people overseeing more than 1,500 platforms.[100] After the 1969 blowout in the Santa Barbara Channel spurred national concerns about offshore drilling, the Department of the Interior issued the first rules in which it claimed authority to prohibit leasing where environmental risks were too high. Since the heyday of activism in the 1970s, there has been backsliding. The Obama administration allowed the 1981 moratorium on offshore drilling on the Atlantic and Pacific coasts to die a quiet death, although the White House changed course again in late 2011, proposing to follow the earlier ban while opening up more development in Alaska and the Gulf of Mexico.[101]

The report to the president concludes with the far-flung hope that "enormous political effort and leadership" might create and implement a more sustainable national energy policy.[102] The fact that Cuba is initiating an offshore program in the Gulf of Mexico, in cooperation with the Russian company Gazprom, may do more than any domestic environmental lobbying to inspire rigorous federal standards and regulatory oversight. The United States needs to regulate its own industry so that it can negotiate similar restrictions on Cuba and Russia.[103]

Of course Texas also has begun to develop a profitable wind industry, although this renewable energy isn't slated to take the place of oil any time soon. In the Texas Energy Museum, a wind exhibit stands empty on the second floor, behind an animated robotic conversation in which Patillo Higgins, the legendary discoverer of Spindletop, recounts his oil triumph. The wind exhibit had apparently left six months before my visit. Looking into the empty room where a solitary tall glass cylinder stood under track lighting like minimalist sculpture, I thought of a phrase that a colleague tells me is used in the Netherlands to demarcate space set aside in new town sites for future use: "speculation ground."[104] This empty exhibit was a speculation ground, a white room for imagining something not present in the current setting.[105] I was grateful for it.

Conclusion: The Tough Old Future

When the art historian Neil Harris writes of the operational aesthetic, he recognizes it as a symptom of an American philosophy of taste that developed in the nineteenth century, in the museums of P. T. Barnum and in a variety of popular media. Harris even identifies the operational aesthetic in nineteenth century America's maritime literature, for example Richard Henry Dana's *Two Years before the Mast* (1842). In the operational aesthetic we see the pragmatic question "how does it work" translated into an aesthetic problem, a matter of imagination and play, through museum hoaxes like Barnum's Feejee Mermaid or Dana's detailed treatments of sailing. The operational aesthetic "narrowed the task of judgment" for the mass public in the United States, Harris argues.[106] Potentially philosophical debates about beauty or morality that required a kind of education not widely available in the States could be transformed into evaluative problems when audiences were directed toward the question of how, or whether, something functions. The energy museums of east Texas proved, to me, that the operational aesthetic still holds power. It explains the enduring popularity of those science and industry museums that historians indict for their vacuity and propaganda.

I came away from these museums impressed by the engineering feats of men and women who relied upon 3-D models—before computer drafting software!—to enter the deep oceans. The Space Age rhetoric that carried Big Oil through the twentieth century also ironically spawned one leg of the environmental movement, as I've noted, originating from Buckminster Fuller through Stewart Brand and the *Whole Earth Catalog*. Environmental literatures of fabrication, about autonomous solar-powered house building, for example, also rely upon the operational aesthetic to convey the charisma of building toward a better world. Part of the pleasure involved in reading about, say, a D.I.Y. energy-efficient stove, made from recycled cans, inheres in wondering, will it work? The operational aesthetic can do good. It also can encourage a forgetting of the collateral damages of some technological systems—such as that 20 percent unemployment rate in African-American Port Arthur or the grisly deaths of porpoises resulting from ultradeep miscalculation and haste in the Gulf. Still, I admit that I enjoyed sitting in the Cyberbase Drilling Chair, pushing buttons supposedly rigged to remote underwater systems. This mid-twentieth-century oil complex tied to so many accidents, wars, and the planetary crisis of a changing climate implies a centuries-old American way of taking pleasure in the world, through the mulling over of technical problems meant to seem remote or abstract.

Rick Bass has written eloquently about the charisma of the oil business, from the point of view of a nature lover. I say "nature lover" since Bass does not present himself as a fully developed environmentalist in his early writings about oil. In the 1980s, when deepwater drilling fought for its life against a record slump in oil prices, Bass, a petroleum geologist, wrote the following: "It's so much like life, this business of oil, at least what used to be life."[107] Bass could have been talking about the price slump when he wrote this line, but mostly he was talking about geology and wonder. He conducted oil exploration in Mississippi and Alabama. His memoir, *Oil Notes* (1989), returns to the sense of constancy he experiences from a resource that takes him into the earth's bowels, to "the old sea" where oil was made, from plant life compressed for hundreds of thousands of years under sliding rock and salt, the splayed components of oceans.[108] "It is like getting married," Bass writes of oil—indicating its certainty within doubt. "It is wonderful," he states plainly.[109] "It really does feel as if the whole earth is swaying, and that that oil locked in, trapped beneath the rocks down there, is all that is constant."[110] Only the sea offers an apt analogy for oil's immensity and deep time. "Maybe when you look at the sea, at night, have you ever done that? That is the same type of thought as knowing about oil and wanting somehow to get it out of the ground."[111] Rachel Carson made much the same point when she incorporated oil mining into the concluding chapters of *The Sea around Us* (1951) as a complement to the larger argument of that book, about the priority and expanse of nature in comparison to human endeavor.

We might recognize in Carson and Bass naive poetry of the Anthropocene, in which mining—the earth's oceans, Alabama's red dirt—figures as a form of transcendence, of getting to the "spiritual facts" that Ralph Waldo Emerson, early in his career, claimed were behind, beneath, and inside the world of matter.[112] Mining is touching nature's soul, just temporarily, and didn't Henry David Thoreau, of all people, make a similarly aggressive metaphor about digging head first in earth?[113] Or perhaps it was Robert Smithson or Michael Heizer, one of those mostly male, American Land Artists of the 1960s who dug and bulldozed and built in the belief that some more natural form of value might be derived from doing so, outside the commodification zone of the gallery. Nature was permanent, indifferent, shifting through time but eternal. Didn't North Americans know that better than anyone, after confronting the West? "There's truly an amount of trust," Rick Bass writes of oil, contrasting the "deceit in writing" to the relative purity of petroleum geology, where you find out, definitively, whether or not it works. "The earth lies there, still, and obeys certain rules. I have faith that I am not going to let myself believe something that is not true."[114] "Lies there, still" and "obeys certain rules"—neither assertion about the earth seems quite true, given the explosive history of oil mining. But writing is an approximate craft, as Bass himself laments. Oil signifies for Bass that which surely is there, that "inland sea" (to quote Thoreau) traceable to the philosophies of the Transcendentalists as a mirror image of self.[115] Those same American Romantics could be held responsible for the frustrating, metaphysical, and at times egoistic nature concept in Bill McKibben's *The End of Nature* (1989), which of course is the first popular treatment of anthropogenic climate change and which was published in the same year as *Oil Notes*.

What might Rick Bass have said to Bill McKibben about the relationship of oil and anthropogenic climate change, back then? "Burning hydrocarbons causes good things and bad," Bass writes (perhaps this is what he might have said): "The bad things are getting worse."[116] Bass segregates the American "people of the thirties, forties, fifties, sixties, and seventies who used Too Much Gasoline, Too Much Energy" from his generation, young in the 1980s when there is "a little more awareness," presumably of the greenhouse effect and its relation to fossil fuels.[117] "There is a good taking for granted and a bad taking for granted, and at least theirs was good then," Bass writes. "Fun, travel, pleasure, quick energy."[118] The future as it was imagined circa the Seattle or New York World's Fair, when airplane travel made a man (gender explicit) worldly, when mobility promised peace. With Vietnam, the oil shocks, and the outright nostalgic deception of the Reagan era, energy politics got harder for nature lovers. But what American could turn her back entirely on the twentieth century's "fun, travel, pleasure, quick energy"—and the tenuous innocence of a once "mass" middle class, swelled with working-class arrivistes? Bass reminds us that oil contains the argument for its own innocence, nature. Again, it is "the old sea." Fossils, evidence of the oceans from which oil was slow cooked over the millennia, play a large role in the museums of east Texas, just as the fossiliferous sea proves a touchstone for Bass. Oil's former life, as ocean microplants, shows itself in fossils, which the museums display and sell in core samples that have been drilled for exploration. These fossils testify not just to life's recurrence, but to its recurrence in better, concentrated forms. As metaphor, oil builds unreasonable expectations.

Some of the failures of these expectations that life and oil, too, will just keep getting better are visible as material ruins in east Texas, in the form of defunct oil rigs and platforms. In these old hulls, the future crashes back down to earth and rust. There are approximately 6,000 oil drilling platforms off U.S. shores.[119] In the Gulf of Mexico alone there are approximately 4,000 platforms[120] and 31,000 miles of pipeline, much of it buried in the sea floor.[121] Every day, this hardware is aging. Currently about twenty-seven offshore platforms in California are scheduled to be decommissioned within five to twenty years, and debate continues about whether they should be removed—which typically involves the use of explosives and thus shock waves that destroy marine life—or "reefed," which implies partial removal or toppling.[122] Both the oil industry and the federal and state governments that oversee offshore drilling save money when rigs are reefed. The effect of reefing on marine environments isn't yet clear, although one significant study found that rockfish and shellfish seem to benefit from it, without retaining unusual amounts of volatile organic compounds or other industry-related toxins.[123] The question of what to do with unusable pipeline is rarely broached. Most of these pipes inadvertently get reefed. The Ocean Star Offshore Drilling Rig and Museum prides itself upon being an example of creative industry recycling, since the Ocean Star was an actual rig that got decommissioned in the 1980s. Yet defunct rigs fill Galveston harbor, mostly semi-submersibles and jack-up rigs that haven't been scrapped or "reimagined." [FIGURE 4.2] There's even a rare cement oil tanker sticking its nose out of the harbor's entrance to the Gulf. This is a remnant from World War I, when steel was so scarce that the U.S. government commissioned cement tankers from Mexico. "Some ideas are not good ideas," our laconic harbor tour guide remarked, about the cement tanker.[124] Or some ideas were good once, until they no longer were good.

My favorite prediction for obsolete offshore hardware brings us back to the Space Age, and to outer space, the twentieth-century ocean's sister frontier. It involves the conversion of old platforms into "space elevators," an idea promoted in the History Channel/A&E's film *Oil Rigs* (2007), a fifty-minute documentary that can be bought at the Offshore gift shop in Galveston.[125] Since 2006, NASA has sponsored the Space Elevator Games to promote the design of a projected 62,000-mile elevator made of carbon nanotubes that will bring

FIGURE 4.2 *Scrap Rigs, Galveston Harbor. Photograph by Author.*

cargo into space.[126] The cable will be held taut by the force of Earth's rotation, and its cargo capacity will outweigh that of the space shuttles. Of course the operational aesthetic is highly stimulated by this almost Barnumesque proposition: *Will it work?* The elevator promises to provide a much cheaper way for space tourists to leave the planet than the shuttles have done. For about $20,000—as compared to $2 million for a shuttle flight—you can see for yourself that you live on a spherical spaceship, with limited carrying capacity, as Bucky Fuller warned back in 1964. "All of a sudden, space will be open for real activity," quips Brad Edwards, a former Los Alamos astrophysicist.[127] Supposedly, the "space elevator" will be bound to Earth by a structure in the ocean "like an offshore oil platform," although nothing in the news media addressing the elevator suggests that actual decommissioned oil platforms will be used.[128] The film *Oil Rigs* argues that defunct rigs are ideal anchors to outer space.[129]

Like life itself, the oil business fights to establish its niche on this planet and elsewhere, with a tenacity once attributed to nature, a concept that has fallen out of favor with cultural critics because it implies that life might be conceived as separate from human history in a manner that is no longer believable as wildfires, superstorms, and unprecedented droughts seize the planet. If one single, material presence, a thing as opposed to a thing-concept (e.g., the atom), signifies the mucking up of human and natural histories, our deep travels together in the long twentieth century, that substance is oil. Like a lenticular image, oil shows itself as a double thing, both within and beyond our sensory field, nature and media, life and simulation. As a twenty-first-century American, I want to stop turning the card. There are dimensions to the field of vision that aren't available in that old magic trick, such as the decoupling of our supposedly democratic governments from corporate greed and the reclaiming of the idea of the public, meaning people and our common resources, our civic ground.

Epilogue

The question of how to stop writing about oil proves as challenging as the question of how, or where, to start writing about it.

One way to end this book: Note viable alternatives to Tough Oil World and diverse efforts toward energy sustainability. Again, consider Germany's model, minus the recent uptick in coal usage. Appreciate the creative scenarios designed by peak oil thinkers, which can be used to continue a dynamic public conversation about oil futures. Consider efficient energy measures, such as cool roofs, anaerobic composting processes that help transform our wastes into clean energy, and lower-carbon transportation fuels, particularly those that are waste-derived. Appreciate that lightweight plastic bags, a ubiquitous petroleum product that blocks storm drains, kills livestock, traps birds, and contributes to ocean pollution, have been banned in more than eighty U.S. communities, taxed in many nations, and banned outright in major countries like South Africa and China. Such political victories recognize the relevance of ecology to sovereignty in the everyday, and that the ordinary conveniences of modern living indebted to petroleum can have persistent damaging effects. Honor, and fund, the efforts of environmental justice groups, from New Orleans to Nigeria to the Arctic, to protect the health of their communities from the incursions of ultradeep oil and gas mining and the related, potentially devastating effects of global climate change. Publicize Bill McKibben's anti–climate change group 350.org, and its latest campaign encouraging university campuses to divest from the fossil fuel industry.[1] Whether practical or no, the divestment idea makes a sharp reply to those universities who invite fracking onto their campuses to compensate for the more robust state funding that students deserve. Be glad that Hollywood warmed to *Gasland*, that your community center (like mine) may be showing it to senior citizens, and that Matt Damon, too, made a frack movie. When your county holds fracking workshops for its residents, as mine did, be sure to attend, or at least talk with your neighbor who did. A good deal of the intelligence available on the topic of oil isn't in the academy or even in the United States, let alone in humanities departments. That said, I can also end this book with the assertion that academic humanists in the United States and elsewhere, particularly those interested in the production of narratives across a variety of media, have something to contribute to a future that challenges Tough Oil. That "thing" is narrative itself. We can disseminate it, and we can make it.

Throughout the process of writing this book I have been overwhelmed and almost shamed by the resilience of ordinary and extraordinary people who have answered Tough Oil World with staunch claims to the rights and privileges of citizenship, speaking for places of various scales, from region to planet. I've also been shocked at the difficulty of putting together oil stories—heroic and otherwise—that are coherent. My complaint echoes Amitav Ghosh's well-known remarks in the essay "Petrocriticism," but it also diverges from his central claims. What surprised me was less the representational slipperiness of oil as transnational capital than the challenge of collating varied sources of intelligence and memory about oil's material effects, even in small-scale neighborhoods that have been or are energy districts.

The larger problem that this book led me to is that of materializing the ecologies of modernity, an investigative and creative task that has much to do with how energy infrastructures have evolved, in relation to each other and to other modern systems. The problem of materializing oil as coherent narrative kept leading me, somewhat unwittingly, to the problem of materializing water, be it the energy-producing water of the rivers or the oceans and groundwater that carry the unwanted by-products of modern lives. Rivers—the Columbia, the Los Angeles, the Mississippi, the Niger, the Buffalo Bayou—run through my book about oil. I did not intend for them to, and upon reviewing the book for publication I had to think about why they do. For me, rivers suggest a narrative through-line from which to see oil, and its possible futures, more clearly. They tell a story both socially and materially more coherent than that of oil, as they visibly connect us and carry our refuse through space and time. Watersheds have long suggested maps of ecologically attuned community for bioregionalists, people arguing that political commitments ought to be organized around natural systems.[2] As Richard White showed, rivers make the point, aesthetically and historically, that energy is connected to real bodies, material things, the work that humans and nonhumans have done.

When I consider materializing the ecologies of modernity as my own narrative task, at least one I aspire to, I do so in part because I like the connotations of the verb "to materialize." In its most fundamental sense, the verb means "to make material or represent"—hence its relation to acts of narrative. One of the earliest contexts for "materialize" as a transitive verb was the nineteenth-century religious movement known as Spiritualism, which was practiced primarily through the séance and focused on calling up the dead. Henry James famously mocks Spiritualism in *The Bostonians* (1885), equating it, tellingly, with the concurrent rise of feminism and of popular print media such as the magazine. To materialize means, within the context of Spiritualism, "to cause (a spirit, etc.) to appear in bodily form," or—in relation to conjuring—"to make something (seem to) appear."[3] The attempt to express embodiment requires not only a conviction that bodies matter in social history and in the production of culture but also a willingness to accept that bodies can be made to *seem* to appear—in relation to other bodies, in partial view—but not made to appear fully in language. Metaphor and metonymy, substitution and deferral, plague the materialization of bodies, in any kind of writing. The problem of representing oil that Ghosh famously notes is also a problem of representing bodies that matter generally. Oil, in its multiform liquidity and imbrication in networks of power, brilliantly brings the representational problem that *is* narrative to crisis. Yet the effort to materialize a modern ecology, always disappearing into the charismatic term "energy," need not be denigrated as mere stagecraft. That is, if the process of investigation is valued over the more elusive goal of making things appear, finished and whole.

As I completed this book, I learned that I was living in a historic oil district, in a newly active frack zone, almost next door to a petroleum Superfund site, and in a neighborhood of particular hydrological interest. I began to realize that the ecological histories of modernity were evolving beneath my feet, in my house, my water. That could be said of most anyone, certainly of any North American. But my local situation began to seem ironic, even severe. What follows is the unfinished detective story that this book engendered—one still without resolution, but not without commitment or hope.

Oil Town Palimpsest: A Penultimate Methods Test

At the California Oil Museum in Santa Paula, California, two docents are talking about the recent labor rights debacle in Michigan, and a concurrent strike at the Port of Los Angeles. "I've got a friend in construction who moved to Arizona, one of those right-to-work states," says one docent, an older man. "He says he can't make a living there." Then he adds, "But those girls who clerk at the Port shouldn't get six figures, if that's true." The other docent, a middle-aged woman, bustles to the gift counter to rearrange some Unocal oil tanker toy trucks, whose blue and orange boxes advertise authentic "lighted headlights" and "PVC tires." She says, "My ex-husband's in Michigan. He's a union guy."

At this point I'm standing about five feet from the docents, trying not to listen to them, on the trail of a modern ecology and its local history. As the docents chat, I'm reading a text box in front of a scale model of a petrochemical refinery located about three miles from my home in Ventura, California, which is roughly twenty miles from Santa Paula, site of the museum. It was at the California Oil Museum, about four years ago, that I began to want to write about oil. "In the early 1950s, Shell Oil Company constructed a urea fertilizer plant on a 96-acre site located several miles northwest of downtown Ventura,"

FIGURE E.1 *California Oil Field. Photo-color postcard by Merle Porter. Reprinted with permission of Beverly Porter Ogg.*

the text box says. "Urea," it explains, "is a concentrated nitrogen-based fertilizer" whose manufacture depends heavily on natural gas.[4] Shell piped in the gas from the Ventura Oil Field, which extends from the hills north of my home into an industrial district of Ventura Avenue, my neighborhood's main drag. [FIGURE E.1] The field started in 1915 after the General Petroleum Corporation—now ExxonMobil—made a discovery there. Memories of the field's origins are scattered widely in county archives and print, much of it industry history. Particularly vivid memories can be found in an interview with "Pretz" Hertel, recorded by a county museum docent in the late 1970s. "Pretz"—short for "Pretzel," the nickname given him during World War I because of his German ancestry—came to the Ventura oil patch in 1921. He worked as a petroleum geologist for Shell, after receiving a degree in geology from Stanford. In the 1880s, Pretz notes, the Ventura field had been a ranch, one of many apricot, walnut, and cattle properties in the area. A man named A. B. Barnard drilled a well on his property that "started spittin' out...salt water."[5] Then "a little bit of gas comin' along with it." Abandoning the idea of watering his orchard, Barnard put up a sign—at the time, an ironic one, reading "Oil, gas, and salt here."[6]

To orient ourselves to this liquid geography, let's imagine a map. Consider that Barnard's ranch and the Ventura oil field transect and inhabit the Ventura River watershed, which moves through a valley surrounded by high hills. The hills to the southeast support a seven-mile-long raised aqueduct. The county's historic preservation society believes that the aqueduct was built by Chumash

Indians (known as "neophytes" in the California Mission culture) who had been trained by skilled Mexican masons who had either read the Roman architect Vitruvius or been instructed in his masonry techniques by the *padres* at the Mission San Buenaventura. The aqueduct begins within the northern quadrant of the oil district, where the trickly San Antonio Creek intersects with the Ventura River, and it terminates at the old mission, located southeast of oil country, about a half mile from the Pacific coast. The petrochemical plant—remember that, the one built to produce urea in the 1950s?—sits almost atop the Ventura River. This has been an unhappy proximity. The archives of the *Ventura County Star Free Press* record accidents, spills. In 1977, an accident at the plant fatally burned one worker and injured four others.[7] The rupture of a fuel oil line resulted in a spill into the Ventura River, and a photograph of fuel-shimmery river water made the front page of the *Ventura Star*.[8] By this time the urea plant had been converted into a gasoline refinery by USA Petrochem, who bought the plant from Shell in 1972. Court records reveal a lawsuit brought against USA Petrochem by a local environmental group in the early 1980s, when the plant was being considered for retrofitting so that it could again produce fertilizer.[9] Thanks in part to the Clean Air Act, the environmentalists won the day, the retrofitting never happened, and the refinery itself ceased operations in 1984—one year shy of the one-hundred-year anniversary of Barnard's "discovery" on his Ventura ranch.

What drew me back to the California Oil Museum was what appears to be a new sign posted at the now decrepit USA Petrochem facility. I noticed the sign one afternoon when I casually rode my bike onto the edge of the old refinery to take some photographs. It reads: "EPA SUPERFUND REMOVAL SITE." A quick search of local newspaper archives revealed that the Environmental Protection Agency's criminal investigation division has begun looking into charges that USA Petrochem illegally stored toxic and flammable petroleum waste on this site. An inspector on an unannounced visit in 2011 reported seeing what appeared to be petroleum leaking onto the ground from cut pipes and "about 46,872 gallons" (a fabulously precise estimation) of sludge in tanks.[10] The open concrete tanks, leakage, and contamination of the Ventura River are acute current concerns, almost thirty years after the site shut down. Materializing the history of the oil district took on a personal urgency in light of this news. I searched the EPA Superfund database only to find the site "archived" and inaccessible, then talked with an EPA officer in San Francisco who told me that it isn't Superfund. The Freedom of Information Act claim that I filed won me a four-page document listing exactly which hazardous chemicals the EPA identified in the underground storage tanks onsite in the 1980s, when its preliminary investigation failed to result in a Superfund listing. As to why an apparently brand-new sign appears at the refinery with the EPA's name and the word Superfund on it, my EPA contact said that she didn't know. Local environmental organizations like Surfrider and Channelkeeper—both of which monitor watershed health—have long considered the old refinery a horror.[11] The two docents at the Oil Museum mentioned only that "gangs" and "homeless" hang out there. They hadn't heard about the recent investigation.

The docents directed me away from unpleasant current concerns to the museum's cable-drill rig exhibit room, where I read, again, about drilling techniques in California circa 1900. Fundamentally, this museum is about the kind of ordinary and largely accepted horror exemplified by the old petrochem refinery, even as it also narrates a proud heritage of bold innovation. Oil history is inevitably a history of high-risk technological experiment, of the perceived crisis of getting oil out of the ground because of its super-utility— a crisis repeatedly met by experiments meant to push technology to catch up with the challenge of getting at the oil, and the accidents accompanying these experiments, deep in earth. The majority of artifacts in the California Oil Museum's cable-drill exhibit are "fishers," fittings that attach to the drill shaft and are meant to pull out objects, like bits, that might break off in the process of drilling or fall into the pit. The sheer variety of fishers attests to how many times things went at least a little bit wrong. Sometimes what fell into the pit was people, like the fictional Joe Gundha who smothers in the drill pit in Upton Sinclair's 1927 novel *Oil!*, basis for the Paul Thomas Anderson film *There Will Be Blood*. Parts of that film were shot in the upstairs rooms of the California Oil Museum, whose building is the former business office of Union Oil. One of the earliest pipelines to carry California crude to the Pacific Coast, like the one we see Daniel Day-Lewis surveying in Anderson's film, was recently removed from the Santa Paula municipal golf course. "I don't think anything was in those old pipes," a docent told me, adding that relic pipelines can be found all over our region. Leakage, like subsidence, suggests a slow and incoherent infrastructural melancholy.

The question of how to materialize the ecology of an oil district quickly becomes one of thinking about leaking, about the quiet, slow accidents that become too ordinary to conceive as accident or threat. Thomas D. Beamish has written an entire book about such "crescive troubles," focusing on the thirty-eight year leaking of an estimated 9-to-20 million gallons of oil under the beach dunes at Guadalupe, a town some 100 miles north of Ventura.[12] For me, there is the specific problem of how not to forget, in the process of merely living as an American modern, that the water table is porous and penetrable, particularly when it lies as near to the surface as it does in my town. Here, the water table has been as shallow as ten feet below the surface, although currently it's estimated at thirty-five feet. A recent Environmental Impact Report (EIR) treating the historic North Ventura Avenue oil district within the larger city of Ventura uses fire insurance maps to identify "49 addresses that may have historically impacted the shallow soils or groundwater of the study area."[13] This EIR defines as a "recognized environmental condition" the "presence or likely presence of any hazardous substances or petroleum products on a property under conditions that indicate an existing release, a past release, or a material threat of a release of any hazardous substances or petroleum products into structures on the property or into the ground, groundwater, or surface water of the property. The term includes hazardous substances or petroleum products even under conditions in compliance with laws."[14] Appendix 4.7 of the EIR, listing "recognized environmental conditions," is 811 pages long. Reading it, I learn that there are thirteen sites near my neighborhood that have been "on the road" to the National Priorities List (NPL), then delisted. There are also sixty-four sites classified as "ERNS," which stands for the "Emergency Response Notification System."[15] At these addresses, reports were made to the EPA of releases of hazardous substances. A list of street-by-street properties includes a few saddled with the potentially playful acronym "LUST," indicating a leaking underground storage tank.

As Susanne Antonetta wrote caustically in her intimately materialized memoir of hazardous waste interpenetrating her own cells and the landscapes of southern New Jersey, *Body Toxic* (2001), we Americans like to make lists.[16] With Whitmanian bombast, we make lists like the NPL that then become a primary and sometimes a sole form of action. As I learned, I am one of the few persons interested in my neighborhood's water systems to be surprised by the inconsistency of official designations given to toxic sites, and by the number of such sites. One neighbor, who used to work for an environmental consulting firm, said flatly, "EPA designations are political." At least the EPA can be commended for responding to the county's (perhaps belated) report that they were "having trouble" with the old oil refinery. Approximately 150 old tanks had been removed from the Ventura Avenue area, where I live, as of 2009.[17] Grassroots organizing on the "westside," the part of town where I am, just south of the heaviest industry sites, has resulted in efforts on the part of the city and county to imagine, and implement, improvement. The city-sponsored booklet *Transforming Urban Environments for a Post-Peak Oil Future* includes fully realized "scenarios," much like speculative fiction, that beautifully sketch designs for a community where 50 percent of the food supply is grown within city limits and 75 percent of urban irrigation needs are supplied by gray water and roof water.[18] My search for the historical *matter* of my oil district works, as noted, as a test of methods, really an apprenticeship for a kind of collaborative documentary-form that I recognize as kin to the novel. Precisely where the urban ecology appears most likely to materialize is where, too, it is most likely to *dematerialize*, often in the contradictory narrative accounts of diverse public actors.

The bodies of discourse that I call by the approximate names (1) "environmental policy discourse"—including documents such as EIRs and the EPA archives—and (2) "civic history and planning"—including documents like historic context reports and surveys, the city's peak oil plan, and recommendations for historic preservation—contain dissonant plots. For example, some of the same sites listed as potentially hazardous in the latest EIR for my area appear in a historic context and survey report also commissioned by the city as places of noteworthy "historic integrity." The *USA Petrochem Plant itself* appears in the survey as an example of exemplary post–World War II (circa 1948) period "forms."[19] A quick search of the Web turns up the refinery within a veritable pornography of industrial ruins, with the site Atlas Obscura featuring "the Ventura Oil Refinery" amongst its "definitive guide to the world's wondrous and curious places," the blogger Sandi Hemmerlein listing the refinery as a not-to-miss opportunity on her blog site "Avoiding Regret: Making up for Lost Time and Missed Opportunities, One Adventure at a Time," and a YouTube bike tour video featuring the site as a worthy attraction.[20] Of course I, too, rode my bike out there to take photographs, in the process discovering the Superfund notice. Call it documentary pleasure. The consultants who designated my own home, built to accommodate oil workers in 1929, with a status code of 5D3, meaning that it's slated to become a "contributor" to a historic district (theme: 1920s Working Class Streetscape) used as one of their primary archival sources another consulting firm's report on contaminated brownfields in the same area. The historic context report translates the brownfields history into questions of thematic unity, exemplary styles. With more self-consciousness, I move between the poles of toxicity and petroleum aesthetics in this book. When narrating the ecologies of modernity, must we choose between contamination and historicism?

Defined by the Oxford English Dictionary as the belief in the value of historicity expressed through style and characteristic forms, *historicism* is a word that gets flung, sometimes pejoratively, at architects, urban planners, and literary and cultural critics.[21] That a site could be both potentially Superfund and a contributor to post–World War II historic period integrity initially seems absurd. Yet city planners write with inspiring earnestness, and their speculative fictions have some chance, at least, of interesting the sort of stakeholders who might invest in a moribund energy district and make it new. When heritage is toxic, as in industrial modernity, it inevitably will be—how can it be embraced without, almost immediately, dematerializing into cultural capital that overwrites the contamination? This problem of how place gets deracinated and thematized to attract capital and inspire gentrification plagues the geographer David Harvey in his somewhat ironically titled *Spaces of Hope*. Harvey wasn't thinking particularly about how place might be played out in a region of brownfields, where underground storage tanks compete for investment with authentic, working-class streetscapes. Not to mention the historic aqueduct, which might, if properly preserved, serve as an affirmative means of marking the complex relations of water and oil that have long defined my neighborhood around energy. In addition to providing water for the mission's residents and its crops, the aqueduct powered a grain mill.

Which counts for more, toxicity or historicism, and whether both can be recognized as players in an historical–ecological relationship worthy of commemoration, is important. Of course there's nothing wrong with instilling pride in a still largely working-class, semi-industrial district in its industrial heritage. The grassroots boosters of the "westside" have looked to historicity as one means of attracting investment in a community that has been written off by some city residents—not just because of its semi-industrial character but also because its residents are primarily Latino. I am proud to live in a designated "5D3" home, although my presence here represents gentrification. Yet such recognition has the potential to strengthen everyone's community, so long as the old petrochem plant is really cleaned up, all (not most) leaking underground storage tanks are removed, and historic integrity doesn't mask a more urgent history taking place out of sight, underground. Recall Richard White's eloquent description of work as that which "involves human beings with the world so thoroughly that they can never be disentangled" from it. In his analysis of how the Columbia was used to harness hydropower, "energy" becomes a way to talk about how both humans and nonhumans do work. I would add that "energy" also functions as a metaphor that obscures our laboring bodies, offloading work as a grounding concept of our species onto other entities, such as water, wood, coal, and oil.

This leads me back to labor, the point at which we entered our conversation about the effort to materialize modern ecologies, with the discussion of labor politics in Michigan by the docents at the California Oil Museum. Labor—work—has to play a role in the effort of materializing historic modern ecologies, because it *is* the nexus of ecology and history, the site where bodies (human and otherwise) rearranged each other in order to bring modernity, as material practice and infrastructure, into being. Since the time of this Epilogue's first writing, America's "Motor City," Detroit, has declared bankruptcy. Burtynsky's most poignant voiceover in the app version of his photo essay *Oil* treats "Detroit Motor City" and the early aspirations of Henry Ford to create workplace efficiency.[22] With the rust-belt keenly suffering, an environmental lawyer in Ventura told me, fracking has come to look like salvation—a way back to good industrial jobs, except without the environmental regulations, fair industry taxes, and in some cases even the labor rights that were hard-won in the twentieth century. Michigan, Ohio, Pennsylvania (and now Texas, again, and the San Joaquin Valley, and Ventura)—these are important points of reference for contemporary environmentalists, overtaking, perhaps, the once central role of Los Angeles in the study of how modern infrastructure forgot human and non-human health, eliding working bodies. In line with White, I recognize a history without ecology as one that fundamentally disregards working people and other agents capable of remaking worlds through their physical force. Let me reiterate that water is one of the least appreciated of such workers.

Susanne Antonetta relates the problem of energy in the twentieth century, which for her centers around nuclear energy and its unresolved, horrific waste crisis, to the "docetism" of her Christian Scientist grandmother.[23] Like Mark Twain, Antonetta recognizes Mary Baker Eddy's faith as deeply complicit with American ideologies of progress—for if bodies don't *matter* (the central tenet of "docetism" that underlies Christian Science, as Antonetta understands it) then what leeches into the ground from our waste storage tanks or runs into the storm drains from our paved streets can't matter, either. All that does matter, in fact, is energy, the efficient rearrangement of matter toward the acute goal of power, which is in its every iteration a metaphysical ideology. White recognized this plot, moving through bodies at work to energy to power, as one which ultimately depleted the cultural and natural ecologies of the Columbia watershed. Now fracking plagues the Ventura River watershed, as I've noted. A verified incident of fracking took place on the hillside above my neighborhood.[24] Our local Monterey shale formation promises a motherload of oil and natural gas. Last year a tony winery in Santa Barbara County was fracked, the vineyard owner claiming that a pipeline of contaminated, industry-"produced" water ran right through his grapes.[25] Here two kinds of ecological narrative, the story of local, artisanal food production and the sacrifice of the rural outlands to toxic degradation, make an unexpected and unhappy marriage. Imagine *Sideways* hooked up to *Gasland*.

Fracking *is* troubling, particularly because of the lack of accountability it enjoys due to the famous "Halliburton loophole" in the Energy Policy Act of 2005, which sets it free of the Safe Drinking Water Act and other federal regulations, including the Clean Air Act, the Clean Water Act, and the Community Right to Know Act.[26] This loophole represents the sort of political evil that could steer Tough Oil World into dystopian scenarios more acute than any I have imagined. Yet fracking offers not quite the discontinuous rupture with older petroleum and natural gas technologies that the phrase Tough Oil suggests. For not only has fracking been happening for about sixty years, albeit with lesser degrees of toxicity in the "produced" water and without the horizontal onshore/offshore drilling at great depths that causes particular concern in my region, but also it's a technique that in many respects only extends the misrecognition of liquid systems as immaterial that we see in petroleum production from the beginning, with its profound disregard for the water table—so permeable, so close. Even if frack chemicals do not contaminate groundwater when they're injected thousands of feet below the water table, as some studies suggest, studies have shown that natural gas leaks near the surface of frack wells can get into our drinking water and into the atmosphere itself, making fracked natural gas a dirtier kind of fuel, in terms of climate change, than we hoped.[27] And what of the seismic consequences in a region like southern California of fracturing naturally occurring faults? With our planners and civic historians and novelists and literature professors living primarily at eye

level—within view corridors, streetscapes, extant exemplary structures, documentary photography, film, and print text—and not within a rich imaginary
of vertical systems, the USTs and the LUSTs and fault lines and the (unselfconsciously) "reefed" pipelines that run through municipal golf courses, how can
we conceive fracking, as threat or as a promised bridge to cleaner, renewable
energy, within a fully realized context of material history?

Memory that calls up infrastructure as a meeting point of ecology and history is, again, scattered. A segment of Pretz Hertel's interview about historic
oil mentions a water-intensive secondary recovery technique called "flooding"
taking place in Ventura in the 1940s causing "serious" landslides. According
to Hertel, his company "fixed" the problem by filling in the canyons below
the drill sites so that the sliding land would have nowhere to go.[28] I live just
one house away from the high hills that form the Ventura River watershed's
eastern boundaries, and ever since I moved in some of my neighbors have
been afraid of landslides. In the late 1980s, the city sent a notice to residents of
my street and a few others that we might be in a slide zone—apparently this
followed a slide to the north of us at a clay-mining facility that long served the
oil industry. My next-door neighbor at the time told me that if I saw the trees
moving down the hillside, I ought to remember to "stop, drop, and roll." Later,
she informed me that she suffers from a delusional disorder. I would counter
that we're all a bit delusional, positioning our lives beneath frack zones that are
also geologically sensitive hillsides, and going on every day, driving, consuming the multiform products of petroleum feedstock, happily recycling plastics
that must be shipped to China to be broken down.

The effort of rematerializing the ground slipping beneath our feet, let alone
collating and retelling the rhetorically inflected information of EIRs, EPA
documents, city surveys, and the oral histories collected by local museums,
is a narrative and literary one. It's the humanistic complement to the work
of engineers and geologists and hydrologists and city planners and county
health agencies and environmental justice activists to create a more resilient
energy regime. Where typically the kind of narrative work that I intend falls
into the toxic discourse genre, with the memoir of environmental illness or
suburban contamination as its most representative type—from which I chose
Antonetta as an exquisite example—I think it also possible to conceive of the
effort of narrative recovery in novelistic terms. For what qualifies as "novelistic," I borrow from Mikhail Bakhtin, Ian Watt, and, more tangentially, Clifford
Geertz. Therefore, I mean heteroglossic—incorporating the multiple linguistic registers of the time, dialogic—inviting interpretive response, thickly
descriptive, and demanding a reader or listener's commitment to time with a
multifaceted plot.

The best examples of this kind of thick narrative recovery are, to my mind,
coming out as hybrid works of environmental justice and narrative art, sometimes in new media, as apps and podcasts that may be complemented by print

text. There is, as I've mentioned already, the Burtynsky app. The more explicitly situated Invisible-5 project, a downloadable app that offers a "critical audio tour" of California's Interstate 5 from San Francisco to Los Angeles—with distinct tours for driving south to north versus north to south—remakes a transport corridor rarely seen culturally or aesthetically as a phenomenological event and a series of lived-in places.[29] Interstate 5 is a major corridor of natural gas and oil transshipment, oil production, and hydrological manipulation, marking some of the most sublime infrastructures of the California State Water Project, as it sends water from the Sacramento delta to thirsty Los Angeles. Most of this oil, gas, and water infrastructure—and the communities that support it—can't be seen from the highway. The many kinds of sound utilized in Invisible-5, from field interviews to "found sound" to archived recordings, create a dense soundscape of modern America in the way that some of the most ambitious novels, for instance Dos Passos's USA Trilogy, also attempt to do. With its multiple "characters" in the environmental justice activists whose stories intermingle to create a corridor of sociability pressing on the highway and dissolving its mythic status as a nonplace, Invisible-5 outdoes the classic road novels, both in the force of its intimacies and in the scope of its eco-social panorama. Its sounds fill your car, peopling the road, invading that dreamed-of place for feeling only the buoyant mobility of your privacy, as you drive.

There are other ways to redo the road narrative, and to deeply imagine oil, natural gas, water, and life. I first experienced the "visible" Interstate 5 on a Center for Land Use Interpretation (CLUI) bus tour of the so-called Grapevine, a section of Interstate 5 between Los Angeles and the San Joaquin Valley.[30] Here I saw energy and hydrology, in electric lines, pump stations, pipelines, and the California Aqueduct's sublime 2,500-foot water lift—after which water from the Sacramento delta moves south in two directions, toward the Los Angeles municipal system to the west and the agricultural "Inland Empire" to the east. In the sociable space of a bus—the same antiquated space of mobile community that enlivens so much of Kerouac's On the Road—people talked about "the 5," its resonance, who lives there, the energy corridor, and what California's State Water Project means—historically, environmentally, and in terms of sustainability. My point being both that hope resides in multimedia narrative forms that help us reimagine modernity and in the fact that people will sign up for a daylong bus tour of an industrial transit corridor. An even greater number of people will download an educational app about the same transit corridor. Many of us want a relationship with the world, in all its intransigence and its evidences of our ignorance and missteps.

That hunger for entanglement is where I locate the hope at the end of my unresolved detective story, for my four-page list of hazardous chemicals at the Ventura petrochem refinery from the EPA did not generate resolution, and in fact it only left me in bemusement that, as of 1985, the refinery site had been marked for no further action because it supposedly was being overseen by the Ventura County Environmental Health Department. The EPA's work has once again started up on that old refinery, as noted. Meanwhile I have yet to collate the multiple voices of my neighborhood into a narrative that satisfies my expectations, as a literature professor, for density and coherence. When I do, I may choose to publish it in a form other than traditional print media. For the time being, it braces me that so many of my neighbors are eager to think about living within oil, all that this has meant in the past, what it might mean now. They think in diverse ways about it, to be sure. But most are more interested in the future than afraid of it. In other words, they're moderns, rather than victims of modernity. We're letting go, moving forward through Tough Oil and beyond it, imagining renewable futures, post-peak cities, regulatory fixes, fair industry taxes, fair labor protections, and the possibility of a genuine conversation about the same with the energy industry and our politicians. Until that conversation happens, stay tuned for more counter-narratives to the petroculture of the American twentieth century. Those stories will come, because they can't afford to stop.

Introduction

The following Life Cycle Assessment was created by Sougandhica Hoysal, a graduate of UC Santa Barbara's Bren School of Environmental Science and Management. Ms. Hoysal's research is meant to express with the baldest honesty the energy inputs required to make this book. As Ms. Hoysal suggests, by leaving the production of paper out of her analysis, she makes the book seem more ecologically innocent than it is, given the heavy environmental taxes connected with making paper. Perhaps you're reading the ebook version, so you don't have to think about paper. Sadly, we weren't able to generate figures for exactly how much your ebook burdens the energy grid. You may find comparative statistics online about the footprint of ebooks versus print books, but from my own findings on this topic I'd say that the research on whether etext is more sustainable than print in the long term hasn't been entirely conclusive. Still, I would prefer to forgo paper. However, I also will say that, comparatively speaking, the news isn't entirely bad for this or any academic book in print.

What is apparent in the Coda to Ms. Hoysal's Appendix, titled "Book v. Cheeseburger," is that, in comparison to a cheeseburger, an academic book has a fairly low impact on the planet. First of all, the likelihood of any one person consuming six hundred copies of my book in a year or a lifetime is nil, so a comparison of the energy consumed in the production of a fleet of my books (600) versus the average number of cheeseburgers eaten by Americans yearly (96) doesn't make much sense. Better to compare the energy costs of one copy of my book to the energy costs of ninety-six cheeseburgers, since average consumption of a single academic book will come nowhere near to the normal habits of industrial food consumption. Many of my books will go to libraries where they will have multiple users, and if students or fellow scholars buy individual copies of the book, they, too, are likely to resell it. Of course they might also throw the book away, and Ms. Hoysal makes a strong point (one valuable to consider retroactively, in the context of *Farenheit 451*) about how books do not fare well as waste. As an academic and lifelong nerd, it's hard for me to imagine throwing a book into the garbage, or even into the recycling bin. I hope I am not unique. I am willing to venture that, for the general public, the "disposability" factor that applies to cheeseburgers and mass-produced print products such as glossy magazines doesn't apply to academic books, which, even when they aren't loved, tend to circulate in limited numbers for years, sitting on library shelves and moving through many pairs of hands.

When in 2008 Dr. Rajendra Pachauri, chair of the United Nations Intergovernmental Panel on Climate Change, asked the world's population to reduce its meat consumption, his bold imperative surprised and offended some people.[1] Certainly the average American, eating ninety-six cheeseburgers per year, might understand Dr. Pachauri's directive as evidence of a vegetarian bias—rather than an indication that meat production in fact counts for one fifth of global greenhouse gas emissions, with the methane emitted by ruminants such as cows being 23 times more effective than carbon dioxide as an agent of global warming. So Ms. Hoysal's Appendix both implicates my method of cultural production in the problem that launched my writing in the first place, making for a necessary confession, and it places the energy footprint of cultural objects such as books and films into perspective. Agriculture demands more gas and diesel than other sectors of the world economy.[2] So before we stop reading, viewing, writing, and printing books—the latter a possibility worth considering, and made realizable by e-text—we're going to have to stop eating. Or, at least, we in the United States will have to stop eating the way that we do, as omnivores within an industrial food system that sends items to our plates by an average distance of 1,500 miles. Enjoy this book, and if you don't enjoy it, resell it.

*Bee Duffell in Fahrenheit 451 (1966). Provided courtesy of Universal Pictures/Photofest.
© Universal Pictures.*

{APPENDIX 2}

Life Cycle Assessment of a Conventional Academic Print-Book

Sougandhica Hoysal

AN APPENDIX TO

LIVING OIL: PETROLEUM CULTURE IN THE

AMERICAN CENTURY

Stephanie LeMenager

Table of Contents

The 'book' referred to in this paper is Dr. Stephanie LeMenager's book titled *Living Oil: Petroleum Culture in the American Century* and an LCA has been been conducted on this item.

1. Introduction

This research paper is aimed at investigating the amount of energy used to publish the book *Living Oil: Petroleum Culture in the American Century,* by Stephanie LeMenager. It is estimated that every year the United States uses 71 million tons of paper and paper products. Also on a yearly basis around 2 million books are published.[1] Apart from the resources used to print the book, many other processes like transportation of the books consume a considerable amount of energy. This study aims to quantify the energy used during some of these processes. Given the complexity and ambiguity of the process involved in the life cycle of this book (or any book), the system boundary for the study will be clearly established. For the energy calculations pertaining to the process outside the system boundary, scientific literature will be referred to.

2. System Description

To decide which processes would be considered for this study, it was necessary to identify the different steps or processes involved in the life cycle of a standard conventional print book. Figure 1 shows the processes such as material production (paper and ink), distribution and disposal of books involved in the life cycle of a print-based book.

A. SYSTEM BOUNDARY

Figure 2 depicts the various processes in the life cycle of the book used in this study. As it can be seen, the system boundary is clearly established around 3 specific processes. The energy inputs will be quantified and considered from these three processes only. Processes such as raw material (paper) manufacturing, use phase and disposal of the book are excluded from the system boundary.

Life Cycle Model Elements: Conventional Print-Based Book

Material Production	Manufacturing	Distribution	Use	TEnd of Life Management
Ink Production Paper Production	Document Creation Book Printing Operations	Textbook Delivery	Facility Infrastructure Collection and Storage Personal Transportation Book Retrieval and Viewing	Book Disposition

FIGURE 1 *Steps in the LCA of a Print Book.*
Source: Kozak and Keoleian 2003.

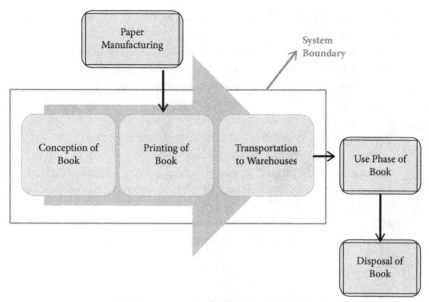

FIGURE 2 *Process Flow Diagram and System Boundary.*

B. FUNCTIONAL UNIT

A functional unit (FU) is a reference unit which is used as the common unit against which all results of the LCA will be compared to (Weidema et al. 2004). All the input and output flows will be referred to this FU. For example, in this study the FU could be *the energy needed to publish 600 copies of the book Living Oil: Petroleum Culture in the American Century from the printing facility in Massachusetts.* If so, all the energy inputs will be quantified considering this FU as a reference unit.

So in this study the FU will be the *energy needed to write and transport **one copy** of the book Living Oil: Petroleum Culture in the American Century to the warehouses.*

C. GENERAL ASSUMPTIONS AND PARAMETERS

To conduct the LCA, a few assumptions were made and parameters were established. They are listed as follows:

1. The book contains approximately 90,000 words which translate to around 275 pages.
2. The number of hours spent writing the book was 1825 hours.
3. The book was written on Dell Optiplex 775 desktop.
4. The book is printed in Massachusetts. Initially 600 copies are being printed.

5. After this, the printed books will be transported to the warehouses for storage. The books sold in U.S. and Canada will be stored in the warehouse situated in Cary, North Carolina, U.S. The books sold everywhere else will be stored in Northampton, Massachusetts.

6. It will be assumed that the book that is being studied in this LCA will be stored in the warehouse situated in Cary, NC. Also that the distance between the warehouse and the printer is 700 miles.

7. It will be assumed that the first batch/run from the printers consisting of 600 books will be transported to the warehouse through standard ground shipping methods using a freight truck of 6 to 10 miles per gallon mileage (EIA 2010). So taking the average, it will be 8 mpg here.

8. All energy values will be presented in kWh.

9. It is assumed that there will be only one reader per book.

3. Life Cycle Inventory and Energy Calculations

This section aims to quantify all the energy flows inside the system boundary and conduct the calculation on each of the processes within this boundary.

A. CONCEPTION PHASE

The book was written on the desktop mentioned before in Ventura, CA. So as the wattage of this device is 280 Watts and was used for 1,825 hours, the total electricity consumption to write the book is 511 kWh (kilo-Watt-hours) as shown in Table 1. Since there will be 600 books printed in the first run, the amount of electricity used for the conception or writing of the book is one sixth of the above value. Therefore, the amount of electricity used for the conception of one book is 0.85 kWh.

B. PRINTING PHASE

The book will be printed in the state of Massachusetts. Given the variation in the types of printing processes and machinery used, an average value is used

TABLE 1 Energy Consumption during Conception Phase

Device Name	Wattage	Hours Used	Total Electricity Consumption for 600 Books (kWh)	Total Electricity Consumption for 1 Book (kWh)
Computer	280	1825	511	0.85

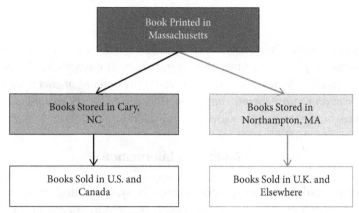

FIGURE 3 *Flow Diagram—Path Taken by Printed Books.*

here to quantify the amount of electricity used to print one book. This average value is extrapolated from scientific reports. The amount of electricity used to print a book will be 0.11 kWh (Durme et al. 2011).

C. TRANSPORTATION TO WAREHOUSE AND STORAGE

The printed books will be transported to two different warehouses in the U.S. and distributed to corresponding retailers from there as shown in Figure 3.

As mentioned in the Section 2.c, the book considered in this study will be stored in the warehouse in Cary, NC. It is assumed that diesel is used as fuel and the calorific value of 1 liter of the same is approximated to be 34.8 MJ. So the calorific value of the fuel consumed is converted to its kWh equivalent as shown in Table 2.

4465.47kWh is needed to transport the first run or batch of books to the warehouse in NC as shown in Table 2.

Since there are 600 books in the first batch, the energy needed to transport one single book will be one by six hundredth of 2570 kWh. This is equal to 4.3 kWh.

TABLE 2 Transportation Energy Calculation

Transportation Type	Mileage (MPG)	Travel Distance (Miles)	Fuel Consumed (Gallons)	Fuel Consumed (Liters)	kWh Equivalent	Total Energy for 1 Book
Freight Truck	8	700	87.5	331.2	**3213**	5.3 kWh

3. Interpretation

Table 3 summarizes the energy consumption in the three different phases. The transportation phase consumes the biggest share of energy and the printing phase consumes the least. Or in other words the *amount of energy needed to write, print and transport* **one copy** *of the book Living Oil: Petroleum Culture in the American Century to the warehouse* is 6.2 kWh.

4. Additional Information

Information gathered on the process outside the system boundary during literature survey and research has shown interesting trends. For example one particular scientific report shows that paper production has the greatest amount of environmental impact among all the other paper and printing processes. This phase of the paper printing process translates to 40 percent-80 percent of the total impacts (Durme et al. 2011). This can be observed in Figure 4 below.

TABLE 3 Summary of Phase Energy Consumptions

Phase	kWh Consumption
Conception Phase	0.85
Transportation Phase	5.3
Printing Phase	0.11

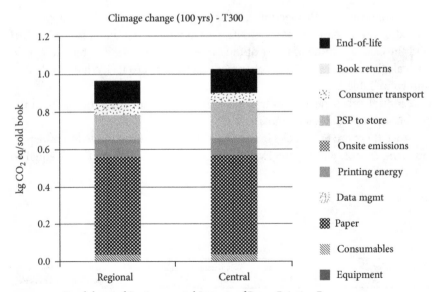

FIGURE 4 *Breakdown of Environmental Impacts of Paper Printing Processes.*
Source: Durme et al. 2011.

By extrapolating, this might correspond to the amount of energy consumption too. So even though the printing phase seems to occupy a small share of the energy consumption in this study, if paper were to be included in the system boundary it might have shifted the energy share percentages between the processes considerably.

5. Conclusions

To reiterate, the amount of energy needed to write and transport **one copy** of the book *Living Oil: Petroleum Culture in the American Century* to the warehouse in Cary, North Carolina is 6.2 kWh. This LCA's system boundary does not include some energy intensive processes which would also have major environmental impacts. This includes paper manufacturing and disposal phases. In the disposal phase, depending on the state and country, the book will be recycled, incinerated or transported to landfills. Various states in the United States have different recycling rates. For example states like California and New York have recycling rates ranging from 80 percent-100 percent.[2] On the other hand states such as Colorado and Mississippi have rates ranging from 0 percent- 19 percent. And these different recycling rates and types of disposal methods will have varying energy demands and environmental effects.

6. References

G. v. Durme, F. Charron-Doucet, É. Clément, and T. Strecker. 2011. Environmental Life Cycle Assessment of Paperback Book Printing Alternatives in the USA. In edited by H. Packard: Quantis: Sustainability Counts.

EIA. *Transportation Sector Key Indicators and Delivered Energy Consumption* 2010. Available from http://www.eia.gov/oiaf/servicerpt/table9.pdf.

G. L. Kozak, and G. A. Keoleian. 2003. Printed Scholarly Books and E-book Reading Devices: A Comparative Life Cycle Assessment of Two Book Options. *IEEE*:291–296.

B. Weidema, H. Wenzel, C. Petersen, and K. Hansen. 2004. The Product, Functional Unit and Reference Flows in LCA. *Environmental News 70*.

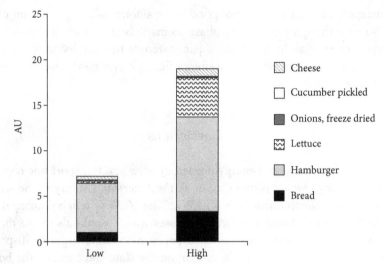

FIGURE 1 *Energy Use (MJ) per Ingredient of a Burger.*
Source: Carlsson-Kanyama and Faist 2000.

7. Coda

BOOK VS. CHEESEBURGER

It is estimated that an American consumes between 1 to 3 burgers (or 2 burgers on an average) every week which totals up to 96 burgers on a yearly basis
(Cascio 2008). So in this section, the average energy needed to produce
a cheeseburger will be estimated. A report titled 'Energy Use in the Food
Sector' by Carlsson-Kanyama and Faist calculates all the energy flows that are
involved in producing a burger. The different ingredients that are considered
are cheese, pickled cucumbers, onion, lettuce, beef patty or 'hamburger' and
bread. The authors categorize the results into two different scenarios—'high'
and 'low' energy consumptions which depend on the processes and the equipment used to process the ingredients. So in this study, the average value of
the two scenarios will be taken into consideration. Figure 1 shows the energy
intensity of production of the different ingredients. It can be observed that the
meat production is the most energy intensive process in both scenarios.

The total energy needed to produce the cheeseburger according to this
report is 7.3 MJ (Mega Joules) in the low intensity and 20 MJ in the high intensity scenario (Carlsson-Kanyama and Faist 2000). The average is 13.65 MJ or
3.79 kWh (kilo Watt hour). Table 1 below summarizes the energy needs of the
book and the burger.

TABLE 1 Comparison - Energy Needs of Book and Burger

Item	Processes Included in LCA	Energy Needed to Produce 1 Single Item		Number of Items	Total Energy Needed to Produce Fleet
Book	Conception, Printing and Transportation	6.2 kWh	Number of Books Published in First Run ->	600	2570 kWh
Burger	Manufacture of Ingredients, Production and Delivery of Product	3.79 kWh	Burgers Consumed by One American/ Year on an Average->	96	363.84 kWh

Coda References

A. Carlsson-Kanyama, and M. Faist. 2000. Energy Use in the Food Sector: A data survey. In *AFN report 291*: Swedish Environmental Protection Agency, Stockholm, Sweden.

J. Cascio. *The Cheeseburger Footprint* 2008. Available from http://www.open-thefuture.com/cheeseburger_CF.html

{NOTES}

Introduction

1. Jacobsen writes that "there may be 40 billion barrels of oil lying underneath the deep Gulf. There may be more. Worldwide, there are more than a trillion barrels of oil reserves—more oil in the ocean depths than Peak Oilers ever dreamed." Rowan Jacobsen, *Shadows on the Gulf: A Journey through Our Last Great Wetland* (New York: Bloomsbury, 2011) 38.

2. Michael T. Klare, "A Tough Oil World: Why Twenty-First Century Oil Will Break the Bank—and the Planet," *Huffington Post*, posted March 13, 2012, accessed December 15, 2012, http://www.huffingtonpost.com//. See also Michael T. Klare, *The Race for What's Left: The Global Scramble for the World's Last Resources* (New York: Metropolitan Books, 2012).

3. Jacobsen, *Shadows on the Gulf*, 38.

4. Klare, *The Race*, 9.

5. For one of many articles on the rapid advance of tough or tight oil technologies, see Vince Beiser, "The Deluge," *Pacific Standard* 6 (March/April 2013): 38–45.

6. Thanks to Imre Szeman for the insight that in fact only 23 percent of the world's oil resources are open to private development, and that this development model produces a different kind of culture than nationalized resources do. Imre Szeman, personal communication via email, July 21, 2012.

7. Charles C. Mann, "What If We Never Run Out of Oil?," *The Atlantic*, April 24, 2013, accessed May 3, 2013, http://www.theatlantic.com/magazine/archive/2013/05/what-if-we-never-run-out-of-oil/309294/.

8. Richard White, *The Organic Machine: The Remaking of the Columbia River* (New York: Hill and Wang, 1995), 7.

9. In *PMLA*, Patricia Yaeger and others introduced the rubric "Literatures of Energy" as a field imaginary to address the kinds of cultural concerns that White recognized as fundamental to energy use. See Patricia Yaeger, "Editor's Column: Literature in the Ages of Wood, Tallow, Coal, Whale Oil, Gasoline, Atomic Power, and Other Energy Sources," *PMLA* 126 (March 2011): 305–10.

10. Ralph Waldo Emerson, quoted in White, *Organic Machine*, 35.

11. Andrew Nikiforuk, *The Energy of Slaves: Oil and the New Servitude* (Vancouver: Greystone Books, 2012). The metaphorical idea of "energy slaves" presents itself at the very start of Nikiforuk's book, with a riff on Donella Meadows's description of herself as a virtual slaveholder because of her debts to fossil fuels. Reference to cause-and-effect relationships between fossil fuel development and abolitionism more explicitly occurs starting on pp. 22–26.

12. John J. McLaurin, *Sketches in Crude Oil* (Harrisburg, Penn.: self-published, 1896), 372. Thanks to Mike Ziser for making me aware of McLaurin's book.

13. Frederick Buell, "A Short History of Oil Cultures; or, The Marriage of Catastrophe and Exuberance," *Journal of American Studies* 46, Special Issue 2 (May 2012): 282. Buell ultimately conceives coal as productive of a "culture" and oil of an "aesthetics" by a different analytical route than my own, although I agree with his conclusions. I would add that it is social history that coal most readily produces, more explicitly the history of social movements such as urbanization and the organization of labor. This becomes a factor reliant upon the infrastructure of oil systems in Timothy Mitchell's provocative book *Carbon Democracy: Political Power in the Age of Oil*, which details the fact that coal transport systems were narrow, purpose-built channels—typically railroad lines—subject to sabotage, whereas oil transport systems were always variable, reliant upon a diverse set of conductors and especially ocean routes, and often removed from industrial population centers where workers might organize to strike.

14. Philip Auslander, *Liveness: Performance in a Mediatized Culture* (1999; New York: Routledge, 2008), 35, 63.

15. Stefan Helmreich, *Alien Ocean: Anthropological Voyages in Microbial Seas* (Berkeley: University of California Press, 2009), 3.

16. Louise Osborne, "German Renewable Energy Drive Brings Emissions Cuts Success," *Guardian Online*, November 26, 2012, accessed December 21, 2012, www.guardian.co.uk.

17. Stefan Nicola, "Germany, China Sign Agreement to Push Renewable Energy Expansion," *Bloomberg*, January 14, 2013, accessed January 17, 2013, http://www.bloomberg.com//.

18. Mann notes the irony of increased German and European coal consumption in "What If We Never Run Out of Oil?"

19. The destruction of the Edison–Ford dream of battery-generated cars and homes is told with great dramatic flair in Edwin Black, *Internal Combustion: How Corporations and Governments Addicted the World to Oil and Derailed the Alternatives* (New York: St. Martin's Press). See especially chapter 8.

20. Michael Ziser, "Home Again: Peak Oil, Climate Change, and the Aesthetics of Transition," in *Environmental Criticism for the Twenty-First Century*, ed. Stephanie LeMenager, Teresa Shewry, and Ken Hiltner (New York: Routledge, 2011), 181–95.

21. Rob Nixon, "Neoliberalism, Genre, and 'The Tragedy of the Commons,'" *PMLA* 127 (May 2012): 593–99.

22. Amory Lovins, *Soft Energy Paths: Toward a Durable Peace* (San Francisco, Calif.: Friends of the Earth International, 1977), 15.

23. President Barack Obama, quoted in Steve Coll, "Gusher: ExxonMobile's PAC Power," *New Yorker*, April 9, 2012, 32.

24. Ibid., 34.

25. Exemptions and loopholes that protect fracking from federal laws are neatly laid out by Santa Barbara's Environmental Defense Center: http://www.edcnet.org/learn/current_cases/fracking/federal_law_loopholes.html.

26. Leonardo Maugeri, *Oil: The Next Revolution: The Unprecedented Upsurge of Oil Production Capacity and What It Means for the World* (Cambridge, Mass.: Geopolitics of Energy Project, Belfer Center for Science and International Affairs, President and Fellows of Harvard College, 2012), 4, 2.

27. Timothy Mitchell critiques the Belfer Center's research findings in "Peak Oil and the New Carbon Boom," *Dissent: A Quarterly of Politics and Culture*, June 25, 2013, accessed June 28, 2013, http://www.dissentmagazine.org/online_articles/peak-oil-and-the-new-carbon-boom.

28. Bill McKibben, "Global Warming's Terrifying New Math," *Rolling Stone*, August 2, 2012, accessed January 18, 2013, http://www.rollingstone.com.

29. These figures also come from McKibben, "Global Warming's Terrifying New Math."

30. Information about Ventura and Santa Barbara County fracking has been published in diverse local papers, including Natalie Cherot, "Hooked on Frack? Where Oil Companies Could Be Fracking in Santa Barbara County," *Santa Barbara Independent*, November 15, 2012, accessed December 15, 2012, www.independent.com; Shane Cohn, "Fracking: Full Disclosure Not Required," *Ventura County Reporter*, June 7, 2012, accessed December 15, 2012, www. vcreporter.com; Zeke Barlow, "Oil Fracking in State and County Raises Questions," *Ventura County Reporter*, January 16, 2012, accessed December 16, 2012, www.vcreporter.com; Natalie Cherot, "Fracking Offshore: Lack of Transparency for the Controversial Practice Raises Major Concerns for Locals," *Ventura County Reporter*, December 13, 2012, accessed December 30, 2012, www.vcreporter.com; Paul Wellman, "Fracking Friction," *Santa Barbara Independent*, September 8, 2011, accessed December 15, 2012, www.independent.com.

31. Amitav Ghosh, "Petrofiction," New Republic, March 2, 1992, 29–34.

32. Ibid.

33. Imre Szeman, "Literature and Energy Futures," *PMLA* 126 (March 2011): 324.

34. For some excellent results of this archiving effort, see Szeman's special issue of the *American Book Review* on petrofiction (33 [March/April 2012]).

35. Jennifer Price, "Thirteen Ways of Seeing Nature in LA," in *Land of Sunshine: An Environmental History of Metropolitan Los Angeles*, ed. William Deverell and Greg Hise (Pittsburgh: University of Pittsburgh Press, 2005), 224.

36. See *Land of Oil and Water, Aboriginal Voices on Life in the Oil Sands* (Warren Cariou, 2009). Cariou is also set to publish a novel and a graphic novel treating petroleum culture in indigenous Canada and beyond.

37. Ibid., 564.

38. Allan Sekula, *Fish Story* (Düsseldorf: Richter Verlag, 2003), 12.

39. According to the Refinery Rankings compiled by the U.S. Energy Information Administration (http://www.eia.gov/energyexplained/index.cfm?page=oil_refining#tab4), a majority of the largest U.S. refineries are in southeast Texas. In 1996 the Texas comptroller reported that "petrochemical plants along the Texas Gulf Coast—the largest such complex in the world—supply nearly two-thirds of the nation's major petrochemicals, while petroleum products from the Texas Gulf Coast refineries account for more than 20 percent of U.S. capacity. Nearly 80,000 Texans were employed in the Gulf Coast petrochemical and refining industries in 1994" (http://www.window.state.tx.us/comptrol/fnotes/fn9604.html). In 2008, Texas refineries as a whole processed 4.7 million barrels per day (more than any other state), while Gulf Coast refineries processed 2.3 million barrels per day (http://www.window.state.tx.us/specialrpt/tif/gulf/indProfiles.php#oil).

40. Martin V. Melosi, "Houston: Energy Capitals," New Geographies, special issue on Landscapes of Energy, 2 (2009): 99.

41. Frampton didn't coin the term, but this essay is typically cited as its point of origin. See Kenneth Frampton, "Towards a Critical Regionalism: Six Points for an Architecture of Resistance," in *The Anti-Aesthetic: Essays on Postmodern Culture*, ed. Hal Foster (Seattle: Bay Press, 1983), 19.

42. Ibid., 25.

43. Ibid., 21.

44. Ibid., 27.

45. Critical realism has jumped the fence into petrocriticism as an effective means of writing oil. Shortly before this manuscript went to the publisher, I was fortunate to receive a brilliant, evocative reading of Sekula against the befuddling capital project of the Alberta tar sands, by Imre Szeman and photographer/artist Maria Whiteman. I heartily agree with Szeman's remarks that critical realism, as Sekula defines it, be proposed as a means of reading oil "to challenge the comforts of incapacity (or comfortable incapacity) that all too often attends the identification of global capital as an unrepresentable system." Imre Szeman and Maria Whiteman, "Oil Imag(e)inaries: Critical Realism and the Oil Sands" (unpublished manuscript), 13. Szeman and Whiteman's manuscript reminds us, too, of the roots of critical realism in the work of Fredric Jameson. I would go back even farther, to Georg Lukács. See Fredric Jameson, "The Case for Georg Lukács," *Salmagundi* 13 (Summer 1970): 3–35.

46. One could look to many publications by Heise or Adamson to make this point, but I see the most influential as their groundbreaking books. See Ursula Heise, *Sense of Place and Sense of Planet: The Environmental Imagination of the Global* (New York: Oxford University Press, 2008), and Joni Adamson, *American Indian Literature, Environmental Justice, and Ecocriticism: The Middle Place* (Tucson: University of Arizona Press, 2001).

47. Postcolonial cultural studies often delivers fine-grained analyses of resource conflicts in global regions formerly under colonial rule—some of the best work of environmental cultural studies on oil falls into the postcolonial studies rubric. See Michael Watts, "Petro-Violence: Community, Extraction, and Political Ecology of a Mythic Commodity," in *Violent Environments*, ed. Nancy Lee Peluso and Michael Watts (Ithaca, N.Y.: Cornell University Press, 2001); Rob Nixon "Fast-Forward Fossil: Petro-Despotism and the Resource Curse," in Nixon, *Slow Violence and the Environmentalism of the Poor* (Cambridge, Mass.: Harvard University Press, 2011), 45–67; Jennifer Wenzel, "Petro-Magic-Realism: Toward a Political Ecology of Nigerian Literature," *Postcolonial Studies* 9, no. 4 (2006): 449–64.

48. Graeme Macdonald, "Oil and World Literature," *American Book Review* 33 (March/April 2012): 7.

49. As will be noted more explicitly in chapter 1, this book owes a debt to the dynamic turn toward oceanic studies in literary and cultural history, exemplified in literary criticism by *PMLA*'s special issue on oceans. See Yaeger, "Editor's Column," 537 and throughout. See also Teresa Shewry, "Pathways to the Sea: Involvement and the Commons in Works by Ralph Hotere, Cilla McQueen, Hone Tuwhare, and Ian Wedde," in LeMenager, Shewry, and Hiltner, *Environmental Criticism for the Twenty-First Century*, 247–59.

50. In ecocriticism, Joni Adamson has led the cultural study of environmental justice as a movement and theoretical frame; Julie Sze, David Pellow, and of course Robert Bullard also come to mind as scholars who've both explicated and promoted environmental justice. Cheryll Glotfelty begins the important work of rehistoricizing mainstream environmental movements as also committed to aspects of social justice in her excellent essay, "Reclaiming NIMBY: Nuclear Waste, Jim Day, and the Rhetoric of Local Resistance," in LeMenager, Shewry, and Hiltner, *Environmental Criticism for the Twenty-First Century*, 196–215.

51. This figure comes from a new series that admirably includes "Energy" among the interests of natural history. See Art Rosenfeld, "Less Is More: California's Energy Legacy," Preface to Peter Asmus, *Energy in California: California Natural History Guides*, no. 97 (Berkeley: University of California Press, 2009), xiii.

52. Margonelli laments that what to her are hyperbolic claims by frack boosters and by environmentalists obscure the arguments for regulation and taxation that North Americans need to have about fracking. See Lisa Margonelli, "The Energy Debate We Aren't Having," *Pacific Standard* 6 (March/April 2013): 30–34. Margonelli's is one of several critical journalistic responses to the optimism about re-industrialization and the revitalization of labor in the United States expressed in "Move Over OPEC—Here We Come," an op-ed published in the *Wall Street Journal* by Ed Morse, head of Global Commodities Research at Citigroup.

53. In "The Energy Debate We Aren't Having," Margonelli examines exaggerated job figures associated with unconventional oil and natural gas development in the United States (32).

54. See the following: Louisiana, which accounts for 40 percent of total U.S. wetlands, loses a football field every thirty-eight minutes, at http://coastal.louisiana.gov/index.cfm?md=pagebuilder&tmp=home&pid=112, accessed August 10, 2012. A scholar at Tulane University in New Orleans offers data to support the loss of one football field's worth of land every fifteen minutes, or twenty-five to thirty-five square miles per year, accounting for 80 percent of total yearly wetland loss in the United States, at http://www.tulane.edu/~bfleury/envirobio/enviroweb/LandLoss/LandLoss.htm, accessed August 10, 2012. The Harte Research Institute of Gulf of Mexico Studies (Texas A&M Corpus Christi) confirms the above numbers (every twenty minutes a loss of thirty-five square miles per year) and says that the Gulf as a whole has already lost 50 percent to subsidence, channelization, and other development, at http://www.harteresearchinstitute.org/the-institute/why-gulf, accessed August 10, 2012.

55. For the term "aggressive realism," see Sule E. Egya, "The Aesthetic of Rage in Recent Nigerian Poetry in English, Olu Oguibe and Ogaga Ifowodo," *Journal for African Culture and Society* 39 (2011): 102

56. Jacques Derrida, *Sovereignties in Question, the Poetics of Paul Celan*, ed. Thomas Dutois and Outi Pasanen (New York: Fordam University Press, 2005), 67, 75.

57. Nelson argues against the supposed "problem" of spectatorship, responding to Susan Sontag: "As Sontag has justly observed … focusing on the question of whether or not an image retains the capacity to produce a strong emotion sidesteps the problem that having a strong emotion is not the same thing as having an understanding, and neither is the same thing as taking an action." Maggie Nelson, *The Art of Cruelty* (New York: Norton, 2011), 61.

58. Susan Sontag, *Regarding the Pain of Others* (New York: Picador, 2003).

59. My definition of "sociability," a term I use throughout this book, comes in part from Georg Simmel, "The Sociology of Sociability," trans. Everett C. Hughes, *American Journal of Sociology* 55, no. 3 (November 1949); see especially the relation of sociability to "play-form," 258. In large part, this essay by Simmel is convoluted in its argument, perhaps due to a flowery translation. Still, his mobilization of the term compels. It reminds me, too, of Winnicott's work on play, and of the contemporary arts practice of social sculpture.

60. Peter Linebaugh, *The Magna Carta Manifesto* (Berkeley: University of California Press, 2008), 6.

61. Sydney Brownstone, "Pennsylvania Fracking Law Opens up Drilling on College Campuses," *Mother Jones*, October 12, 2012, accessed December 27, 2012, www.motherjones.com/; Eve Troeh, "Pennsylvania Allows Fracking on Public College Campuses," *Marketplace*, October 12, 2012, accessed October 25, 2012 http://www.marketplace.org.

62. Discussion of fracking in the environs of the University of California, Santa Barbara, campus broke in the media in Cherot, "Fracking Offshore."

63. The most recent study to conclude that the risks of fracking have more to do with well construction and surface or near-surface level emissions than groundwater contamination from chemicals injected thousands of feet below the surface came out of the Department of Energy. See Kevin Begos, "Pennsylvania Fracking Study Shows Chemicals Did Not Contaminate Water," *Huffington Post*, July 19, 2013, accessed July 19, 2013, http://www.huffingtonpost.com/2013/07/19/pennsylvania-fracking-study_n_3622512.html.

Chapter 1

1. David W. Orr, *Earth in Mind: On Education, Environment, and the Human Prospect* (Washington, D.C.: Island Press, 1994), 54.

2. Paul Relis, in-person interview by Stephanie LeMenager, February 4, 2012.

3. Bryan Hopkins et al. quotations from author's notes taken during postfilm conversation, *Dirty Energy* screening, Santa Barbara Film Festival, February 2012.

4. Ibid.

5. Bryan D. Hopkins, ibid.

6. Bryan D. Hopkins, personal communication by email, May 15, 2013.

7. Orr, *Earth in Mind*, 55.

8. Ibid., 54.

9. Harriet Miller, Earth Day Speech, Santa Barbara, California, 1970. Get Oil Out (GOO) Collection, ca. 1969–1990, SBHC Mss 10, Department of Special Collections, Davidson Library, University of California, Santa Barbara.

10. Ibid.

11. Diane di Prima, "Revolutionary Letter #16," in *The Portable Sixties Reader*, ed. Ann Charters (New York: Penguin, 2003), 559.

12. Susan Faludi offers a compelling reading of the Port Huron Statement as "about a yearning for bonds of brotherhood" no longer available in the rapidly decentralizing, privatizing United States in *Stiffed: The Betrayal of the American Man* (New York: William Morrow, 1999), 306–7.

13. My conception of "ecology" versus "environmentalism" owes some debts to Carolyn Merchant's delineation of "social ecology" in terms that suggest the radical ecological critiques of the early 1970s. Merchant describes social ecology as either a back-to-the-land or a Marxist movement in the amusing scenario that opens her longer discussion of the movement. Carolyn Merchant, *Radical Ecology: The Search for a Livable World* (New York: Routledge, 2005), 139.

14. Donald Worster, *Nature's Economy: A History of Ecological Ideas*, 2nd ed. (Cambridge: Cambridge University Press, 1995). See chapter 16, "Healing the Planet."

15. For an excellent accounting of Earth Day and its long-term accomplishments toward "eco-infrastructure," see Adam Rome, *The Genius of Earth Day: How a 1970 Teach-In Unexpectedly Made the First Green Generation* (New York: Hill and Wang, 2013), 118.

16. Kenneth P. Cantor, "Warning: The Automobile Is Dangerous to Earth, Air, Fire, Water, Mind and Body," in *The Environmental Handbook, Prepared for the First National Environmental Teach-In*, ed. Garrett De Bell (New York: Ballantine/Friends of the Earth, 1970), 197.

17. Ibid., 209.

18. Editorial, *Ramparts* 8, no. 11 (May 1970): 4.

19. The Isla Vista bank burning occurred two weeks after students at the University of California at Santa Barbara campus angrily protested the denial of tenure to William Allen, a popular assistant professor of anthropology. This controversial decision (linked to Allen's political radicalism) resulted in a petition signed by 7,776 students and faculty. Allen's personnel case got mixed up in the oil spill legacy when he staged a "wharf-in" to commemorate the one-year anniversary of the spill in the midst of the controversy surrounding his tenure. The radicalization of the university in terms of student demands for cogovernance in the Allen case complemented larger radical themes, including the burgeoning ecology movement and anti-Vietnam sentiment. The "student" charge on police that preceded and made possible the bank burning, which took place on February 25, 1970, has since been attributed both to students and to a Federal Bureau of Investigation Counter Intelligence Program operation meant to discredit student radicals. This latter interpretation is controversial. See James F. Short, Jr., and Marvin E. Wolfgang, eds., *Collective Violence* (Piscataway, NJ: Transaction, 2009), 256.

20. Editorial, *Ramparts* 8, no. 11 (May 1970): 4.

21. Katherine Barkley and Steve Weissman, "The Eco-Establishment," *Ramparts* 8, no. 11 (May 1970): 56.

22. Historian Robert Sollen offers useful context for the Santa Barbara Declaration of Environmental Rights in *An Ocean of Oil: A Century of Political Struggle over Petroleum off the California Coast* (Juneau, Alaska: Denali Press, 1998), 67.

23. James Ridgeway, "Para-Real Estate: The Handing Out of Resources," *Ramparts* 8, no. 11 (May 1970): 33 (emphasis mine).

24. See Rob Nixon's acute critique of Hardin in Rob Nixon, "Neoliberalism, Genre, and 'The Tragedy of the Commons,'" *PMLA* 127 (May 2012): 593–99.

25. Garrett Hardin, "The Tragedy of the Commons," *Science* 162 (1968): 1249. For discussion of the historical inaccuracies of Hardin's influential essay, see Susan Jane Buck Cox, "No Tragedy on the Commons," *Environmental Ethics* 7 (Spring 1985): 49–62.

26. Ramachandra Guha, "Radical American Environmentalism and Wilderness Preservation: A Third World Critique," *Environmental Ethics* 11 (Spring 1989): 73.

27. Paul R. Ehrlich, "Mankind's Inalienable Rights," in De Bell, *Environmental Handbook*, 233.

28. "Mr. Nixon: Population" (petition), in ibid., 360.

29. Rome reports that "Ballantine alone had twenty-eight eco-titles by mid-1971, with nearly 7 million copies in print. Half of that astounding total came from *The Population Bomb* (two million plus) and *The Environmental Handbook*." Ian Ballantine had begun a partnership with David Brower in 1967, and by the early 1970s the two brainstormed about what "a survival library" should include (240).

30. Jerry Mander, "The Media and Environmental Awareness," in ibid., 258.

31. Barkley and Weissman, "Eco-Establishment," 56.

32. "Smokey the Bear Sutra," in *Environmental Handbook*, 2.

33. Keith Lampe, "Earth Read-out," in ibid., 4.

34. Mander, "Media and Environmental Awareness," 261.

35. "Smokey the Bear Sutra," 3.

36. Lampe, "Read-out," 6.

37. Ibid., 8.

38. Barkley and Weissman, "Eco-Establishment," 58.

39. While the word "public" comes up frequently in *The Environmental Handbook*, interestingly it appears with special frequency in the essays treating ocean and energy. See Wesley Marx, "The Tainted Sea," 51–66, and Garrett De Bell, "Energy," 66–75.

40. Michael V. McGinnis, "Negotiating Ecology: Marine Bioregions and the Destruction of the Southern California Bight," *Futures* 38, no. 3 (May 2006): 388.

41. Rome, *Genius of Earth Day*, 209, 210.

42. The story of Nelson's role in the creation of Earth Day appears in Philip Shabecoff, *A Fierce Green Fire: The American Environmental Movement* (Washington, D.C.: Island Press, 2003), 105.

43. Todd Gitlin, *The Whole World Is Watching: Mass Media in the Making and Unmaking of the New Left* (Berkeley: University of California Press, 2003), 238.

44. Relis, interview.

45. Ibid.

46. Harvey Molotch, "Santa Barbara: Oil in the Velvet Playground," *Ramparts* 8 (November 1969): 44. See also Molotch, "Oil in Santa Barbara and Power in America," *Sociological Inquiry* 40 (Winter 1970): 131–44.

47. Molotch, "Oil in the Velvet Playground," 51.

48. Ross MacDonald, *Sleeping Beauty* (1973; repr., New York: Vintage Books, 2000), 4.

49. Ibid.

50. Judy Smith, quoted in David Snell, "Iridescent Gift of Death," *Life* 66, no. 23 (June 13, 1969): 26.

51. John Berger, "Uses of Photography," in *About Looking* (New York: Pantheon, 1980), 57.

52. Jacques Rancière, quoted in Maggie Nelson, *The Art of Cruelty: A Reckoning* (New York: Norton, 2011), 45; see also Jacques Rancière, "The Emancipated Spectator," in *The Emancipated Spectator*, trans. Gregory Elliott (London: Verso, 2009), 1–25.

53. John Keeble, *Out of the Channel: The Exxon Valdez Oil Spill in Prince William Sound* (Cheney: Eastern Washington University Press, 1999), 187.

54. Alan Trachtenberg, *Reading American Photographs: Images as History, Mathew Brady to Walker Evans* (New York: Hill and Wang, 1989) 74.

55. Ibid., 187.

56. Ibid., frontispiece.

57. Berger, "Uses," 51.

58. Finis Dunaway writes eloquently of Banerjee's role in the visual politics of environmentalism in "Reframing the Last Frontier: Subhankar Banerjee and the Visual Politics of the Arctic National Wildlife Refuge," in *A Keener Perception: Ecocritical Studies in American Art History*, ed. Alan C. Braddock and Christoph Irmscher (Tuscaloosa: University of Alabama Press, 2009) 254–74.

59. Susan Sontag, quoted in Berger, "Uses," 55.

60. Again, I thank Imre Szeman for sharing with me his coauthored essay on Sekula and the photography of the Alberta tar sands, shortly before this book went to press. Szeman and Maria Whiteman offer a nuanced reading of Sekula's efforts to "map global space and to do it in a 'concrete' or material way." Imre Szeman and Maria Whiteman "Oil Imag(e)inaries: Critical Realism and the Oil Sands" (unpublished manuscript, 10).

61. Allan Sekula, *Fish Story* (Rotterdam: Witte de With, Center for Contemporary Art; Düsseldorf: Richter Verlag, 1995), 12.

62. Ibid., 12.

63. Jay Prosser, *Light in the Dark Room: Photography and Loss* (Minneapolis: University of Minnesota Press, 2005), 29.

64. Andrew Ross, *The Chicago Gangster Theory of Life: Nature's Debt to Society* (London: Verso, 1995).

65. See Mick Gidley, *Photography and the USA* (London: Reaktion Books, 2011), 13; Drew Gilpin Faust offers a rich account of photography as a means of consolation for mourning families, and soldiers dying far from home, in *The Republic of Suffering: Death and the American Civil War* (New York: Knopf, 2008).

66. Berger, "Uses," 56–57.

67. Dick Smith, "Dead Porpoise Incident," typewritten manuscript in Richard Jay [Dick] Smith Collection, Special Collections, Davidson Library, University of California, Santa Barbara.

68. On the underreporting of bird death in the wake of the Santa Barbara spill, see Robert Easton, *Black Tide: The Santa Barbara Oil Spill and Its Consequences* (New York: Delacorte Press, 1972). Easton writes: "The California Fish and Game Department listed 3,686 known dead during the spill's first four months. Questioned about the rigor of the count, the department admitted that it had no way of knowing how many birds died at sea or on remote stretches of island and mainland shore....Some experts believe that the number of dead birds that can be accounted for after an oil spill represents one-fifth of the total dead. Thus the number of birds that died as a result of the Santa Barbara Spill can be reasonably estimated at between 6,000 and 15,000" (261). Another useful source is Harry R. Carter, "Oil and California's Seabirds: An Overview," *Marine Ornithology* 31 (2003): 1–7.

69. Jacques Derrida, "Plato's Pharmacy" (abridged), trans. Barbara Johnson, in *A Derrida Reader: Between the Blinds*, ed. Peggy Kamuf (New York: Columbia University Press, 1991), 133.

70. Untitled photograph, Dick Smith Archive.

71. Susan Sontag, "Photography within the Humanities," in *The Photography Reader*, ed. Liz Wells (London: Routledge, 2003), 63.

72. Sally Stein, "The Graphic Ordering of Desire: Modernization of a Middle-Class Women's Magazine, 1919–1939," in *The Contest of Meaning: Critical Histories of Photography*, ed. Richard Bolton (Cambridge, Mass.: MIT Press, 1989), 145.

73. Snell, "Iridescent," 23.

74. Peter Wollen, "Fire and Ice," in Wells, *Photography Reader*, 78.

75. Henry Booth Luce, quoted in Terry Smith, "'Life'-Style Modernity: Making Modern America," in *Looking at Life Magazine*, ed. Erika Doss (Washington, D.C.: Smithsonian Institution Press, 2001), 2.

76. Smith, "'Life'-Style Modernity," 11.

77. Ibid., 11.

78. Snell, "Iridescent," 23.

79. Barthes's introductory discussion of the "stadium" and "punctum" as means of visual knowledge appears in his *Camera Lucida, Reflections on Photography* (New York: Farrar, Straus and Giroux, 1980), 26–27.

80. Susan Sontag, *Regarding the Pain of Others* (New York: Farrar, Straus and Giroux, 2003), 117.

81. Ibid., 116. See also John Berger, "Photographs of Agony," in *About Looking*, 40.

82. Sontag, *Regarding*, 121.

83. Snell, "Iridescent," 23.

84. Ibid., 23–24.

85. Albert Rosenfeld, "Challenge to the Miracle of Life," *Life* 66, no. 23 (June 13, 1969): 50.

86. Ibid.

87. Ibid.

88. Ernest Callenbach, *Ecotopia* (1975; repr., Berkeley: Banyan Tree Books, 2004), 64.

89. Ibid.

90. "We tyrannize and frustrate ourselves by expecting more than the world can give us or than we can make of the world," Daniel J. Boorstin laments in his introduction to *The Image: A Guide to Pseudo-Events in America* (1961; repr., New York: Vintage Books, 1992), 5.

91. "Gulf Oil Spill: Animal Disaster." *Life Online*, June 10, 2010, accessed February 7, 2012, http://web.archive.org/web/20100610195922/http://www.life.com/image/first/in-gallery/43401/gulf-oil-spill-animal-disaster?xid=liferss.

92. Nelson quips, "Well intentioned and effective as the operation may be, scrolling through such choices makes me feel as though I've arrived at the hub of a problem rather than its solution." See Nelson, *Art of Cruelty*, 38.

93. For savvy discussion of Brower's innovation of the Sierra Club exhibit book, see Finis Dunaway, *Natural Visions: The Power of Images in American Environmental Reform* (Chicago: University of Chicago Press, 2005), 117–48. John McPhee's now-classic *Conversations with the Archdruid* also touches on Brower's use of print media to evoke powerful emotional response.

94. *The Huffington Post* has created an online gallery of oil spill images, testifying to the global reach, variety, and injury built into everyday petroleum production. The gallery strikes me as incredibly useful—but, again, targeted: Who searches for it, and who looks? See http://www.huffingtonpost.com/news/oil-spill/.

95. Kevin Michael DeLuca, *Image Politics: The New Rhetoric of Environmental Activism* (New York: Guilford Press, 1999), 4.

96. Ibid., 3.

97. Of television media routines, Gitlin writes: "Battlefield footage in Vietnam, for example, might in its bloodiness fight against the government's we-can-see-the-light-at-the-end-of-the-tunnel frame, which is relayed, however skeptically, by the correspondent's voice-over narrative. The closer to air time the story breaks, the fewer hands and minds may intervene to process the film into the dominant frames. But most of the time discrepancies [between words and pictures] are flattened out by producers and editors splicing the piece together in New York (or another major bureau). Commonly the lecture is unitary and controlling." See Gitlin, *Whole World*, 265.

98. Tiziana Terranova's theoretical gloss on the micropolitics of our digital "network culture" includes both optimism and doubt. She writes, "It can reproduce the rigid segments of the social and hence its ghettos, solipsisms, and rigid territorialities. And it also offers the potential for a political experimentation, where the overall dynamics of a capillary communication milieu can be used productively as a kind of common ground." By "capillary communication milieu" Terranova indicates the embodiment of the "mass" public and the primarily affective intensities of images, which have lost much of their indexical relationship to the social. See Tiziana Terranova, *Network Culture: Politics for the Information Age* (London: Pluto Press, 2004), 156.

99. John Gennari, "Bridging the Two Americas: *Life* Looks at the 1960s," in *Looking at Life Magazine*, 275.

100. For a fairly typical web treatment of Meisel's fashion essay, see "*Vogue Italia* Takes on the Gulf Oil Spill," accessed July 31, 2012, http://www.styleite.com/media/steven-meisel-water-oil-photos/#0.

101. I was not able to secure permission to reprint this image, but readers can find it on the Internet at http://www.google.com/search?q=Steven+Meisel+Oil+and+Water&client=safari &rls=en&tbm=isch&tbo=u&source=univ&sa=X&ei=ywXmUZnsMcKfiALwvYCYCA&ved =0CC8QsAQ&biw=1024&bih=627.

102. Orr, *Earth in Mind*, 54.

103. Ibid.

104. Ibid.

105. Patricia Yaeger, "Editor's Column: Sea Trash, Dark Pools, and the Tragedy of the Commons," *PMLA* 125, no. 3 (May 2010): 537 and throughout. Authors such as Elizabeth DeLoughrey have long made the oceans a site for postcolonial critique. For an explicit discussion of the concept of the commons in relation to literary and artistic representation of the oceans, see also Teresa Shewry, "Pathways to the Sea: Involvement and the Commons in Works by Ralph Hotere, Cilla McQueen, Hone Tuwhare, and Ian Wedde," *Environmental Criticism for the Twenty-First Century*, ed. Stephanie LeMenager, Teresa Shewry, and Ken Hiltner (New York: Routledge, 2011) 247–59. See, finally, Callum Roberts, *An Unnatural History of the Sea* (Washington, D.C.: Island Press, 2007).

106. *Santa Barbara News-Press* article, in Anonymous Scrapbook, GOO archives.

107. Kevin Starr, *Golden Dreams: California in an Age of Abundance 1950–1963* (New York: Oxford University Press, 2009), 219.

108. Rachel Carson, *The Sea around Us* (1950; repr., New York: Oxford University Press, 1989), 3.

109. For the history and cultural reach of the association of ocean and eternity, see Philip E. Steinberg, *The Social Construction of the Ocean* (Cambridge: Cambridge University Press, 2001). See also Kimberley C. Patton, *The Sea Can Wash Away All Evils: Modern Marine Pollution and the Ancient Cathartic Ocean* (New York: Columbia University Press, 2007).

110. Carson, *Sea*, 19.

111. Ibid., 195, 196.

112. Ibid., 212.

113. Lawrence Buell neatly chronicles Carson's change of heart in regard to ocean pollution in *Writing for an Endangered World: Literature, Culture, and Environment in the U.S. and Beyond* (Cambridge, Mass.: Harvard University Press, 2001).

114. Captain J. Y. Cousteau, with Frédéric Dumas, *The Silent World* (1950; repr., New York: Harper and Brothers, 1953), 8.

115. Stewart Brand, interviewed in *Earth Days*, directed by Robert Stone (PBS Films/American Experience, 2009), DVD.

116. Stefan Helmreich, *Alien Ocean: Anthropological Voyages in Microbial Seas* (Berkeley: University of California Press, 2009), 16.

117. Faludi, *Stiffed*, 26–27.

118. Joan Didion, *Where I Was From* (New York: Vintage Books, 2003), 113.

119. Bud Bottoms, in-person interview by Stephanie LeMenager, February 8, 2012.

120. Ibid.

121. Ibid.

122. John Lilly, *The Mind of the Dolphin, a Nonhuman Intelligence* (New York: Doubleday, 1967), 2, 34, 39. The intertextuality of midcentury dolphin writing is impressive. In tribute to Loren Eiseley, Lilly writes: "Sometimes we reach out from our aloneness for someone else who may or may not exist. But at least we reach out, however primitively. They reach toward those of us who are willing to reach toward them. It may be that someday not too far distant we both can draw to an end the 'long loneliness'..." (John Lilly, "A Feeling of Weirdness," in *Mind in the Waters*, ed. Joan McIntyre [San Francisco: Sierra Club Books, 1974], 77). On the question of hands, see, in the same volume, Gregory Bateson, "Observations of a Cetacean Community," 146–68.

123. Loren Eiseley, "The Long Loneliness," in *The Star Thrower* (New York: Times Books, 1978), 43.

124. Thomas I. White, *In Defense of Dolphin: The New Moral Frontier* (Malden, Mass.: Blackwell, 2007), 41–45, 25, 17.

125. D. Graham Burnett, "A Mind in the Water: The Dolphin as Our Beast of Burden," *Orion Magazine*, May/June 2010, accessed February 11, 2012. http://www.orionmagazine.org/index.php/articles/article/5503/ The *Orion* article derives from Burnett's magisterial *The Sounding of the Whale: Science and Cetaceans in the Twentieth Century* (Chicago: University of Chicago Press, 2012).

126. Buell traces the dramatic American awakening to the fragility of the ocean commons in the late twentieth century to both hard evidence of such facts as ocean contamination and dwindling fish stocks and to "the creation of icons of endangerment," such as whales and, to a lesser extent, dolphins. Buell, *Endangered World*, 201.

127. As Corbin reminds us, this has been so since about 1750. In *The Lure of the Sea*, he writes of the upper classes' love affair with the seashore: "The elite of society feared their artificial desires, their listlessness, and their neuroses. They felt threatened by social death from their own particular types of fevers and passions, because they were unable to participate in the rhythms of nature. This is the perspective within which the sea-shore began to develop its appeal in the middle of the eighteenth century. Remember that, even more than the countryside, the ocean represented indisputable nature which was more than just scenery, and which remained unaffected by falsehood" (Alain Corbin, *The Lure of the Sea: The Discovery of the Seaside in the Western World, 1750–1840*, trans. Jocelyn Phelps [Berkeley: University of California Press, 1994], 62).

128. For discussion of Cunningham-Shell and the larger sanctuary concept as it applies to Santa Barbara, see Sollen, *Ocean of Oil*, 23–24.

129. Snell, "Iridescent," 24.

130. Linesch quoted in Maggie Bellows, "Landscaped Modernistic Towers Actually Disguised Oil Derricks," *Marysville Appeal-Democrat*, July 16, 1967.

131. For discussion of the THUMS islands in the larger context of Long Beach architecture, see Cara Mullio and Jennifer M. Volland, *Long Beach Architecture: The Unexpected Metropolis* (Santa Monica, Calif.: Hennessey and Ingalls, Inc., 2004), 220.

132. Mary Ellis Carlton, "With Glamour of High-Rise Hostelries, Drilling Islands to Be Beautiful," *Long Beach Independent Press-Telegram*, Feb. 26, 1966, 8 (A).

133. Bellows, "Landscaped Modernistic Towers."

134. D. J. Waldie, *Where We Are Now: Notes from Los Angeles* (Los Angeles: Angel City Press, 2004), 150.

135. Linesch to Art Seidenbaum, Los Angeles, 14 February 1972, Joseph H. Linesch papers, Architecture and Design Collection. Art Design & Architecture Museum, UC Santa Barbara.

136. For an account of these protests, see Sollen, *Ocean of Oil*, 68.

137. Discussion of the living ocean as an ecological and lively beauty appears throughout the GOO archives. This quote comes from an article in a GOO file regarding the dangers of supertankers. See Ellen Winchester, "Oil and Water Still Don't Mix," *Sierra Club Bulletin* (August/September 1975) 21. For a local defense of beauty as way of life, see Mrs. Alan Weingand to R.E Foss, Executive Vice President of Sun Oil Company, November 26, 1969, Get Oil Out (GOO) Collection.

138. Elaine Scarry, *On Beauty and Being Just* (Princeton, N.J.: Princeton University Press, 1999), 114.

139. Ibid., 114.

140. Jenny Perry, letter to *Santa Barbara News-Press*, February 8, 1969, in Scrapbook, GOO Collection.

141. Keeble, *Out of the Channel*, 126.

142. James Bud Bottoms, *Davey and the GOM* (Buellton, Calif.: Summerland Publishing, 2008), 32.

143. I want to thank Elaine Scarry for bringing the nuclear submarines to my attention, and to the attention of a large audience at the University of California, Santa Barbara, at the conference *Beyond Environmentalism* in May 2009.

144. Sollen, *Ocean of Oil*, 129 and 129–34.

145. For more on the National Marine Sanctuaries Act, see McGinnis, "Negotiating Ecology," 392.

146. These details about the biodiversity of the channel come from ibid., 7.

147. Discussion of increased channel traffic can be found in ibid., 20.

148. Beamish's important book about the chronically underreported, massive oil spill under California's Guadalupe Dunes, *Silent Spill*, explores the media salience of spill events— and the factors that either discourage or encourage the institutional monitoring of them. The treatment of a spill as normative and unworthy of redress depends, Beamish finds, upon "the interplay of selective perceptions, limited organizational attentions, and a propensity to accommodate socially and psychically low-intensity and non-extreme events" (14). See Thomas D. Beamish, *Silent Spill: The Organization of an Industrial Crisis* (Cambridge, Mass.: MIT Press, 2002).

149. "Last Oil Barge Leaves Ellwood Terminal," Press Release, Environmental Defense Center, February 21, 2012.

150. Natalie Cherot, "Fracking Offshore: Lack of Transparency for the Controversial Practice Raises Major Concerns for Locals," *Ventura County Reporter*, December 13, 2012, accessed December 30, 2012, www.vcreporter.com.

151. Kit Stolz, "Tar on Your Foot: The Down and Dirty about Ventura County's Oil Legacy," *Ventura County Reporter*, April 16, 2009, accessed December 30, 2012, www.vcreporter.com.

152. Conyus, "The Santa Barbara Oil Disaster; or, A Diary," accessed January 23, 2010, http://alyoung.org/2010/05/26/conyus-the-great-santa-barbara-oil-disaster-2/. All further quotations from the poem refer to this site. I thank Professor Candace Waid for first introducing me to Conyus's poem.

153. Conyus Calhoun, personal communication with author via email, January 31st, 2012.

154. Keeble, *Out of the Channel*, 196.

155. Ibid., 196.

Chapter 2

1. Discussion of the relationship of anthropogenic climate change, peak oil, and water scarcity is drawn from Catherine Gautier, *Oil, Water, and Climate: An Introduction* (Cambridge: Cambridge University Press, 2008), 81–82 and throughout.

2. Marc Herbst, *Fashion 2012: A Relational Style Guide for the Next Decade* (Los Angeles: Journal of Aesthetics and Protest Press, 2009), 9, 10, 15, 16.

3. Rob Hopkins, "Rob Hopkins Transition Handbook," last modified February 28, 2008, accessed May 28, 2009, http://www.youtube.com/watch?v=kGHrWPtCvg0&feature=related/.

4. James Howard Kunstler, *World Made by Hand* (New York: Grove Press, 2008), 35.

5. Frank Kaminski, "The Post-Oil Novel: A Celebration!," *Energy Bulletin*, last modified May 12, 2008, accessed May 28, 2009, http://www.energybulletin.net/node/44031.

6. Hopkins, "Transition Handbook."

7. Mimi Sheller, "Automotive Emotions: Feeling the Car," *Theory, Culture and Society* 21, no. 4–5 (2004): 229.

8. Susanne C. Moser, "More Bad News: The Risk of Neglecting Emotional Responses to Climate Change Information," in *Creating a Climate for Change: Communicating Climate Change and Facilitating Social Change*, ed. Susanne C. Moser and Lisa Dilling (Cambridge: Cambridge University Press, 2007), 69.

9. Kate Soper, "Alternate Hedonism, Culture Theory, and the Role of Aesthetic Revisioning," *Cultural Studies* 22 (September 2008): 571.

10. Herbst, *Fashion 2012*, 7.

11. Buell points to the "pragmatism that plays a major part in shaping all agendas of discussion" as stalling the recognition of the discourse of toxicity that he eloquently delimits in "Toxic Discourse," *Critical Inquiry* 24 (Spring 1998): 640.

12. Bruno Latour, *We Have Never Been Modern*, trans. Catherine Porter (Cambridge, Mass.: Harvard University Press, 1993), 7.

13. Estha Briscoe Stowe, *Oil Field Child* (Fort Worth: Texas Christian University Press, 1989). Stowe makes reference to "oil field weather" throughout and in reference to specific fires, as on 56.

14. Upton Sinclair, *Oil! A Novel* (1927; repr., New York: Penguin Books, 2008), 8. Internal citations hereafter refer to this edition.

15. Elaine Scarry, *Dreaming by the Book* (New York: Farrar, Straus and Giroux, 1999), 14–15.

16. Michael Winship, "Manufacturing and Book Production," in *A History of the Book in America*, vol. 3, *The Industrial Book, 1840–1880*, ed. Scott E. Casper, Jeffrey D. Groves, Stephen W. Nissenbaum, and Michael Winship (Chapel Hill: University of North Carolina Press/ American Antiquarian Society, 2007), 40–70.

17. Jim Milliot, "Toward a Greener Future," Publishers Weekly, March 10, 2008, 26; Erika Engelhaupt, "Would You Like That Book in Paper or Plastic?," *Environmental Science and Technology*, June 15, 2008, accessed December, 22, 2009, http://pubs.acs. org | doi:10.1021/es087144e/; Greg Kozak, *Printed Scholarly Books and E-Book Reading*

Devices: A Comparative Life Cycle Assessment of Two Book Options (Ann Arbor: University of Michigan Press, 2003), 23–34, http://css.snre.umich.edu/; John C. Ryan and Alan Thein Durning, "Newspaper," in *Stuff: The Secret Lives of Everyday Things* (Seattle: Northwest Environment Watch, 1997), 13–20.

18. Ray Bradbury, *Fahrenheit 451* (1950; repr., New York: Random House, 1953), 6.

19. Ibid., 117.

20. Ibid., 115.

21. Friedrich A. Kittler, *Gramophone, Film, Typewriter*, trans. Geoffrey Winthrop-Young and Michael Wutz (Stanford, Calif.: Stanford University Press, 1999), 16.

22. Ibid., 32.

23. Ibid., 12.

24. Jerry Mander quoted in Kenneth Frampton, "Towards a Critical Regionalism: Six Points for an Architecture of Resistance," in *The Anti-Aesthetic: Essays on Postmodern Culture*, ed. Hal Foster (Seattle: Bay Press, 1983), 19.

25. Brian Ladd, *Autophobia: Love and Hate in the Automobile Age* (Chicago: University of Chicago Press, 2008), 89.

26. Ray Bradbury, "The Pedestrian," in *Writing Los Angeles: A Literary Anthology*, ed. David L. Ulin (New York: Literary Classics of the United States, 2002), 373.

27. For Guy Debord's "Theory of the Dérive," accessed December 22, 2010, http://www.bopsecrets.org/SI/2.derive.htm.

28. Bradbury, "Pedestrian," 374.

29. Ibid., 274.

30. Jenny Price, personal interview conducted at Price's home in Venice, California, on August 5, 2011.

31. Donna Haraway, "The Promises of Monsters: A Regenerative Politics for Inappropriate/d Others," in *The Haraway Reader* (New York: Routledge, 2004), 68.

32. Bradbury's remarks that Disney was "the only man in the city who can get a working rapid transit system built without any more surveys, and turn it into a real attraction" appear in Reyner Banham, *Los Angeles: The Architecture of Four Ecologies* (Berkeley: University of California Press, 1971), 64.

33. David Harvey, *Spaces of Hope* (Berkeley: University of California Press, 2000), 160.

34. Le Corbusier, "Foreward," in *The City of To-Morrow and Its Planning*, trans. Frederick Etchells (1929; repr., New York: Dover Publications, 1987), xxiii; Kenneth T. Jackson, *Crabgrass Frontier: The Suburbanization of the United States* (New York: Oxford University Press, 1985), chapters 11 and 12; Marshall Berman, *All That Is Solid Melts into Air: The Experience of Modernity* (New York: Penguin Books, 1982), 290–312; James Howard Kunstler, *The Geography of Nowhere: The Rise and Decline of America's Man-Made Landscape* (New York: Touchstone, 1993), 97–100.

35. Harvey, *Spaces*, 177.

36. Louis Marin, "Frontiers of Utopia: Past and Present," *Critical Inquiry* 19 (Winter 1993): 413.

37. Barbara Adam, *Timescapes of Modernity: The Environment and Invisible Hazards* (New York: Routledge, 1998), 41.

38. Banham, *Los Angeles*, 94, 109.

39. Ibid., 19, 20.

40. Ibid., 198.

41. "City Hunting for Source of 'Gas Attack,'" *Los Angeles Times*, July 27, 1943, ProQuest Historical Newspapers, *Los Angeles Times*, 1881–1986.

42. Ibid., 1.

43. Chip Jacobs and William J. Kelly, *Smogtown: The Lung-Burning History of Pollution in Los Angeles* (Woodstock, N.Y.: Overlook Press, 2008), 176–78; Daniel Sperling and Deborah Gordon, *Two Billion Cars: Driving toward Sustainability* (New York: Oxford University Press, 2009), 188.

44. "Atmospheric Freak Holds 'Smog' Over City," *Los Angeles Times*, September 24, 1944, ProQuest Historical Newspapers, *Los Angeles Times*, 1881–1986.

45. "Want to Beat Smog and Heat? Put on a Mask and Start a Fan," *Long Beach Press-Telegram*, September 27, 1956, 1 (Home Edition); "London Plays Deadly Game in the Smog," *Oakland Tribune*, December 3, 1953, 11(S); Fitzhugh White, "In 50 Years," letter to the editor, *Los Angeles Times* A4, December 22, 1954, accessed June 15, 2009, ProQuest Historical Newspapers, *Los Angeles Times*, 1881–1986; Jacobs and Kelly, *Smogtown*, 131–32, 111.

46. Susan Sunshine, "House and Home," *Los Angeles Times*, January 31, 1886, accessed May 28, 2009, ProQuest Historical Newspapers, *Los Angeles Times*, 1881–1986.

47. "Want to Beat Smog and Heat?"

48. Jacobs and Kelly, *Smogtown*, 29.

49. Ibid., 35.

50. The report's concern about the "dwindling" of "scenic resources" specifically cites development of beach properties that preclude "the enjoyment of views out over the sea from the highways along the shore" ("Parks, Playgrounds, and Beaches for the Los Angeles Region" [Los Angeles, 1930], repr. in Greg Hise and William Deverell, eds., *Eden by Design: The 1930 Olmsted-Bartholomew Plan for the Los Angeles Region* [Berkeley: University of California Press, 2000], 23).

51. Jackson, *Crabgrass Frontier*, 75.

52. "Parks, Playgrounds," 29. Eric Avila points to the effects of later-century freeway screening in *Popular Culture in the Age of White Flight: Fear and Fantasy in Suburban Los Angeles* (Berkeley: University of California Press, 2004): "Dense landscaping or concrete walls alongside freeway arteries, for example, obstructed the driver's passing glance at the sights of the city. This kind of visual screening sustained ignorance of, or indifference to, the surrounding built environment and negated a sense of passing through the city's landscapes of work and community" (213).

53. Marshall McLuhan, *Understanding Media: The Extensions of Man*, ed. W. Terrence Gordon (Corte Madera, Calif.: Gingko Press, 2003), 70.

54. "Parks, Playgrounds," 25.

55. Walter Benjamin, "The Work of Art in the Age of Mechanical Reproduction," in *Illuminations*, ed. Hannah Arendt, trans. Harry Zohn (New York: Harcourt, Brace, and World), 222–23.

56. Roland Barthes, *Mythologies*, trans. Annette Lavers (New York: Hill and Wang, 1972), 97.

57. "Parks, Playgrounds," 23.

58. Ibid., 66–67.

59. Mike Davis's strong reading of the "underproduction of public space" in Los Angeles bears out this larger point in the chapter "How Eden Lost Its Garden," *Ecology of Fear: Los Angeles and the Imagination of Disaster* (New York: Henry Holt and Company, 1998), 61–67 and throughout.

60. Sinclair, *Oil!*, 17.

61. Ibid., 15, 6.

62. Ibid., 14.

63. Frederick Law Olmsted, Jr., *Report of State Parks Survey of California* (Sacramento, 1929), 29.

64. The term "premodern" is from Gabrielle Barnett, "Drive-By Viewing: Visual Consciousness and Forest Preservation in the Automobile Age," *Technology and Culture* 45 (January 2004): 32.

65. Barnett, "Drive-By," 34; Warren Belasco, *Americans on the Road* (Cambridge, Mass.: Harvard University Press, 1979), 22.

66. Edward Abbey, "Industrial Tourism and the National Parks," in *American Earth: Environmental Writing since Thoreau*, ed. Bill McKibben (New York: Literary Classics of the United States, 2008), 423.

67. Raymond Williams, *Television: Technology and Cultural Form* (1974; repr., London: Routledge, 2003), 19.

68. McLuhan distinguishes hot from cool media in *Understanding Media*: "Hot media do not leave so much to be filled in or completed by the audience. Hot media are, therefore, low in participation, and cool media are high in participation or completion by the audience" (36).

69. Ladd, *Autophobia*, 13.

70. Paternite offers an Internet gallery of his work: http://www.spaternite.com/frame/frames/fr/fr_0720.html.

71. Jean Baudrillard, *The System of Objects* (New York: Verso, 2006), 70.

72. Ibid., 140.

73. Ibid., 141.

74. Lionel Trilling, "The Last Lover," in *The Moral Obligation to Be Intelligent: Selected Essays* (1958; repr., New York: Farrar, Straus and Giroux, 2000).

75. The art historian Karal Ann Marling tartly describes the typical car of the 1950s as "a chorus girl coming, a fighter plane going—a semiotic anagram." Karal Ann Marling, *As Seen on T.V.: The Visual Culture of Everyday Life in the 1950s* (Cambridge, Mass.: Harvard University Press, 1996), 141.

76. Vladimir Nabokov, *The Annotated Lolita*, ed. Alfred Appel, Jr. (1955; repr., New York: Vintage, 1991), 23.

77. Ibid., 256.

78. Brand goes so far as to argue that Nabokov sets up Humbert Humbert to test the failures of aestheticism within the context of twentieth-century commercial culture. Dana Brand, "The Interaction of Aestheticism and American Consumer Culture in Nabokov's Lolita," *Modern Language Studies* 17 (Spring 1987): 19.

79. Sloanism discussed in Marling, *As Seen*, 136.

80. David Riesman with Nathan Glazer and Reuel Denney, *The Lonely Crowd* (1961; repr., New Haven, Conn.: Yale University Press, 2001), 129 and throughout.

81. Both quotations are from Jack Kerouac, *On the Road* (1957; repr., New York: Penguin, 1976), 269, 58. All internal citations henceforth refer to this edition.

82. Louis Menand, "Drive, He Wrote: What the Beats Were About," *New Yorker*, October 1, 2007, 91. Menand explicitly links what he sees as nostalgia to changes in the U.S. auto infrastructure: "When 'On the Road' came out, there was roughly the same amount of highway [as there was when Kerouac was traveling] but there were thirty million more cars and

trucks. And the construction of the federal highway system, which had been planned since 1944, was under way."

83. Avila, *Popular Culture*, 194.

84. See ibid., 5–6 and throughout, for a detailed discussion of the cultural geographies of white flight.

85. Ibid., 11.

86. Nabokov, *Lolita*, 88.

87. Ibid., 210

88. Ibid., 174

89. Ibid., 154.

90. Ibid., 175, 298.

91. Ibid., 152.

92. Ibid., 153.

93. Ibid.

94. Ibid., 211.

95. Ibid.

96. Ed Ruscha, quoted in Richard D. Marshall, *Ed Ruscha* (New York: Phaidon Press, 2003), 62.

97. Nabokov, *Lolita*, 309.

98. Kerouac, *On the Road*, 22, 168.

99. Kerouac, quoted in Paul Maher, Jr., *Jack Kerouac's American Journey: The Real-Life Odyssey of "On the Road"* (New York: Thunder's Mouth Press, 2007), 12.

100. Kerouac, *On the Road*, 27.

101. Ibid., 89.

102. Ibid., 98.

103. Ibid., 181.

104. Avila discusses the discrepancy between suburbanites possessed of a freeway geographical imaginary and "circumscribed" inner-city residents in relation to a 1971 survey by the Los Angeles Department of City Planning to assess how residents of Los Angeles perceived their environment, in *Popular Culture*, 222.

105. Kerouac, *On the Road*, 80.

106. McWilliams discusses this fantasy past in relation to Helen Hunt Jackson's popular novel *Ramona*, the pageants that transformed the novel into legend, and the preservation of the Catholic missions, in chapter 4 of *Southern California: An Island on the Land* (1946; repr., Salt Lake City: Peregrine Smith Books, 1973), 70–83.

107. Kerouac, *On the Road*, 81.

108. Ibid., 97.

109. Ibid., 93.

110. Ibid., 299.

111. Here I consider the first strong flourishing of the American road genre as the 1920s, although earlier American road narratives, such as Theodore Dreiser's *Hoosier Holiday* (1916), should be noted.

112. After presenting this chapter as a conference paper in 2009 and writing it as an article, I discovered that some fellow travelers had fallen into similar themes. The adjacent criticism on roads and oil is well worth reading in the "Literatures of Energy" special issue of *PMLA*. Although I don't agree with Patricia Yaeger's take on Kerouac, I admire her field vision, in

Yaeger, "Editor's Column: Literature in the Ages of Wood, Tallow, Coal, Whale Oil, Gasoline, Atomic Power, and Other Energy Sources," *PMLA* 126 (March 2011): 305–10. Michael Ziser extends my list of road fictions, mostly through film, in his witty essay "Oil Spills," *PMLA* 126 (March 2011): 321–23.

113. Ladd writes: " 'Autophobia' is an obscure psychiatric diagnosis of 'fear of oneself.' Fear, or hatred, of automobiles is quite a different thing. Yet the automobile has become such a central tool (and toy) of modern life that it might make sense to claim that fear of cars is tantamount to fear of being human in the automobile age." *Autophobia*, 11.

114. Nabokov, *Lolita*, 306.

115. Kerouac, *On the Road*, 237.

116. Bruno Latour, *Reassembling the Social: An Introduction to Actor-Network-Theory* (Oxford: Oxford University Press, 2005), 63–121. Environmental criticism establishes a rich conversation with science studies and corporeal feminism in Stacy Alaimo and Susan Hekman, *Material Feminisms* (Bloomington: Indiana University Press, 2008).

117. Bakhtin, from *Rabelais and His World*, quoted in Andrew Stott, *Comedy* (New York: Routledge, 2005), 87.

118. Michael Watts, "Petro-Violence: Community, Extraction, and Political Ecology of a Mythic Commodity," in *Violent Environments*, ed. Nancy Lee Peluso and Michael Watts (Ithaca, N.Y.: Cornell University Press, 2001), 212. For more discussion of the magic and violence attributed to oil production, see Jennifer Wenzel, "Petro-Magic-Realism: Toward a Political Ecology of Nigerian Literature," *Postcolonial Studies* 9 (December 2006): 449–64.

119. Quoted in Watts, "Petro-Violence," 212.

120. Ibid., 191.

121. Myrna I. Santiago, *The Ecology of Oil: Environment, Labor, and the Mexican Revolution* (Cambridge: Cambridge University Press, 2006), 338–39; Paul Sabin, "Beaches versus Oil in Greater Los Angeles," in *Land of Sunshine: An Environmental History of Metropolitan Los Angeles*, ed. William Deverell and Greg Hise (Pittsburgh: University of Pittsburgh Press, 2005), 95–114.

122. Frederick Buell, "A Short History of Oil Cultures; or, The Marriage of Catastrophe and Exuberance," *Journal of American Studies* 46 (2012): 282.

123. See Stowe, *Oil Field Child*.

124. Bill Brown, "How to Do Things with Things (A Toy Story)," *Critical Inquiry* 24 (Summer 1998): 935.

125. Santiago, *Ecology of Oil*, 164.

126. Robert Vitalis, *America's Kingdom: Mythmaking on the Saudi Frontier* (New York: Verso, 2009), 22.

127. Vitalis notes that the term "coolie," in reference to Arab employees, was used by Aramco executives through the early 1950s. See ibid., 59.

128. Wallace Stegner, *Discovery: The Search for Arabian Oil*, abridged for Aramco World Magazine (Beirut: An Export Book, 1971), 35.

129. Vitalis recounts the complex narrative of Stegner's publication for Aramco in the preface to *America's Kingdom*. See also Robert Vitalis, "Wallace Stegner's Arabian Discovery: Imperial Blind Spots in a Continental Vision," *Pacific Historical Review* 76, no. 3 (August 2007): 405–38.

130. W. J. Archer and Edward L. Doheny, *Mexican Petroleum*, ed. Archer (New York: Pan American Petroleum and Transport Company, 1922), 102.

131. Ibid., 96.

132. Carleton Beals, *Black River* (Philadelphia, Penn.: J. B. Lippincott, 1934).

133. Santiago, *Ecology of Oil*, 125.

134. Archer and Doheny, *Mexican Petroleum*, 98.

135. Rahman Badalov, "Oil, Revolution, and Cinema," *Azerbaijan International* 5 (Autumn 1997): 57.

136. Robin L. Murray and Joseph K. Heumann, "The First Eco-Disaster Film?," *Film Quarterly* 59 (Spring 2006): 50.

137. Ibid., 48.

138. Jean Baudrillard, "The Dramatization of Economics," in *Utopia Deferred: Writings from Utopie* (1967–1978), trans. Stuart Kendall (New York: Semiotext(e), 2006), 197. For a discussion of convivial modernity and varied architectural responses to the 1973 oil shock, see Giovanna Borasi and Mirko Zardini, eds., *Sorry, Out of Gas: Architecture's Response to the 1973 Oil Crisis* (Montreal, Canada, and Mantova, Italy: Canadian Centre for Architecture and Maurizio Corraini, 2007).

139. Kent Jones, "Triumph of the Will," Film Comment, January/February 2008, 25.

140. Paul Thomas Anderson, *There Will Be Blood: Final Shooting Script* (Paramount/Vantage), 3. Copyright (c) 2007 Paramount Pictures and Miramax Film Corp. All Rights Reserved.

141. Ibid., 48.

142. Linda Williams, "Film Bodies: Gender, Genre, and Excess," *Film Quarterly* 44 (Summer 1991): 3–6.

143. Stuart Klawans, "A Hard Man," *The Nation*, January 28, 2008, 33.

144. I enjoy conceiving this reading of Day-Lewis in conversation with the "new kind of bio-energetics...produced by oil" that Frederick Buell notes in relation to the character of Dad Ross—animated by a new, oil-based personality trait called "pep," in the Sinclair novel *Oil!* See Buell, "Short History," 287.

145. UCLA Institute of the Environment, *Sustainability in the Motion Picture Industry* (Sacramento: California Integrated Waste Management Board, 2006), 25.

146. Elswit, quoted in Michael Goldman, "Old-Fashioned Filmmaking," *Millimeter—The Magazine of Motion Picture and Television Production* 35, no. 6 (2007), http://gateway.proquest.com/openurl?url_ver=Z39.88-2004&res_dat=xri:iipa:&rft_dat=xri:iipa:article:citation:iipa00455256.

147. Ibid.

148. Ibid.

Chapter 3

1. Glenn Blake, "Chocolate Bay," in *Drowned Moon* (Baltimore, Md.: Johns Hopkins University Press, 2001), 78.

2. Ibid., 86.

3. Ibid., 85, 91.

4. Ibid., 94.

5. Ibid., 92.

6. "Millions of Barrels of Oil Safely Reach Port in Major Environmental Catastrophe," *The Onion*, August 11, 2010, accessed August 15, 2010, http://www.theonion.com/articles/millions-of-barrels-of-oil-safely-reach-port-in-ma,17875.

7. Rebecca Solnit, "Diary," *London Review of Books*, August 5, 2010, accessed August 10, 2010, http://www.lrb.co.uk/v32/n15/rebecca-solnit/diary/print. The U.S. Geological Survey offers several helpful definitions of Volatile Organic Compounds (VOCs). For instance, "Many VOCs are human-made chemicals that are used and produced in the manufacture of paints, adhesives, petroleum products, pharmaceuticals, and refrigerants. They often are compounds of fuels, solvents, hydraulic fluids, paint thinners, and dry-cleaning agents commonly used in urban settings. VOC contamination of drinking water supplies is a human-health concern because many are toxic and are known or suspected human carcinogens," accessed July 20, 2012, http://toxics.usgs.gov/definitions/vocs.html.

8. Mike Davis, "Los Angeles after the Storm: The Dialectic of Ordinary Disaster," *Antipode* 27 (Summer 1995): 221–41.

9. Rob Nixon, "Neoliberalism, Slow Violence, and the Environmental Picaresque," *Modern Fiction Studies* 55 (Fall 2009): 443–48. See also Curtis Marez, "What Is a Disaster?," *American Quarterly* 61 (September 2009): ix–xi; this entire special issue of *American Quarterly*, edited by Clyde Woods, creates a strong template for cultural studies of disaster.

10. Paul Connerton, *How Societies Remember* (Cambridge: Cambridge University Press, 1989).

11. Guy Debord, *Society of the Spectacle*, trans. Ken Knabb (London: Aldgate Press, 2005).

12. Drew Landry, "BP Blues," accessed August 10, 2010, http://www.youtube.com/watch?v=6E9HyoOyHg8.

13. Catriona Mortimer-Sandilands, "Melancholy Natures, Queer Ecologies," in *Queer Ecologies: Sex, Nature, Politics, Desire*, ed. Catriona Mortimer-Sandilands and Bruce Erickson (Bloomington: Indiana University Press, 2010), 333.

14. Ibid., 333.

15. Bruno Latour, *Politics of Nature: How to Bring the Sciences into Democracy*, trans. Catherine Porter (Cambridge, Mass.: Harvard University Press, 2004), 23. Hereafter referred to as *PN*.

16. Solnit discusses the feeling of being in New Orleans and breathing in VOCs, with a periodic "gas station smell," in "Diary."

17. Timothy Morton, "The Mesh," in *Environmental Criticism for the Twenty-First Century*, ed. Stephanie LeMenager, Teresa Shewry, and Ken Hiltner (London: Routledge, 2011), 19–30.

18. When I refer to the degree that "U.S. modernity" has taken hold in the Deep South, I consider both proximity to the grid and fulfillment in this region of the now ordinary U.S. landscape of highways, low-density suburbs, strip malls, fast-food and gasoline-service islands, and shopping centers ringed by parking lots or parking towers.

19. Barack Obama, "Text of Obama's Speech on Gulf Oil Spill," *New Haven Register*, July 16, 2010, page 2, accessed July 25, 2010, http://www.nhregister.com/articles/2010/06/15/news/doc4c184f9627d4f201824265.txt.

20. Ibid., page 4.

21. Hannah Arendt, *The Origins of Totalitarianism* (New York: Harcourt, 1968); Giorgio Agamben, *Homo Sacer: Sovereign Power and Bare Life*, trans. Daniel Heller-Roazen (Stanford: Stanford University Press, 1998).

22. Ramachandra Guha and Juan Martinez-Alier, *Varieties of Environmentalism: Essays North and South* (London: Earthscan Publications, 1997), 12–13.

23. Robert D. Bullard, *Dumping in Dixie: Race, Class, and Environmental Quality* (Boulder, Colo.: Westview Press, 1990), xiii.

24. Lawrence Buell, "Toxic Discourse," *Critical Inquiry* 24 (Spring 1998): 641.

25. Bullard, *Dumping in Dixie*, 32.

26. "Lewis Black's Spill Solution: Declare War, Invade BP," *Raw Story*, June 10, 2010, accessed July 25, 2010, http://www.rawstory.com/rs/2010/06/lewis-blacks-spill-solution-de clare-war-invade-bp.

27. Mike Tidwell, *Bayou Farewell: The Rich Life and Tragic Death of Louisiana's Cajun Coast* (New York: Vintage, 2003). Hereafter referred to as *BF*.

28. Louisiana Coastal Wetlands Conservation and Restoration Task Force and the Wetlands Conservation and Restoration Authority, *Coast 2050: Toward a Sustainable Coastal Louisiana* (Baton Rouge: Louisiana Department of Natural Resources, 1998), 1–2.

29. Discussion of these figures and the fate of *Coast 2050* can be found in Mark Fischett, "Drowning New Orleans," *Scientific American*, October 2001, 78–85.

30. Tom McGuire, *History of the Offshore Oil and Gas Industry in Southern Louisiana*, volume II: *Bayou Lafourche—Oral Histories of the Oil and Gas Industry* (Washington, D.C.: U.S. Department of the Interior, Minerals Management Service, Gulf of Mexico OCS Region, 2008), vii. Hereafter referred to as *BL*.

31. Martha Serpas, "Decreation," in *The Dirty Side of the Storm* (New York: W. W. Norton, 2007), 79. Hereafter referred to as *DSS*.

32. W. Lance Bennett discusses the Greenpeace/Adbusters's Coke "Spotlight" campaign and other environmental activism via the Internet in "New Media Power: The Internet and Global Activism," in *Contesting Media Power: Alternative Media in a Networked World*, ed. Nick Couldry and James Curran (Lanham, Md.: Rowman and Littlefield, 2003).

33. Hannah Arendt, *The Human Condition* (Chicago: University of Chicago Press, 1958), 201.

34. See, again, Bennett, "New Media Power."

35. Ulrich Beck, *Ecological Enlightenment: Essay on the Politics of the Risk Society*, trans. Mark A. Ritter (Atlantic Highlands, N.J.: Humanity Books, 1995), 13.

36. Bethany Halford, "Scientists Use Social Networking to Study Spill," *Chemical and Engineering News* 88 (June 2010): 24.

37. In California, the web-based California King Tides initiative similarly calls on citizens to document the highest seasonal tides on that state's coasts.

38. Sadly, as of the time of the writing of this book, Project Tantalus does not seem to be up and running, and its primary director, Olsen, does not answer email inquiries about its status. Since I take this to be an exemplary project, one among many forecasted for the present and near future, I don't see the status of Tantalus per se as a refutation of my larger—tentatively hopeful—argument.

39. Ulrich Beck, *World Risk Society* (Cambridge: Blackwell, 2001).

40. Poppy Z. Brite, *Dispatches from Tanganyika: The Journal of Poppy Z. Brite*, "'This a lotta shit,' someone said, but Ignatius ignored the voice," last modified June 29, 2010, accessed July 11, 2010, http://docbrite.livejournal.com/739298.html.

41. Hartman's analysis moves between a widely applicable critique of empathic cooptation and an explicit analysis of how the fungibility of black bodies in chattel slavery enables the "projection of others' feelings, ideas, desires, and values." Hartman's ironic use of "enjoyment" indicates the pleasures of feeling another's pain but finds its primary context in the legal definition of "enjoy" as "to have, possess." Saidiya V. Hartman, *Scenes of Subjection: Terror,*

Slavery, and Self-Making in Nineteenth-Century America (New York: Oxford University Press, 1997), 22–23.

42. Brite, quoted in mf, "Treme Is Not OK," *Back of Town: Blogging Treme*, March 23, 2010, accessed July 11, 2010, http://backoftown.wordpress.com/2010/03/23/treme-is-not-ok.

43. Ibid.

44. Brite, "'This a lotta shit.'"

45. "wanderingastray," "Comments," *Dispatches from Tanganyika*, June 30, 2010, 4:10 a.m., accessed July 11, 2010, http://docbrite.livejournal.com/739298.html.

46. Brite, "Comments," June 30, 2010, 4:14 a.m.

47. "wanderingastray," "Comments," June 30, 2010, 4:22 a.m.

48. Hartman, *Scenes of Subjection*, 18.

49. John Wathen quoted from his Internet video (as "hccreekkeeper"), "BP Slick THE SOURCE 05.07.10," accessed June 10, 2010, http://www.youtube.com/watch?v=uG8JHSAVYT0. See also Wathen's blog at http://www.bpoilslick.blogspot.com.

50. Lauren Berlant, "Trauma and Ineloquence," *Cultural Values* 5 (January 2001): 44.

51. Jerry W. Ward, Jr., *The Katrina Papers: A Journal of Trauma and Recovery* (New Orleans: University of New Orleans Press, 2008), 206.

52. Ibid., 53.

53. See Michael Ziser's brilliant discussion of the relative carbon weight of culture in new media systems in "Home Again: Peak Oil, Climate Change, and the Aesthetics of Transition," in *Environmental Criticism for the Twenty-First Century*, ed. Stephanie LeMenager, Teresa Shewry, and Ken Hiltner (New York: Routledge, 2011), 181–95.

54. Ward, "Katrina Papers," 180.

55. Ibid., 53–54.

56. Ibid., 114.

57. Ibid., 183.

58. Jeff Newelt, comics editor at *Smith*, contends that web publication could produce a graphic novel that "sells 60,000 or 70,000 copies instead of 5,000." Newelt, quoted in Dave Itzkoff, "The Unfinished Tale of an Unlikely Hero," *New York Times*, September 5, 2010.

59. Josh Neufeld, *A.D.: New Orleans after the Deluge Presented by SMITH Magazine*, January 1, 2007, accessed August 9, 2010, http://www.smithmag.net/afterthedeluge/2007/01/01/prologue-1.

60. Scott McCloud, *Understanding Comics: The Invisible Art* (New York: HarperCollins, 1993), 30–37.

61. Sean Cubitt, *Digital Aesthetics* (London: Sage, 1998), 14.

62. Josh Neufeld, *Katrina Came Calling: A Gulf Coast Deployment* (Brooklyn: Josh Neufeld Comix and Stories, 2005–2006), 2, 82.

63. Neufeld, "Afterword," *Katrina*.

64. Harriet Russell, "An Endangered Species, Oil," in *Sorry, Out of Gas*, ed. Giovanna Borasi and Mirko Zardini (Montreal, Canada, and Mantova, Italy: Canadian Centre for Architecture and Maurizio Corraini, 2007).

65. Michael W. Toffel and Arpad Horvath, "Environmental Implications of Wireless Technologies: News Delivery and Business Meetings," *Environmental Science and Technology* 38 (May 2004): 2963.

66. Robert Weinhold, "A New Pulp Fact? New Research Suggests a Possible Mechanism for Some of the Damage to Fish from Pulp and Paper Mills," *Environmental Science and Technology* 43 (March 2009): 1242.

67. Conner Bailey, Peter R. Sinclair, and Mark R. Dubois, "Future Forests: Forecasting Social and Ecological Consequences of Genetic Engineering," *Society and Natural Resources* 17 (August 2004): 642, 643, 645.

68. Noelle Skodzinski, "Offshoring and the Global Marketplace," *Book Business Magazine*, accessed July 17, 2010, http://www.bookbusinessmag.com.

69. Nathalie Hardy, "A Writer's Green Guide," *Poets and Writers* 37, no.1, accessed July 17, 2010, http://lion.chadwyck.com.proxy.library.ucsb.edu:2048; Michael J. Ducey, "Paper's Environmental Agenda," *Graphic Arts Monthly*, July 2001, accessed July 17, 2010, http://www.gammag.com.

70. Neufeld, "Afterword," *A.D.*, 193.

71. I'm referring to the controversial study of mirror neurons as a subpersonal ground for empathy and more broadly for the recognition of common humanity. For example, see Vittorio Gallese, "The 'Shared Manifold' Hypothesis: From Mirror Neurons to Empathy," *Journal of Consciousness Studies* 8 (2001): 43. By "the shared manifold," Gallese intends the states we share with others, including "emotions...body schema...our being subject to pain" (44).

72. Patricia Smith, "34," in *Blood Dazzler* (Minneapolis, Minn.: Coffee House Press, 2008), 57.

73. Félix Guattari, *The Three Ecologies*, trans. Ian Pindar and Paul Sutton (New York: Continuum International, 2000), 20.

74. Martin V. Melosi, "Houston: Energy Capitals," *New Geographies* (Special Issue on Landscapes of Energy) 2 (2009): 99.

75. Brooks sees the detective story as indicative of the self-reflexivity of all narrative acts. "The detective story, as a kind of dime-store modern version of 'wisdom literature,' is useful in displaying the double logic most overtly, using the plot of the inquest to find, or construct, a story of the crime which will offer just those features necessary to the thematic coherence we call a solution, while claiming, of course, that the solution has been made necessary by the crime." Peter Brooks, *Reading for the Plot: Design and Intention in Narrative* (New York: Knopf, 1984), 29.

76. Carl D. Malmgren, "Anatomy of Murder: Mystery, Detective, and Crime Fiction," *Journal of Popular Culture* 30, no. 4 (Spring 1997): 123. Jameson writes of Raymond Chandler's fiction as reconfiguring the social relations that make a feeling of lived place in the decentered spaces of Los Angeles. In Fredric Jameson, "On Raymond Chandler," *Southern Review* 6, no. 3 (July 1970): 633.

77. I want again to offer gratitude to those critics and writers involved in the immensely productive "oceanic turn" in cultural and literary studies, including Elizabeth DeLoughrey, Teresa Shewry, Peter Alagona, Nicole Starosielski, Patricia Yaeger, Kimberley C. Patton, Callum Roberts, Philip E. Steinberg, and D. Graham Burnett.

78. Helon Habila, *Oil on Water* (New York: W. W. Norton, 2010), 96.

79. "The Niger Delta is undergoing rapid subsidence being a sedimentary basin where oil and gas are being intensely extracted. In combination with predicted sea level rise as a result of global warming, about 40Km wide strip of the Niger Delta could be submerged in the next 30 years." Those were the declarations of Professor Dagogo M. J. Fubara in the "Niger Delta

Environment Position Paper," presented in Abuja during one of several stakeholder prepara-
tory consultative sessions conducted by the Federal Ministry of Environment and aimed at har-
nessing inputs from relevant sectors in the Country Report/National Position for the United
Nations Conference on Sustainable Development (Rio+20), which was held in Rio de Janeiro,
Brazil, in June 2012. Fubara, quoted in Michael Simire, "Rio + 20: Chronicling, Resolving
the Niger Delta Crisis," *ecojournalism*, accessed September 25, 2012, http://ecojournalism.org/
en/march2012/articles/230/Rio20-Chronicling-resolving-Niger-Delta-crisis-Michael-Simir
e-niger-delta-rio20.htm?tpl=6.

80. Timothy Morton, *The Ecological Thought* (Cambridge, Mass.: Harvard University
Press, 2010).

81. Antonia Juhasz, *Black Tide: The Devastating Impact of the Gulf Oil Spill* (Hoboken,
N.J.: John Wiley & Sons, 2011), 100–105.

82. Ibid., 104–5, 100.

83. Joye, interviewed in ibid., 113.

84. Jennifer Wenzel, "Behind the Headlines," a review essay on *Oil on Water* by Helon
Habila, *American Book Review*, Special Issue on Petrofiction, 33, no. 3 (March/April 2012),
accessed August 2, 2012, online version through ProjectMuse.

85. Cyril Obi and Siri Aas Rustad, *Oil and Insurgency in the Niger Delta* (London: Zed
Books, 2011), 3. For a somewhat out-of-date but still striking account, see also Ike Okonta and
Oronto Douglas, *Where Vultures Feast: Shell, Human Rights, and Oil in the Niger Delta* (San
Francisco: Sierra Club Books, 2001).

86. Rob Nixon, *Slow Violence and the Environmentalism of the Poor* (Cambridge,
Mass.: Harvard University Press, 2011), 106.

87. Obi and Rustad, *Oil and Insurgency*, 5–6.

88. Ibid., 7–8. See also Ken Saro-Wiwa, *A Month and a Day, a Detention Diary*
(New York: Penguin, 1995).

89. Nixon writes that "by the time Saro-Wiwa was executed, the Nigerian military and
Mobile Police force had killed 2,000 Ogoni through direct murder and the burning of villages." In Nixon, *Slow Violence*, 107. Elsewhere, Nixon notes the remarkable environmental
racism of Shell Oil in Africa, in terms of their policies on flaring. "A 1995 World Bank report
noted that 76 percent of the natural gas resulting from petroleum production in Nigeria was
flared (at temperatures of 14,000 degrees Celsius), while in Britain only 4.3 percent and in the
United States a mere 0.6 percent was flared" (113).

90. Habila, *Oil on Water*, 79.

91. Ibid., 5.

92. Brooks, *Reading for the Plot*, 29.

93. This quotation from Nixon, *Slow Violence*, 107.

94. Wenzel, "Behind the Headlines."

95. Habila, *Oil on Water*, 38.

96. Ali Erritouni, "Postcolonial Despotism from a Postmodern Standpoint: Helon Habila's
Waiting for an Angel," *Research in African Literatures* 41, no. 4 (Winter 2010): 145.

97. Kwame Anthony Appiah, "Is the Post- in Postmodernism the Post- in Postcolonial?,"
in *Theory of the Novel, a Historical Approach*, ed. Michael McKeon (Baltimore, Md.: Johns
Hopkins University Press, 2000), 891.

98. Habila, *Oil on Water*, 38.

99. I thank Byron Caminero-Santangelo for pointing me toward Nigerian poetry, in particular the works of Ifowodo and Tanure Ojaide. Thanks to Byron, too, for generously reading an early draft of this chapter section.

100. Ogaga Ifowodo, "Jese," in *The Oil Lamp* (Trenton, N.J.: Africa World Press, 2005), 7.

101. Greg Campbell, "The Killing Fields: Oil Ravages the Niger Delta," *InTheseTimes.com*, June 25, 2001, accessed August 13, 2012, http://www.inthesetimes.com/issue/25/15/campbell2515.html.

102. Ifowodo, "Jese," 16.

103. Ifowodo, "Cesspit of the Niger Area," in *The Oil Lamp*, 55.

104. Ifowodo, "Jese," 3.

105. Lisa Margonelli, *Oil on the Brain: Petroleum's Long, Strange Trip to Your Tank* (New York: Broadway Books, 2007), 245.

106. Monica Mark, "Nigeria's Penalty for Gas Flaring Will Not Curb Emissions, Say Campaigners," *The Guardian*, May 31, 2012, accessed May 14, 2013, http://www.guardian.co.uk.

107. Wenzel, "Behind the Headlines."

108. Habila, *Oil on Water*, 193.

109. Ibid., 239.

110. Lisa Merkl, "UH Geologists Find Parts of Northwest Houston Sinking Rapidly," *University of Houston News and Events*, September 28, 2010, accessed September 25, 2012, http://www.uh.edu/news-events/stories/2010articles/Sept2010/09282010KhanFaultLines.php. Merkl attributes the sinking of northwest Houston to groundwater withdrawal reflecting population increases and real estate development (in other words, not a direct correlation with the oil industry). In contrast, the dramatic sinking over time of Houston's Brownwood neighborhood near Baytown—which was destroyed by Hurricane Alicia in 1983—has been explicitly linked to the petrochemical industry's massive groundwater withdrawal in the area around the Houston Ship Channel.

111. Attica Locke, *Black Water Rising* (New York: Harper Perennial, 2009), 217.

112. Ibid., 265.

113. Ibid.

114. Ibid., 271.

115. Fredric Jameson, "The Case for Georg Lukács," *Salmagundi* 13 (Summer 1970): 9.

116. Ibid.

117. Locke, *Black Water*, 22.

118. Ibid., 427.

119. Ibid., 119.

120. Ibid., 351.

121. Stephen Tatum, "Spectral Beauty and Forensic Aesthetics in the West," *Western American Literature* 41 (Summer 2006): 123–45. See especially the final section, "The Open Space of Spectral Beauty."

122. Appiah, "Is the Post-," 893.

123. Tanure Ojaide, "I Want to Be an Oracle: My Poetry and My Generation," *World Literature Today* 68, no. 1 (Winter 1994): 21.

124. Tanure Ojaide, "Delta Blues," in *Delta Blues and Home Songs* (Ibadan, Nigeria: Kraft Books, 1997), 21.

125. Ojaide, "I Want to Be an Oracle," 16.

126. Sule E. Egya, "The Aesthetic of Rage in Recent Nigerian Poetry in English, Olu Oguibe and Ogaga Ifowodo," *Journal for African Culture and Society* 39 (2011): 102.

127. Ian Watt, "From *The Rise of the Novel: Studies in Defoe, Richardson, and Fielding*," in *Theory of the Novel: A Historical Approach*, ed. Michael Mckeon (Baltimore, Md.: Johns Hopkins University Press, 2000), 463.

128. For percentages of oil imports from Nigeria, see a purportedly unbiased account at NPR Online, at http://www.npr.org/2012/04/11/150444802/where-does-america-ge t-oil-you-may-be-surprised, accessed September 25, 2012. The U.S. State Department (also purportedly unbiased) confirms these figures. See http://www.state.gov/r/pa/ei/bgn/2836. htm, accessed September 25, 2012.

129. The term "instrumental aesthetics" is Nixon's, *Slow Violence*, 108.

130. Reyner Banham, quoted in *Ephemeral City: Cite Looks at Houston*, ed. Barrie Scardino, William F. Stern, and Bruce C. Webb (Austin: University of Texas Press, 2003), 3.

131. For a brief history of Houston's many monikers, see Bruce C. Webb's "Introduction" to *Ephemeral City*, 4–5. Other names include "Freeway City," "Strip City," and "Mobility City."

132. Phillip Lopate, "Pursuing the Unicorn: Public Space in Houston," in *Ephemeral City*, 11.

133. See *Ephemeral City*.

134. Lopate, "Pursuing the Unicorn," 14.

135. Webb, "Introduction," 7.

136. "CLUI Opens Field Office in Houston: Gulf States Logistics Site Supports Programs in Region," in *On the Banks of Bayou City*, ed. Rachel Hooper and Nancy Zastudil (Houston: Blaffer Gallery, the Art Museum of the University of Houston, 2009), 16.

137. Robert Venturi and Denise Scott Brown, quoted in Britt Savlesen, *New Topographics* (Göttingen: Steidl, 2010), 51.

138. "On Residence, in Place: Matthew Coolidge in Conversation with Bree Edwards," in *On the Banks of Bayou City*, 21.

139. See the CLUI newsletter, *Lay of the Land*, Winter 2011, http://clui.org/newsletter/ winter-2011/houston-report, accessed March 8, 2012.

140. "Amidst a Petrochemical Wonderland: Points of View along the Houston Ship Channel," *Lay of the Land*, Summer 2004, republished in *On the Banks of Bayou City*, 8.

141. "On Residence," *On the Banks of Bayou City*, 24.

142. Salvesen, *New Topographics*, 38.

143. Quote from the CLUI Field Station, "Corporate Boardroom," Exhibit.

Chapter 4

1. Jeffrey Wallen, "Narrative Tensions: The Archive and the Eyewitness," *Partial Answers* 7, no. 2 (2009): 262.

2. Tess L. Takahashi, "The Imaginary Archive: Current Practice," *Camera Obscura* 22, no. 3 (2007): 179. To access the CLUI's American Land Museum, go to: http://www.clui.org/page/ american-land-museum.

3. Pierre Nora, "Between Memory and History: Les Lieux de Mémoire," *Representations* 26 (Special Issue: "Memory and Counter-Memory," Spring 1989).

4. David Wilson, "Nikolai Federov, Konstantin Tsiolkovsky and the Roots of the Russian Space Program" (lecture, University of California, Santa Barbara, April 13, 2011).

For discussion of Wilson's ironic relationship to the natural history endeavor, see Lawrence Weschler, *Mr. Wilson's Cabinet of Wonder* (New York: Vintage, 1995).

5. Bennett is particularly concerned with how the relatively new time-scheme of the nation-state could be annexed to the universal natural history idea. See Tony Bennett, "The Exhibitionary Complex," *New Formations* 4 (Spring 1988): 88–89.

6. Robert E. Kohler, *All Creatures: Naturalists, Collectors, and Biodiversity, 1850–1950* (Princeton, N.J.: Princeton University Press, 2006): 2, 3, 9; Steven Conn, *Museums and American Intellectual Life, 1876–1926* (Chicago: University of Chicago Press, 1998), 72.

7. Some curators resent the emphasis on information technology as the key to the continuing relevance of their collections, arguing, for instance, that "there is a tendency to divorce data from objects," "museums are the cornerstone of an object-oriented approach to the natural world," and "the useful life of...specimens" outlasts the analyses made of them. See, for example, Leonard Krishtalka and Philip S. Humphrey, "Can Natural History Museums Capture the Future?," *BioScience* 50 (July 2000): 612.

8. Alison Griffiths extensively historicizes interactive exhibits and the concept of "interactivity," suggesting alternatives to the explicitly digital or even technological application of the concept, in *Shivers down Your Spine: Cinema, Museums, and the Immersive View* (New York: Columbia University Press, 2008). The journal *Curator* features frequent articles on interactivity and a 2004 special issue on the topic that includes useful reflections from museum practitioners, for example, John H. Falk, Carol Scott, Lynn Dierking, Leonie Rennie, and Mika Cohen Jones, "Interactives and Visitor Learning," *Curator* 47 (April 2004): 171–98.

9. Conn, *Museums*, 40; a key critical discussion of the popular exhibit versus the disciplinary role of the museum is Bennett, "Exhibitionary Complex," 86.

10. Michel Foucault, *The Order of Things: An Archeology of the Human Sciences* (London: Tavistock, 1970), 132; see also Tony Bennett, "Pedagogic Objects, Clean Eyes, and Popular Instruction: On Sensory Regimes and Museum Didactics," *Configurations* 6, no. 3 (1998): 345–71.

11. For a thoughtful general treatment of ecomuseums, see Peter Davis, *Ecomuseums: A Sense of Place* (London: Leicester University Press, 1999).

12. Andreas Huyssen, *Twilight Memories: Marking Time in a Culture of Amnesia* (London: Routledge, 1995), 33.

13. An overview of the rhetorical transformation of bitumen into "oil"—and brief reference to the Oil Sands Discovery Museum—can be found in Andrew Nikiforuk, *Tar Sands: Dirty Oil and the Future of a Continent* (Vancouver: Greystone Books, 2010). My general comments refer to a personal visit that I made to this museum, for research purposes, in August 2011.

14. Tony Bennett, "Civic Laboratories: Museums, Cultural Objecthood, and the Governance of the Social," *Cultural Studies* 19 (September 2005): 525.

15. Jonathan Spaulding, "*L.A.: light/motion/dreams*: Developing an Exhibition on the Natural and Cultural History of Los Angeles," *Environmental History* 10 (April 2005): 295–313.

16. Griffiths, *Shivers*, 168.

17. Andrea Witcomb offers a strong set of alternative definitions of "interactivity" and rebuttal to the screen-mania of multimedia exhibit promoters in *Re-Imagining the Museum: Beyond the Mausoleum* (London: Routledge, 2003). See especially chapter 6.

18. "Gail," docent, George C. Page Museum of La Brea Discoveries Outdoor Tour, April 17, 2011.

19. Linda Williams, "Film Bodies: Gender, Genre, and Excess," *Film Quarterly* 44 (Summer 1991): 2–13.

20. "Imperial Mammoth Struggling in Asphalt Pool" (undated postcard), George C. Page Museum of La Brea Discoveries.

21. Hannah Arendt, *The Human Condition* (Chicago: University of Chicago Press, 1958), 201.

22. "Gail," Discoveries Outdoor Tour.

23. Thomas H. Benton (pseud. for William Pannapacker), "Preserving the Future of the Natural History Museum," *Chronicle of Higher Education*, October 30, 2009; see also Benton, "Getting Real at Natural-History Museums," *Chronicle of Higher Education*, July 1, 2010, and "Getting Real at the Natural-History Museum, Part 2," *Chronicle of Higher Education*, August 1, 2010.

24. Witcomb, *Re-Imagining the Museum*, 102.

25. Dana W. Bartlett, "Progress Made in Developing Tomb of Giants: Creation of New Park at La Brea Pits Gives City Unique Monument," *Los Angeles Times*, March 27, 1927, ProQuest Historical Newspapers, *Los Angeles Times*.

26. Eva G. Taylor, "By the Way," *Los Angeles Times*, February 1, 1928, ProQuest Historical Newspapers, *Los Angeles Times*.

27. William L. Fox, *Making Time: Essays on the Nature of Los Angeles* (Emeryville, Calif.: Shoemaker and Hoard, 2007), see especially 34–37.

28. Although I see Adorno's discussion of the "museal" as ripe for critique, exhibited fossils speak rather literally to his sense that museum objects are dead, by virtue of separation from other cultural relations. Theodor Adorno, "Valery Proust Museum in Memory of Hermann von Grab," in *Prisms*, ed. Theodor Adorno (London: Garden City Press, 1967), 175–85.

29. Griffiths, *Shivers*, 252.

30. Max Poschin, "What Has Happened to Our Priorities?," letter to the *Los Angeles Times*, May 2, 1970, ProQuest Historical Newspapers, *Los Angeles Times*.

31. George Miller, quoted in John Kendall, "Fossil Dig to Be Phased Out: Firing Clouds La Brea Pit Study," *Los Angeles Times*, January 16, 1972, ProQuest Historical Newspapers, *Los Angeles Times*.

32. See Paul D. Brinkman, *The Second Jurassic Dinosaur Rush: Museums and Paleontology in America at the Turn of the Twentieth Century* (Chicago: University of Chicago Press, 2010).

33. Quoted in Kendall, "Fossil Dig."

34. Howard Kegley, "Something Bigger Than Barnum," *Los Angeles Times*, March 10, 1940, ProQuest Historical Newspapers, *Los Angeles Times*.

35. Ibid.

36. "Body Hunted in Tar Pits: Missing Girl's Hint Recalled," *Los Angeles Times*, October 26, 1935, ProQuest Historical Newspapers, *Los Angeles Times*.

37. "Tar Pits Suicide Hoaxer Jailed as Extortion Suspect," *Los Angeles Times*, January 23, 1939, ProQuest Historical Newspapers, *Los Angeles Times*.

38. "Life in Asphalt: New Petroleum-Degrading Bacteria Found at Rancho La Brea Tar Pits in Los Angeles," *Astrobiology Magazine*, accessed August 31, 2010, http://www.astrobio.net/pressrelease/2336/life-in-asphalt.

39. Ibid.

40. Conn, *Museums*, 44–45.

41. For example, see some of the bioarchitectural model cities in Lucas Cappelli and Vicente Guallart, eds., *Self-Sufficient City: Envisioning the Habitat of the Future* (Barcelona: Institute for Advanced Architecture of Catalonia, 2010).

42. Latour's discussion of the entangled agency of quasi-objects, nonhumans, and "matters of concern" runs throughout his work. One might begin with the explicitly political argument of a more recent book, for example, Bruno Latour, *The Politics of Nature: How to Bring the Sciences into Democracy*, trans. Catherine Porter (Cambridge, Mass.: Harvard University Press, 2004). Here's Latour discussing the "tangled beings" that are the concern of political ecology: "Political ecology does not shift attention from the human pole to the pole of nature; it shifts from certainty about the production of risk-free objects (with their clear separation between things and people) to uncertainty about the relations whose unintended consequences threaten to disrupt all orderings, all plans, all impacts" (*Politics*, 25).

43. Heather Wax, "Engineering the Magic: Disney Imagineers Give Robots Personality, Charm—and Even a Smile," *IEEE "Women in Engineering" Magazine*, Summer 2008, 22.

44. Nikiforuk, *Tar Sands*. In the twenty-two-point "Declaration of Political Emergency" that begins Nikiforuk's book, he writes—under XVIII—"A business-as-usual case for the tar sands will change Canada forever. It will enrich a few powerful companies, hollow out the economy, destroy the world's third-largest watershed, industrialize nearly one-quarter of Alberta's landscape, consume the last of the nation's natural gas supplies, and erode Canadian sovereignty" (4).

45. Ibid., 48.

46. Alexandra Fuller, "Boomtown Blues," *New Yorker* 82, no. 48 (2007): 38–44.

47. Kathryn J. Brasier, Matthew R. Filteau, Diane K. McLaughlin, Jeffrey Jacquet, Richard C. Stedman, Timothy Kelsey, and Stephan J. Goetz, "Residents' Perceptions of Community and Environmental Impacts from Development of Natural Gas in the Marcellus Shale: A Comparison of Pennsylvania and New York Cases," *Journal of Rural Social Sciences* 26, no. 1 (2011): 47, 50.

48. James MacPherson, "North Dakota Litter Problem Rises with Oil Boom," *Huff Post Green*, March 26, 2012, http://www.huffingtonpost.com/2012/03/26/north-dakota-litter-oil_n_1379286.html.

49. Mike Wallace, *Mickey Mouse History and Other Essays on American Memory* (Philadelphia: Temple University Press, 1996), 12–13.

50. Imre Szeman tells me that, for some oil sands professions, U.S. workers can now pick up a work visa at the airport. Szeman pointed me to the following, well worth a read: http://www.edmontonjournal.com/Simons+hopeful+immigrants+promise+faster+citizenship/6954381/story.html. Huge thanks to Imre for his generous and quick reading of this piece.

51. Jim Bentein, "Workers in the New Wave," *Oilsands Review*, September 2011, 51.

52. Deborah Jaremko, "Why and How America Really Can Love the Oilsands: Q and A with John Davies, Founder and Chief Executive officer, Davies Public Affairs," *Oilsands Review*, September 2011, 104.

53. Nikiforuk, *Tar Sands*, 53.

54. Ibid., 11.

55. David Finch, *Pumped: Everyone's Guide to the Oil Patch* (Calgary: Fitzhenry and Whiteside, 2007), 112–14.

56. Nikiforuk, *Tar Sands*, 107.

57. Imre Szeman and Maria Whiteman perform a wonderful reading of this so-called recovery project in "Oil Imag(e)inaries: Critical Realism and the Oil Sands" (unpublished manuscript, 25).

58. Griffiths, *Shivers*, 252.

59. Lawrence Buell, *The Environmental Imagination: Thoreau, Nature Writing, and the Formation of American Culture* (Cambridge, Mass.: Harvard University Press, 1995), 267.

60. For a light but informative overview of this midcentury U.S. future, see chapter 3 of Lawrence R. Samuel, *Future: A Recent History* (Austin: University of Texas Press, 2009), 77–108.

61. I use the term "intangible heritage" self-consciously, after Barbara Kirshenbblatt-Gimblett, "Intangible Heritage and Metacultural Production," *Museum International* 56, nos. 1–2 (2004): 53.

62. Much of this history of "technical museums" comes from Eugene S. Ferguson, "Technical Museums and International Exhibitions," *Technology and Culture* 6, no. 1 (Winter 1965): 30–46. See also Michael McMahon's exhibit review essay on the occasion of the opening of the National Air and Space Museum: "The Romance of Technological Progress: A Critical Review of the National Air and Space Museum," *Technology and Culture* 22, no. 2 (April 1981): 282–85.

63. Goode, quoted in Ferguson, U.S. National Museum *Annual Report*, Part 2 (1896–1897), "A Memorial of George Brown Goode," 197.

64. Ferguson, *Annual Report*, 42.

65. T. R. Adam, *The Museum and Popular Culture* (New York: American Association for Adult Education, 1939), 130.

66. Ibid., 14–15.

67. Ibid., 128.

68. Ferguson, *Annual Report*, 46.

69. McMahon, "Romance of Technological Progress," 296. McMahon delves into debates that would continue into the following decades about whether the National Air and Space Museum ought to exhibit the darker histories of aerospace technologies, in particular the World War II bomber *Enola Gay.*

70. Wallace, *Mickey Mouse*, 17.

71. J. Arwel Edwards and Joan Carles Llurdés i Coit, "Mines and Quarries, Industrial Heritage Tourism," *Annals of Tourism Research* 23, no. 2 (1996): 342–45.

72. Brochure, Ocean Star Offshore Drilling Rig and Museum. For more information about the museum, see http://www.OceanStarOEC.com.

73. Peder Anker, *From Bauhaus to Ecohouse: A History of Ecological Design* (Baton Rouge: Louisiana State University Press, 2010), 81. As noted, Anker's reading of technocratic management as a continuation of high modernism focuses on Buckminster Fuller. For an "ecological" take on the pleasures of automation, see R. Buckminster Fuller, *Operating Manual for Spaceship Earth* (1969; repr., Baden, Switzerland: Lars Müller Publishers, 2008–2011).

74. Quotations cited from author's notes treating the American eagle display case at the Texas Energy Museum, Beaumont, Texas.

75. Fuller, "Boomtown Blues," 43.

76. Text from oil refinery model exhibit, Texas Energy Museum.

77. "Escape Capsule," *OCEAN STAR Offshore Drilling Rig and Museum Tour Guide Book* (Houston, Tex.: T.G.I. Printed, 2007), 12.

78. Samuel, *Future*, 115.

79. Mike Wallace, "Industrial Museums and the History of Deindustrialization," Public Historian 9, no. 1 (Winter 1987): 13–14.

80. Ibid., 17.

81. Neil Harris, *Humbug: The Art of P. T. Barnum* (Boston: Little, Brown, 1973), 67–79.

82. Lisa Margonelli takes a particularly measured approach to the exaggeration of "tight oil" opportunities for labor in "The Energy Debate We Aren't Having," Pacific Standard 6 (March/April 2013): 32–24.

83. Lisa Margonelli discusses the environmental health dimension of refineries and the local activists who have led the way toward more effective regulatory measures in *Oil on the Brain: Petroleum's Long, Strange Trip to Your Tank* (New York: Broadway Books, 2007), 57–60,

84. Stephen Greenblatt, "Resonance and Wonder," Museum Studies: An Anthology of Contexts, ed. Bettina Messias Carbonell (Malden, Mass.: Blackwell, 2004), 550.

85. "Underwater Construction," *OCEAN STAR Guide*, 9.

86. Ibid., 10.

87. See *Oil Rigs* (A&E Television Networks, 2007); *Diver Down* (National Geographic Channel, 2009).

88. An image that doesn't do full justice to the Devils Tower exhibit can be found in the *OCEAN STAR Guide*, 19.

89. Ibid., 23.

90. Ibid., 25.

91. Arthur W. Baum, "They Gamble on Offshore Oil," *Saturday Evening Post*, May 28, 1955, 39, 96.

92. Dow Plastics Advertisement for Seat Covers Woven of Wonderful Saran, ibid., 102.

93. Baum, "Gamble," 102.

94. Ibid.

95. National Commission on the BP Deepwater Horizon Oil Spill and Offshore Drilling, Report to the President, *Deep Water: The Gulf Oil Disaster and the Future of Offshore Drilling*, January 2011, 53.

96. For an efficient history of offshore drilling technologies, see chapter 2 in ibid.

97. Lang, quoted in Rowan Jacobsen, *Shadows on the Gulf: A Journey through Our Last Great Wetland* (New York: Bloomsbury, 2011), 43.

98. Jacobsen writes that "there may be 40 billion barrels of oil lying underneath the deep Gulf. There may be more. Worldwide, there are more than a trillion barrels of oil reserves— more oil in the ocean depths than Peak Oilers ever dreamed." Ibid., 38.

99. Ibid., 39.

100. *Deep Water*, 28–29.

101. [101.] See http://www.nytimes.com/2011/11/09/science/earth/us-to-open-new-areas-to -offshore-drilling.html, accessed August 1, 2012.

102. *Deep Water*, 305.

103. Ibid., 300.

104. Sara Daleiden, personal interview. September 1, 2011.

105. Sara Daleiden of the Los Angeles Urban Rangers, in person interview by Stephanie LeMenager conducted at midnight in a tent in front of the Los Angeles MOCA, at the LA Urban Rangers' "Critical Campout," September 1, 2011.

106. Harris, *Humbug*, 78.

107. Rick Bass, *Oil Notes* (Dallas, Tex.: Southern Methodist University Press, 1989), 70.

108. Ibid., 27.

109. Ibid., 62

110. Ibid., 58.

111. Ibid.

112. Emerson, "Nature," *The Norton Anthology of American Literature*, 3rd ed., vol. 1, ed. Nina Baym et al. (1836; repr, New York: W. W. Norton and Company, 1989), 911. In Emerson's now famous formulation, "The use of natural history is to give us aid in supernatural history. The use of the outer creation is to give us language for the beings and changes of the inward creation."

113. Thoreau's famous mining metaphor begins: "My head is hands and feet....My instinct tells me that my head is an organ for burrowing, as some creatures use their snout and fore-paws, and with it I would mine and burrow my way through these hills." Henry David Thoreau, *Walden*, ed. William Rossi (1854; repr. New York: W.W. Norton & Company, 1992), 67.

114. Bass, *Oil Notes*, 165.

115. Thoreau, *Walden*, 214.

116. Bass, *Oil Notes*, 91.

117. Ibid., 171.

118. Ibid.

119. The total number of offshore platforms (6,000) is estimated in a report now eight years old. See Donna M. Schroeder and Milton S. Love, "Ecological and Political Issues Surrounding Decommissioning of Offshore Oil Facilities in the Southern California Bight," *Ocean and Coastal Management* 47 (2004): 22.

120. According to NOAA.gov, the exact number is 3,858. See http://oceanexplorer.noaa. gov/explorations/06mexico/background/oil/media/platform_600.html, accessed August 1, 2012.

121. The number for the pipeline comes from *USA Today*. See Doyle Rice, "Undersea Oil Pipelines Vulnerable to Hurricanes," *USA Today* Online, updated June 2, 2012, accessed August 25, 2012, http://www.usatoday.com/weather/storms/hurricanes/2010-06-01-oil-hurricanes_N.htm.

122. According to Sean B. Hecht, J.D., "Southern California Environmental Report Card 2010," there are (as of 2010) twenty-seven offshore rigs along the California coast, all slated for decommission within five to twenty years because they will cease being productive by then, and state and federal law requires decommissioning after that. See Hecht, "California's New Rigs-to-Reefs Law," the UCLA Institute of the Environment and Sustainability, Fall 2010, accessed August 25, 2012, http://www.environment.ucla.edu/reportcard/article. asp?parentid=9389. As of June 2010, there were 3,500 drilling rigs and platforms offshore of the United States, 79 of them deepwater wells. With 62 inspectors nationwide (at that time), on average each inspector would be responsible for 56 rigs. See "Ask CBS News: How Many Offshore Rigs Are There?," June 11, 2010, accessed August 23, 2012, http://www.cbsnews. com/8301-18563_162-6573602.html. For more on the debates in California about how to decommission—via reefing or removal—see Schroeder and Love, "Ecological and Political Issues," 24–27.

123. Ibid., 38.

124. Personal communication, tour guide, Galveston Harbor.

125. See *Oil Rigs*.

126. Georgia Flight, "The 62,000-Mile Elevator Ride," *CNNMoney*, March 1, 2006, http://money.cnn.com/magazines/business2/business2_archive/2006/03/01/8370588/index.htm.

127. Edwards, quoted in ibid.

128. Ibid.

129. See *Oil Rigs*.

Epilogue

1. The campus divestment campaign of 350.org can be accessed at http://gofossilfree.org/toolkit-fossil-fuel-divestment-on-campus//. McKibben's *Rolling Stone* article "Global Warming's Terrifying New Math" also explains the campaign, in the context of the new certainties of global climate change and its relation to the fossil fuel industries.

2. Lawrence Buell insightfully incorporates bioregionalist thinking into questions of aesthetics in the chapter "Watershed Aesthetics" in his *Writing for an Endangered World: Literature, Culture, and Environment in the U.S. and Beyond* (Cambridge, Mass.: Harvard University Press, 2001), 243–65. See also Michael Vincent McGinnis, *Bioregionalism* (New York: Routledge, 1998).

3. "Materialize." *Oxford English Dictionary Online* (Oxford: Oxford University Press, 2012). Accessed January 12, 2013.

4. Shell Refinery Exhibit text, California Oil Museum, Santa Paula, California, December 20, 2012.

5. Francis W. Hertel, interviewed by Allen Stauch, September 1, 1979, "Petroleum Industry in Ventura County, Especially the Ventura Avenue Field," p. 4 (Ventura County Museum Library).

6. Hertel interview, 4.

7. A neat summary of complaints about the refinery through the 1970s and early 1980s can be found in Constance Sommer, "Homes Proposed at Site of Old Refinery: Ventura: The Council Will Consider USA Petroleum's Bid for a Zoning Change. Environmentalists Voice Opposition," *Los Angeles Times*, January 7, 1995. From *Los Angeles Times* archive (1985–present), accessed January 3, 2013, at http://articles.latimes.com// through the University of California at Santa Barbara online articles database. For a vintage spill photograph, see "Crews Mop Up Oil Spill at River Mouth," *Ventura County Star Free Press*, section A-1, October 23, 1970.

8. "Petrochem Spill Was Reported, Tape Reveals," *Ventura County Star Free Press*, April 1, 1977, section A-1.

9. Citizens to Preserve the Ojai v. County of Ventura et al., Defendants and Respondents; USA Petrochem Corporation, Real Party in Interest and Respondent. 176 Ca. App. 3d 421; 222 Cal. Rptr. 247 (Dec. 1985).

10. Cheri Carlson, "EPA Investigates Reports of Possible Toxic Waste at Old Refinery Near West Ventura," *Ventura County Star* online, November 29, 2012, accessed December 22, 2012, htttp:/www.vcstar.com/news/.

11. Paul Jenkins, Surfrider Organization, personal communication.

12. Again, I refer to Beamish's *Silent Spill: The Organization of an Industrial Crisis*.

13. The information-gathering techniques about forty-nine sites are described in the Executive Summary of Appendix 4.7, "Hazards and Hazardous Materials Study," *Preliminary*

Environmental Site Assessment and Identification of Areas of Potential Concern Westside Community Planning Project, Ventura, California. Ref. No. 0161-39P. Available at the City of Ventura online, accessed December 27, 2012, http://www.cityofventura.net/page/community-plan-amp-development-code.

14. Ibid.

15. Ibid.

16. Susanne Antonetta, *Body Toxic: An Environmental Memoir* (Washington, D.C.: Counterpoint Press, 2001).

17. The salutary news of local clean-up—as of 2009, appears in Kit Stolz, "Tar on Your Foot: The Down and Dirty about Ventura County's Oil Legacy," *Ventura County Reporter,* April 16, 2009, accessed January 10, 2012, www.vcreporter.com. Surfrider's Paul Jenkins also credits the city with responding to community members' concerns about hazardous waste, while still acknowledging that "we have a long way to go." Jenkins, personal communication.

18. 606 Studio (Yarnie Chen, Matt Deines, Henry Fleischmann, Sonya Reed, Isby Swick), *Transforming Urban Environments for a Post-Peak Oil Future* (Pomona: Department of Landscape Architecture, California State Polytechnic University, 2007), available at the City of Ventura online, "Green Ventura," accessed January 3, 2012, http://www.cityofventura.net/greenventura.

19. "Very good examples of industrial buildings from this era [post–World War II] include 2220 North Ventura Avenue and 4777 Crooked Palm Road [the USA Petrochem refinery]." City of Ventura, *Westside Historic Context and Survey Report,* prepared by Galvin Preservation Associates, Inc., January 2011, 37.

20. See http://www.atlasobscura.com/places/ventura-oil-refinery, http://www.avoidin-gregret.com/2012/07/photo-essay-ventura-oil-refinery.html, and http://www.youtube.com/watch?v=puDwHD7m2Xk. Accessed January 10, 2013.

21. "Historicism." *Oxford English Dictionary Online* (Oxford: Oxford University Press, 2012), accessed January 12, 2013.

22. Edward Burtynsky, *Oil,* Apple iTunes Store, Version 1.1, Melcher Media, May 23, 2012, accessed March 10, 2013, https://itunes.apple.com/us/app/burtynsky-oil/id524467450?mt=8.

23. Antonetta, *Body Toxic.*

24. See Shane Cohn, "Fracking: Full Disclosure Not Required," *Ventura County Reporter,* June 7, 2012, accessed December 15, 2012, www.vcreporter.com; Zeke Barlow, "Oil Fracking in State and County Raises Questions," *Ventura County Reporter,* January 16, 2012, accessed December 16, 2012, www.vcreporter.com; Natalie Cherot, "Fracking Offshore: Lack of Transparency for the Controversial Practice Raises Major Concerns for Locals," *Ventura County Reporter,* December 13, 2012, accessed December 30, 2012, www.vcreporter.com; Paul Wellman, "Fracking Friction," *Santa Barbara Independent,* September 8, 2011, accessed December 15, 2012, www.independent.com.

25. Natalie Cherot, "Hooked on Frack? Where Oil Companies Could Be Fracking in Santa Barbara County," *Santa Barbara Independent,* November 15, 2012, accessed December 15, 2012, www.independent.com.

26. Exemptions and loopholes that protect fracking from federal laws are neatly laid out by Santa Barbara's Environmental Defense Center. See http://www.edcnet.org/learn/current_cases/fracking/federal_law_loopholes.html.

27. Charles C. Mann reports in "What If We Never Run Out of Oil?" that if a frack well leaks more than 3 percent of its methane production into the air, then it's dirtier than coal.

A recent federal study (released to the press in mid-July 2013) showing the relatively limited danger to groundwater from fracking promises to challenge some common beliefs about fracking risks and to raise questions about other kinds of risk, for years to come. Lisa Margonelli reminds us of earlier studies showing fracking to be less a threat to groundwater per se than, more broadly, an unevenly regulated and inherently risky industry in "The Energy Debate We Aren't Having."

28. Hertel interview, 9, 23.

29. See http://www.invisible5.org/.

30. For the CLUI's "Through the Grapevine" exhibit, see their online newsletter, *The Lay of the Land*, at http://www.clui.org/newsletter/winter-2011/through-grapevine-exhibit.

Appendix 1: Introduction

1. Juliette Jowit, "UN says eat less meat to curb global warming," September 6, 2008. *The Guardian* online. http://www.guardian.co.uk, accessed September 12, 2012">, accessed September 12, 2012.

2. See http://www.ogj.com/articles/print/vol-110/issue-5b/general-interest/iea-global-oil-demand-growth-accelerating.html. See also p. 82 of this USDA report, with numbers up to 2005, which breaks down into gasoline and diesel use, along with other energy sources: http://www.usda.gov/oce/climate_change/AFGG_Inventory/5_AgriculturalEnergyUse.pdf.

Appendix 2: Life Cycle Assessment of a Conventional Academic Print-Book

1. U.S Environmental Protection Agency. Wastes—Resource Conservation—Common Wastes & Materials—Paper Recycling, http://www.epa.gov/osw/conserve/materials/paper/faqs.htm#sources

2. Paper Industry Association Council 2012. http://stats.paperrecycles.org/maps/ Comparative LCA

{INDEX}

CPSIA information can be obtained
at www.ICGtesting.com
Printed in the USA
BVHW032022300721
612370BV00006B/166

9 780190 461973